Albert Bushnell Hart, Edward Campbell Mason

The Veto Power

Its Origin, Development, and Function in the Government of the United States,

1789-1889

Albert Bushnell Hart, Edward Campbell Mason

The Veto Power
Its Origin, Development, and Function in the Government of the United States, 1789-1889

ISBN/EAN: 9783337187712

Printed in Europe, USA, Canada, Australia, Japan

Cover: Foto ©ninafisch / pixelio.de

More available books at **www.hansebooks.com**

HARVARD UNIVERSITY PUBLICATIONS

Harvard Historical Monographs

No. 1

THE VETO POWER

ITS ORIGIN, DEVELOPMENT AND FUNCTION IN THE GOVERNMENT OF THE UNITED STATES
(1789–1889)

BY

EDWARD CAMPBELL MASON, A.]
INSTRUCTOR IN POLITICAL ECONOMY

EDITED BY

ALBERT BUSHNELL HART, PH.D.
ASSISTANT PROFESSOR OF HISTORY

BOSTON, U.S.A.
PUBLISHED BY GINN & COMPANY
1891

COPYRIGHT, 1890, BY

THE PRESIDENT AND FELLOWS OF HARVARD COLLEGE.

SECOND EDITION.

Presswork by John Wilson and Son,
University Press.

EDITOR'S PREFACE.

AMONG the many subjects in the constitutional development of the United States on which no formal treatise has been written, none seems more to deserve the attention of a scholar than that chosen by Mr. Mason and here presented as the first number of the Harvard Historical Monographs. The veto power is the most important of the institutions connecting the national executive with the legislature; the provision for a revision by an enlarged majority of the legislature is original, to the United States; the vetoes have appertained to some of the most interesting episodes of American history; the power is in frequent exercise, yet has of late been somewhat disputed.

In a work of this kind, based on records sometimes defective and usually badly indexed, perfection is almost impossible. The greatest pains have, however, been taken to make the list of vetoes complete. In the Report made to the Senate in 1886, by the Senate Committee on Printing, there are printed, with some other matter, two hundred and thirty-seven veto messages, which were supposed by the Committee to include all that had ever been rendered. Mr. Mason has discovered ten additional vetoes, to which reference is made in appendix A; and he has added references to one hundred and eighty-six messages submitted since the date of the report.

The Editor's function has been that of advice, suggestion, and revision; the labor of preparation is entirely Mr. Mason's own. All important points of opinion have been discussed between us, but in every case Mr. Mason has stated his own views and assumes all responsibility for them. Although the work deals with political subjects, many of which are still subjects of debate, both

Editor and Author have endeavored to avoid political bias; the vetoes are condemned or approved upon what seem to us sound principles of constitutional law and political expediency, irrespective of the attitude of present parties. The effort has been made in the notes and appendices to furnish all the apparatus necessary for following out and testing the Author's conclusions, and for pursuing the subject further.

It had been intended to add a chapter on the workings of the veto in the States, and another on the veto power in modern constitutions. The discussion of the veto in the national system of government in the United States has required more space than had been anticipated: the two additional chapters have therefore been omitted. But, for purposes of comparison, there has been introduced as an appendix a tabulation of the provisions of state constitutions. In another appendix will be found a list of the vetoes of the President of the Confederate States of America. The material for it has been kindly furnished for this Monograph by Mr. John Osborne Sumner, a member of the Graduate Department, from the manuscript Journals of the Confederate Congress, which he has been the first historical scholar to study.

I desire also to express my obligation to Dr. Charles Gross, of Harvard University, for his careful revision of the proofs; and to Professor J. B. Thayer, of the Harvard Law School, for helpful suggestions.

ALBERT BUSHNELL HART.

CAMBRIDGE, April 12, 1890.

AUTHOR'S PREFACE.

THE object of the present Monograph is, to trace the development and operation of the veto power in the government of the United States. The work is almost wholly the result of an examination of the sources. Indeed such a course was almost a necessity since very little has been written upon the subject. The basis of the study is a list of the Presidential vetoes, compiled from the records of Congress, and covering the period from the foundation of the present form of government in 1789, to the end of President Cleveland's administration, March 4, 1889.

For convenience of comparison, the vetoes have been classified according to subject; and to the discussion of these classes the greater part of the work is devoted. It has, however, seemed essential in a full treatment of the subject to prefix a brief account of the origin in English and Colonial precedent of that particular form of the veto power which is found in the United States: and to add a chapter on the constitutional points which have arisen concerning the operation of the veto power; and another on the gradual development of the power during the century of the national government.

The preparation of the thesis began in the fall of 1887, in one of the Historical Research Courses in Harvard University, and has been continued most of the time since, as undergraduate and graduate work, in connection with the University, under the direction of Professor Albert Bushnell Hart, the editor of the Monograph. I desire to express my obligation to Dr. William Everett, of Quincy, Mass., for information in regard to the decline of the veto in England; and to Mr. Herman V. Ames, a member of the Graduate Department of Harvard College, who has kindly furnished me with a list of proposed amendments which concern the veto power. The authorities used will be found enumerated in Appendix C. As the work is based upon the voluminous Government Records, special pains have been taken to verify every reference, both in the text and appendix. Nevertheless, errors may have crept in, owing either to errors in the originals or to inadvertence. I shall be happy to acknowledge the correction of such mistakes as may be discovered. The deductions have been made after long and careful thought; but are subject to the errors into which a person not directly connected with the administration of affairs is always liable to fall. Here again, corrections and criticisms will be gladly received.

The results of the study of this somewhat neglected portion of American constitutional history are given to the public in the hope that they may aid in the further investigation both of the question here considered and of other related and unsolved problems in United States history and law.

EDWARD CAMPBELL MASON.

CAMBRIDGE, April 12, 1890.

CONTENTS.

CHAPTER I.

GENESIS OF THE VETO POWER.

§ 1. Origin of the Veto Power................................... 11
§ 2. Legislative Power among the Teutonic Tribes 11
§ 3. Legislative Power in England down to the Appearance of the Royal Veto... 12
§ 4. Extension of Royal Legislative Power: Proclamation, Suspension, and Dispensation 13
§ 5. Limitations on Royal Legislative Power; the Veto....................... 14
§ 6. Disappearance of the Veto in England 15
§ 7. The Veto Power in the American Colonies.............................. 17
§ 8. The Veto Power in the First State Constitutions 18
§ 9. The Veto Power under the Articles of Confederation..................... 19
§ 10. The Veto Power in the Federal Convention 20
§ 11. The Veto Clause in the Constitution of the United States................. 22

CHAPTER II.

VETOES AFFECTING THE FORM OF GOVERNMENT.

§ 12. Executive Methods of treating a Bill 24
§ 13. Classification of the Vetoes 25
§ 14. Vetoes affecting the Form of the National Legislature 25
§ 15. Vetoes affecting the Form of the National Judiciary...................... 27
§ 16. General Effect of Vetoes considered in this Chapter 30

CHAPTER III.

VETOES AFFECTING THE DISTRIBUTION OF THE POWERS OF GOVERNMENT.

§ 17. Classification of Vetoes in this Chapter 31
§ 18. Executive Claims to Legislative Power supported by the Veto.,........... 32
    § 19. The Bank Veto.. 32
    § 20. Removal of the Deposits....................................... 33
§ 21. Vetoes for the Protection of the Executive from Legislative Encroachment.. 35
    § 22. Power over Foreign Affairs: the Treaty Power..................... 36
        § 23. Establishment of Consular and Diplomatic Offices............. 37
        § 24. Diplomatic Intercourse..................................... 39

§ 25. The Power of Appointment.................................... 39
　§ 26. Requiring Names of Candidates for Appointment 40
　§ 27. Requiring Papers relative to Removals from Office 41
　§ 28. The Tenure of Office Act................................. 42
　§ 29. The Fitz-John Porter Bill................................. 43
§ 30. Protest for the Protection of the President's War Power............. 44
§ 31. Protest and Veto for the Protection of the President's Personal Rights under the Constitution.. 45
　§ 32. Covode Investigation 45
　§ 33. The President's Salary 45
§ 34. Use of the Veto in Controversies arising out of the Civil War........ 46
§ 35. Riders on Appropriation Bills.................................. 47
§ 36. General Effect of the Vetoes for the Protection of the Executive 49

CHAPTER IV.

VETOES AFFECTING THE EXERCISE OF THE POWERS OF GOVERNMENT.

§ 37. Classification... 52
§ 38. Relation of the National Government to Individuals...................... 52
　§ 39. Question of the Establishment of Religion.......................... 53
　§ 40. Naturalization... 54
　§ 41. The Indians.. 54
　§ 42. The Negro... 57
　§ 43. The Chinese 58
　§ 44. General Remarks on the Power over Individuals 59
§ 45. Territorial Powers; Public Land 59
　§ 46. Early Land Vetoes... 60
　§ 47. Public Lands and the Constitution; Land Grants.................... 61
　§ 48. Later Land Vetoes on Grounds of Expediency 64
　§ 49. Effect of the Public Land Vetoes.............................. 66
　§ 50. Admission of States.. 67
　§ 51. Criticism of the Colorado and Nebraska Vetoes..................... 68
§ 52. Financial Powers.. 69
　§ 53. The Tariff 69
　§ 54. Refunding the Direct Tax................................... 72
　§ 55. Bank Charter Vetoes 74
　　§ 56. Madison's Bank Veto 74
　　§ 57. Jackson's Bank Veto................................... 74
　　§ 58. Tyler's Bank Veto..................................... 76
　　§ 59. Criticism of Bank Vetoes............................... 78
　§ 60. Currency and Coinage...................................... 78
　　§ 61. Inflation Bill... 80
　　§ 62. The Bland Silver Bill 81
　§ 63. Expenditure of Public Money................................ 82
　　§ 64. French Spoliation Claims............................... 83
　　§ 65. Relief Bills... 85
　　　§ 66. Bills defrauding the Government of Money............ 85

§ 67. Bills relieving Deserters from the Army 86
§ 68. Bills relieving former Army Officers of Disability......... 86
§ 69. Bills carelessly drawn 86
§ 70. Miscellaneous Relief Bills............................. 87
§ 71. Pension Vetoes... 87
 § 72. Bills conveying no Benefit............................ 88
 § 73. Unnecessary Increase of Pensions..................... 88
 § 74. Injuries not received "in the Line of Duty"........... 88
 § 75. Dependent Relatives: Dependency not proved.......... 88
 § 76. Miscellaneous Pension Bills 88
 § 77. Dependent Pension Bill............................... 89
 § 78. President Cleveland's Pension Policy................. 90
  § 79. Expediency of the Pension Vetoes............... 91
  § 80. Constitutionality of the Pension Vetoes.......... 92
 § 81. Summary of the Question of Pension Vetoes........... 93
§ 82. Commercial Powers... 93
§ 83. Internal Improvements 94
 § 84. Madison's Veto of a General Bill 94
 § 85. Monroe's Cumberland Road Veto. Constitutionality of Improvements 95
 § 86. Jackson's Vetoes. Jurisdiction and Local Character........... 96
 § 87. Tyler's Vetoes. Improvement of Water-Ways................ 99
 § 88. Polk's Vetoes. Local Improvements 100
 § 89. Pierce's Vetoes. Implied Powers......................... 101
 § 90. Buchanan's Vetoes. Constitutional Grounds 103
 § 91. Grant's Veto and Refusal to carry out a Bill................. 103
 § 92. Arthur's Veto. Local Objects............................ 104
 § 93. Public Buildings 105
 § 94. General View of Internal Improvement Vetoes 106
§ 95. Measures based on the General Welfare Clause......................... 107
 § 96. Texas Seed Bill....................................... 107
§ 97. War Powers 108
§ 98. General Effect of the Veto on the Exercise of the Powers of Government.... 109

CHAPTER V.

CONSTITUTIONAL PROCEDURE AS TO VETOES.

§ 99. The Action of the President... 111
 § 100. Is the Exercise of the Veto a Legislative Power?................... 112
 § 101. Constitutionality of Pocket Vetoes. The Legal Ten Days........... 113
 § 102. May a Bill be vetoed without stating Reasons?..................... 114
 § 103. May a Bill be signed after the Adjournment of Congress?............ 115
 § 104. May a President refuse to carry out an Act ?....................... 116
 § 105. The President's Right of Protest................................... 117
 § 106. Is the Signature of the President Essential to Constitutional Amendments ?.. 117
§ 107. The Action of Congress... 118
 § 108. Has the Executive a Right to recall a Veto?....................... 118

§ 109. What is a Two-thirds Majority?......................... 119
§ 110. Has the Speaker a Right to vote on Reconsideration?............. 120
§ 111. Second Reconsideration of a Veto......................... 120
§ 112. Failure to enter the Veto Message in the Journal 122
§ 113. Frequent Neglect of Reconsideration...................... 122
§ 114. Comparative Unimportance of Constitutional Details................... 123

CHAPTER VI.

POLITICAL DEVELOPMENT OF THE VETO POWER.

§ 115. Reasons for Chronological Treatment................................. 124
§ 116. Statistics of Vetoes 124
§ 117. Personal Element in the Veto... 126
    § 118. Presidents who vetoed No Bills 126
    § 119. Presidents who vetoed Few Bills 126
    § 120. Presidents who vetoed Many Bills.............................. 126
§ 121. Reasons expressed for Vetoes 129
    § 122. The Constitution and Expediency 129
    § 123. Cause of the Increasing Use of Expediency as a Reason for Vetoes.. 130
§ 124. Effect of the Veto on Parties 131
§ 125. Effect of the Veto on Legislation 132
    § 126. Prevention of Unwise Measures 133
    § 127. Prevention of Unwise Lines of Policy............................ 133
    § 128. Indirect Influence of the Veto on Legislation 134
    § 129. Vetoes which have failed of their Object 134
§ 130. Popular Objections to the Veto.. 135
§ 131. Proposed Constitutional Amendments 136
    § 132. Attempts to destroy the Power.................................. 136
    § 133. Attempts to diminish the Power................................. 136
    § 134. Attempts to enlarge the Power.................................. 137
§ 135. The Veto Power in 1789 and in 1889................................... 138

APPENDICES.

APPENDIX A.
Chronological List of Presidential Vetoes with References (1789–1889) 141

APPENDIX B.
Chronological List of Presidential Protests (1789–1889) 208

APPENDIX C.
Chronological List of Vetoes sent to the Confederate Congress (1861–1865)....... 210

APPENDIX D.
Legislative Activity of the Presidents (1789–1889)............................. 214

APPENDIX E.
Provisions of State Constitutions relative to the Veto........................... 215

APPENDIX F.
Bibliography of the Veto Power.. 220

CHAPTER I.

GENESIS OF THE VETO POWER.

§ 1. Origin of the veto power.
§ 2. Legislative power among the Teutonic tribes.
§ 3. Legislative power in England down to the appearance of the royal veto.
§ 4. Extension of royal legislative power: proclamation, suspension, dispensation.
§ 5. Limitations on royal legislative power: the veto.
§ 6. Disappearance of the veto in England.
§ 7. The veto power in the American Colonies.
§ 8. The veto power in the first State constitutions.
§ 9. The veto power under the Articles of Confederation.
§ 10. The veto power in the Federal Convention.
§ 11. The veto clause in the Constitution of the United States.

§ 1. **Origin of the veto power.**—The veto power which to-day seems purely a power to prevent the passage of proposed laws, originated as a part of the power to make them. This paradox is explained by the fact that legislation includes the right of the legislating body either to accept or to reject the propositions which it discusses. It has a positive and a negative function, and this latter function is in its nature a power to veto or deny. Among our German political ancestors both legislative functions were exercised by the same authority. Since the time of the Teutonic tribes a change has gradually been taking place, and now in the United States two authorities are interested in the making of laws: Congress, which, like its early prototype, can either accept or reject proposed legislation; and the President, who is entirely separate from Congress, but has a qualified power of rejection which is similar to the negative power of Congress.

The steps by which the change has taken place are clearly to be seen in English history.

§ 2. **Legislative power among the Teutonic tribes.**— In the Germany of Tacitus legislative power was lodged with the freemen. These men, who formed a majority of the tribe, met in assemblies and transacted in a rude way the business of the tribe.[1]

---

[1] Freeman, Growth of the English Constitution, 12.

We find among these peoples *principes* or nobles, and in some cases even kings, who were chosen by popular vote, and who had full authority in minor matters.[1] But the weightier affairs of state could be settled only by the assembly, although even in these cases the questions were prepared by the *principes* for the action of the freemen.[2] The people, therefore, really made their own laws, yet we see the germs of that kingly influence on legislation which in early English history became well-nigh supreme.

§ 3. **Legislative power in England down to the appearance of the royal veto.** — When the Teutonic tribes conquered England, they brought with them their political constitution and set it up in the conquered land, practically unchanged. The people were still sovereign. Little by little, however, the King acquired power, and always at the expense of popular authority. In the first place, as the English kingdom spread further and further out over the island, the King, from the very fact of this growth, became more and more powerful.[3] Again, there were certain persons in the nation to whom the King sustained the relation of personal lord. As the King became a more powerful personage, it of course became more of an honor to be the King's servant or Thegn,[4] and in a comparatively short time all the chief men in the nation became in this way the personal supporters of the King. His position was thus very materially strengthened.

The growing power of the King was nowhere more clearly seen than in the national council, the *Witenagemot*. At first, just as in the assemblies among the Teutonic tribes, all the freemen of the kingdom attended.[5] As the English extended their territory, personal presence became practically an impossibility for the great majority of freemen, and, in the end, only the chief men of the nation, many of whom were the "King's men," attended these meetings.[6] Thus the legislative power which had been exercised formerly by the whole people came to be exercised by a comparatively small number of men who were summoned and practically controlled by the King.

The Norman Conquest strengthened the legislative power of

---

[1] Stubbs, Select Charters, 4.
[2] Tacitus, De Moribus Germaniæ, c. 7–13.
[3] Freeman, Growth of the English Constitution, 36.
[4] Ibid., 50.   [5] Ibid., 60.
[6] Stubbs, Select Charters, 11.

the kings; and consequently the duties of Parliament became more than ever a mere matter of form. Parliament held the shadow of power, while the King enjoyed the substance.[1] Supremacy over Parliament was retained by the King well down to the reign of Edward III; and during this period, the subjects of legislation as well as the mode of dealing with them rested with the royal will. In many cases a mere proclamation by the Sovereign created law.[2] Generally, however, the matter was laid before the council, but even then the King's authority was a condition precedent to the action of the council.[3]

§ 4. **Extension of royal legislative power: proclamation, suspension, and dispensation.** — There were three outgrowths of royal legislative power which lasted long after the surrender of the unlimited right to make laws, but which should be considered at this point. They were: the power of creating substantive laws by royal proclamation; the power of suspension; and the power of dispensation.

From early times it had been customary for the kings of England to issue proclamations for the enforcement of law. The custom grew until at last the King commenced to issue proclamations, not for the enforcement, but for the creation of law. As a rule, this power was exercised only when Parliament was not in session, and when some urgent necessity called for immediate legislation. The propriety of the King's action in such cases was generally recognized and acquiesced in.[4] As the country grew, the royal proclamations became more frequent and their necessity less evident; consequently they encountered a great deal of opposition from the people. In 1610, when James I and Parliament were quarrelling, the Commons issued an address to the Crown, complaining of the frequency of proclamations.[5] The King consulted the judges in reference to the matter, and they declared against proclamations creating law. The practice was not ended by this decision, however; and during the time of Charles I proclamations were more frequent than ever.[6] The question was not finally settled until 1766, when an act of Parliament[7] recognized the illegality of proclamations creating law.

[1] Stubbs, Select Charters, 17-35.
[2] Hearn, Government of England, 37.
[3] Ibid., 52, quoting Bracton in support of the statement.
[4] Ibid., 38.   [5] State Trials, II, 519.
[6] Hearn, Government of England, 40.   [7] 7 George III, c. 7.

Laws passed by Parliament sometimes worked in unexpected ways which caused great hardship, and as the hardship generally became apparent after Parliament had been dissolved, it gradually became the custom for the King to suspend the troublesome act until it could be reconsidered.[1] This was the suspending power.

Closely connected with the power just considered, was the dispensing power of the Crown, by the exercise of which the King could exempt particular persons from the operation of a law. Like the suspending power, it was in its exercise a partial repeal of law.[2]

Both the power of dispensation and the power of suspension were acquiesced in by the people for a considerable time. Their disappearance, like the disappearance of many of the other powers of the Crown, dates from the overthrow of the Stuarts. The last two kings of this dynasty, in their attempts to remove the disabilities of Catholics and Dissenters, freely used the powers which we are considering. This action roused their opponents to an unreasonable pitch,[3] and the powers were taken away from the Crown in the first year after the Revolution of 1688.[4] The three incidents which we have just been considering, well illustrate the extensive legislative power of the early English kings. They show that not only was the royal authority necessary for the enactments by Parliament, but that the Sovereign, wholly without consent of Parliament, could both make and repeal laws.

§ 5. **Limitations on royal legislative power; the veto.**—As has already been said, the period during which the kings of England had their greatest control of legislation lasted until about the time of Edward III. Then the House of Commons began to have a distinct influence in the making of laws, and the royal legislative power took on a new and less important character. In this period, as before, the King was the real power in legislation; but hitherto he had acted as prompted by his own will, while now he makes use of his legislative power only when requested by the Parliament so to do. The usual method of procedure was as follows. The Commons petitioned the King to make a law on a given subject. The King received the petition and made such a law as he thought fit.[5] When once the power was set in motion,

---

[1] Taswell-Langmead, English Constitutional History, 313. [2] Ibid., 313.
[3] Hallam, Constitutional History of England, III, 62.
[4] 1 William and Mary, Sess. 2, c. 2, 1st Sec. Bill of Rights.
[5] Hearn, Government of England, 55.

the King could exercise it much as in former days, when he himself took the initiative in legislation. The sovereigns were not slow to take away the effect of the privilege of the Commons, by granting laws which were in no sense an answer to the petitions upon which they were based. The practice was of course exceedingly distasteful to the Commons, and they objected strenuously, but to no purpose; for the King continued to ignore the petitions. Finally the Commons drew up a petition in the precise form of an Act of Parliament. The Crown assented to it in the exact form in which it was drawn up. From this grew the custom of accepting or rejecting as a whole the petition of the Commons.[1] The custom grew stronger as time went on, and by the beginning of the sixteenth century it was a fixed practice.[2] The results of the new method were far-reaching. The King was almost wholly deprived of his positive power in legislation. All that was left him was the negative power of disapproval. He could refuse his assent to a law, but he was not directly concerned in the making of law, however much he might accomplish by his influence with the legislature.

Here at last we come upon the veto as we find it in the Constitution of the United States, — the right of the executive to refuse his assent to the laws which the legislature has framed. It is apparent that the veto is a remnant of the more extensive legislative power formerly held by the English kings. The power of legislation was cut down little by little, until at last only the veto was left. In time, as we shall see,[3] an authority similar to the English veto was transferred to the chief executives of the American Colonies, and at last embedded in the Constitution of the United States.

§ 6. **Disappearance of the veto in England.** — We have now traced the rise of the veto in England; and, before passing to its history in America, let us examine briefly the manner of its disappearance in the mother country. From the time of the Tudors down to the Revolution of 1688, the King's right to refuse his assent to bills of Parliament was practically unquestioned.

The Stuarts, instead of vetoing bills, generally preferred lightly

---

[1] This custom grew up in the reign of Henry VI. Hallam, Middle Ages (N. Y. 1869), III, 89, and note 3.
[2] Hearn, Government of England, 58.
[3] *Post*, §§ 7, 8, 9, 10, 11.

to assent to laws which they intended to dispose of by the power of dispensation or of suspension; although James I, in assenting to all the measures passed in Parliament in 1606, explained that he did so "as a special token-of grace and favor, being a matter unusual to pass all acts without exception."[1] Charles I, however, was more outspoken in his opposition to Parliament. His evasive approval of the Petition of Right[2] was practically an attempt to extend the principle of the powers of dispensation and suspension; while his refusal to assent to the Militia Bill,[3] and other ordinances, is considered by Mr. Hallam one of the direct causes of the Revolution of 1643.[4] Parliament afterwards gave the Militia Bill the force of law without the King's signature;[5] a fact which may have been in the minds of the Massachusetts Constitutional Convention when, in 1780, they gave to the governor the suspensive veto which was afterwards adopted by the Federal Convention.

From 1688 the veto was used more circumspectly, although it was still active down through the reign of William III.[6] After his death, the royal assent to a bill was refused only once. In the sixth year of the reign of Queen Anne[7] a bill was passed for settling the militia of that part of Great Britain called Scotland. It became known to the Queen and her advisers that the Pretender was on his way to Scotland, and it was therefore thought unwise to carry out the measures proposed by the bill. As the bill had not yet gone through the formality of presentation for the royal signature, the Queen, under advice, refused her assent to it rather than to wait for repeal. From that time to this, no sov-

---

[1] Hearn, Government of England, 61.

[2] 1628. Taswell-Langmead, English Constitutional History, 544–545.

[3] February 16, 1642.

[4] Hallam, Constitutional History of England (6 ed.), I, 554, 559; Bright, History of England, II, 658. For the text of the veto of the Militia Bill, see Parliamentary History, II, 1077, 1106–7, 1110.

[5] The words used in assenting to a bill were and are "Soit droit fait comme est desiré," or " Le roy le veult," or " Soit fait comme il est desiré." May, Law, Privileges, etc., of Parliament, 6th ed., p. 496. A veto was expressed in the words "le roy s'avisera."

[6] Macaulay refers to at least four bills which William III refused to sign. Macaulay, History of England, IV, 183, 371, 479, 687. Dr. William Everett speaks of two more vetoes by William III. Proceedings of the Massachusetts Historical Society, Second Series, V, 160 (January, 1890).

[7] 1708. Ibid., Second Series, V, 159 (January, 1890).

ereign of England has vetoed a bill of Parliament. Mr. Bagehot puts the case in a graphic though exaggerated form when he says that the Queen "must sign her own death-warrant if the two Houses send it to her."[1] Bills have been defeated by the announcement that the Sovereign would consider its promoters unfriendly; they have been defeated by royal influence or royal bribes, but never since 1708 has the signature of the Sovereign been refused to a measure which has obtained a majority of both Houses of Parliament.

§ 7. **The veto power in the American Colonies.** — At the time of the constitutional struggle in England between the Crown and the representatives of the people, English colonies were growing up in America. And here both the Crown and the royal governors exercised with great vigor and inflexibility the power which was gradually disappearing in the mother country.

From the earliest times, the power to establish colonies was admitted to be a royal prerogative; the King alone could form or sanction colonial constitutions, and by the King, except in the two colonies of Rhode Island and Connecticut, the governors were appointed. In each of the thirteen colonies which later revolted, the governor could, under charter, proprietary grant or royal instructions, veto any measure of the legislature; and in each of the colonies, except proprietary Maryland and the charter colonies of Rhode Island and Connecticut, the King could prevent a bill from becoming a law, even after it had been approved by the governor. In all cases where the veto was exercised it was absolute.[2]

The King used his power over the Colonial legislatures with great freedom, and a bill which was obnoxious to any interest or policy of the mother country was almost sure to be vetoed promptly. Indeed, the disallowance of Colonial acts was a part of the system of controlling the Colonies for the advantage of the mother country which made reconciliation impossible. As an illustration, which could be easily multiplied not only from the history of Virginia, but from that of the other Colonies,[3] it may be noted that by this process were annulled the acts of the Virginia

---

[1] Bagehot, English Constitution, 83.   [2] Elliot, Debates, IV, 620.
[3] Documents relating to the Colonial History of the State of New York, V, 157, 158, 529. Quincy, History of Harvard University, I, 77, contains an account of the veto of the Colonial act of 1692, granting a charter to Harvard College.

legislature restricting the slave-trade.[1] In fact, the abuse of the veto power by the Crown was so universally felt that the first clause in the Declaration of Independence set forth as a reason for the separation of the Colonies from the mother country: "He [the King] has refused his assent to laws most wholesome and necessary for the public good."

More distasteful to the people even than the abuse of the royal veto was the abuse of the Governor's veto. In Maryland, indeed, the governor's right to veto was not admitted by the Burgesses. None of the other colonies went quite so far; but in all, save Connecticut and Rhode Island, where governors were chosen by the people for a single year,[2] and could not be expected to take a firm stand against popular measures, there were loud complaints because the governors refused to allow acts of the legislature to become laws. Nor was the feeling groundless. In many of the colonies the governor was sent over seas, with little sympathy for his people. In all he was bound to regard the instructions of the Lords of Trade. When conflicts with the legislatures arose, the governor made use of the veto power to secure grants or even the payment of his salary. Franklin says that in Pennsylvania "it became at last a regular practice to have orders on the treasury in his (the governor's) name presented along with bills to be signed, so that he might actually receive the former before he should sign the latter."[3]

§ 8. **The veto power in the first State constitutions.** — In view of the use to which the King and the royal governors put the veto power, it is hardly to be wondered that, in the state governments which were formed after the breaking out of hostilities with England, this power was greatly limited. In several states a commission took the place of a governor. In no state but Massachusetts

---

[1] Bancroft, United States (last revision), II, 77.

[2] Arnold, History of Rhode Island, I, 202; Bancroft, United States (last ed.), I, 272.

[3] Elliot, Debates, IV, 621. Examples of vetoes by royal governors may be found in Documents relating to the Colonial History of New York, IV, pp. 426, 536. In Quincy, History of Harvard University, I, 302-305, is an account of a bill presented by the General Court of Massachusetts June, 1722, altering the constitution of the Corporation of Harvard College. Gov. Shute returned it with the following conditional approval: "I consent to these votes provided the Rev. Mr. Benjamin Wadsworth and the Rev. Mr. Benjamin Colman and the Rev. Mr. Appleton are not removed by said orders, but still remain Fellows of the Corporation." The House declared that the proviso "has a tendency to defeat entirely the design and purpose of these votes"; but Shute carried his point.

did the governor have even a qualified veto on the acts of the legislature;[1] and in that state the governor was not given this qualified veto until the constitution of 1780 was adopted.[2]

§ 9. **The veto power under the Articles of Confederation.** — The fear of executive power which was so evident in the State Conventions at this time, was even more plainly to be seen in the Articles of Confederation. Under the national government thereby established there was not even so much as an executive commission, except the "Committee of States" which managed the affairs of the nation during the time that Congress was not in session, and other minor committees appointed and controlled by Congress. In such a form of government it is hardly necessary to say that there was no executive veto. In fact, the Articles went to the other extreme and granted to five states, and in some cases to a single State, the authority which was so feared in the executive: for the assent of nine of the thirteen States was required to all important acts, and unanimous assent was required to Amendments to the Articles. This latter provision in practice resembled very nearly the "liberum veto" of the Polish diet, and the principle which was thus recognized, namely, that a single State could declare an act

---

[1] Hildreth, United States, III, 377.

[2] The provision in the Massachusetts Constitution of 1780 is as follows (Chap. I, Sec. I, Art. II): "No bill or resolve of the senate or house of representatives shall become law, and have force as such, until it shall have been laid before the governor for his revisal: and if he, upon such revision, approve thereof, he shall signify his approbation by signing the same. But if he have any objection to the passing of such bill or resolve, he shall return the same, together with his objections thereto, in writing, to the senate, or house of representatives, in whichsoever the same shall have originated, who shall enter the objections sent down by the governor, at large, on their records, and proceed to reconsider the said bill or resolve; but if, after such reconsideration, two-thirds of the said senate or house of representatives shall, notwithstanding the said objections, agree to pass the same, it shall, together with the objections, be sent to the other branch of the legislature, where it shall also be reconsidered, and if approved by two-thirds of the members present, shall have the force of law; but in all such cases the vote of both houses shall be determined by yeas and nays; and the names of the persons voting for or against the said bill shall be entered upon the public records of the Commonwealth.

"And in order to prevent unnecessary delays, if any bill or resolve shall not be returned by the Governor within five days after it shall have been presented, the same shall have the force of law." — Poore, Charters and Constitutions, I, 960.

The fact that this provision is so similar to the one in the United States Constitution, taken in connection with the fact that Mr. Gerry of Massachusetts introduced the resolve in the Federal Convention upon which the veto power was based, leads almost inevitably to the conclusion that the national provision as to the veto power is but an improved copy of this early Massachusetts provision.

of the National Legislature null and void, if the State set up the plea of unconstitutionality, bore unpleasant fruit in 1798-9, in 1832, and again in 1860.

§ 10. **The veto power in the Federal Convention.** — The whole machinery of the government under the Articles of Confederation was so defective that after six years' experience it became evident that a change must be made. The Constitutional Convention met at Philadelphia, made the change, and the change restored the veto power.

In the deliberations of the Convention it was early admitted that a national executive was a necessity, and, with some reluctance, that this executive should be endowed with the veto power. There was, however, a great difference of opinion as to the degree of the power. Should it be absolute or qualified? If the latter, what number of votes in each house of Congress should be required to override the veto? Should the power be exclusively vested in the President, or should it be entrusted to the President jointly with some other department of the government? These and other questions of a like nature arose and were settled by the Philadelphia Convention.

The matter was first brought up on May 29, 1787, when, in the series of resolves introduced by Randolph of Virginia, appeared the following clause:[1] "The executive and a convenient number of the national judiciary ought to compose a Council of Revision, with authority to examine every act of the National Legislature before it shall operate and every act of a particular legislature before a negative thereon shall be final; and the dissent of the said Council shall amount to a rejection unless the act of the National legislature be again passed, or that of a particular legislature be again negatived by —— of the members of each branch." Mr. Randolph's views in this matter may have been based on a suggestion made in a letter written to him by Mr. Madison a few weeks previous. Mr. Madison proposed a negative by the national government of the same nature "in all cases whatsoever, on the legislative acts of the States, as the King of Great Britain heretofore had."[2]

---

[1] Randolph plan, § 8, in Elliot, Debates, IV, 622.
[2] Elliot, Debates, IV, 623; V, 108. The plan here suggested has been adopted in the Dominion of Canada, British North America Act, Art. 90.

The so-called Pinckney plan contains a veto clause much as we have it now.¹ The only other scheme of government of any importance which was introduced at this time was the "Jersey Plan"; but as it had no executive, there was no provision for a veto.

The main discussion in regard to the veto power centred around the resolve of Mr. Randolph. On June 4, Mr. Gerry of Massachusetts moved to amend Randolph's resolve so that it should read: "that the national executive shall have a right to negative any legislative act which shall not afterwards be passed by —— parts of each branch of the National Legislature."² Hamilton, with his characteristic zeal for a strong central government, moved to strike out the last fifteen words of the Amendment, but the motion was unanimously rejected.³ At this point Franklin attempted to have a suspensive veto substituted for a negative veto, but the attempt failed.⁴ The blank in Gerry's substitute resolve was then filled by the words "two-thirds," and the whole resolution was adopted by a vote of eight states to two.⁵ The resolution allowed the President to retain bills for seven days, and did not apply to joint resolutions, orders, or votes. Later on, the plan was changed so that the President could retain a bill for ten days, and could veto joint-resolutions, orders, and votes as well as bills.⁶

On June 18th Hamilton introduced his scheme of government which entrusted the executive with an absolute veto on both state and national legislation.⁷ The scheme was too pronounced to have any chance of acceptance in the Convention, and was at once rejected.

On August 15th Madison brought up for the third time the question of including the judges of the Supreme Court with the President in the exercise of the veto power. The plan was one the success of which Madison apparently had very much at heart, but it was defeated.⁸ Two reasons seem to have led to this result. In the first place, it was considered that the judges who were to be the interpreters of the law "might receive an improper bias

---

¹ Elliot, Debates, IV, 622. ² Ibid., IV, 623.
³ Ibid., IV, 623. ⁴ Ibid., IV, 623.
⁵ Mass., N. Y., Penn., Del., Va., N. Car., S. Car., Ga., voted "aye." Conn., Md., voted "no."— Madison Papers, II, 791.
⁶ Ibid., III, 1548. ⁷ Elliot, Debates, IV, 632.
⁸ The vote stood: Aye, 3 States — Del., Md., Va.; No, 8 States — N. H., Mass., Conn., N. J., Pa., N. Car., S. Car., Ga. Madison, Papers, III, 1333.

from having given a previous opinion in a revisionary capacity."[1] In the second place, it was deemed wise to keep the judiciary as far removed as possible from any connection with political schemes which the President might wish to bring forward or influence either by his approval or disapproval of legislation. The Convention acted wisely in rejecting Madison's proposal, and the experience of a century has shown how fortunate was their decision. It is certainly a dangerous thing "to place the judges in a position to be either corrupted or influenced by the executive."[2]

One of the curious incidents of the discussion of the veto power in the Convention was the fluctuation of opinion regarding the proportion of votes in each branch of Congress which should be necessary to override an executive veto. August 15, on motion of Mr. Wilson, it was decided by a vote of six states to four, to change it from two-thirds to three-fourths;[3] on September 12th, this decision was exactly reversed by an exactly similar vote of six states to four, made on the motion of Mr. Wilson.[4] The reason which he assigned for his change of front was that the three-fourths rule gave the President too much power. Mr. Madison pointed out that when the three-fourths rule was adopted the President was to be elected by the legislature, and for seven years, but that since that time a change had been made, and he was now to be elected by the people, and for four years.[5] Partly on account of these circumstances Mr. Madison favored the retention of the three-fourths requirement.[6]

§ 11. **The veto clause in the Constitution of the United States.** — Such is, in brief, the history of the veto as it appears in the Constitution of the United States. The scope of the present work precludes more than a mere outline of the origin of the power, — a sketch of a growth to which a volume might profitably be devoted. Before passing to the discussion of the veto messages of the Presidents of the United States, which will occupy the body of the work, the result of the deliberations of the Convention should be stated. Article I, section 7, §§ 2 and 3 of the Constitution, reads as follows: "2. Every bill which shall have passed

---

[1] Story, Commentaries, § 886.
[2] Story, Commentaries, § 886.
[3] Elliot, Debates, V, 431
[4] Ibid., V, 536.
[5] Elliot, Debates, V, 538.
[6] Had the three-fourths ratio been retained, few bills would have been passed over the veto. See § 116.

the House of Representatives and the Senate shall, before it become a law, be presented to the President of the United States; if he approve, he shall sign it; but if not, he shall return it, with his objections, to that house in which it shall have originated, who shall enter the objections at large on their journal, and proceed to reconsider it. If, after such reconsideration, two-thirds of that house shall agree to pass the bill, it shall be sent, together with the objections, to the other house, by which it shall be likewise reconsidered, and if approved by two-thirds of that house, it shall become a law. But in all such cases the votes of both houses shall be determined by yeas and nays, and the names of the persons voting for and against the bill shall be entered on the journal of each house respectively. If any bill shall not be returned by the President within ten days (Sundays excepted) after it shall have been presented to him, the same shall be a law in like manner as if he had signed it, unless the Congress by their adjournment prevent its return, in which case it shall not be a law.

"Every order, resolution, or vote to which the concurrence of the Senate and House of Representatives may be necessary (except on a question of adjournment) shall be presented to the President of the United States; and before the same shall take effect, shall be approved by him, or, being disapproved by him, shall be repassed by two-thirds of the Senate and House of Representatives, according to the rules and limitations prescribed in the case of a bill."

CHAPTER II.

VETOES AFFECTING THE FORM OF GOVERNMENT.

§ 12. Executive methods of treating a bill.
§ 13. Classification of the vetoes.
§ 14. Vetoes affecting the form of the national Legislature.
§ 15. Vetoes affecting the form of the national Judiciary.
§ 16. General effect of vetoes considered in this chapter.

§ 12. **Executive methods of treating a bill.** — There are five ways in which a President of the United States may treat a bill which has duly passed both houses of Congress and has been presented to him: 1. In the first place, he may sign it, and in this case, the bill at once becomes a law. 2. Or if he is not satisfied with a bill, but nevertheless considers it inadvisable to veto it, he may sign it, and at the same time send to Congress a protest against those provisions in the measure of which he disapproves. This is a method of treating a bill which is not recognized by the Constitution. 3. Again, if a bill be presented to the President more than ten days before the close of a session of Congress, he may leave it unsigned; in this case in ten days it becomes a law without his signature. 4. If a measure be presented to the executive *within* ten days of the end of a session of Congress, and he fails to sign it, the bill does not become a law. This method of dealing with bills is the well-known "pocket-veto." 5. Lastly, a President may veto a bill; that is, may refuse to sign it, and send his reasons for such refusal to Congress.[1] Of course, if a bill has been presented within ten days of the end of a session, simple withholding of the President's signature kills it; but in many such cases the President has preferred to return the bill at once with his objections.

In the discussion to follow, and in the Appendices, every formal veto message, and all formal protests have been included, but no attempt has been made to sift out of the mass of abortive legisla-

---

[1] Constitution, Art. I, sec. vii, §§ 2 and 3. Quoted, *ante*, § 11.

tion the many bills which have failed for want of approval, and have never been referred to by the executive in his communications to Congress.

§ 13. **Classification of the vetoes.** — Before beginning the examination of the vetoes themselves, a word in explanation of their classification may be proper. All measures of Congress relate either to the form of the government or to the exercise of its powers. All the vetoes may therefore be conveniently divided into two corresponding classes. The classes will be considered in the order mentioned above, partly because it is natural to consider the form of a government before its powers, and partly because the vetoes of the second class are the more numerous and important.

Attempts at radical changes of the form of government have usually appeared in Congress as resolutions to amend the Constitution, and consequently the first class of vetoes is small. For resolutions to submit amendments do not require the assent of the President. The great majority of Congressional measures which have required the assent of the President have had reference to the scope of the powers granted by the Constitution, and it is under this head that we find the greatest number of vetoes. Within the various classes and sub-classes into which the vetoes have been divided the order in the discussion will be chronological.

§ 14. **Vetoes affecting the form of the national Legislature.** — The first bill vetoed under the Constitution was one authorizing a change in the form of the legislative branch of the government. In 1792 a bill passed Congress entitled, "An Act for an Apportionment of Representatives among the several States." April 5, 1792, President Washington vetoed the bill in a message addressed to the "Gentlemen of the House of Representatives," and signed simply "G. Washington."[1]

The reasons given for the veto were as follows: "First. The Constitution has prescribed that Representatives shall be apportioned among the several States according to their respective numbers; and there is no proportion or divisor which, applied to the respective numbers of the States, will yield the number and allot-

---

[1] See Appendix A, No. 1. See also Hildreth, History of the United States, IV, 303; Schouler, History of the United States, I, 189; John C. Hamilton, Life of Alexander Hamilton, IV, 334; Writings of Thomas Jefferson, VII, 594, IX, 115; Writings of James Madison, I, 544–546, 549, 550, 552, 554.

ment of Representatives proposed by the bill. Second. The Constitution has also provided that the number of Representatives shall not exceed one for every thirty thousand: which restriction is, by the context, and by fair and obvious construction, to be applied to the separate and respective numbers of the States; and this bill has allotted to eight of the States more than one for every thirty thousand." The President sent this message to Congress only after the most anxious thought. In Mr. Jefferson's diary [1] is to be found a most interesting account of the matter. The vote on the bill had been a sectional one, the North favoring and the South opposing the measure. Washington expressed to Mr. Jefferson the fear lest his veto should be considered as favoring the South, and also lest the Union should be dissolved on account of the sectional feeling which was beginning to show itself, — a foreboding which would seem to denote a deep insight into the future development of political questions. Mr. Jefferson reassured the President, and advised him to veto the bill. Influenced by this advice, and by his own strong feeling that the apportionment was unconstitutional, the President refused to sign the bill, and sent his reasons for that refusal to Congress.

The only other instance of the use of the veto power to preserve the form of the legislative branch of the government occurred in Jackson's administration. May 31, 1836, a bill passed Congress which provided that in the future Congress should assemble on the first Monday in November and should adjourn on the second Monday in May.[2] The President vetoed the measure [3] on the ground that no Congress had the power to fix the time of adjournment for future Congresses. Jackson based his statement upon the fourth clause of the fifth section of the first article of the Constitution, which declares "that neither house, during the session of Congress, shall, without the consent of the other, adjourn for more than three days, nor to any other place than that in which the two houses shall be sitting." The President also quoted, as a reason for his opposition, the clause in the Constitution which authorizes the executive to adjourn Congress in case the two houses cannot agree upon a day for adjournment.

When the veto message came up in the Senate, Clay, Webster,

[1] Elliot, Debates, IV, 624.
[2] Congressional Debates, XII, Part II, 1649.
[3] Appendix A, No. 20.

Calhoun, Clayton, and others opposed it.[1] Mr. Goldsborough, one of the opponents, argued [2] that the clause upon which the veto was founded [3] referred to temporary adjournments of either house pending the adjournment of the session, but not to the close of the session. Furthermore, he pointed out that, granting the President's statement that one Congress could not fix the time of adjournment for future Congresses, it should have no weight in the present case, since the bill particularly provided that future Congresses might adjourn at any other time than that set down in the act, if only both houses should agree to the change. Mr. Goldsborough's criticism seems just. Jackson's conclusion can hardly be drawn from his premises, and even if his argument were unassailable, his objection would hardly apply to the bill he was vetoing.

§ 15. **Vetoes affecting the form of the national Judiciary.** — The veto has been called into use to protect not only the form of Congress, but also the form of the national judiciary, and the attempted changes in this latter department which have not met with executive approval have been of no greater importance than those which related to Congress.

The first of these judiciary vetoes was interposed by President Madison, April 3, 1812, to a bill entitled: "An act providing for the trial of causes pending in the respective District Courts of the United States, in case of the absence or disability of the judges thereof."[4] The bill was intended primarily to give relief to the district courts of New York State, which were some seven hundred cases behind in their work. The President refused his assent to the bill for four reasons, the most important of them being as follows. In the first place, the new district judges contemplated by the act were to be the Supreme Court judges, who were already Circuit Court judges. The law allowed appeals from the district to the circuit courts. But as the act contemplated making the same man both circuit and district judge, the President thought that the advantage of an appeal would be lost. In the second place, the act left it with the President to determine when it should be necessary for the justices of the Supreme Court to perform the duties of District Court justices. Mr. Madison very wisely considered that this was "an unsuitable relation of members of the judiciary

---

[1] Congressional Debates, XII, Part II, 1859.
[2] Ibid., XII, Part II, 1878.
[3] Art. I, Sec. V, § 4.   [4] Appendix A, No. 5.

department to a discretionary authority of the executive department." Lastly, the President vetoed the bill because it virtually appointed the justices of the Supreme Court to new offices, thereby usurping a power which belonged to the executive branch of the government.[1] The President's objections were evidently considered sound, for the Senate sustained the veto by a large vote.[2]

December 14, 1842, President Tyler sent to the House of Representatives his reasons for the "pocket veto" at the last session of Congress of a bill entitled: "An act regulating the taking of testimony in cases of contested elections, and for other purposes."[3] Mr. Tyler did not sign the bill, because it had been presented to him so near the end of the session that he could not find time to read it through before Congress adjourned.

The practice of deluging the President in the last moments of a session of Congress with bills requiring his signature is very injurious to the interests of good legislation. Little or no time can be given to the consideration of each act, and as a result, bills become laws which even a slight examination would cause to be rejected.[4] Under such circumstances, a President would be justified in refusing to sign a measure of which he knew nothing. In the case under consideration, the President's failure to approve may have come wholly from an unwillingness to sign a measure of whose provisions he was ignorant. But the great care with which Mr. Tyler elaborates his reason for the veto raises a suspicion that he objected less to the time of presentation than to the measure itself. In the last paragraph of the message he betrays such knowledge of the provisions of the bill as to show that he had spent much time upon it after the adjournment of Congress.

January 22, 1873, the veto was again made use of to preserve the form of the judiciary. On that day, President Grant refused to sign a bill entitled: "An act in relation to new trials in the Court of Claims."[5] The purpose of this act was to modify an existing act of Congress which allowed the government to suspend payment for two years on judgments obtained against it in the

---

[1] *Post*, § 16.   [2] Appendix A, No. 5.   [3] Appendix A, No. 27.
[4] President Cleveland stated to Mr. Kenna in February, 1888, that he had received one hundred bills at the end of the preceding session, one of which, an important appropriation bill, he had not had time even to read. — MS. letter of Senator G. F. Hoar to Professor Hart, Feb. 11, 1888.
[5] Appendix A, No. 87.

Court of Claims. If evidence came to light within that time which showed the claim to be unjust, the United States could move for a new trial. The privilege of suspending judgment was only exercised in doubtful cases where fraud was suspected. The act under consideration reduced the time during which the government could suspend payment from two years to six months. The President refused to sanction the bill, on the ground that, by reducing the time during which judgment was suspended, it greatly increased the opportunities for defrauding the government. On the other hand, he pointed out that perfectly good claims would gain nothing by the new law, since, under the old law, claims which were evidently meritorious were settled without delay. The President's message was referred to the Committee on the Judiciary and ordered to be printed; but no attempt was ever made to pass the bill over the veto.

May 26, 1876, President Grant vetoed a bill entitled: "An act providing for the recording of deeds, mortgages, and other conveyances affecting real estate in the District of Columbia."[1] The bill was vetoed because it was drawn with such indefiniteness and uncertainty that it would lead to serious complications in regard to transfers of real estate, if it should become a law.

Only once since President Grant's administration has the executive refused to sign a bill affecting the national judiciary. March 6, 1878, President Hayes vetoed a bill entitled: "An act to authorize a special term of the Circuit Court of the United States for the southern district of Mississippi, to be held at Scranton, in Jackson County."[2] The President objected to the bill for two reasons. In the first place, because the time between the passage of the bill and the proposed session of the Circuit Court was not sufficient to allow the notice of the extra term to be published in the manner contemplated by the bill. In the second place, because although the United States was interested in forty-nine of the suits which it was proposed to bring in the extra term, it was shown that the government could not prepare for trial on such short notice, since no fund appropriated by Congress could be made available for that purpose. When the message was read in the House there was a little desultory debate as to just how many cases the proposed court would have to try. Then the veto was referred to the Committee on the Judiciary, and no further action was taken by Congress.

[1] Appendix A, No. 100.   [2] Ibid., No. 118.

§ 16. **General effect of vetoes considered in this chapter.** — The vetoes already considered, although few in number, are the only ones in our history which have directly protected the form of the government. The executive has frequently disagreed with Congress as to the powers which the Constitution has granted to Congress and to the States, and in some of the clauses of that document different meanings have been attached to almost every word; but though there have been differences in regard to the nature of the instrument, there have been few attempts essentially to change the form of government established under it. This is the more remarkable when it is remembered that Congress had a very large share in fixing the form of government, the outlines of which alone were settled by the Constitution. Indeed, only one of the unsuccessful attempts at change which we have just examined was of any constitutional importance. This was the apportionment bill that Washington vetoed: a bill which did seem to threaten in some degree the constitutional method of assigning representatives. But even this attack on the form of the legislature was probably unintentional. The other vetoes were called out either because the proposed legislation seemed inexpedient, or because it seemed corrupt. Jackson to be sure tried to base his veto of the bill regulating the length of the sessions of Congress on constitutional grounds, but he hardly made out his case.

In summing up this comparatively unimportant branch of the subject, we may say that the vetoes included here do not stand for any great constitutional principles, nor even for any connected policy of mere expediency, but are isolated endeavors of the executive to prevent the legislature from passing useless, or worse than useless, laws.

CHAPTER III.

VETOES AFFECTING THE DISTRIBUTION OF THE POWERS OF GOVERNMENT.

§ 17. Classification of vetoes in this chapter.
§ 18. Executive claims to legislative power supported by the veto.
　§ 19. The Bank veto.
　§ 20. Removal of the deposits.
§ 21. Vetoes for the protection of the executive from legislative encroachment.
　§ 22. Power over foreign affairs: the treaty power.
　　§ 23. Establishment of consular and diplomatic offices.
　　§ 24. Diplomatic intercourse.
　§ 25. The power of appointment.
　　§ 26. Requiring names of candidates for appointment.
　　§ 27. Requiring papers relative to removals from office.
　　§ 28. The Tenure of Office Act.
　　§ 29. The Fitz-John Porter Bill.
　§ 30. Protest for the protection of the President's war power.
　§ 31. Protest and veto for the protection of the President's personal rights under the Constitution.
　　§ 32. Covode Investigation.
　　§ 33. The President's salary.
　§ 34. Use of the veto in controversies arising out of the Civil War.
　§ 35. Riders on appropriation bills.
§ 36. General effect of the vetoes for the protection of the Executive.

§ 17. **Classification of vetoes in this chapter.** — The second of the two great divisions into which the vetoes have been separated includes those vetoes which concern either the distribution or the exercise of the powers of government. The vetoes relating to the distribution of powers will be taken up in the present chapter; those relating to the exercise of powers will be considered in Chapter IV.

On each of the three branches of the government has been conferred a separate authority, a distinct portion of the power which the people ceded to the national government. As between the legislature and judiciary, and between the judiciary and executive, the distribution has generally been acquiesced in,[1] or at least such

---
[1] President Jackson in the bank veto, however, claimed power belonging to the Supreme Court. *Post*, §§ 19, 57.

contentions as have occurred have not given rise to vetoes. But the distribution as between the executive and the legislative departments has not been undisputed. Congress has at various times attempted, either consciously or unconsciously, to usurp power belonging to the President, and many of these attempts have been frustrated by the veto. The wisdom of the Convention in providing a veto is thus vindicated; for one of the main objects of the power was that the President might protect his office from legislative encroachment.

Since the President has no definite power of initiative in legislation, and absolutely no power of amendment, it is evident that the veto cannot be used as a means of positive encroachment on the powers of Congress. It was intended as a means of defence, not as an instrument of attack. It is therefore remarkable that the first case of the use of the veto in any contest over the distribution of power between the President and Congress was a case of executive aggression.

§ 18. **Executive claims to legislative power supported by the veto.** — Jackson's bank veto is the one instance in our history where the veto has been used to convey a counter-proposition to Congress. In this case the President used the power less as a protection of the executive against an attack from Congress than as a cover for an attack by the executive against Congress.

§ 19. **The Bank veto.** — The Second United States Bank, which had been chartered in 1816 for a term of twenty years, applied, in 1832, for a new charter, and a bill for this purpose passed Congress on July 3, 1832.[1] On the tenth of the same month it was vetoed by President Jackson.[2] The financial side of the veto will be considered in another place.[3] Here we must consider the new and strange doctrines as to executive power advanced in the message.

The President first offered the novel suggestion that if he had been called upon he could have laid before Congress a measure to which no objection would have been made. This plan of waiting for the President's draft of a proposed law does not seem at all in

---

[1] A laborious search in the printed records of the government and in newspapers fails to disclose the text of this bill.

[2] Appendix A, No. 14; Von Holst, Constitutional History of the United States, II, 31–75; Schouler, History of the United States, IV, 44–54, 68–70, 132–147; Sumner, Jackson, Chapters XI–XIV; Parton, Jackson, Chapters XX, XXIX, XXX.

[3] *Post*, § 57.

keeping with the Constitution, which delegates legislative power to Congress, reserving to the President only a qualified veto. Jackson's claim was in effect that he should have had a hand in the details of the law, or in other words, that he should have initiated the legislation.[1]

But the President went further, and in the face of an act of Congress, duly approved by President Madison, and of a decision of the Supreme Court,[2] declared the new charter unconstitutional. The position was based not on a fundamental constitutional objection to the chartering of the bank, but on his individual opinion that some other provisions might have better served the purpose for which the bill was drawn. Dr. Von Holst states the case forcibly but in a much exaggerated form when he says: "The Supreme Court of the Union has its own Constitutional law; each President has his own; each new majority in Congress its own; and the public law of the Union is in principle the chaos of law, and the decision of a question of law lies outside the realm of possibility."[3]

It would be difficult and useless to attempt to trace all the remote consequences to which these principles of Jackson's would lead. It is enough for the present purpose to notice that the President laid claim to a power of initiative which belonged to Congress, and that the veto was used to fortify and defend this claim.

§ 20. **Removal of the deposits.** — In pursuance of the policy outlined in the bank veto of July 10, 1832, Jackson, through his Secretary of the Treasury, Taney, in September, 1833, ordered the removal of the government's deposits from the United States Bank. The order led to the famous Senate resolution,[4] censuring the President, and to his equally famous protest[5] against the censure. While this protest is not legally a veto, it had many of the effects of a veto, and is intimately connected with the question we are considering; for the protest was used by the executive to fortify the position taken in the veto of the Bank Bill, and to lay claim on behalf of the executive to still greater power.

---

[1] Von Holst, Constitutional History of the United States, II, 45.
[2] McCulloch v. State of Maryland, 4 Wheaton, 423; 3 Stats. at Large, 266.
[3] Constitutional History of the United States, II, 49.
[4] Debates of Congress, Vol. X, Part I, 58.
[5] Appendix B, No. 1.

Jackson defended the removal of the deposits on the ground that the placing of government funds in the bank was discretionary with the Secretary of the Treasury; furthermore, the President maintained that, since the treasury was one of the executive departments, the President had full authority to control the Secretary, and therefore to direct the removal of the deposits on his own responsibility. In both particulars the action of the President was open to exception.

In the first place, let us examine the Secretary of the Treasury's authority to remove the deposits at his discretion. The Secretary's power in the matter was not unlimited; for although the wording of the statute was very general,[1] the meaning was limited. So careful and accurate a writer as Mr. Story says that it was generally understood that the deposits were not to be removed by the Secretary except for "high and important reasons of state, upon unexpected emergencies."[2] The Secretary, it is true, may have considered that he was face to face with an "unexpected emergency," but he had no right to make that assumption in the face of the favorable report of the bank's condition which had been made by a Committee of Congress, many of whom were personally opposed to the renewal of the bank charter.[3] In short, the cause for the removal of the deposits was not the "unexpected emergency," but Jackson's personal determination that they should not be allowed to remain in the United States Bank. If this was not contrary to the letter of the Act of 1816, it was most certainly contrary to its spirit; and an usurpation of Congressional power.

The further assumption of Jackson that, in case the Secretary of the Treasury would not remove the deposits, the President himself could and would undertake the responsibility, was equally bold. He supported it by saying that the Constitution had conferred all executive authority upon him.[4]

---

[1] "The deposits of the money of the United States, in places in which the said bank and branches thereof may be established, shall be made in said bank or branches thereof, unless the Secretary of the Treasury at any time otherwise order and direct; in which case the Secretary of the Treasury shall immediately lay before Congress, if in session, and if not, immediately after the commencement of the next session, the reason of such order or direction." — 3 Stats. at Large, 274.

[2] Life and Letters of Story, II, 156.

[3] Debates of Congress, XI, 605, 638; XII, 191.

[4] Dr. Von Holst sarcastically observes that even if this were true, it could evidently only mean "all the executive powers granted by the Constitution, not all authority which

The President, in saying that all executive authority was conferred upon him, meant that the heads of the different departments were responsible to him alone. The claim was contrary to the practice of the government; the office of Secretary of the Treasury was created by law, his duties defined by law, and his control over public money was limited by law. In the case of Marbury v. Madison,[1] the Supreme Court of the United States had already emphatically declared that Congress could impose duties on the heads of the executive departments, and that the officers on whom such duties were imposed were solely responsible for the performance of these duties, and were responsible only to the law imposing the obligation. This decision directly covers the present case; and even if the heads of the departments were in general subject to the will of the chief executive, in the particular instance under discussion the President was not warranted in ordering the removal of the deposits, contrary to the will of Congress.

To sum up: President Jackson, in the first place, gave his own construction to an act of Congress, and it was a construction which only a most rigid adherence to the strict letter of the law could justify. In the second place, Jackson assumed power over the acts of the heads of the departments, which was not granted by the Constitution, which had not been conceded by Congress, and which had been expressly denied by the Supreme Court of the United States in an important decision. It was this stretch of prerogative which President Jackson's protest of April 15, 1834, justified and glorified.

§ 21. **Vetoes for the protection of the executive from legislative encroachment.**[2] — None of President Jackson's successors have laid

should, according to any political theory whatever, or according to any view of any person whatever, belong to the highest possessor of executive power." — Constitutional History of the United States, II, 63.

[1] 1 Cranch, 165, 166.

[2] One veto should be included at this point which comes properly under the main head of vetoes for the protection of the executive, but which cannot be classed under any of the following subheads. February 14, 1877, the President vetoed a bill which amended the statutes in such a manner that the clerk of the House of Representatives should select the newspapers throughout the United States in which the advertising of the executive departments should be placed (Appendix A, No. 115). Prior to 1867 this work had been done by the heads of the departments. In that year the advertising in ten of the States which had seceded was placed in the hands of the clerk of the House of Representatives. The President objected to the bill because it made general and permanent a

claim to the extended executive power asserted by his veto of the Bank Bill and his protest against the Senate resolution of censure. On the contrary, the executive has generally been satisfied to defend himself from the encroachments of Congress, and it is interesting to notice that Jackson himself was the first who was obliged to contend for his constitutional rights.

§ 22. *Power over foreign affairs: the treaty power.* — On October 14, 1832, a treaty between the United States and the Two Sicilies was signed, by which the King of the Two Sicilies was to pay an indemnity to merchants of the United States whose vessels had been destroyed in 1809, 1811, and 1812 by ships under the control of the Two Sicilies.[1] Certain claimants under this treaty petitioned the Senate, December 15, 1834, for an immediate settlement of the claims against the Two Sicilies at a reduced rate. In a word, they wished to discount their claims against the foreign government. A bill was drawn in accordance with this petition and passed both houses of Congress. It was vetoed by Jackson, March 3, 1835,[2] because it authorized "the Secretary of the Treasury to compromise the claims allowed by the commissioners under the treaty with the King of the Two Sicilies." The President declared that the Constitution granted the executive full authority to negotiate with a foreign power, and Congress need not, in fact could not, empower him to act in the matter.

The compromise which was desired was of course nothing but a new treaty with the King of the Two Sicilies; and as the President, by and with the consent of the Senate, is empowered by the Constitution to make all treaties,[3] it certainly would seem to be an assumption on the part of Congress to authorize the President to enter into negotiations. To be sure, the Senate may amend, and has amended, treaties submitted to it;[4] and it might also, with per-

provision only intended to be local and temporary; because the law could hardly fail to work unsatisfactorily; and because it was an encroachment on the rights of the executive departments. Two other vetoes of minor importance call for mention here. One was President Tyler's veto of a bill regulating the construction of revenue cutters (Appendix A, No. 30). The other was President Buchanan's veto of a resolution increasing the speed of mail carriers on certain postal routes (Appendix A, No. 43). Both bills were vetoed because, among other reasons, they encroached upon the authority of the executive.

[1] United States Treaties and Conventions, 855.
[2] Appendix A, No. 19; Senate Journal, 2 sess., 23 Cong., p. 233.
[3] Treaties of all descriptions are included in the grant of power by the Constitution. — Story, Commentaries, § 1502.
[4] Von Holst, Constitutional Law, 201.

fect propriety, request the President to enter into negotiations with a foreign power; but it is certain that the chief executive would be under no obligations whatever to heed the request.[1] The President alone has full power to take the preliminary steps in making a treaty, and he derives this power, not from Congress, but directly from the Constitution.

Under these circumstances, President Jackson's treatment of the bill under discussion was constitutionally correct. He was defending in a constitutional manner a power which constitutionally belonged to the executive. Had he suffered the action of Congress to stand, he would have given his sanction to its arrogation of authority, and the affair would have become a precedent for future Congressional attempts, perhaps more intent than the present one on depriving the President of the treaty-making power.

§ 23. **Establishment of consular and diplomatic offices.** — In President Grant's administration, Congress again attempted to encroach upon the power of the executive in foreign affairs. The first of these attempts was met by a strong protest; the second by a veto. August 14, 1876, President Grant signed a bill entitled "An act making appropriations for the consular and diplomatic services of the government for the year ending June thirtieth, eighteen hundred and seventy-seven, and for other purposes"; but in signing the bill he protested against a provision in the act which directed that notice be sent to certain diplomatic and consular officers to close their offices.[2] The President admitted the right of Congress to refuse to appropriate money for the salaries of consular and other public ministers, but he denied the right of Congress to order the closing of any diplomatic or consular offices. This claim he based on that section of the Constitution[3] which provides that the President "shall nominate, and by and with the advice and consent of the Senate, shall appoint ambassadors or other public ministers and consuls." The Constitution nowhere makes provision for the removal of these officers, and consequently the power of removal is vested in the department having the power of appointment. This last statement was apparently admitted by all, and hence the real contest related to the power of appointment.

The President's position seems sound and reasonable, yet when the protest was read in the House of Representatives, it caused

[1] Von Holst, Constitutional Law, 202.
[2] Appendix B, No. 8.   [3] Art. II, Sec. II, § 2.

much discussion. Mr. Holman of Indiana opened the debate, and asserted that the House of Representatives could alone close a foreign diplomatic office, and his reason for this statement was that the foreign diplomatic missions were created, or at least authorized, by statute.[1] General Garfield then challenged him to name an instance in point, — a challenge which Mr. Holman was unable to meet. Mr. Tucker of Virginia then took up the argument which the "Great Objector" had dropped, and in a much more logical way maintained that, while the Constitution authorized the creation of diplomatic offices, Congress created them; that until Congress had passed appropriations for the salaries of the various foreign diplomatic agents, the President could not appoint them; that Congress must determine how many embassadors, ministers, and other diplomatic officers were necessary, and that then it is in the executive's power to fill such offices; that the President's refusal to fill offices thus created would be an impeachable offence. In short, Mr. Tucker argued that Congress created the diplomatic offices, and could therefore destroy them if it saw fit.[2] On the other hand, it was held by General Garfield, Mr. Lawrence, and others that the Constitution created the diplomatic offices, and that it rested entirely with the President to appoint men to fill as many such offices as he chose.

The great argument against the protest seemed to be that the appropriations for the various offices in some way created the offices. This cannot be true, since in the early days of the government, when it was in the hands of those who drew up the Constitution, and who presumably knew better than any one else what that document meant, a sum in gross was appropriated for the expenses of the diplomatic service, and it was left to the executive to determine the grade of the officers, and the countries to which they should be sent.[3] The weight of argument would therefore seem to be in favor of the President.[4] The hostility which the President's protest provoked shows its necessity, and throws a strong light on the encroachments which are constantly and imperceptibly being made by the legislative branch of the government upon the executive.

[1] Congressional Record, 44 Cong., 1 sess., 5684.   [2] Ibid., 5686–5688.
[3] Senate Miscellaneous Documents, 49 Cong., 2 sess., No. 53, p. 402. See also 1 Stats. at Large, 128, 299, 345.
[4] The same view is taken by Dr. Von Holst in his Constitutional Law of the United States, 199, note 2.

§ 24. **Diplomatic intercourse.** — Within a year the President was again called upon to protect his authority in foreign affairs. December 15, 1876, Mr. Swann introduced into the House, from the Committee on Foreign Affairs, two resolutions entitled respectively, "Joint resolution relating to congratulations from the Argentine Republic," and "Joint resolution in reference to congratulations from the Republic of Pretoria, South Africa." The resolution directed the Secretary of State to convey to the respective nations the thanks of Congress for their congratulations.

These resolutions passed the Senate January 11, 1877, and on January 26 they were vetoed.[1] The President refused his assent to the resolutions because the Constitution vested in the executive the reception and conduct of all correspondence with foreign states. President Grant based his claim on the clause in the Constitution which entrusts to the President solely the reception of "embassadors and other public ministers,"[2] a clause which the President correctly considered to include all intercourse with foreign powers. If it be claimed that this clause in the Constitution needs support in order to sustain the President's position, it is only necessary to turn to the act of Congress establishing what was then the Department of Foreign Affairs, but which is now the Department of State.[3] The language used in that act gives no countenance to the theory that Congress has anything to do with diplomatic correspondence.

Apparently President Grant's protest in regard to closing the diplomatic offices had borne good fruit, for there was no discussion of the veto in the present case. The message was referred immediately to the Committee on Foreign Affairs, and ordered to be printed.

§ 25. **Vetoes for the protection of the President's power of appointment.** — Among the cases of legislative encroachment in foreign affairs which have just been examined, the protest against the

[1] Appendix A, No. 112.   [2] Constitution of the United States, Art. 2, Sec. 3.
[3] The Secretary of State is to "perform and execute such duties as shall from time to time be enjoined or entrusted to him by the President of the United States, agreeable to the Constitution, relative to correspondence, commissions, or instructions to or with public ministers or consuls from the United States, or to negotiations with public ministers from foreign states or princes, or to memorials or other applications from foreign public ministers or other foreigners, or to such other matters respecting foreign affairs as the President of the United States shall assign said department: And furthermore the said principal officer (Secretary of State) shall conduct the business of the said department in such manner as the President of the United States shall from time to time order or instruct." — 1 United States Stats. at Large, 28.

closing of the consular offices would seem also to relate to the power of appointment. But it did not. The objectionable bill did not attempt to appoint any one to an office, nor to provide for the manner of appointment, nor to remove any one from an office. What the bill proposed was to close the office itself; a principle which could not be applied as a general one without stopping the wheels of government altogether.

In a number of other instances, however, the President has been obliged directly to protect from an overbearing Congress his right of appointing to office. The first case we have already considered in the examination of President Madison's veto of the act increasing the number of United States district judges.[1] That bill in reality appointed the judges of the Supreme Court to the new district judgeship, and was thus an unintentional but nevertheless an undeniable infringement of executive power.

§ 26. **Requiring names of candidates for appointment.** — The next Congressional attempt at usurpation was in President Tyler's administration. On February 21, 1842, the House of Representatives passed a resolution requesting the President and heads of the various departments to furnish the House with lists of the names of the members of the twenty-sixth and twenty-seventh Congresses who had been applicants for office.[2] The President refused to comply with the request. This refusal is of course in no sense a veto, since resolutions passed by only one of the two houses of Congress do not require the President's approval. In the present case, however, the refusal of the President to comply with the resolution defeated it more effectually than a veto could have defeated a bill, since the resolution could not by any majority be made effective against the refusal.

The President supported his action on the ground that the power of appointment was conferred on him without reserve or qualification, and that therefore the House of Representatives had no constitutional right to make its request. It would seem that in making this statement the President must have meant the power of nomination instead of the power of appointment, since it could hardly be maintained that the Senate had no share in the appointment of those officers whose confirmation depended upon the consent of the Senate.[3]

[1] *Ante*, § 11.
[2] Appendix B, No. 3; House Journal, 27 Cong., 2 sess., 421.
[3] Constitution of the United States, Art. II, Sec. 2, § 2.

But even if we suppose President Tyler to have meant what he said, his argument is forcible; for under no circumstance could the House have a share in the power of appointment to office. The power was vested solely with the President and Senate, and so long as legal proceedings of impeachment were not pending, any body of citizens would have as much right as the House of Representatives to inquire into the reasons for an appointment. But if we suppose President Tyler referred to nominations instead of to appointments, the case becomes stronger yet; for even the Senate has no right to call upon the executive for his reasons in nominating a certain man. It can refuse to confirm the nominee, but that is the limit of its power.

If the call for information about nominations would have had no force, the request of the House was even more unjustifiable, since it called for the names of those who had applied to the President for office, whether they were nominated by him or not. The fact that the resolution verged on the ridiculous was appreciated by some of the representatives; for, in the debate pending its adoption, various amendments were offered, each one of which enlarged the scope of the proposal. The last of these amendments was offered by Mr. Snyder, and was to the effect that the President be requested to state whether or not he slept in a four-post bed.[1] This amendment was gravely voted down, but it certainly had as broad a basis of constitutional right as the original resolution.

§ 27. **Requiring papers relative to removals from office.** — Closely akin to the question just considered is the controversy which arose between President Cleveland and the Senate in regard to removals from office.

In July, 1885, George M. Dustin, United States District Attorney for the Seventh District of Alabama, was removed by the President, and John D. Burnett designated to perform the duties of the office. When the question of Burnett's confirmation came up in January, 1886, the Senate called on the Attorney General for all the papers filed in the Department of Justice relative to the removal of Dustin.[2] The Attorney General at the direction of the President refused this request, and pointed out that the

---

[1] Niles, Register, LXII, 61.
[2] Congressional Record, 49 Cong., 1 sess., 1585.

Senate already had all the papers relating to the nomination of Burnett.[1]

The Senate criticised the President's position severely.[2] It was maintained that the papers were essential to the decision of the question as to whether a nomination was necessary; that letters to public officers in their public capacity are official papers. In short, it was held that the Senate had the right to call for and should receive any papers on file in the archives of the Departments, and that therefore the President's position was untenable.

The President, on the other hand, declared that the papers in question, although on file in the Department of Justice, were private, and therefore not subject to the call of the Senate. The President then took up the real question at issue, and denied in a most emphatic manner the right of the Senate to "review or reverse the act of the executive in the suspension during the recess of the Senate of federal officials."[3]

The decision of the dispute must turn on the question last touched upon. Can the Senate "review or reverse" the suspension of federal officials during the recess of the Senate? It would seem that it cannot. For when the Tenure of Office Act was amended in 1869, the suspension of officials during the recess was left wholly to the discretion of the President, and the provision requiring him to report to the Senate the evidence and reason for his action was abandoned.[4] Under these circumstances the Senate had no right to demand the papers relative to the suspension of Dustin, and the President in refusing the request was only defending his legal and constitutional rights.

§ 28. **The Tenure of Office Act.** — In President Johnson's administration arose a much more serious question with reference to the power of appointment. President Johnson had always advocated rotation in office in its most flagrant form,[5] and when he came into power he used the patronage of the government to destroy the political organization which had placed him in power, but which was not willing to accept his policy. In the summer of 1866 he openly defied Congress, and declared that he would "kick out" the office-holders hostile to him as fast as he could.[6] Congress and the country felt that something must be done, and, after re-

[1] Congressional Record, 49 Cong., 1 sess., 1585. [2] Ibid. [3] Ibid., 1902-1903.
[4] 16 Stats. at Large, 6.
[5] Miss Salmon, Appointing Power of the President, 89. [6] Ibid., 89, note.

jecting the Civil Service Bill, offered by Mr. Jenckes of Rhode Island, passed the Tenure of Office Act.[1] This bill abandoned the past policy of the government, and provided that in all cases where the confirmation of the Senate was required, no removal could be made by the President without the approval of the Senate.

President Johnson's veto was based on constitutional grounds. The President showed that the First Congress had construed the Constitution as conferring the power of removal on the President alone;[2] that Madison considered this to be a correct construction of the Constitution; that Justice Story and Chancellor Kent considered the ruling of the First Congress binding; and that Mr. Webster, although opposed to removal by the President alone, admitted "that it was settled by construction, settled by precedent, settled by the practice of the government, and settled by statute." The President's position was perfectly sound, from a constitutional point of view, and his argument was of great weight. The fact was that Congress, in attacking President Johnson's notoriously flagrant abuse of power, had attacked it from the wrong direction. If Mr. Jenckes' measure had been adopted, the President would have had no constitutional arguments to oppose to it.[3]

Congress was in no mood to be opposed, however, and in spite of the President's logic, passed the bill over his veto.[4]

§ 29. **The Fitz-John Porter Bill.** — The last of the vetoes for the protection of the power of appointment, like the first one in the class, frustrated action which was much like an actual appointment to office on the part of Congress. The bill was entitled "An act for the relief of Fitz-John Porter," and it was vetoed by President Arthur July 2, 1884.[5] The bill authorized the President to appoint Porter to his old position as Colonel in the Army.

One of the reasons for the veto was that the measure was an infringement of the executive power of appointment. It is unconstitutional for Congress to authorize the President to make any

[1] Senate Journal, 39 Cong., 2 sess., 423; 14 Stats. at Large, 430.
[2] Annals of Congress, 1 Cong., 1 sess., 368–383.
[3] Mr. Jenckes' Bill would have prevented the appointment of unfit men, but would have left the President's power of removal untouched. — Miss Salmon, Appointing Power of the President, 90.
[4] Appendix A, No. 62. The act was partially repealed in 1869, and wholly repealed in 1887. It has generally been considered both inexpedient and unconstitutional.
[5] Appendix A, No. 132. Porter had been cashiered by court-martial in 1863 for alleged insubordination.

appointment. The Constitution gives the President power to make appointments to certain offices which it names, as well as to all others not otherwise provided for by the Constitution which shall be established by law. The only limit on this power is the provision that "Congress may by law vest the appointment of such inferior officers as they think proper in the President alone, in the Courts of the law, or in the heads of the departments."[1] Congress is omitted from this carefully enumerated list of possible possessors of appointing power, and, in consequence, cannot legally claim such power. To be sure, in the bill under discussion Congress merely authorized the President to appoint, and did not assume to make the appointment or even to command the President to make it. The bill was, however, an attempt to ensure the appointment of Porter to his old position, and this attempt was in spirit, if not technically, a violation of the Constitution.[2]

§ 30. **Protest for the protection of the President's war power.** — The President has been obliged to defend his power in foreign affairs and his power of appointment by the use of the veto. Still another executive power has been attacked by Congress and defended by the President. This is the War Power. In 1867, Congress passed an act making appropriations for the army, to which was tacked a rider[3] practically depriving the President of his power as Commander-in-chief of the Army.[4] The President signed the bill on account of the urgent need for the appropriation, but he sent to Congress a vigorous protest against the rider.[5]

Here, as in the veto of the Tenure of Office bill, Johnson had the Constitution on his side. That instrument says clearly that "the President shall be Commander-in-chief of the Army and Navy of the United States."[6] Congress has no voice in the matter. It can appoint no one but the President Commander-in-chief, and can withdraw from him not the slightest part of the power pertaining to the office.[7] The only remedy for a misuse of the power is an impeachment.

[1] Constitution of United States, Art. II, Sec. 2, § 2.
[2] The bill also relieved Porter of his disabilities. This side of the measure will be referred to in § 68.
[3] 14 United States Stats. at Large, 487.
[4] The act provided that all orders should be given through the commanding general, then General Grant.
[5] Appendix B, No. 6.
[6] Art. II, Sec. 2, § 1.   [7] Von Holst, Constitutional Law, 192.

§ 31. **Protest and veto for the protection of the President's personal rights under the Constitution.** — Congress, besides infringing the powers of the executive in foreign affairs, over appointments and over the Army and Navy, has, in two instances, attempted to deprive the President of what might be called his personal rights under the Constitution.

§ 32. **Covode Investigation.** — The first of these attempts occurred in President Buchanan's administration and was met by a protest. The affair is known as the Covode investigation, and was based on a resolution appointing a committee to see if the President had, "by money patronage or improper means, sought to influence the action of Congress, or any committee thereof, for or against the passage of any law appertaining to the rights of any State or Territory." [1] The friends of the measure upheld it on the ground that it was but an exercise of the power which the House of Representatives possessed in the matter of impeachment. The President pointed out in his protest [2] that, with the exception of the power of impeachment, the Constitution vests the House of Representatives with no jurisdiction over the President, and that in such proceedings all precedents demanded the presentation of particular charges, and an open and impartial investigation of those charges. In the Covode Investigation the accusations were of the vaguest possible character, and the investigation was conducted by an *ex parte* committee in secret session. In view of these facts, the protest seems justified; and this conclusion is strengthened when we consider that the resolution calling for the investigation was rushed through the House under cover of the previous question, that no attempts to point out the lack of specific charges were allowed to succeed, that the accuser was made one of the judges, and that the evidence was taken in an unfair way. It was, in short, little more than a scheme to inculpate the administration and render it odious before the country.[3]

§ 33. **The President's salary.** — One other attempt to encroach upon what I have called the personal rights of the executive is to be noticed. On April 18, 1876, President Grant vetoed a bill to reduce the President's salary from $50,000 to its old figure,—

---

[1] Congressional Globe, 39 Cong., 1 sess., 1437.
[2] Appendix B, No. 4; Senate Miscellaneous Documents, 49 Cong., 2 sess., No. 53, 274.
[3] Curtis, Life of Buchanan, 248.

$25,000.[1] The bill was an avowed attempt at reform, — a return to the former simplicity of the government,—and was brought forward, largely for party purposes, not long before a national election. The President vetoed the bill [2] because the salary as fixed by the measure was insufficient to support the office of chief executive of a great nation with becoming dignity. He argued that $25,000 was enough at the beginning of the government, when the nation numbered only three millions of people and when the country had not yet recovered from a long and exhausting war; but since that time the size and dignity of the country and the needs of the office had greatly increased, and now $50,000 was not too much. The good sense of the country has approved the President's position, and no serious attempt has since been made to reduce the President's salary.

§ 34. **Use of the veto in Controversies on questions arising out of the Civil War.**[3] — In the discussion of the veto as a protection to the executive, one class of vetoes remains for special consideration, namely, the vetoes of measures which grew out of the Civil War. Some of these vetoes have already been considered under other heads. Here it becomes necessary to determine what bearing the questions raised had on the mutual relations of the executive and legislative branches of the government.

The reconstruction vetoes claim our attention first.[4] President Johnson had a definite plan with regard to reconstruction. He desired to have the Rebel States readmitted into the Union at once, and on their former footing.[5] Congress objected for two

---

[1] The increase was made in 1873 by a rider tacked to the legislative appropriation bill. The rider also increased the salaries of Congressmen, and was known as the "Salary Grab."

[2] Appendix A, No. 99.

[3] Two vetoes which are connected with the later reconstruction policy of the government should be mentioned at this point. They both apply to the United States laws covering Southern elections, and occurred in President Hayes's administration. The first veto was of a bill to prohibit military interference at elections (Appendix A, No. 121). President Hayes objected to it because it would prevent the exercise of force necessary at times to support the Constitution and laws of the United States (see § 35). The other vetoed bill was entitled "an act regulating the pay and appointment of deputy marshals" (Appendix A, No. 127). Under the guise of regulating the appointment of these officers the act took from them the power by which they were enabled to preserve order and prevent fraud at elections. For this reason the President refused to sign the bill (see § 35).

[4] The bills discussed here can be found in Appendix A, numbered as follows: 53, 54, 57, 59, 62, 63, 64, 65, 66, 67, 68, 69, 70, 71, 72. The important measures are elsewhere considered according to subject matter.

[5] Conkling, Executive Powers, 76; McPherson, Reconstruction, 45-100 passim; Callender, Stevens, 111-112, 123; Wilson, Slave Power, III, 590-602, 614.

reasons: in the first place, it had a plan of its own which it very much preferred; and in the second place, rather as a corollary to the first reason, Congress disapproved of the manner in which the President attempted to carry out his scheme. Congress claimed that the President acted in an unconstitutional manner, and the President abusively charged Congress with proceeding in an unconstitutional manner. Congress passed act after act in furtherance of its plan, acts which were regularly vetoed, and almost as regularly passed over the veto. The President called hard names, and strove to carry out his plan by means of proclamations and executive orders to the Army, the effect of which Congress counteracted.

No ordinary rules of judgment can be applied to these discussions, since the circumstances were abnormal and wholly unforeseen by the founders of the government; measures were needed for which neither constitutional provisions nor precedent could be cited. The plan proposed by President Johnson seems more in accord with the principles of the Constitution, although less practical, than the Congressional plan.

In so far as the veto was used in this contest, it cannot be said to have been used to defend the President from unconstitutional attack, save in the case of the Tenure of Office Act.[1] Incidentally he was deprived of his command over the army[2] and his power of appointment. But in the contest over the main question, that of reconstruction, none of the President's rights under the Constitution were touched.

§ 35. **Riders on appropriation bills.** — At one other period in our history questions arising out of the Rebellion have called for the use of the veto to protect executive power. In this case the veto was used for its own protection; that is, for the protection of the President's right to refuse to sign a bill.

The law of 1865 provided that troops might be used at the polls on election days to repel armed enemies of the United States, and to keep the peace.[3] The election law of 1870, as amended February 28, 1871, provided for the appointment of two supervisors of elections in each election district or voting precinct. These supervisors were to be appointed by the Federal circuit judges and were personally to count each ballot.[4]

[1] *Ante*, § 28.
[2] *Ante*, § 30.
[3] Rev. Stats., §§ 2002, 5528.
[4] 16 Stats. at Large, 434.

The Democrats disliked this legislation, and opposed it unsuccessfully in Congress. In time they got control of that body and at once set about the repeal of the obnoxious laws. President Hayes was opposed to the undertaking, and Congress therefore attempted to accomplish its purpose by means of riders.[1]

A rider was attached to the Army appropriation bill of 1878, taking away from the government the right to employ the Army as a *posse comitatus*.[2] The President signed this bill, and emboldened by success, Congress redoubled its efforts. Within a short time five appropriation bills were furnished with riders, whose object was the repeal of the objectionable election laws.[3] But they did not meet with the success which attended the first one. In short, they were all vetoed.

The President vetoed the measures on the ground that the Constitution had granted the executive the privilege of refusing his sanction to Congressional proposals, and that he would not allow Congress to brow-beat him out of his privilege. It was a bold step to take, for riders had been very numerous in the years since the war, and had come to be considered almost as a matter of course.[4] The President's position was, however, constitutionally sound. He was brave enough to stand by his convictions, and the fact that his opponents did not have a two-thirds majority in Congress gave

---

[1] The practice of attaching riders to appropriation bills and other important measures began in 1820, when the bill for the admission of Missouri was "tacked" to the bill for the admission of Maine. In 1849 the Senate tacked to an appropriation bill a clause extending the Constitution and Revenue laws to the newly-acquired Mexican territory. This attempt at coercion failed. In 1856 the House tacked a provision to an Army appropriation bill, forbidding the use of Federal troops for the enforcement of territorial law in Kansas. The Senate refused to be coerced, and Congress adjourned without passing any Army appropriation. An extra session was called, in which the House yielded and passed an Army appropriation bill without the rider. These early riders were attempts by one house of Congress to coerce the other. In President Johnson's administration riders were first prominently used to coerce the President. They have been exceedingly numerous in the last twenty-five years. The most important were: the rider depriving President Johnson of the war power; Senator Kellogg's rider providing for Federal supervisors of elections (1872); "the salary grab" (1873); and the riders in Hayes' administration. — Horace Davis, American Constitutions (in Johns Hopkins University Studies, Third Series).

[2] 20 Stats. at Large, 152.

[3] The bills will be found in Appendix A, numbered: 120, 122, 123, 125, 126.

[4] It is said that 387 riders were attached to appropriation bills between 1862 and 1875. — Davis, American Constitutions, 30.

him complete victory. The rules of the House of Representatives in 1888–89 forbade the "tacking" of any measure of general legislation to an appropriation bill unless it was germane to the subject of the bill.

§ 36. **General effect of the vetoes for the protection of the Executive.** — The veto power, as the present chapter shows, has been used many times, and often successfully, as a defence to the executive. The power of the executive in foreign affairs, the power of appointment, his power over the Army, and lastly his power to veto bills, have all been asserted and maintained against legislative encroachment.

In other instances, however, the veto has not proved the complete protection to the President which the Constitutional Convention anticipated. Mr. Horace Davis, in his "American Constitutions,"[1] points out three ways in which Congress has encroached on the executive. In the first place, Congress has invaded the treaty-making power, and, in the face of the Constitution, abrogated treaty provisions by statute.[2] This was conspicuously the case in 1798, when our treaty relations with France were thus abrogated.[3] Again, the House of Representatives claims the right to pass upon all treaties touching the revenue, by refusing the appropriations necessary to carry them into effect, on the ground that the House alone has the right to originate money bills. This claim was acknowledged in the Hawaiian Reciprocity treaty, in which there was a provision that the treaty should not become binding until the passage of an act of Congress to carry it into effect.[4] Both of these claims Mr. Davis considers as invasions of the President's treaty-making power, which might have been resisted, perhaps successfully, by the veto. They were, however, not resisted, and are probably both too strong now to be overthrown.

In the second place, Congress both directly and indirectly has invaded the President's power of appointment to and removal from office. As we have already seen, the Tenure of Office Act deprived the President of power in making removals which the uniform interpretation of the Constitution has accorded him. But Con-

[1] Johns Hopkins University Studies, Third Series
[2] In support of this claim by Congress, see Taylor *v.* Morton, 2 Curtis, 454.
[3] Davis, American Constitutions, 28.
[4] 19 Stats. at Large, 627.

gress, although powerful enough to seize this power in spite of the veto, has since relinquished it voluntarily.[1]

The President by the relinquishment obtained merely the shadow of power, for he had already lost the substance through the "courtesy of the Senate." As far back as President Jackson's administration party leaders began to claim the right to control the President's power of nomination by suggesting suitable candidates. This claim became stronger, and by President Johnson's time it was looked upon as an undoubted right, so that nominations were practically made, not by the President, but by the Senators, and even by members of the House of Representatives.

It is clear that an invasion of the President's power in regard to nominations to office cannot be reached by the veto. It must be met, if at all, by the sturdy refusal of the President to submit to dictation in the matter. It has been met in that way. President Hayes refused to listen to Senatorial dictation;[2] President Garfield's contest with the New York Senators over the "courtesy of the Senate" is famous, and President Harrison is at the present time showing a commendable independence in making appointments not approved by Senators of the states in which they are made.

Congress has encroached upon the executive in one other way, namely, in forcing him to sign bills of which he did not approve, by tacking them as riders to appropriation bills. This assumption of executive power, and President Hayes's successful resistance of it, we have just considered.

Practically, then, Congress has succeeded in partially usurping only one of the President's powers, that of making treaties; and even in this case the veto might have been successfully used. The record forcibly demonstrates the wisdom and foresight of the founders of the Constitution, in their expectation that the veto would be an efficient instrument in maintaining the balance of power between the executive and legislative departments.

[1] The act was finally repealed March 3, 1887. See 24 Stats. at Large, 500.
[2] Davis, American Constitutions, 40.

CHAPTER IV.

VETOES AFFECTING THE EXERCISE OF THE POWERS OF GOVERNMENT.

§ 37. Classification.
§ 38. Relation of the national government to individuals.
    § 39. Question of the establishment of religion.
    § 40. Naturalization.
    § 41. The Indians.
    § 42. The Negro.
    § 43. The Chinese.
    § 44. General remarks on the power over individuals.
§ 45. Territorial powers. District of Columbia.
    § 46. Early land vetoes.
    § 47. Public lands and the Constitution. Land grants.
    § 48. Later land vetoes on grounds of expediency.
    § 49. Effect of the public land vetoes.
    § 50. Admission of States.
    § 51. Criticism of the Colorado and Nebraska vetoes.
§ 52. Financial powers.
    § 53. The tariff.
    § 54. Refunding the direct tax.
    § 55. Bank charter vetoes.
        § 56. Madison's Bank veto.
        § 57. Jackson's Bank veto.
        § 58. Tyler's Bank veto.
        § 59. Criticism of Bank vetoes.
    § 60. Currency and coinage.
        § 61. Inflation Bill.
        § 62. The Bland Silver Bill.
    § 63. Expenditure of public money.
        § 64. French spoliation claims.
        § 65. Relief bills.
            § 66. Bills defrauding the government of money.
            § 67. Bills relieving deserters from the army.
            § 68. Bills relieving former army officers of disability.
            § 69. Bills carelessly drawn.
            § 70. Miscellaneous relief bills.
        § 71. Pension vetoes.
            § 72. Bills conveying no benefit.
            § 73. Unnecessary increase of pensions.
            § 74. Injuries not received "in the line of duty."
            § 75. Dependent relatives: dependency not proved.

§ 76. Miscellaneous pension bills.
§ 77. Dependent Pension Bill.
§ 78. President Cleveland's pension policy.
§ 79. Expediency of the pension vetoes.
§ 80. Constitutionality of the pension vetoes.
§ 81. Summary of the question of pension vetoes.
§ 82. Commercial powers.
§ 83. Internal improvements.
§ 84. Madison's veto of a general bill.
§ 85. Monroe's Cumberland Road veto. Constitutionality of improvements.
§ 86. Jackson's vetoes. Jurisdiction and local character.
§ 87. Tyler's vetoes. Improvement of water-ways.
§ 88. Polk's vetoes. Local improvements.
§ 89. Pierce's vetoes. Implied powers.
§ 90. Buchanan's vetoes. Constitutional grounds.
§ 91. Grant's veto and refusal to carry out a bill.
§ 92. Arthur's veto. Local objects.
§ 93. Public buildings.
§ 94. General view of internal improvement vetoes.
§ 95. Measures based on the general welfare clause.
§ 96. Texas Seed Bill.
§ 97. War powers.
§ 98. General effect of the veto on the exercise of the powers of government.

§ 37. **Classification.** — The vetoes affecting the powers of government may conveniently be subdivided into two classes: those relating to the distribution of powers, and those relating to the exercise of powers. In the last chapter the first of these two divisions was considered; the second and more important claims our attention in the present chapter.

In order to trace the connection between the vetoes of the successive Presidents it is necessary to classify them, according to the nature of the power claimed or exercised, into six sections. 1. The vetoes which affect the government's power over individuals. 2. Vetoes which concern the exercise of the territorial powers of the government. 3 and 4. Vetoes which involve the financial and commercial powers of the government. 5. Vetoes of measures based upon the general welfare clause. 6. Vetoes which affect the war power of Congress.

§ 38. **Relation of the national government to individuals.** — Although the United States is a Federal government, it exercises authority over all individuals in the States. It recognizes and protects certain rights of all persons, and has special powers over certain specified classes of persons. Thus the Constitution guarantees personal and religious liberty, a guaranty which Congress must enforce. Again, the Indians are subject exclusively to the control of the Federal government, and the important matters of naturalization and immigration have also been placed within the jurisdiction of the United States, rather than within that of the States. In the exercise of the duties imposed by or implied in these provisions of the Constitution, the government at Washington is brought directly in contact with the people, and oftentimes in our history the veto has been used to check Congress in what the executive considered an unconstitutional or unwise use of this power over the individual.

§ 39. **Question of the establishment of religion.** — Early in 1789 Mr. Madison brought up in Congress the question of the amendments to the Constitution, which the people demanded as sureties for their liberties.[1] Before the year 1791 ten amendments had become parts of the Constitution. The first of these declares that "Congress shall make no law respecting an establishment of religion, or prohibiting the free exercise thereof." The amendment was passed by men keenly alive to the dangers of an intolerant and powerful state church. It was meant to be a guaranty of religious liberty to every individual in the nation.

In two instances President Madison made use of the veto to protect the first amendment. February 21, 1811, he vetoed a bill entitled, "An act incorporating the Protestant Episcopal Church in the town of Alexandria in the District of Columbia."[2] In so far as the act was merely for the incorporation of the church it was constitutional, since in no other way could a charter be obtained in the District of Columbia. But the bill went beyond the limits of an incorporating act, and established certain unnecessary rules which related purely to the organization and policy of the church. The measure was therefore vetoed.

The President's position seems sound. The bill gave legal force and sanction to certain provisions of the constitution and administration of the church which the simple incorporation of the church did not require. It was, therefore, in so far as it exceeded the necessities of the case, a law "respecting the establishment of religion," and consequently a violation of the first amendment.

When the President's message came up for consideration in the

---
[1] Schouler, History of the United States, I, 102.
[2] Appendix A, No. 3.

House, very little was said. Mr. Wheaton, in support of the bill, declared it to be constitutional, on the ground that it was merely a regulation of the funds of a religious society.[1] This argument seems hardly more than the question at issue stated in a different form, and therefore can have no weight.

February 28, 1811, President Madison withheld his assent from a bill entitled "An act for the relief of . . . the Baptist Church at Salem Meeting-House in the Mississippi Territory."[2] The President vetoed the bill because it reserved a portion of the land of the United States for the use of the Baptist Church. This he considered a "principle and precedent" for the appropriation of the funds of the United States for the use of religious societies, which would be contrary to the first amendment to the Constitution.

Since 1811 there has been no attempt by Congress to link church and state together. Indeed, the two bills above described were not intended to have such an effect. President Madison was nevertheless wise in preventing what might have been used afterwards as a confusing or dangerous precedent. For in spite of the fact that our Constitution is a written one, custom and precedent have a great influence upon it.

§ 40. **Naturalization.** — Under authority granted by Art. I, Sec. VIII, of the Constitution, Congress, in 1812, passed a bill entitled, "An act supplementary to the acts heretofore passed on the subject of a uniform rule of naturalization." The bill reached the President late in the session, and he took no action upon it. It was subjected to what later became known as the "pocket veto." At the next session of Congress President Madison briefly explained as his reason for withholding his signature from the bill, that the privileges which it granted were liable to abuse by aliens having no real purpose of becoming naturalized.[3]

§ 41. **The Indians.** — The Indians have always been a troublesome factor in the regulation of our internal affairs. The government has not wilfully wronged the Red man: nevertheless, through carelessness, inefficiency, and perhaps, most of all, through sheer ignorance, it has given ground for the charge that our treatment of the Indians has been careless and unjust. The treatment is, to a certain extent, reflected in the veto messages.

[1] Annals of Congress, 11 Cong., 3 sess., 984.
[2] Appendix A, No. 4.
[3] Ibid., No. 6.

On December 29, 1835, the Cherokee Indians agreed to leave the State of Georgia and move West, on consideration of the payment to them of $5,600,000.[1] During the last hours of the third session of the twenty-seventh Congress a joint resolution was passed, directing the payment of certificates or awards issued by the commissioners under the treaty with the Cherokee Indians.[2] President Tyler disposed of this resolution by a pocket veto, and sent his reasons for so doing to the next Congress. He disapproved of the resolution, because it was unjust to the Indians. Congress had not provided sufficient funds for satisfying in full the claims which the resolution professed to provide for; nor was any system of *pro rata* payment substituted for full payment. The consequence would have been that the first claim presented would have been paid, while the claims last presented, although equally entitled to consideration, would have gone unsatisfied. The President prevented this injustice, and suggested the propriety of making some provision for a *pro rata* payment of claims: a course which would seem most reasonable since the last of the money due under the treaty was appropriated by the resolve under consideration.

On February 3, 1876, President Grant vetoed a bill entitled, "An act transferring the custody of certain Indian trust funds from the Secretary of the Interior to the Treasurer of the United States."[3] The bill had been drawn at the request of the Interior department, but it was so carelessly phrased that the Secretary of the Interior feared it would not accomplish the purpose desired. It was therefore vetoed.

August 15, 1876, President Grant vetoed a bill entitled, "An act to provide for the sale of a portion of the reservation of the Confederated Otoe and Missouri, and the Sacs and Foxes of the Missouri tribe of Indians, in the States of Kansas and Nebraska."[4] The message was sent to the Senate, but before any action could be taken upon it a second message was received from the President, requesting that the bill be returned to him, in order that he might approve it. An interesting discussion then arose as to the power of the President to recall a veto message which had been received by Congress.[5] It was generally held that the President had no

---

[1] Schouler, History of the United States, IV, 235.
[2] Appendix A, No. 28.   [3] Ibid., No. 96.   [4] Ibid., No. 108.
[5] Congressional Record, 44 Cong., 1 sess., 5664; see also *post*, § 108.

power to recall a veto when once it had been delivered, and that the only effect, and, in fact, the intended effect, of the President's second message was to destroy the persuasive influence of the first message, — to invite Congress to pass the bill over the veto. In accordance with this view the bill was passed over the veto by large majorities in both houses of Congress.

July 7, 1886, President Cleveland returned to the Senate, with his objections, a bill entitled, "An act granting to railroads the right of way through the Indian reservation in Northern Montana."[1] The President vetoed the bill: first, because it granted a general right of way to all railroad companies, regardless of the needs of the community, or of the rights and interests of the Indians; and secondly, because it specified no limit of time within which the construction of railroads should be begun or completed. The door was thus opened to a speculative occupation of the reservation, for an indefinite period, by corporations whose only object would be to sell the land at some future time to a genuine railroad company. Senator Dawes, in criticising this message, pointed out[2] that by the treaty of October 17, 1855, the United States reserved the right to construct roads of every description in the Indian reservation in Northern Montana. The President, however, in vetoing the bill under discussion, recognized this fact, and based his objection, not upon the granting of a right of way, but upon the granting of a right of way in such a loose manner that the grant could hardly fail to be abused. The Senate referred the President's message to the Committee on Indian Affairs, and no further action was taken.

President Cleveland, by his veto of May 7, 1888,[3] justly interfered in a case in which the rights of the Indians had been grossly violated. Certain New York Indians had been granted land in Kansas. Most of the Indians were prevented by threats or actual violence from taking possession of their lands. Some of the more venturesome, however, entered upon the land, but they were speedily killed or driven off. The white robbers then settled upon the land. The government professed to be powerless to help its "wards," and as the only reparation possible sold a part of the land in 1873, at the rate of four dollars and a half an acre, and turned the pro-

---

[1] Appendix A, No. 232.
[2] Congressional Record, 49 Cong., 1 sess., 6613.
[3] Appendix A, No. 293.

ceeds over to the Indian owners. The present bill authorized the government to sell the remainder of the land at two dollars and a half an acre. This the President considered most unjust to the Indian owners; the land was certainly worth what it was in 1873, and he accordingly refused his assent to the bill.

July 26, 1888, the President vetoed a bill granting a right of way to the Fort Smith, Paris, and Dardanelle Railway Company, through the Indian territory, on the ground that the grant violated the treaty rights of the Indians.[1]

§ 42. **The Negro.** — It is a remarkable fact that, although the negro problem has been one of great political importance since 1775, the veto power has never been employed directly either to attack or defend slavery. The nearest approach to anything of the kind was the well-known determination of Taylor to veto the Compromise of 1850. The veto has been used, however, since the Civil War in connection with questions arising out of the status of the former slaves.

March 13, 1866, a bill passed Congress entitled, "An act to protect all persons in the United States in their civil rights and furnish the means of their vindication."[2]

March 27, 1866, President Johnson vetoed the bill. His objections to it may be grouped under four heads. First, he denied the constitutional power of Congress to declare a body of persons citizens of the United States. Secondly, even admitting the first point, the President did not think that Congress had the right to settle the question when eleven States were unrepresented in that body. Thirdly, the President considered the bill, on the grounds of expediency, an unjustifiable mistake. The negroes were ignorant, and it would be a serious danger to make them citizens. Lastly, the President objected to the bill on account of its interference with State rights.

When the message came up in the Senate, the President's first and most important argument was very severely criticised. Senator Trumbull showed[3] that Frenchmen, Mexicans, Indians, and Spaniards had been admitted to citizenship by act of Congress.[4] The Senator further maintained that a citizen of the United States might also be a citizen of any state, and quoted in support of this

---

[1] Appendix A, No. 345. [2] Ibid., No. 54.
[3] Congressional Globe, 39 Cong., 1 sess., 1756 *et seq.*
[4] Lawrence, Wheaton's International Law, 897–899.

statement the decision of the Supreme Court of the United States in the case of Gassies v. Ballow.[1]

The last three arguments in the President's message refer to the difference that existed between himself and Congress as to the proper reconstruction policy. That question has already been discussed in another connection.[2]

§ 43. **The Chinese.** — In 1868 Mr. Burlingame negotiated a treaty between China and the United States,[3] under which citizens of either country could visit or reside in the other. Almost immediately the dangers and evils of Chinese immigration into the United States became manifest. The Chinese came here with no idea of becoming citizens, and never in any degree became infused with American ideas. The people of the Pacific slope early became alarmed, and finding state legislation ineffectual, memorialized Congress to check the inflowing stream of Mongolians. In 1879 Congress passed a bill restricting Chinese immigration. March 1, 1879, President Hayes vetoed it.[4] The message is long, but its point may be stated in a word. The President objected to the bill because it put an end to a treaty without notice. He did not question the power of Congress to take the step, but in the state of our relations with China he considered it inadvisable and harmful to approach the subject in that way.

The veto was sustained by Congress, and the President at once appointed a commission to treat with China in regard to a modification of the Burlingame treaty. These negotiations were successful, and a treaty was obtained from China which was duly ratified by the Senate.[5] It reserved to the United States the right of regulating the immigration of the Chinese to this country.

Before the treaty had been in operation a year, a bill was passed by Congress prohibiting all Chinese immigration into the United States for twenty years. April 4, 1882, President Arthur vetoed this bill.[6] He objected to it because in his opinion the treaty did not give Congress the power to exclude the Chinese for so long a period. It had not been expected, he said, that the United States would suspend immigration for more than three, or possibly five, years.

[1] 6 Peters, 762.   [2] *Ante*, Chap. III, § 34.
[3] United States Treaties and Conventions, 165.
[4] Appendix A, No. 119; Blaine, Twenty Years in Congress, 651–656.
[5] 22 United States Stats. at Large, 826.
[6] Appendix A, No. 129.

The action of President Arthur was justified by the intention of the negotiations; and though the meaning of a treaty, like that of any other law, is not to be deduced from the opinion of the framers, the President exercised a proper discretion in withholding his assent. After some discussion [1] the Senate attempted to pass the bill over the veto, but did not succeed.

§ 44. **General remarks on the power over individuals.** — The class of vetoes which concern the power of the general government over individuals is not an important one. Perhaps the most significant is President Madison's refusal to sign the bill granting public land to the church in Mississippi. Had the bill become law, it might have led to other similar demands, which the government could not consistently have ignored, and in time precedents would probably have been created which would have involved the government in grave difficulties. The only effect of the vetoes of the Chinese immigration bills was to prevent Congress from moving with unjust haste. President Johnson's refusal to sign the civil rights bill had no practical effect, since that bill was passed over the veto. The Indian vetoes have been too few seriously to affect the policy of the government.

§ 45. **Territorial powers. District of Columbia.** — No power of government has caused so much discussion in the United States as that over territory. The annexation of each successive parcel has been the subject of long diplomacy and of fierce debates; the administration of territory involved the slavery question, and was the occasion of the Civil War. But the great struggles over the territories, the Compromises of 1820 and 1850, the Kansas-Nebraska, Lecompton, and English bills, led to no conflict between Congress and the President. It is otherwise with the public lands. Ever since 1789 the disposition of the public lands has been a recurring subject of dispute, and has led to a series of interesting vetoes.

Before entering upon that subject, however, it may be well to dispose of several unimportant vetoes which relate to the local administration of the District of Columbia.

August 14, 1876, President Grant vetoed a bill in regard to the repairing of Pennsylvania Avenue, in Washington, on the ground that the time within which the contractors must complete the work was not definitely stated.[2]

[1] Congressional Record, 47 Cong., 1 sess., 2609, 2614.
[2] Appendix A, No. 107.

January 23, 1877, President Grant vetoed a bill removing the police of the District of Columbia from the control of the Police Commissioners, on the ground that certain gross violations of the law could be prevented only in case the then existing arrangement was continued.[1]

April 26, 1886, President Cleveland vetoed a bill which provided for the delivery of certain dead bodies to medical colleges in the District of Columbia, on the ground that the measure did not guard carefully enough against abuses liable to arise in the treatment and disposition of the bodies.[2]

§ 46. **Early land vetoes.**[3] — The first of the vetoes affecting the public lands was the refusal of President Madison, in 1811, to sign a bill granting land to a church in Mississippi.[4] The ground upon which it rested was the constitutional provision against the union of church and state, and the question was not discussed as to whether the grant would have been proper for other purposes.

December 5, 1833, President Jackson sent to Congress a message giving his reasons for failing to sign at the last session a bill entitled, "An act to appropriate for a limited time the proceeds of the sales of public lands of the United States, and for granting lands to the States."[5] This document is, in many respects, the best of Jackson's veto messages. He begins by tracing the history of the public land, and comes to the conclusion that it was ceded to the United States on the express condition that it should be disposed of for the common benefit of the States, "according to their respective proportions in the general charge of expenditure."[6] The President then points out that this compact is violated by the present bill in two respects. In the first place, a portion of the land was confessedly not to be distributed equally among the States;[7]

---

[1] Appendix A, No. 111. [2] Ibid., No. 135.
[3] For general accounts of the public land policy of the United States, with bibliography, see Shosuki Sato, in Johns Hopkins University Studies, Series IV; Albert Bushnell Hart, in Quarterly Journal of Economics, I, 169-183, 251-254.
[4] *Ante*, § 39; Appendix A, No. 4.
[5] Appendix A, No. 17. In reference to this bill Henry Clay wrote to Madison, asking him whether, in his opinion, the President had not violated the Constitution by retaining the bill, instead of returning it approved or disapproved. To this inquiry Madison returned a rather equivocal answer.— Madison, Works, IV, 299. The same question was discussed at length when the President's message was read. — Debates of Congress, Vol. X, Part I, 14-18; see *post*, § 101.
[6] Senate Miscellaneous Documents, 49 Cong., 2 sess., No. 53, p. 111.
[7] Ibid., 113.

and, in the second place, the distribution of the remainder was to be made according to the population, instead of according to the share of each State in the general charge and expenditure.[1]

The President also objected to the bill because it appropriated the land and its proceeds for local improvements, — a procedure which he considered identical with the appropriation of money lying in the treasury. He declared that the money derived from the sales of the land should be turned into the treasury, to form a part of the aggregate revenue of the government.[2]

December 14, 1842, President Tyler sent to Congress his reasons for having failed at the close of the preceding session to sign a bill entitled, "An act to repeal the proviso of the sixth section of the act entitled, 'An act to appropriate the proceeds of the sales of the public lands and to grant pre-emption rights,' approved September fourth, eighteen hundred and forty-one."[3] The proviso suspended the distribution of the proceeds of the sales of the public land among the States whenever the customs duties were over twenty per cent. The proviso was considered by President Tyler an important part of the compromise tariff of 1833; and as he objected to the bill, not from the point of view of the public land, but from the point of view of the tariff, his position will be fully considered later on in connection with his veto of the tariff bills.[4]

§ 47. **Public Lands and the Constitution. Land grants.** — In 1854 we come upon a veto which follows President Jackson's discussion of the proper constitutional disposition of the public lands. On May 3 of that year President Pierce refused his sanction to a bill entitled, "An act making a grant of public lands to the several States for the benefit of indigent insane persons."[5] In the debates upon this bill its friends had argued[6] that land was different from money in the vaults of the treasury; and that although Congress could appropriate money only in certain limited ways, its power over the public land was absolutely unlimited.

The President dismissed this argument with a word, declaring that he could see no difference between public land and money in

---

[1] Senate Miscellaneous Documents, 49 Cong., 2 sess., No. 53, p. 114.   [2] Ibid., 112.
[3] Appendix A, No. 26.
[4] *Post*, § 53; see also Appendix A, Nos. 24, 25.
[5] Appendix A, No. 34.
[6] See Congressional Globe under the dates given in the Appendix; and United States Constitution, Art. IV, Sec. 3, § 2.

the treasury. He placed his objection to the bill on the broad ground that it assumed for the general government a power over local affairs in the States which was not granted either directly or impliedly by the Constitution. The only clause from which the measure could hope to obtain support, in the President's opinion, was the "general welfare" clause, and he declared that to admit the authority of that clause in the present case would be to deprive the Constitution of its meaning. "All the pursuits of industry, everything which promotes the material or intellectual well-being of the race, every ear of corn or boll of cotton which grows, is national in the same sense; for each of these things goes to swell the aggregate of national prosperity and happiness of the United States." The President argued further that the land in question was pledged as security for the debt contracted by the act of January 28, 1847, and to sell it would be a breach of the national faith.

February 24, 1859, President Buchanan vetoed a bill entitled, "An act donating public lands to the several States and Territories which may provide colleges for the benefit of agriculture and the mechanic arts."[1] In order to secure the grant each State was required to provide within five years not less than one college. The President objected to the bill, in the first place, because the government needed the revenue from the sale of the lands to meet its expenses; in the second place, because the low price at which the land was to be sold would induce speculators to buy it in large blocks, thus retarding the development of the country; lastly, the President doubted the constitutional power of Congress to pay for these State colleges. If public land and the proceeds from its sale were to be treated as were the funds in the treasury, there was, he considered, no question of the unconstitutionality of the measure. The argument in favor of the bill was substantially the same as in 1854; it was said that public land stood upon a different footing from other public property, and that the power which Congress had to "dispose of"[2] the public lands included the right to give them to the States for any purposes whatever. Against this doctrine Buchanan set himself strongly: he declared that Congress was in the position of a trustee for the people, and that no trustee would be justified in giving away trust property, merely because he was instructed to "dispose" of it.

[1] Appendix A, No. 44.
[2] Constitution, Art. IV, sec. 3, § 2.

The President met the argument that Congress had previously granted land to the States for educational purposes, with the same reasoning employed by Pierce in 1854. The gifts, he said, had been almost universally to new States, and were for the purpose of enhancing the value of the remaining public land in the States to which the grants were made. The acts were merely those of a "prudent proprietor."

June 22, 1860, President Buchanan again refused his assent to an act relating to the public land. The bill was entitled, "An act to secure homesteads to actual settlers on the public domain, and for other purposes."[1]

The measure provided that any citizen of the United States who was a head of a family, and any foreigner who should declare his intention of becoming a citizen, could obtain one hundred and sixty acres of public land at a nominal cost. The important condition was that the settler should remain on the land five years before receiving the title. It was further provided that all the unsold public land which had been subject to sale for thirty years should be granted to the State within whose boundaries it lay.

The President considered the bill unconstitutional, both on account of the donation to the States, and because it practically gave the land to the settlers. For his reasons he referred to the message which has just been considered in regard to grants of land for the establishment of agricultural colleges. He also objected to the bill because it opened a vast field to speculation; because the government needed the revenue from the public land; and because it was unjust to the settlers who had already bought land.

The message gave rise to a long debate in Congress in which each of the President's arguments was attacked.[2] The only important point that was effectually met, however, was that in regard to the revenue. Here it was pointed out that the bill took away no essential resource of the government; because in times of war or distress when the government needed revenue most, the public lands sold very slowly.[3] A more occult reason for the opposition of both Presidents was the feeling of some Southern politicians that the lands were being used to attract foreigners to the West, and thus to strengthen the North and to increase the number of

---

[1] Appendix A, No. 48.
[2] Congressional Globe, 36 Cong., 1 sess., 3263–3272.
[3] Ibid., 3272.

Northern States.[1] Whatever the reasons, the attempt made by Pierce and Buchanan to check the generosity of Congress was ineffectual. Acts were eventually passed granting lands to the States for agricultural colleges, establishing the homestead system, and making "donations" of unsold lands to the older interior States.

§ 48. **Later land vetoes on grounds of expediency.**— Since the war a number of bills relating to the public lands have failed to obtain executive approval, but in these bills the only points raised have been those of expediency.

June 15, 1866, President Johnson vetoed a bill which authorized the New York and Montana Mining Company to pre-empt mineral and timber lands in the Territory of Montana.[2] The provisions of the pre-emption laws in regard to residence on and cultivation of the land, the limit to the amount of land which could be pre-empted by a single individual, and the rule requiring payment for the land within a certain time, were all suspended by the bill under discussion. Furthermore, it allowed the mining company to acquire a patent to the land before the Indian title was extinguished. The President considered such an act to be hostile to the policy of the pre-emption laws, and a great injustice to the Indians.

July 28, 1866, President Johnson vetoed an act which, under the pretext of erecting the Territory of Montana into a surveying district, practically granted to the New York and Montana Mining Company the rights which the President had objected to in his message of June 15.[3]

January 15, 1877, President Grant vetoed an act relating to the proof required in homestead entries.[4] The reasons for the veto accompanied the veto message in a separate document which does not appear in the Journals of Congress.

In President Cleveland's administration, six bills relating to the public land met with executive disapproval. March 11, 1886, the President vetoed a bill entitled, "An act to quiet the title of settlers on the Des Moines River lands in the State of Iowa, and for other purposes."[5] In 1846 Congress had granted to Iowa a strip of the public land lying along the Des Moines River. The act was so worded that the title to a portion of the land was in doubt. The State claimed it, and a few years later the claim was admitted

---

[1] Von Holst, U. S., VI, 302.
[2] Appendix A, No. 56.
[3] Ibid., No. 58.
[4] Ibid., No. 110.
[5] Ibid., No. 134.

by the United States, and the land was certified to the State by the Secretary of the Interior. The State then deeded it to the Des Moines Navigation and Railroad Company in consideration of improvements made by that company along the Des Moines River. The company afterward wound up its affairs and distributed the land. In 1859 the Supreme Court of the United States decided that the certification of the lands to Iowa was unauthorized and void, and that the title was still in the United States. Thereupon in 1861 and 1862 acts of Congress were passed which relinquished to Iowa all the title of the United States in these lands. The Supreme Court has since then held repeatedly that these acts made good the title of the Des Moines Navigation and Railroad Company, and of those claiming under that company.

The present act in the face of the previous acts of Congress, and of the decisions of the Supreme Court, declared the lands to be the property of the United States. Furthermore, the claims of all settlers on these lands prior to 1880, who had taken possession with intent to obtain the lands under the pre-emption and homestead laws, were made good. This seemed to the President " An interference with the determination of a co-ordinate branch of the government, an arbitrary annulment of a public grant made more than twenty-five years ago, an attempted destruction of vested rights, and a threatened impairment of lawful contracts," and he therefore vetoed the bill.

May 18, 1888, President Cleveland vetoed a joint resolution authorizing the city of Boston to make use of Castle Island in Boston Harbor as a park.[1] Fort Independence, one of the important defences of Boston, is situated on this island, and the President objected to the resolution, on the ground that the use of the island as a place of recreation would be entirely inconsistent with its necessary use as a defence.

August 7, 1888, the President was again compelled to interfere to prevent the destruction of a portion of the national defences. The vetoed bill granted to the city of Tacoma, Washington Territory, the right to use a military reservation in the neighborhood of the city as a park.[2] This reservation was considered by the military authorities an important element in the national defence.

[1] Appendix A, No. 298.   [2] Ibid., No. 347.

The President objected to the bill, on the ground that the use of the reservation as a park would impair or destroy its usefulness from a military point of view.

In 1862 land was granted to such of the States as should establish agricultural colleges. In case a State should select lands whose value had been raised to double the minimum price in consequence of railroad grants, the act provided that the number of acres granted to the State should be diminished proportionately. The grant to Kansas had been decreased in this way. A joint resolution passed Congress in 1888, authorizing the Secretary of the Interior to certify lands to Kansas for the benefit of her agricultural college, on the ground that the railroad which made the State land more valuable had been abandoned; that the land had in consequence fallen to the minimum value; and that, therefore, the State was entitled to more land. The President vetoed the resolution September 24, 1888,[1] on the ground that although the original railroad had been abandoned, new ones had been located in its place, and that in consequence only about three hundred acres of the Kansas grant had fallen to the minimum.

On the same day that the resolution just considered was vetoed, the President sent to the House of Representatives his objections to a bill entitled, "An act to provide for the disposal of the Fort Wallace military reservation in Kansas."[2] President Cleveland objected to the measure because it had been drawn in such a careless manner that it would be likely to lead to the unjust treatment of certain private interests.

February 21, 1889, President Cleveland vetoed a bill entitled, "An act to quiet the title of settlers on the Des Moines River lands, in the State of Iowa, and for other purposes."[3] The reasons for the veto were identical with those assigned for the veto of March 11, 1886.

§ 49. **Effect of the public land vetoes.** — A comparison of the vetoes affecting the public lands brings out clearly two respects in which the executive has differed from the legislative department. On questions of expediency the executive has been a conservative element, unwilling to enter on untried schemes and standing as a protector of settled and vested interests, as against the sweeping and often ill-considered action of Congress. In the end, however, a lavish disposition of the public lands has prevailed. In like

[1] Appendix A, No. 386.   [2] Ibid., No. 387.   [3] Ibid., No. 425.

manner the second principle for which several Presidents have striven, has in the end been overborne. Pierce and Buchanan were right in their assertion that public land may lawfully be used for the same purposes as public money, and for no other: but the practice of the government has since been firmly established that the lands may be used to attract settlement, in ways in which money could not be used; and the principle set forth by the vetoes may be considered as superseded by the accepted practice of the government.

§ 50. **Admission of States.** — The territorial power of Congress enables it not only to control the management of the public lands and the government of the Territories, but also to admit the Territories into the Union whenever it sees fit. In several cases, all of which occurred in President Johnson's administration, the executive has prevented the exercise of this power.

The first of the bills to which the President objected was entitled, "An act for the admission of the State of Colorado into the Union." President Lincoln's administration had been distinctly favorable to the admission of new free States. Encouraged by this fact, both Colorado and Nebraska had applied for and obtained from Congress enabling acts.[1] In 1866 both States applied for admission, and Congress passed acts admitting them.

The Colorado bill was passed first, and when it reached the President, it found a man by no means so favorably disposed to the admission of Northern States as his predecessor had been; and on May 15, 1866, it was vetoed.[2] The President's objections were threefold. In the first place, in his opinion the population in the territory was not sufficient to warrant its admission as a State. Secondly, he doubted whether the people in the Territory really wished to change the Territory into a State. Lastly, the President did not think it just to admit new States while eleven of the existing States were unrepresented in Congress. This last argument was borrowed from the larger controversy between Congress and the President in regard to reconstruction.[3]

The Nebraska bill was passed later in the session, and was quietly disposed of by a pocket veto,[4] of which Congress never received official notice.

[1] Blaine, Twenty Years in Congress, II, 276.
[2] Appendix A, No. 55.   [3] *Ante*, § 34.
[4] Blaine, Twenty Years in Congress, II, 277.

At the beginning of the next session of Congress[1] Senator Wade again introduced bills for the admission of both Colorado and Nebraska into the Union. Both bills passed Congress, but as a preliminary to the passage of the acts both Territories were obliged expressly to guarantee the right of suffrage to the negroes.

The Colorado bill reached the President first, and was promptly vetoed.[2] The reasons for the veto were substantially those for the veto of the first bill with a few additions. The most important of the new objections was directed against the clause which prescribed that the State should never interfere with the right of the negroes to vote.

January 29, 1867, the President vetoed the bill for the admission of Nebraska.[3] The President urged that the population of Nebraska was scarcely sufficient to warrant its admission; but his main objection to the bill was that it prohibited the State from ever interfering with the right of the negroes to vote. The bill was reconsidered and passed over the veto.

§ 51. **Criticism of the Colorado and Nebraska vetoes.** — The discussion of both vetoes in Congress was bitter and partisan. It was mainly carried on in the Senate.[4] It can hardly be doubted that, in the light of the circumstances governing the admission of other States, the President was justified in his course. Florida, Oregon, Kansas, and Nevada had, it is true, been admitted into the Union with a population not sufficient justly to entitle them to one representative. But Florida had been admitted to make a slave State, and Kansas to settle a great national controversy.

Without doubt, Congress had exclusive power in such cases, and could admit new States upon such terms as it chose. But the President was also a part of the legislative power, and could set his conditions. The truth was that Congress in its eagerness to increase the number of Northern States had hastened to admit unfit communities, and the President, although actuated by equally partisan motives, maintained a higher principle of public interest.

The President objected in the second place to the restriction which Congress proposed to place upon the new States in regard

---

[1] 2 sess., 39 Cong.
[2] Appendix A, No. 60.   [3] Ibid., No. 61.
[4] Colorado bill: Congressional Globe, 2 sess., 39 Cong., 818, 1922, 1927. Nebraska bill: Congressional Globe, 2 sess., 39 Cong., 851, 1096.

to the right of suffrage. The question was only one phase of the larger one as to whether Congress may impose conditions of any kind on the admission of new States. Restrictions have not been uncommon, and some of them, as for example requiring from the new State a waiver of any claim to tax the lands of the United States, or fixing the boundary of the State, are undoubtedly binding.[1] Such conditions as those imposed on Nebraska and Colorado cannot however have any force. One of the fundamental rules for the admission of new States is that each one shall be received into the Union on a footing with the States already existing, and with all their rights and privileges. One of these privileges is the power to amend the State Constitution, and the condition imposed on Nebraska and Colorado interfered with that privilege. Here, again, the President, although actuated by motives of hostility to the majority of Congress, was acting upon principles of strict constitutional justice.

§ 52. **Financial powers.** — In considering the vetoes relating to the exercise of the powers of government, we have so far been concerned only with those touching either the rights of individuals or the territorial power of Congress. The class which next presents itself includes those vetoes which in one way or another affect the financial powers of the government. They are by far the most important and numerous of those to be examined. Such vetoes will be discussed in the following order : first, those which concern the raising of the revenue ; next, those which concern the safe-keeping of government funds ; thirdly, those which concern the circulating medium ; and lastly, those which concern the spending of the revenue.

§ 53. **The tariff.** — The raising of revenue seems so well recognized a prerogative of Congress, that no tax bill has ever been vetoed upon financial grounds, or even from constitutional considerations unmixed with personal animus. With a single unimportant exception, the only tariffs vetoed have been the two bills presented by the Whigs to President Tyler in the summer of 1842, when his struggle with the party which placed him in power was at its height.

The reduction of duties under the Compromise Tariff of 1833 had gone so far that by 1842 the expenses of the government were

[1] Cooley, Principles of Constitutional Law, 177.

greater than its receipts. To meet this deficiency, Congress, in June, 1842, passed a temporary revenue act which raised the duties above the twenty per cent average. Tacked to this bill was a provision for the continuance of the distribution of the proceeds from the sales of public land. The addition would have been virtually a repeal of the act of 1841 for the distribution of the proceeds of the public land sales; it was therein provided that, if the duties should be raised above twenty per cent, the distribution should cease.[1] To the President's mind the act of 1841 was a vital part of the Compromise of 1833, and he therefore vetoed the present bill.[2] When the message was received by Congress, it created great excitement in that body.[3] The Whigs were charged by their opponents with sending the bill to the President for the purpose of having it vetoed. The Whigs themselves expressed great indignation at the suggestion, and declared that the purest motives of patriotism alone had influenced them.

August 5, 1842, a permanent revenue bill passed the Senate and was sent to the President. This bill, like its predecessor, contained a clause providing for the distribution of the proceeds of the public land sales. August 9, President Tyler vetoed the bill.[4] As in the case of the preceding bill, the President expressed no objection to the revenue clauses of the bill, but based his opposition on the distribution clause.

When the message was received by the House, it was referred to a select committee of thirteen.[5] On August 16, this committee made three reports: a majority report through Adams, the chairman,[6] a minority report signed by Ingersoll and Roosevelt,[7] and a report signed by Gilmer.[8] The majority report attacked the President's whole course, and severely censured his use of the veto power. The report closed with a recommendation for a constitutional amendment, providing that a simple majority vote of all the members of both Houses of Congress should be sufficient to pass a bill over the President's veto. When this report appeared, the President sent a written protest to the House.[9] The House

---

[1] The same question came up in Tyler's veto of the act to repeal the provision. See *ante*, § 46; Appendix A, No. 26. [2] Appendix A, No. 24.
[3] Congressional Globe, 27 Cong., 2 sess., 694, 699, 708, 712, 716.
[4] Appendix A, No. 23.
[5] Congressional Globe, 27 Cong., 2 sess., 877. [6] Ibid., 894. [7] Ibid., 899.
[8] Ibid., 896. [9] Appendix B, No. 3.

returned as a reply a verbatim copy of the resolutions which the Senate had adopted on the occasion of President Jackson's protest, and for which Tyler, as a Senator, had voted.

In the debate over the veto, members of Congress indulged in the most gloomy forebodings as to the future of the country. The President was charged with crushing out freedom. Mr. Lane of Indiana affirmed that[1] "If the proud eagle of American liberty should ever sink, it would be cloven down by the sword of the executive." The records show that even the most sensible men on the Whig side of the House appeared to share the fear grandiloquently expressed by Mr. Lane. Much of the criticism was of course mere party talk; but one point of more than partizan interest was touched upon in the strife. It was maintained that it was entirely contrary to the spirit of the Constitution for the executive to veto a revenue bill.[2] It was indeed true that the Constitution had reserved to the House the exclusive right to originate such bills;[3] but the Senate was not prohibited, either expressly or by implication, from rejecting or amending them; nor was the President precluded from vetoing them. Analogies were drawn from the English procedure in similar cases, but were misleading. We have already seen that the veto power in England had totally disappeared more than one hundred years before the time of President Tyler's administration. Moreover, the English kings were dependent upon Parliamentary votes for their revenues, and therefore would not have refused their assent to appropriation bills even if they had not lost the veto. It would have been vetoing their own means of support. The error in the argument becomes even more apparent when we consider that, during the time that the English veto was becoming obsolete, the American veto was growing in strength and scope. In the United States the power had long ceased to be used simply as a check upon unconstitutional measures, and had come to be freely used when a President considered a bill inexpedient.

If there was nothing in the Constitution condemning these vetoes, was there anything in that document requiring them? There was not. They were, however, directly confirmatory of the act of 1841 already referred to. This act, with its proviso, was con-

[1] Congressional Globe, 27 Cong., 2 sess., 700.
[2] Von Holst, Constitutional History of the United States, II, 460.
[3] Art. I, Sec. 7, § 1.

sidered an important element of the Compromise of 1833. That compromise, while it was of course not a part of the Constitution, nevertheless bore a peculiar character as a settlement between the sections of the country of a great question of policy. It had, in consequence of this character, been recognized by the Supreme Court of the United States as somewhat above an ordinary act.[1] While it is impossible to consider the tariff vetoes a defence of the Constitution, it is equally impossible to call them mere measures of expediency or the exercise of the President's personal whims. They occupy a curious and somewhat anomalous position midway between expediency and constitutionality.

February 22, 1869, President Johnson vetoed a bill increasing the duty on the import of copper and copper ores.[2] The bill was passed in the interests of certain mines on Lake Superior which were in a much depressed condition. It was, in short, a bill for the protection of home industries, and was vetoed by the President on the ground that it would diminish the revenue of the government by curtailing imports, would impose an additional tax on an already overburdened people, and would destroy certain manufactories which were much more extensive and important than the industry it was proposed to protect. He also pointed out that the bill could not be called a protective measure in any fair acceptation of the term, since it appeared to assume that the need for which provision was to be made was inherent and permanent.

In the House, a sharp debate arose upon the veto. The question was mainly as to the advisability of a policy of protection in general and in this particular instance. It was argued that other industries had been protected; therefore copper should be.[3] Mr. Schenck took occasion to remark that the veto should only be used to protect the executive and to prevent unconstitutional legislation.[4] These two views, together with the natural animosity of Congress toward President Johnson, procured the passage of the bill over the veto.

§ 54. **Refunding the direct tax.** — Bills affecting the relations between the States and the general government have seldom been called in question by the President. Twice, however, the veto has

---

[1] Aldrige v. Williams, 3 Howard, 1.
[2] Appendix A, No. 73.
[3] Congressional Globe, 40 Cong., 3 sess., 1461–1466.
[4] Ibid., 1465.

been interposed, in both cases to prevent undeserved payments of money to the States.

July 14, 1832, a bill was presented to President Jackson entitled, "An act providing for the final settlement of the claims of States for interest on advances made during the war." President Jackson disposed of the bill by a pocket veto,[1] and early at the next session of Congress he sent to the Senate his reasons for withholding his approval. It adopted, he said, a principle in regard to the allowance of interest to the States contrary to the rule which had been uniformly followed by the government up to that time.

A more recent and much more important proposition has been that of refunding a tax duly collected from the several States. March 2, 1889, President Cleveland vetoed a bill entitled, "An act to credit and pay to the several States and Territories, and the District of Columbia, all moneys collected under the direct tax levied by the act of Congress approved August fifth, eighteen hundred and sixty-one."[2] The purpose of the bill is sufficiently explained by its title. It was argued in support of the measure that the money due from most of the Southern States never had been paid and could not now be collected, and that therefore it was an act of justice to those States which had paid the tax to refund to them the money they had advanced.

The President objected to the bill first because there was nothing in the Constitution which in his opinion warranted such an appropriation. The original tax was laid and collected in a constitutional manner, and could not be considered in any sense as a debt due by the United States either to the States or to the individuals who had paid the tax. It was, so the President held, a sheer gratuity, and as such was wholly unconstitutional.

But the President objected to the bill on other than constitutional grounds. He considered it most unwise to familiarize the people with the principle that the government might be called upon to repay a tax whose validity and constitutionality were not even questioned, simply because a portion of it had not been collected. He might have added that should this principle be rigidly enforced scarcely one of the multitude of taxes levied by the United States government could remain unrefunded. The last and most practical of the President's objections was that the method of dis-

[1] Appendix A, No. 15.   [2] Ibid., No. 433.

tribution adopted by the bill was extremely unjust, and that in fact distribution on a just basis was an impossibility. The bill provided that in certain cases the money was to go unconditionally into the State treasuries, while in other cases it was to be returned to those who had paid the tax, or to their legal representatives. The President maintained that the tax had been collected from individuals and should in justice be returned to individuals. But in many cases the original tax-payers were neither alive nor represented, while in other cases those alive could not be found. In short it would be impossible to return the money to those who had paid it, or to their representatives, and to return it to any one else, or even to the State, would be wholly unjustifiable.

The bill was passed over the President's veto in the Senate, and in the debate incident to that passage the doctrine was laid down by Senators Sherman and Stewart that bills should be vetoed only upon constitutional grounds,[1] a doctrine which is without foundation, and which sounds strange at the present day.[2]

§ 55. **Bank charter vetoes.** — Turning now from the vetoes relating to the raising of revenue, we come to those which relate to what for lack of a better title may be called the care of the revenue. The place of deposit of government funds has always been a subject of solicitude ever since the government had funds to deposit. Three different Presidents have so far recognized this solicitude as to veto bills granting charters to banks.

§ 56. **Madison's Bank veto.** — January 30, 1815, President Madison vetoed a bill for the charter of the Second Bank of the United States of America.[3] In this message the President passed over the constitutional arguments against the charter of the bank on the ground that the constitutionality of the question had been settled by the repeated recognition of the validity of a national bank. Madison's objection to the charter was based wholly on its inefficiency. The avowed objects of the bill were to strengthen the public credit, to furnish a currency, and to make loans to the government during the existing war. These objects the President thought could not be attained under the present measure, and he therefore vetoed it. This veto was interesting as marking a gradual

---

[1] Congressional Record, 50 Cong., 2 sess., 2612.

[2] A more elaborate discussion of the right of the President to veto bills for reasons of expediency will be found in §§ 121–123.

[3] Appendix A, No. 7.

change in the ground upon which veto messages were based. Most of the earlier vetoes of importance had been founded wholly on constitutional principles; occasionally the argument of expediency was added. In the present case it was upon expediency alone that the President made objections. The veto is one of the first of the long series in which the President has asserted a difference of judgment between himself and Congress as the only reason for refusing assent to a bill.

§ 57. **Jackson's Bank veto.** — In 1816, however, another bank bill was presented to Madison, who signed it; and under the act the second United States Bank was organized. In 1832 an attempt was made to recharter the bank, and Jackson interposed his veto.[1] In this case the question of constitutionality, which President Madison had considered as irrevocably settled in the affirmative, was revived by President Jackson, who insisted that the general question was still open, and further, that the charter contained in the present bill was unconstitutional in details.

In a previous chapter President Jackson's bank veto has been considered in its bearing on the contest between the legislative and the executive branches of the government.[2] It has also an important bearing on the exercise of the financial powers of the government, which must be considered here. The President affirmed that he had as much right as the Supreme Court to declare an act unconstitutional. He then proceeded to justify the veto on constitutional grounds, and quoted the Supreme Court in support of his position. His principle seems to be that the decision of the Supreme Court was good law so far as he agreed with it, but of no effect where he disagreed. The decision to which President Jackson appealed had declared that a bank was a "necessary" means for carrying into effect the powers of government, and that it was therefore constitutional; that Congress might employ this means at its discretion, and that the question of the degree of necessity must be left to Congress. President Jackson then goes on to say that the decision acknowledges the right of Congress to decide whether a bank and the details of its organization are necessary and proper; that the President, as part of Congress, may decide for himself whether the provisions of the act are necessary and proper; and that if the provisions are not in his opinion necessary and proper then the act is unconstitutional. The court declared

[1] Appendix A, No. 14.   [2] *Ante*, § 19.

the action of Congress constitutional, but Jackson succeeded to his own satisfaction in deducing the conclusion that if Congress, or any part thereof, should afterward hold another opinion, the act then in operation was unconstitutional.

Acting in accordance with this rather curious chain of reasoning, the President proceeded to declare the bill for the recharter of the bank unconstitutional, because he disapproved it. He thought it unnecessary that Congress should grant the monopoly without allowing open competition for it, particularly since much of the stock in the bank seeking a recharter was held by foreigners. He thought it unnecessary that the bank should have power to locate its branches where it thought fit. It is impossible in this connection, however, to go into all the curious financial ideas embodied in the veto message. It is sufficient to say that President Jackson reversed the decision of President Madison as to the constitutionality of the bank charter, and supported his position by a distorted argument.

§ 58. **Tyler's Bank veto.** — John Tyler when in the Senate had supported Jackson in his attack on the bank; had agreed with Van Buren in his opposition to the revival of the bank; and felt sure that the "popular voice" approved Van Buren's course. When in 1841 he unexpectedly became President, he found himself obliged to accept the Whig policy of a bank, and agreed to give his assent to any bank bill that was constitutional. Notwithstanding the symptoms of a breach with their President, the Whigs passed a bank bill through Congress. It was not a bill that satisfied any one,[1] but it accomplished the object of forcing an issue with the President. It was generally considered certain that the President would not listen to dictation, at least in this matter;[2] and no one was really very much surprised when the Senate received a message on August 16, 1841, vetoing the bill.[3]

The President's reasons for vetoing the bill were twofold. In the first place he declared that approval would be inconsistent with his previous expressions on the subject.[4] In the second place the

---

[1] Niles, Register, LXI, 93.

[2] Von Holst, Constitutional History of the United States, II, 424.

[3] Appendix A, No. 23; Benton, Thirty Years in the U. S. Senate, II, chaps. lxxv, lxxxi–lxxxiii.

[4] Von Holst declares that "Tyler had too little firmness of character and too much vanity to be able to face the reproach that he had been unfaithful to his earlier convictions, because he did not dare defy the Whigs." — Constitutional History of the United States, II, 425.

President considered the bill unconstitutional because it established a bank with power to locate branches wherever it chose without the consent of the States within whose boundaries the branches were to be placed. This position is scarcely tenable. The Supreme Court had decided that a national bank was a necessary and proper means for carrying on the government, and therefore constitutional. But if the government was to make use of this constitutional agent in the conduct of its affairs, — in collecting revenue, establishing revenue, and furnishing currency, — it must surely have the power to put the bank, or its branches, where they would be most effective; yet this is the very power which is denied by President Tyler. Clearly he was wrong: for if the Constitution gave the government the power to establish a bank without the consent of the States, the consent of the States was not essential for the establishment of necessary branches of the bank.

The Whig leaders at once drew up a bill designed to avoid the objections against the first bill. It was entitled, "An act to provide for the better collection, safe keeping, and disbursement of the public revenue, by means of a corporation to be styled the Fiscal Corporation of the United States." September 9, 1841, Tyler vetoed it.[1] The President's main objection to this bill, as to the last one, appears to be that the bank could establish branches in the various States without their consent. He also objected to the provision which allowed the bank to deal in bills of exchange drawn in one State, payable in another, and running an unlimited time. He further objected to the failure to place a limit on the premium on these bills. Since the measure had been drawn by the Whigs in accordance with the ideas and wishes expressed by the President, the veto greatly enraged them. That portion of the debate in Congress which is reported consists for the most part of a very sharp arraignment of the President by Mr. Botts,[2] in which he discussed in no gentle fashion Tyler's vacillating political policy. During the course of his speech, he took occasion to say "that the President had changed his opinion since this session opened just as often as the sun had risen, and it had lasted now some one hundred and twenty days."[3]

---

[1] Appendix A, No. 23.
[2] Congressional Globe, 27 Cong., 1 sess., 447-449.   [3] Ibid., 448.

§ 59. Criticism of the Bank vetoes. — Whatever the causes of Tyler's vetoes, however unsound his constitutional positions, and however justified the wrath of the Whigs, there can scarcely be any doubt that he did the country good service when he vetoed the bank bills. The creation of such a huge machine as the "Fiscal Corporation," closely connected with the government and parties as it must have been, could not have gained the confidence of bankers and financiers, and would always have been an object of party attack, and a fatally easy means of corruption and political dishonesty.

After the retirement of Tyler, the Whigs never again controlled both Houses and the executive at the same time; the Democrats finally established the independent treasury system inaugurated under Van Buren and repealed in 1841, and were in principle opposed to a bank. The Republican party created the compromise system of numerous so-called national banks, and there has been but one instance in which a President has felt called upon to interpose his veto even against details of bills affecting that system.

Congress in 1881 passed an act retiring the "new fives" issued under the funding act of 1870, and authorizing in their stead three and one-half per cent bonds which were to run forty years. March 3, 1881, President Hayes vetoed the bill on the ground that it was a "step in the direction of the destruction of the national banking system."[1] It provided that after July 1, 1881, no bonds could be deposited by national banks as security which bore a greater interest than three per cent. This provision the President declared would prevent the future establishment of national banks except in the few large financial centres where the prevailing rates of interest are extremely low. The measure would also threaten the existence of the banks already established through the additional disadvantages to which it would subject them. The President then briefly referred to the great success of the national bank system with its almost indispensable advantages, and concluded that he could not approve any measure which, like the present one, unnecessarily attacked that system.

§ 60. Currency and coinage. — Closely connected with the tariff and bank bills, are bills which treat of currency and coinage.

---

[1] Appendix A, No. 128.

Vetoes of such bills have been comparatively few in number, but some of them have been exceedingly interesting.

March 3, 1837, at "11.45 P.M." President Jackson signed the veto of a bill entitled, "An act designating and limiting the funds receivable for the revenues of the United States."[1] The bill was intended to repeal or nullify the specie circular. The friends of the measure had declared it to mean that the deposit banks and the Secretary of the Treasury must receive the notes of all specie paying banks in payment of duties or for public land. The President on the other hand held that the bill merely permitted the secretary and the deposit banks to receive the notes of specie paying banks. In this position he was supported by the Attorney General, who, however, considered the meaning of the bill ambiguous and liable to misinterpretation. The President did not review the bill either as interpreted by himself and the Attorney General, or as interpreted by its friends. He declared it to be ambiguous, and vetoed it for that reason. It is not difficult, however, to read between the lines of the message that the President's real objection to the measure was that it nullified the specie circular.[2]

The disposition made of this veto message is somewhat remarkable and strictly Jacksonian. It was signed within fifteen minutes of the end of the President's term of office. He could not send it to the existing Congress, and when the next Congress met, Jackson would be a private citizen without opportunity to submit a pocket veto message. He was determined, however, that his views on the subject should be left on record; he therefore caused the message, together with the bill and the Attorney General's opinion on it to be deposited in the Department of State.[3] It is the only instance in which a veto message has been thus preserved instead of in the journals of one or both of the Houses.

June 23, 1862, President Lincoln vetoed a bill entitled, "An act to repeal that part of an act of Congress which prohibits the circulation of bank notes of a less denomination than five dollars in the District of Columbia."[4] The President objected to the bill on the ground that if a few banks were privileged to issue such notes, all the banks in the District would issue them, whether

---

[1] Appendix A, No. 21.
[2] Bolles, Financial History of the United States, II, 350.
[3] Senate, Miscellaneous Documents, 49 Cong., 2 sess., No. 53, p. 151.
[4] Appendix A, No. 50.

with or without authorization, and that it would be impracticable to prevent such unauthorized issue. The natural effect would be a deterioration of the currency in the District of Columbia, to the serious injury of trade. The President further suggested that the object contemplated, namely, providing the District with small bills, could be easily and unobjectionably attained by government issues.

§ 61. **Inflation bill.** — April 22, 1874, President Grant vetoed what is commonly known as the inflation bill,[1] providing that the issue of legal tender notes and of national bank-notes should each be increased to four hundred million dollars. The President pointed out that the bill practically increased the paper circulation of the country one hundred million dollars, and would eventually lead to a still greater inflation of the currency. His fear was justified. For it is a fact proved by experience that the more irredeemable paper a government issues, the greater is the call for it, and the greater the apparent scarcity of money.

The President added that not only was he opposed to inflation on principle, but that in this particular instance the government had practically pledged itself to contract the irredeemable currency instead of inflating it. In support of his assertion, he quoted the statement made by Secretary McCulloch at the close of the war to the effect that specie payment should be resumed as soon as possible; and the warm approval of that principle by the House of Representatives on December 5, 1865.[2] Furthermore, on March 18, 1869,[3] Congress had passed an act which solemnly pledged the faith of the United States to make provision at the earliest practicable period for the redemption of the United States notes in coin.

Inflation was urged upon Congress by the "debtor class,"[4] — a class which at that time may even have included some Congressmen. Throughout the country men were eager for inflation as a means of raising prices, and thus diminishing their burdens of debt.[5] The President had argued incidentally that inflation would impair the obligation of contracts, both public and private.

---

[1] Appendix A, No. 92.
[2] Congressional Globe, 39 Cong., 1 sess., 10.
[3] 16 Stats. at Large, 1.
[4] House Report, 43 Cong., 2 sess., No. 328.
[5] Bolles, Financial History of the United States, III, 285.

Arguments put forward in Congress indicated not only that the measure might impair the obligation of contracts, but that such impairment was its very object. The Constitution wisely prohibits such legislation by the States; and justice to the creditors of the nation, and regard to the honor of the government demand that the United States should not be less scrupulous, except in the face of the most urgent national danger.

The veto is to be commended not only on financial grounds and as a defence of the national honor; nor merely because it prevented an unwarranted interference with existing contracts; but on strictly constitutional grounds. At the time the inflation bill was passed, the issue of irredeemable notes as legal tender was considered unconstitutional, except as a necessary incident of the exercise of the war power.[1] Hence President Grant declared the inflation bill not warranted by the Constitution. The fact that the issue of legal tender notes by the government has since been declared constitutional for all purposes did not make it so in 1872. The Constitution is a growth, upon a basis represented by the written document, and the growth has been rapid in many directions in the past fifteen years. Changes have been introduced by custom and by interpretation, without going through the wellnigh impossible process of formal amendment. Thus the principle seems established by legislation and confirmed by judicial decision, that Congress may make government notes legal tender.[2] President Grant's position as to the constitutionality of legal tender issues by the government was therefore sound according to the principles generally accepted in 1872.

§ 62. **The Bland silver bill.** — President Grant's veto practically disposed of inflation through irredeemable paper, and was a striking illustration of the strength of the veto. But although the greenback party rapidly became a thing of the past, the determination to increase the currency remained, and took on the somewhat altered form of the silver movement. One of the measures which resulted was known as the Bland Silver Bill. It passed Congress in February, 1878, and was vetoed on the twenty-eighth of the same month.[3]

---

[1] See 12 Wall., 457; also, the resolutions of the House of Representatives and Secretary McCulloch's statement, to which reference is made above.
[2] 110 U. S. Reports, 421.
[3] Appendix A, No. 117.

President Hayes placed the veto purely on grounds of expediency. The proposed dollar was worth from eight to ten cents less than a gold dollar. The President pointed out that in time, even at the limited rate at which it was to be coined, the silver must drive out the gold, in accordance with the law, so frequently exemplified in our own financial history, that the less valuable money will drive the more valuable from circulation. The result of this process would be an increase in prices and a corresponding scaling of debts, both public and private, contracted on a gold basis.

The President then referred to the public debt, which had been contracted in gold, and which the national honor demanded should be paid in coin of equal value with gold.[1] Furthermore, the President pointed out that when, in his administration, bonds to the amount of about $225,000,000 were refunded at 4 per cent, the government authorized the statement that the government would not "sanction or tolerate the payment of either the principal or interest of those bonds in any coin of less value than gold." Should the depreciation likely to result from the bill set in, these obligations might be cancelled by offering a smaller value in silver. By a decided vote of both Houses, the act was passed over the veto, and during the last twelve years has been in operation. Gold has not yet been driven out; but once or twice the Government has been very near the point where it would have had to pay its regular disbursements on the public debt in silver.[2] Should the time ever come when gold shall have completely disappeared from circulation, the evils predicted by the President may arise. So far, the growth of business has absorbed the additional currency; and the use of certificates has prevented the silver specie from becoming burdensome.

§ 63. **Expenditure of public money.** — The power of taxation in the Constitution of the United States is hedged about by many specific provisions as to the manner and uniformity of levy. The appropriation power is, on the contrary, in its nature connected with the exercise of all the other forms of government. Money may be spent in war, in the public service, for national objects of

---

[1] Mr. Bolles points out that it was intended by both parties to the contract — *i.e.*, the United States and the buyers of the bonds — that they should be paid in gold. Financial History of the United States, III, 391.

[2] February, 1884, and August, 1884. Mill, Principles of Political Economy (Laughlin's edition), 323.

all kinds. Special interests push doubtful measures: private individuals beg for relief or reward. The loose and irresponsible method of conducting financial legislation by unrelated committees leads to waste. It is, therefore, not strange that the largest single class of vetoes relates to the expenditure of public money.

In addition to the riders upon appropriation bills, which are, strictly speaking, financial measures,[1] the most important vetoes of this kind are those affecting the payment of claims on the government, those affecting pensions, and those affecting internal improvements.

§ 64. **French spoliation claims.** — The first of these vetoes in point of time were those of the French spoliation bills. In the course of the Napoleonic wars, three sets of claims arose against France for illegal seizure of vessels and other violations of neutral rights. The first set, arising from 1793 to 1800, were considered in the negotiation of 1800. With the counter claim of France upon the United States for the non-performance of the guaranty of the treaty of 1778, these demands were reserved for future negotiation.[2] The hot-headed blundering of the Senate and the shrewd management of Bonaparte caused the United States afterward altogether to abandon recourse to France;[3] and the merchants and others aggrieved then looked to the United States for reimbursement. Their request was admitted to be just,[4] and attempts were made at various times to secure appropriations to satisfy it; but it was not until 1846 that a bill was passed. It was vetoed by President Polk Aug. 8, 1846.[5] He objected to the bill in the first place because the claims had been before Congress for many years, and, if just, would have been paid long before; in the second place, he urged that, at that precise moment, the country needed all its funds to prosecute the Mexican War. A third objection was that the payment was to be made in land scrip, which, in the President's opinion, would prevent the settlement of the public land, and would be unjust to the States within whose boundaries the public land lay. Finally the President, with a sudden and suspicious thoughtfulness for the claimants, argued that the bill was unjust to them, since it

[1] See *ante*, § 35.
[2] Henry Adams, Administration of Thomas Jefferson, I, 360–363.
[3] Schouler, History of the United States, I, 479.
[4] Ibid., I, 479, note.
[5] Appendix A, No. 32.

obliged them to relinquish all other claims upon the payment of those included in the bill.

In 1855 Congress again passed a bill for the satisfaction of these claims. It was vetoed by President Pierce.[1] He reiterated all the reasons which President Polk had advanced against the measure, dwelling with special emphasis on the fact that such noble patriots as Madison and Jefferson would not have allowed the claims to go unsatisfied if they had been just, but quietly ignoring the fact that Congress must pass the necessary acts before any President could approve them.

The veto message then reviewed the history of the whole discussion between France and the United States, and came to the following conclusions. The United States, by the Consular Convention of 1800, did not give up the claims of American citizens against the French, nor agree to satisfy them herself; all the pretensions which the French could be brought to consider valid were allowed by France in 1803; and it was the allowances then made and paid which the present bill proposed to satisfy a second time. In short, President Pierce was satisfied that the United States had fully discharged her duty to her citizens in pressing their claims; that France had honorably paid all just demands; and that for these reasons the bill should be vetoed.

The President's conclusions were erroneous. In the first place, the Convention of 1800 did surrender the claims of the American ship-owners. Clause 2 of that Convention provided that the spoliation question should be left open for future settlement. The United States Senate struck out this clause. Napoleon ratified the treaty, adding a proviso to the effect that by the retrenchment of the second article each country was understood to renounce the pretensions which constituted its object.[2] The United States Senate ratified the treaty with this proviso attached, thus abandoning the claim which the President said had not been renounced.

In regard to the argument that in 1803 France agreed to pay for all the claims which she could be brought to consider valid, the answer is complete. The sum which France promised to pay was for debts[3] owed by France to citizens of the United States, and did not include spoliation claims. Indeed, it expressly

---

[1] Appendix A, No. 56.
[2] Schouler, History of the United States, I, 479.
[3] United States Treaties and Conventions, 280, Art. I.

excluded indemnity for prizes whose condemnation had been confirmed.[1]

§ 65. **Relief bills.** — Under the Constitution no appropriation of money can be made except by Congress. It follows that no claim can be paid without express provision of law. Hence a considerable part of our legislation is made up of private acts for the benefit or relief of individuals. Since 1861 the usual number of such acts has been increased by claims arising out of the war. Many of the measures have been intended to relieve persons from obligations to the United States, or from punishments inflicted by the United States laws; others are for the purpose of reimbursing soldiers and contractors for pecuniary loss suffered in the national service. As one would naturally expect, there have been among these measures many which defrauded the government of money, or unjustly relieved individuals from their obligations to the government, or from their disabilities under the law. The veto has been freely used in preventing the acknowledgment of these spurious claims, and has in this service amply justified its existence. The vetoes of relief bills can be roughly divided, according to the grounds upon which they rested, into five classes.

§ 66. **Bills defrauding the government of money.** — The first class includes those bills which would have fraudulently secured from the government a grant of money, and also those which would unjustly have relieved individuals from contract obligations to the United States.[2] It comprises, therefore, all such measures as would have unfairly deprived the government of money. This class is very well illustrated by the veto numbered 80. The bill granted money to the children of John M. Baker for his services as *chargé d'affaires* in Rio Janeiro in 1834. The facts were that he had not been *chargé d'affaires* in that year, and on the contrary had been forbidden to enter into diplomatic correspondence with Brazil. The bill was very properly vetoed by President Grant. Another example is the bill granting exorbitant remuneration to contractors for furnishing supplies to the Kansas Indians.[3] The

---

[1] United States Treaties and Conventions, Art. V.

[2] No less than twenty-eight such bills have been vetoed; the first in Pierce's administration, eight by Grant, seventeen by Cleveland. Appendix A, Nos. 37, 47, 49, 76, 77, 80, 86, 89, 93, 98, 101, 133, 210, 250, 271, 272, 278, 282, 291, 299, 316, 346, 366, 372, 388, 390, 407, 411.

[3] Appendix A, No. 93.

second section of the first class includes bills relieving individuals from contract obligations. Among them is a bill to relieve certain mail contractors from loss suffered in complying with the terms of their contract.[1] The loss was caused by curtailing, in accordance with a provision of the contract, the number of trips made by the mail-carriers. Another bill excused a revenue collector from the use of that degree of diligence which the law required him to exercise, or, in other words, absolved him from the results of his own carelessness.[2]

§ 67. **Bills relieving deserters from the army.** — The second class includes four bills relieving deserters from the United States Army from the legal effect of their desertion.[3] One of these bills was passed over the veto on the ground that the man was not a deserter.[4]

§ 68. **Bills relieving former army officers of disability.** — Two bills were vetoed whose object was the restoration of former army officers to the active list, by relieving them of disabilities.[5] The latter of these bills was for the relief of Fitz John Porter, and is of considerable constitutional interest, from the fact that it quite openly attempted to appoint Porter to his old position in the Army. This question has, however, already been considered.[6] Porter had been found guilty by a court-martial duly appointed and composed of officers of distinguished ability, and the sentence had been approved by President Lincoln. President Arthur, in view of these facts, vetoed the bill, not only because it usurped executive authority, but because in relieving Porter it "established a dangerous precedent, calculated to imperil in no small measure the binding force and effect of the judgments of the various tribunals established under our constitution and laws."[7]

§ 69. **Bills carelessly drawn.** — Several relief bills have been vetoed because they were so carelessly drawn that they would not have accomplished their intended objects.[8] The bill for the relief of Daniel H. Kelly may be taken as an example. It was passed

---

[1] Appendix A, No. 49.   [2] Ibid., No. 89.
[3] Ibid., Nos. 94, 97, 103, 114. These vetoes were all in the administration of General Grant, who may be supposed to have felt a special interest in cases of military discipline.
[4] Appendix A, No. 103.   [5] Ibid., Nos. 106, 132.
[6] *Ante*, § 29.
[7] Senate Miscellaneous Documents, 49 Cong., 2 sess., No. 53, p. 457 b.
[8] Appendix A, Nos. 79, 113, 124, 307.

to benefit Kelly's heirs, but it was pointed out in the paper accompanying the veto message that the bill as it stood would be of no advantage to them.

§ 70. **Miscellaneous relief bills.** — The last class includes vetoes which could not be fairly classified under any of the preceding heads.[1] Two of the bills were for the extension of patents which the needs of the government and the public welfare seemed to demand should not be extended. Several of the bills were to compensate the owners of houses and other property destroyed on the ground of military necessity by the United States armies in the Civil War. These bills came up in President Grant's administration, and he objected to them on the ground that the destruction was necessary, and was for the public good, and that if the bills were approved it would open the way for the presentation of a vast number of similar and equally good claims, calling for the expenditure of very large sums of money. The veto for the relief of Major J. T. Turner gave rise to the very interesting question of parliamentary law as to whether a President could recall a veto message before Congress had voted upon it. The question will be discussed in a later chapter.[2]

§ 71. **Pension vetoes.** — With the exception of five unimportant bills disapproved by President Grant, no bill granting a pension has been vetoed by any President save Cleveland. For this fact there are several reasons. In the first place, the veterans of the previous wars almost invariably received land where now pensions would be granted. Furthermore, the government, before 1861, was never rich enough to enter upon an extensive system of money pensions. After the Civil War the circumstances were altered. Good public land was no longer abundant; the government, owing to the prosperous condition of the country, rapidly and easily accumulated large sums of money. This circumstance naturally gave rise to a system of pensions on a large scale. With the increasing surplus, less and less scrutiny was bestowed on private pension bills. In consequence a very great number of wholly unworthy claims received the assent of Congress, and it was against this rising tide of fraudulent or unnecessary pensions that President Cleveland set himself.

---

[1] Appendix A, Nos. 74, 84, 85, 88, 90, 91, 109, 116 (Grant); 373, 406 (Cleveland).
[2] *Post*, § 108.

The pension vetoes comprise two hundred and thirty-three of the four hundred and thirty-three vetoes enumerated in Appendix A, and for the purposes of discussion they have been divided into the following five classes.

§ 72. **Bills conveying no benefit.** — The first group includes thirty-four bills which would have been of no benefit to the claimant, either because of some technical fault in the bill itself, or because the proposed beneficiary would receive at least as great a pension under some general law as under the special act, or because the pension under the general law would begin to run at a much earlier date than under the special act.[1]

§ 73. **Unnecessary increase of pensions.** — The third class includes ten bills increasing pensions which in the President's opinion were already large enough.[2]

§ 74. **Injuries not received "in the line of duty."** — The fourth and largest group of bills includes those granting compensation for injuries which had not been received while "in military service and in the line of duty." Here are found the greatest number, — one hundred and seventy-five, — and the most important of President Cleveland's pension vetoes. It was in regard to these bills that the President and Congress came squarely into conflict.[3]

§ 75. **Dependent relatives: dependency not proved.** — Congress passed many bills granting pensions to persons who claimed to be dependent for their support upon soldiers killed or disabled in the war. Six of these bills failed to obtain the President's approval because the "dependency" of the person pensioned upon the injured soldier was not made out.[4]

§ 76. **Miscellaneous pension bills.** — There are a few bills which do not come legitimately under any of the preceding heads. One granted back pay unjustly;[5] another was the claim of an alleged

---

[1] Appendix A, Nos. 81, 82, 83, 95, 104 (Grant), 137, 168, 178, 189, 194, 196, 204, 208, 211, 219, 233, 248, 249, 255, 258, 265, 266, 267, 275, 284, 290, 318, 337, 340, 358, 391, 400, 424, 430 (Cleveland).

[2] Appendix A, Nos. 138, 160, 165, 203, 242, 268, 269, 270, 323, 432 (Cleveland).

[3] Appendix A, Nos. 140–155, 159, 162–164, 166, 167, 169–177, 179–181, 183–188, 190–193, 195, 197–202, 205, 207, 209, 212–218, 220–226, 228–231, 238–241, 243–246, 251–254, 256, 257, 259, 260, 263, 274, 279, 281, 283, 285–289, 292, 295, 296, 297, 300, 324, 327, 329, 333–336, 338, 339–342, 343, 348–356, 359, 360, 363–365, 367–371, 375–385, 392–396, 398, 399, 402–405, 408–410, 412, 413, 415, 417–423, 426–429, 431 (Cleveland).

[4] Appendix A, Nos. 161, 182, 206, 247, 264, 280 (Cleveland).   [5] Ibid., No. 156.

widow who proved not to be a widow;[1] a third was the claim of a woman who had had a pension as the widow of a soldier killed in the war, but who had lost her pension by remarrying, and who now wished it renewed, although she was still married and was living with her husband.[2] Five granted pensions to men who had deserted from the army.[3]

§ 77. **The Dependent Pension Bill.** — The most important of all the pension bills which encountered the veto was not, however, a private act for the benefit of an individual, but a general and far-reaching law. February 11, 1887, President Cleveland vetoed a bill entitled, "An act for the relief of dependent parents and honorably discharged soldiers and sailors who are now disabled and dependent upon their own labor for support."[4] The bill granted service pensions to all honorably discharged soldiers and sailors who were not at the time of the passage of the act, or who should not, at any future time, be capable of supporting themselves by their own labor, and who are dependent on their daily labor for support, regardless of whether they had received any injury in the service or even had been engaged in battle. The President objected to the bill in the first place because in his estimation the wording of the proposed law was so indefinite as to give rise to conflicting constructions, and to be liable to unjust and mischievous application. In support of his statement he quoted the conflicting opinions in regard to the operation of the bill expressed on the floors of Congress.[5] The looseness of phraseology, and the fact that the proof necessary for the establishment of claims was largely within the knowledge of the claimants alone, would still further stimulate fraudulent applications for pensions and put a "premium on dishonesty and mendacity."[6] The President argued also that the bill was uncalled for, because the soldiers of the Civil War had been better provided for by pay and bounty than any other soldiery "since mankind first went to war," and because most ample laws had been passed which granted pensions for any injury actually received in the service of the United States. Lastly, the President pointed out that the expense of the proposed law would probably be many times the estimate. In support of this argument, he cited the case of the pension granted

[1] Appendix A, No. 330.
[2] Ibid., Nos. 343, 357, 361, 397, 416.
[3] House Journal, 49 Cong., 2 sess., 571.
[4] Ibid., No. 389.
[5] Ibid., No. 261.
[6] Ibid., 572.

in 1853 to the widows of the soldiers of the Revolutionary War, which had cost the government nearly eight times as much as had been expected.

The debate in Congress over the veto was very sharp.[1] The opponents of the veto were both indignant and outspoken; they called attention to the President's inconsistency in signing the Mexican War service pension bill, and characterized his objections as flimsy; they charged him with favoring the solid South and Wall Street.

§ 78. **President Cleveland's pension policy.** — In his veto of the Dependent Pension Bill, President Cleveland took a bold stand against a popular measure, in behalf of economical government. The same general principles appear in the vetoes of private pension bills, classified in paragraphs 71 to 76 above. There the President repeatedly and clearly stated what he considered to be the wise policy; and it was in the discussion of these vetoes that the congressional hostility to the policy was manifested.

The position of the executive may be briefly defined as a desire to check the indiscriminate and often fraudulent granting of pensions. In the veto of a bill granting a pension to Elizabeth S. De Krafft, the President says: "In reviewing the pension legislation presented to me, many bills have been approved upon the theory that every doubt should be resolved in favor of the proposed beneficiary. I have not, however, been able to entirely divest myself of the idea that the public money . . . should be devoted to the indemnification of those who in the defence of the union have worthily suffered."[2] Again he says: "Every relaxation of principle in the granting of pensions invites applications without merit and encourages those who for gain urge honest men to become dishonest. Thus is the demoralizing lesson taught that as against the public treasury the most questionable expedients are allowable."[3] The President was, in short, attempting avowedly to defend the public money, the public morals, and the disabled soldier.

The President's policy was severely attacked in Congress, on the ground that his conclusions as to the unjustifiable character

---

[1] Congressional Record, 49 Cong., 2 sess., 2200, 2202, 2210, 2222.

[2] Appendix A, No. 168; Senate Miscellaneous Documents, 49 Cong., 2 sess., No. 53, p. 489.

[3] Ibid.

of the pensions were incorrect ; and that, even if these conclusions had been correct, his overruling of congressional decisions on matters of fact was unconstitutional.[1] Both of these charges must be examined.

§ 79. **Expediency of the pension vetoes.**— The first charge is of no very great weight. The Senate Committee in their elaborate report admit that the President was legally correct, but claim that Congress should be allowed for equitable reasons to be more lenient than the laws which it had enacted. A reading of the messages and an examination of the evidence will however convince any candid person that even on equitable grounds the President was in most cases correct. At the time the report of the Senate Committee was made, the President had vetoed one hundred and thirty-six pension bills.[2] Out of these, the Senate could find only seven bills in which the apparent injustice of the veto was sufficient to make them the subject of investigation. One of these bills was ultimately discovered to have been wisely vetoed, thus leaving six bills in the treatment of which the Senate Committee claimed that the President had been unjust.[3] The conclusion seems inevitable that in one hundred and thirty cases the President was correct, not only as a matter of law, but also as a matter of justice. The information on which the President acted was in almost every case derived from the pension office; and a few illustrations, which are chosen almost at random and might be multiplied indefinitely, will show more clearly than argument why the Senate Committee was unable to point to any considerable number of cases where the veto was unwisely used. William Bishop was enrolled as a substitute in Indianapolis and served nine days, when he was attacked with the measles; he was shortly afterward mustered out. Fifteen years later the claimant suddenly discovered that his attack of measles had some relation to his army enrollment, and that his disease had settled in his eyes and affected his spinal column.[4] In another case a former soldier was accidentally shot and killed by a neighbor who was attempting

---

[1] Senate Report, 50 Cong., 1 sess., No. 1667.
[2] Ibid., 1667, 3.
[3] These bills are Nos. 310, 289, 315, 281, 309, and 280 of Appendix A.
[4] Appendix A, No. 177; Senate Miscellaneous Documents, 49 Cong., 2 sess., No. 53, p. 478.

to shoot an owl. The widow claimed a pension.[1] Again, James O'Shea applied for a pension on the ground of a sabre-wound and a gun-shot wound received in 1862 while serving in the army. There was no evidence that the man ever received the wounds, a fact which the committee reporting the bill admitted; but in spite of the facts, they were of the opinion "that, situated as he was, he was very liable to, and very probably did receive the wound." [2] These illustrations show the foundation upon which most of the vetoed bills rested. All sorts of diseases and calamities are traced by an almost impossible chain of circumstances to service in the army, one woman tracing her husband's death by drowning to rheumatism contracted in the service, and claiming a pension in consequence.[3]

§ 80. **Constitutionality of the pension vetoes.** — In regard to the second charge, the members of the Senate Committee had more to say. They declared that "it cannot be maintained upon any fair construction of the Constitution that the power of executive disapproval ought to be exercised upon acts of this character for the sole reason that the President differs in opinion from Congress upon a mere question of the weight of testimony, or upon the expediency of a special act, which subserves a proper general purpose and which imperils no power of any other department." [4] They further argued that the veto had been granted to the President as a protection to the executive and to prevent the passage of notoriously bad or unconstitutional laws, and that President Cleveland's policy implied that a factious or usurping President might rightfully subordinate the legislature to his will by an exercise of the veto.[5]

It is only necessary to go back to President Johnson's time to refute the last argument. The statement with regard to the intended scope of the veto power is more difficult to meet, for it is true that in 1789 the veto was regarded as a means of protecting the executive and the Constitution, and was seldom used when the question was simply one of expediency. The gradual increase of

[1] House Journal, 50 Cong., 1 sess., 1811; Appendix A, No. 292.
[2] Appendix A, No. 153; Senate Miscellaneous Documents, 49 Cong., 2 sess., No. 53, p. 476.
[3] Ibid., p. 496; Appendix A, No. 179.
[4] Senate Report, 50 Cong., 1 sess., 1667, p. 2.
[5] Ibid., pp. 3, 4.

the number of vetoes based on expediency will be elsewhere considered.[1] It is sufficient in the present connection to notice that this long growth culminated in President Cleveland's pension vetoes. Here we find Congress protesting against what it calls an unconstitutional use of the veto. It is, however, a use which is permitted by the Constitution, which has frequently been made, which has become more common of late years, and in which President Cleveland persisted unchecked up to the day of his retirement from office. As a result, we must admit what indeed has been conceded practically for many years, that the interpretation of the Constitution in this particular, as in so many others, has somewhat changed, and that, in the future, the right of a President to veto a bill on grounds of expediency cannot be questioned.

§ 81. **Summary of the question of pension vetoes.** — The conclusion in regard to President Cleveland's pension vetoes may be summed up as follows: The facts in the various cases would warrant the refusal of the President to approve the bills on grounds of expediency, and the present interpretation of the Constitution admits the right of the President to assign reasons of expediency for a refusal to approve a bill. Furthermore, the President's action was exceedingly timely. In the first place, it saved the country from what was, to put the best construction on it, a large and useless expenditure of money. The great service which the pension vetoes performed, however, was in checking the spirit of reckless pension legislation. The great prominence which they gave to the question emphatically called the attention of the country to it, gave rise to a strong sentiment against the reckless granting of pensions, quickened the Congressional conscience, and made it more difficult for doubtful claims to succeed.

§ 82. **Commercial powers.** — It is very remarkable that, while the Presidents have relentlessly vetoed financial measures of all kinds, the only great classes of bills affecting commerce which have been selected for executive disapprobation are the tariffs and the bills for internal improvements. Shipping acts, embargoes, bankruptcy acts, and railroad acts have passed unquestioned. The tariff bills have already been considered under the head of taxation,[2] since the veto messages covering them have treated them rather as financial than as commercial measures. Internal improvement bills

---

[1] *Post*, §§ 121, 123.   [2] *Ante*, § 53.

have formed one of the most numerous classes, and present a well-defined succession of vetoes through many administrations.

Before taking up internal improvements, however, it may be well to dispose of a few minor acts relating to commerce.

July 1, 1882, President Arthur vetoed a bill to regulate the carriage of passengers by sea, on the ground that the measure was drawn in such ignorance of the existing method of building ocean steamers that its provisions would render useless for passenger traffic all the modern ocean steamships.[1]

May 17, 1886, President Cleveland vetoed a bill making Springfield, Mass., a port of delivery, on the ground that it would produce confusion and uncertainty in the adjustment of customs duties, and lead to irritating discriminations and probable loss to the government.[2]

§ 83. **Internal improvements.**— The appropriation bills so far considered have authorized government expenditures for the benefit of individuals, as, for example, the pension bills and the French spoliation bills. Another class contains those bills which have authorized expenditures ostensibly for the benefit of all. These are the bills appropriating money for internal improvements; they are bills which have been important and numerous almost since the foundation of the government, and have frequently met with strong opposition from the executive. They have called for the expenditure of enormous sums of money, and are exemplified at the present time by River and Harbor bills and by bills for the erection of public buildings.

§ 84. **Madison's veto of a general bill.**— The first distinct measure for internal improvements was the Cumberland Road Act of 1806. The first veto was interposed by Madison in 1817.[3] The measure was entitled, "An act to set apart and pledge certain funds for internal improvements."

The bill is important as marking the real rise of the question of internal improvements. On all sides it was admitted that internal improvements should be made, but there was a difference of opinion as to whether the Constitution authorized the expenditure of money for that purpose. The supporters of the bill held that it was constitutional because its object was to improve internal commerce between the States and to provide for the common

[1] Appendix A, No. 130. [2] Ibid., No. 139. [3] Ibid., No. 8.

defence. Calhoun argued that the Constitution should be construed "with plain good sense," and that, under such a construction, Congress had power to construct roads and canals as a means of providing for the general welfare.[1]

The President, in his veto message, maintained, as he had suggested in his annual message of December 3, 1816,[2] that the government should undertake internal improvements; but he argued that it could not be done without a constitutional amendment. He maintained that it could not be included under the authority of Congress to regulate commerce; for the present bill was for the purpose of constructing roads and canals, or, in other words, of creating commerce, which he considered a very different thing from regulating it. Furthermore, the President did not think that the power could be included under the general welfare clause. Such a view "would be contrary to the established and consistent rules of interpretation, as rendering the special and careful enumeration of powers which follows the clause, nugatory and improper";[3] it would embrace every act "within the purview of a legislative trust";[4] and would give Congress complete power on every matter not specially excepted, whereas the Constitution particularly reserves to the States all powers not conferred on Congress nor prohibited to the States.[5]

The President was close upon the end of his term of office when he wrote the message. There is every appearance that he intended it as a warning against too free an application of the principle of implied powers in support of the doctrine that internal improvements should be carried on by the national government.

It is of interest to note that, upon the consideration of the President's veto in the House of Representatives, the Speaker, Henry Clay, claimed and exercised the right to vote. There was no tie, but he asserted that the question of the passage of a bill over the President's veto differed in its nature from every other question which could come before the House.[6]

§ 85. **Monroe's Cumberland Road veto. Constitutionality of improvements.** — May 4, 1822, President Monroe, in his only veto

[1] Von Holst, Life of Calhoun, 36–37.
[2] Statesman's Manual, I, 335.
[3] Senate Miscellaneous Documents, 49 Cong., 2 sess., No. 53, p. 17.
[4] Ibid.   [5] Amendment X.
[6] Senate Miscellaneous Documents, 49 Cong., 2 sess., No. 53, p. 18; also Annals of Congress, 14 Cong., 2 sess., 1062. The question is further considered *post*, § 110.

message, refused to sign "An act for the preservation and repair of the Cumberland Road."[1] The President held that Congress had a constitutional right to make appropriations for internal improvements, provided it had the consent of the State in which the improvement was to be made. But the present bill went further, and established tolls and provided for their collection. In the President's opinion, it was implied that Congress had a complete right of jurisdiction and sovereignty over the land of the various States for all the purposes of internal improvement; the bill was therefore unconstitutional. In short, the President considered that Congress had the constitutional power to "apply money" to internal improvements, but did not have authority to construct them. It was a reflection of what Dr. Von Holst calls the "quibble over words,"[2] which characterized the internal improvement discussions of that time. In conclusion, the President pointed out the advantage of having internal improvements carried on by the national government; and, like Madison, he recommended a constitutional amendment to enable this to be done.

President Monroe's position is essentially different from that of President Madison. The latter considered it unconstitutional for Congress to make internal improvements in any way. He did not recognize any distinction between "appropriating money" for, and "constructing," internal improvements. Indeed, this fine distinction was created to avoid the constitutional difficulty raised by President Madison. The country demanded an improvement of its means of internal communication, and it was necessary to find some way out of the hard-and-fast doctrine laid down by Madison. To admit the constitutional right and then to hedge it about with limitations of detail seemed to Monroe a statesmanlike way of meeting the difficulty. His doctrine gave way, however, to a broader view; the difference between "appropriating" and "constructing" was lost, and the only question was: Does Congress have the constitutional authority to appropriate money for internal improvements? And, as we shall see, this query resolved itself into the question whether the intended improvement was or was not national in its character.

§ 86. **Jackson's vetoes. Jurisdiction and local character.** — May 27, 1830, President Jackson vetoed a bill entitled, "An act to

---

[1] Appendix A, No. 9.
[2] Constitutional History of the United States, I, 389.

authorize a subscription of stock in the Maysville, Washington, Paris, and Lexington Turnpike Road Company."[1] In this message the President laid it down as a well-settled rule that the United States could not assume jurisdiction over State territory for the purpose of constructing or maintaining internal improvements. He then went on to say that Congress had power to appropriate money for internal improvements whenever the objects were "general, not local; national, not State."[2] Although this principle had been referred to by President Monroe,[3] it was now for the first time clearly laid down as that by which to test the constitutionality of internal improvements. President Jackson considered the measure before him local in its character, and in accordance with his new rule he vetoed it. He closed his message with an appeal for a constitutional amendment to define clearly the limits of the important power over internal improvements.

When the message came up for consideration in the House of Representatives a most bitter controversy took place. The debate had little or no bearing on the merits of the veto, and was hardly more than a personal attack on the President by his enemies, and a violent defence of him by his friends.[4]

May 31, 1830, President Jackson vetoed a bill authorizing a subscription of stock in the Washington Turnpike Road Company.[5] For his reasons in this case the President referred Congress to his veto of the Maysville Road bill.

December 7, 1830, the President, in his annual message, gave his reasons for the pocket veto of two bills at the last session of Congress, entitled respectively, "An act making appropriations for building light-houses, light-boats, beacons, and monuments, placing buoys, and for improving harbors and directing surveys";[6] and "An act to authorize a subscription of stock for the Louisville and Portland Canal Company."[7] These bills were vetoed like the two already considered, because in the opinion of the President a portion of the authorized expenditure was for purely local improvements.

The last of Jackson's internal improvement veto messages is by

---

[1] Appendix A, No. 10.
[2] Senate Miscellaneous Documents, 49 Cong., 2 sess., No. 53, p. 79.
[3] Ibid., 61.
[4] Congressional Debates, 1829–30, Vol. VI, Part II, 1140–1147.
[5] Appendix A, No. 11.   [6] Ibid., No. 12.   [7] Ibid. No. 13.

far the most interesting. In it he expresses clearly his conception of a constitutional internal improvement, and applies the principle with true Jacksonian simplicity. December 1, 1834, in his annual message, the President sent to Congress his reasons for failing to sign at the last session a bill entitled, "An act to improve the navigation of the Wabash River."[1] In this message the President divides the constitutional question into three parts. He discusses in the first place the "power of the national government to make internal improvements within the limits of a State, with the right of territorial jurisdiction sufficient at least for their preservation and use"; secondly, the right of appropriating money in aid of such works when carried on by a State, or by a company in virtue of State authority, without claim of national jurisdiction; thirdly, the propriety of making appropriations for light-houses, beacons, public piers, and for the removal of sand-bars and other temporary obstructions in navigable rivers and harbors. Jackson's position on the first two points has been sufficiently explained in connection with his previous vetoes. He did not think the government had any jurisdiction over the improvements, but nevertheless thought that money might be appropriated for improvements of a national character. He again insists that there should be a constitutional amendment defining national improvements, and, in his discussion of the third point, lays down a curious rule for determining, in the case of river and harbor improvements, those that are national in character. Expenditures of this character, he said, must be confined to places below the ports of entry or delivery established by law. Since the improvement authorized by the bill under discussion was to be made at a point on the Wabash River above any port of entry or delivery, the President concluded that the bill was unconstitutional. The utter futility of this, or indeed of any hard-and-fast principle, was demonstrated the day after the reception of the President's message. The Senate introduced a resolution for the improvement of the Wabash River identical with the vetoed measure, and included in it a provision making Lafayette, which is situated higher up on that river, a port of entry.[2] The resolution passed the Senate, but was never acted upon by the House. The episode not only illustrates the worthlessness of the President's criterion, but also the impossibility of securing an

[1] Appendix A, No. 18.
[2] Senate Miscellaneous Documents, 49 Cong., 2 sess., No. 53, p. 149.

amendment of the Constitution sufficiently definite to meet the President's suggestion. Indeed, if it could be secured, such an amendment would not be desirable, for the Constitution is a document embodying broad principles, and does not attempt to settle questions of detail or of expediency.

§ 87. **Tyler's vetoes. Improvement of water-ways.** — Like Madison and Monroe, Jackson was not consistent in his vetoes. They all three approved other bills not different in principle from those vetoed. Appropriations continued under Van Buren and Tyler, and it was not till late in the administration of the latter that we find another veto of an internal improvement bill. June 11, 1844, President Tyler returned, with his objections, "An act making appropriations for the improvement of certain harbors and rivers."[1]

In the first place, the President argued that to appropriate money for the improvement of streams is to exercise United States jurisdiction over them, and is accordingly unconstitutional. This conclusion is unsound; for the bill merely appropriated money, and in no way claimed authority over the land or water of any State. The supporters of the measure contended that it came under the clause in the Constitution which gives Congress power to regulate commerce with foreign nations, among the several States, and with the Indian tribes. The President demurred, on the ground that "the plain and obvious meaning of this grant is that Congress may adopt rules and regulations prescribing the terms and conditions on which the citizens of the United States may carry on commercial relations with foreign States or Kingdoms, and on which the citizens or subjects of foreign States or Kingdoms may prosecute trade with the United States, or either of them. But the power to regulate commerce among the several States no more vests Congress with jurisdiction over the water-courses of the States than the first branch of the grant gives authority over the waters of foreign powers."[2] Comment on this remarkable statement is scarcely necessary. At the time it was written it was well-settled law that navigation and intercourse upon the national navigable water-ways is under the regulating control of Congress whenever the water-way is not limited to a single State.[3]

[1] Appendix A, No. 29.
[2] Senate Miscellaneous Documents, 49 Cong., 2 sess., No. 53, p. 182; Appendix A, No. 29.
[3] Cooley's Principles of Constitutional Law, 65; Gibbons v. Ogden, 9 Wheat. 1 (1824).

In closing his message the President hints at a reason upon which the message might have rested, namely, that the bill appropriated money for improvements, some of which are purely local in character. This was a recognition of the principle which was referred to by President Monroe and adopted by President Jackson, and which has since become the main criterion in deciding as to the constitutionality of internal improvements.

§ 88. **Polk's vetoes. Local improvements.** — August 3, 1846, President Polk vetoed a bill making appropriations for the improvement of certain harbors and rivers.[1] The President refused his sanction to the bill on the ground that its provisions were local and not national in character. In endeavoring to determine what are national river and harbor improvements he revived President Jackson's test,[2] and attempted to improve upon it. He admitted that many times ports of entry had been created on paper only, and for the sole purpose of making some intended improvement plausible. He then went on to say that if the test be a sound one it could apply only to bays, inlets, and rivers connected with or leading into such ports as actually have foreign commerce.[3] This amendment hardly improves the test, since it would never be difficult to develop a foreign trade, even from a "paper port" of entry, sufficient to satisfy the Congressional conscience. This veto message met with strong opposition in the House,[4] but mainly from those Congressmen whose districts would have received appropriations under the bill.

On December 15, 1847, President Polk sent to Congress his reasons for not signing at the last session of Congress a bill entitled, "An act to provide for continuing certain works in the Territory of Wisconsin, and for other purposes."[5] The bill was a typical river and harbor bill, and appropriated only six thousand dollars for continuing works in Wisconsin, and more than half a million for improving in other States rivers and harbors, many of which were unknown and valueless.

The President considered that when the country was borrowing money to carry on a war, as was the case at that time, large sums

---

[1] Appendix A, No. 31.
[2] *Ante*, § 86.
[3] Senate Miscellaneous Documents, 49 Cong., 2 sess., No. 53, p. 188.
[4] Congressional Globe, 29 Cong., 1 sess., 1183-1189.
[5] Appendix A, No. 33.

should not be appropriated for improvements. He then took up the constitutional question: he apparently admits the authority of Congress to appropriate money for national improvements, but comes to the conclusion that it is practically impossible to draw any line or principle between deepening a harbor capable of admitting only small sailing craft, and deepening a harbor capable of receiving large ships. "I cannot perceive," he says, "any intermediate ground. The power to improve harbors and rivers for purposes of navigation . . . must be admitted without other limitation than the discretion of Congress, or it must be denied altogether." [1] This difficulty resolves itself into a question of fact and not into a settlement of constitutional points. The constitutional rule is plain enough, but Polk seemed to think the selection of suitable places so far beyond the wisdom of Congress that he considered it unwise for the national government to engage in making internal improvements. The President, however, recognized that some works were indispensable, and suggested that the States be allowed to lay tonnage duties for this purpose. The States may, under the Constitution, lay such duties, with the consent of Congress,[2] and the President referred to many instances where that consent had been given.[3] In conclusion, he advocated the passage of an amendment to the Constitution granting Congress the power to appropriate money for internal improvements, in States in which it was impossible to lay tonnage duties.

The debate on this message was of no particular moment. It was enlivened by a sharp speech of Mr. Schenck,[4] in which he classified, in an amusing manner, the various tests as to the constitutionality of internal improvements, and concluded by practically including all improvements as national in their influence.

§ 89. **Pierce's vetoes. Implied powers.** — Had Tyler been in sympathy with the party which chose him, he would not have opposed internal improvements; the next Whig Presidents, Taylor and Fillmore, vetoed no bill of any kind. Fillmore's Democratic successors, however, again set forth the doctrine to which their predecessors, Jackson and Polk, had given life.

[1] Senate Miscellaneous Documents, 49 Cong., 2 sess., No. 53, p. 198.
[2] Constitution, Art. I, Sec. 10, Clause 2.
[3] Thirteen instances are referred to where tonnage duties were laid with the consent of Congress for the purpose of internal improvements by Mass., Va., N. C., S. C., Ga.
[4] Congressional Globe, 30 Cong., 1 sess., 37.

August 4, 1854, President Pierce vetoed a bill making appropriations for the completion of certain public parks.[1] December 30, 1854, the President sent to Congress a careful statement of his reasons for vetoing the bill, and at the same time took occasion to state his position on the question of internal improvements. He held that the national government should not make appropriations for internal improvements, unless the improvements were necessary to the execution of the enumerated powers of Congress.[2] The President's principle seems to be that when an improvement was plainly and directly for the benefit of the army or the navy, or was necessary for the establishment of post roads or the regulation of commerce, it was constitutional. He does not in terms, call the improvement of rivers and harbors for commercial purposes unconstitutional, but leaves it to be inferred that, in most cases, such improvements would be unauthorized. In closing his message the President recommends a return "to the primitive idea of Congress, which required, in this class of public work, as in all others, a conveyance of the soil, and a cession of the jurisdiction of the United States."[3] Furthermore, he advised that the appropriation for each work be made in a separate bill.[4] The advantages of the last suggestion are obvious, and in recent years the attempt has frequently been made to accomplish much the same end, by allowing the President to veto items in appropriation bills.[5]

In May and August, 1856, President Pierce vetoed five internal improvement bills.[6] The President, in accordance with the rule which he laid down in his message of December 30, 1854, objected to the bills now under discussion, because they were not directly essential to the exercise of the powers of Congress, but were parts of a general system of internal improvements. Congress was not in a mood to submit to the President's views, and it passed each of the five bills over the veto; this was the first case in which an internal improvement veto had failed to check legislation.

[1] Appendix A, No. 35.
[2] Senate Miscellaneous Documents, 49 Cong., 2 sess., No. 53, p. 225.
[3] Ibid., p. 234.   [4] Ibid., p. 235.
[5] See *post*, § 134. There was practically no discussion of this message in Congress, Congressional Globe, 33 Cong., 2 sess., 161.
[6] May 19, Mouth of the Mississippi River, Appendix A, No. 38. May 19, Channel over the St. Clair Flats, Appendix A, No. 39. May 22, Channel over St. Mary's River Flats, Appendix A, No. 40. August 11, Des Moines River, Appendix A, No. 41. August 14, Patapsco River, Appendix A, No. 42.

Several interesting points of procedure came up on the passage of the bills over the veto. On the consideration of the first one (May 19, 1856) the President of the Senate decided that the bill would pass if two-thirds of the Senators present, instead of two-thirds of the entire Senate voted in favor of it. An appeal was taken from the ruling, but it was sustained by a vote of 34 to 7,[1] and remains the principle accepted by the best interpreters of the Constitution.[2]

The Senate on the consideration of the fourth and fifth messages (August 11 and 14) failed in the first attempt to pass the bill over the veto. In each case, however, the vote was reconsidered several days later, and the necessary two-thirds majority was obtained.[3]

§ 90. **Buchanan's vetoes. Constitutional grounds.** — February 1, 1860, President Buchanan sent to the Senate his reasons for failing at the last session of Congress to sign an act making appropriation for the deepening of the channel over the Saint Clair Flats, in Michigan.[4] The channel had already been improved, and the present bill was to provide for additional, and in the President's opinion, unnecessary, dredging. More than this, he considered the bill unconstitutional. For his reasons on the latter point, he referred to President Polk's veto of December 15, 1847,[5] in which, it will be remembered, President Polk argued that it was unconstitutional for the national government to carry on any internal improvements, and advocated the authorization of State tonnage duties. The President restated Polk's reasoning at some length, and added nothing to it.

February 6, 1860, President Buchanan sent to the Senate a message stating that he had failed to sign at the last session of Congress a joint resolution appropriating money for removing obstructions to the navigation of the Mississippi River, for the reasons set forth in his veto message of February 1, 1860.[6]

§ 91. **Grant's veto and refusal to carry out a bill.** — From 1860 to 1882 there were no internal improvement vetoes. The neces-

---
[1] Senate Miscellaneous Documents, 49 Cong., 2 sess., No. 53, p. 255.
[2] *Post*, § 109.
[3] Senate Miscellaneous Documents, 49 Cong., 2 sess., No. 53, pp. 257, 258, *post*, § 111.
[4] Appendix A, No. 45.
[5] *Ante*, § 87.
[6] Appendix A, No. 46.

sities of the Civil War cut off this form of expenditure; and when in 1870 the finances of the government permitted the resumption of the policy, the Republican party was found in much the same attitude as that of the Whigs. August 14, 1876, President Grant in signing a river and harbor bill protested strongly against certain of its provisions. In the first place he objected to numerous appropriations in the bill which were for improvements in no sense national. In the second place the President doubted the advisability of making any appropriations further than to provide for the protection of works already finished and paid for, in view of the probable falling off of the internal revenue. The President declared that he would not have approved the bill had it been obligatory upon the executive to spend all the money appropriated by Congress. Since he was not under such an obligation, the President, although he had signed the bill, informed Congress that he should take care that, during his term of office at least, no public money should be expended upon improvements which were not of a national character. This was a new way of defeating the provisions of an internal improvement bill, and it was a means that could be made very effective during at least one administration.

The authority under which President Grant made the statement is found in the first paragraph of the act which reads: "the following sums of money . . . are hereby appropriated, to be paid out of any money in the Treasury not otherwise appropriated, to be expended under the direction of the Secretary of War, for the repair, preservation, construction, and completion of the following works."[1] It may seem like an unwarranted stretching of the sense of the clause to make it mean that the executive may do as he chooses about carrying out the provisions of a bill; but no objection was made to the President's interpretation. Indeed, it has become the practice of the executive to withhold expenditures upon works plainly of no value; but the open avowal made by President Grant of his determination not to carry into effect a law duly passed by Congress and approved by himself, has not been repeated.[2]

§ 92. **Arthur's veto. Local objects.** — A few years later, the appropriations had so increased in amount that President Arthur

[1] 19 U. S. Stats. at Large, 132.
[2] Gen. Grant vetoed an unimportant internal improvement bill (App. A, No. 102) on the ground that the objects of the appropriations were most of them local.

felt compelled, August 1, 1882, to veto a river and harbor bill. His reason for this action was that the bill contained provisions of a purely local character, and was therefore unconstitutional. The bill was promptly passed over the veto. In the next session the Senate took the unusual course of calling upon the President to name the items in the bill which he considered of local importance. The President pointed out items aggregating almost one million dollars.[1]

§ 93. **Public buildings.** — Besides the bills for the improvement of various means of communication, roads, canals, and water-ways, Congress has passed a large number of measures for improvements of an entirely different kind, the construction of public buildings. The first President to check this legislation was Cleveland. In the messages there could of course be no question of constitutionality; the buildings authorized by the bills were for the accommodation of the United States courts, for post-offices, and for revenue offices — buildings which Congress is expressly authorized to erect in the different States upon such sites as may be purchased with the consent of the State legislatures.[2] The ground which the President took in each of the vetoes was, therefore, that there was no necessity for the erection of the building called for by the bill; that the needs of the government were well satisfied, and the proposed structure was merely to gratify local pride.[3]

§ 94. **General view of internal improvement vetoes.** — Before leaving the subject, it may be well briefly to sum up, in so far as it is possible, the effect of the internal improvement vetoes. President Madison based his dissent on the broad ground that the Constitution as it stood did not authorize such undertakings by the national government. President Monroe agreed with the principle, but held that it applied to cases where the United States undertook to "construct" roads and canals, and not to cases where Congress merely appropriated money for improvements which were national in character, and over which Congress did not claim jurisdiction. After Monroe's time, the distinction between "constructing" and "appropriating" seems to have been almost

---

[1] Papers of the American Historical Association, III, 192.
[2] Constitution, Art. 1, Sec. 8, Clause 17.
[3] The vetoed bills were twelve in number: Appendix A, Nos. 157, 158, 227, 234, 235, 237, 294, 308, 312, 313, 314, 374.

forgotten. The constitutional question has been simply whether Congress has the power to appropriate money for internal improvements; and the existence of such authority has generally been held to depend on the national character of the proposed improvement. The great difficulty has therefore been to decide what was national and what was local. President Jackson's rule in regard to river improvements proved valueless; and President Polk, after trying to find some satisfactory criterion, came to the conclusion that there was none, and that therefore internal improvements were not provided for under the Constitution. As a substitute for national aid he recommended that the States be allowed to lay tonnage duties. This plan was also recommended by President Buchanan, and has many things in its favor. It is in accordance with the principle of local self-government, which was wisely made fundamental in our system, and it would probably put a stop to much of the reckless extravagance in carrying out internal improvements. The consent of Congress which would still be necessary for each State act imposing tonnage duties would probably keep them uniform and just. President Pierce was more liberal than Polk, and advocated such improvements as were essential to the exercise of the well-defined powers of government — as, for example, the war power. But he lays down no definite rule, and he therefore leaves the discussion in the vague state against which President Polk protested so vigorously. The recent internal improvement vetoes have all been based on the local character of the bills, but no attempt has been made to define a "local provision." The Presidents have simply passed upon the items before them.

At present the question of the constitutionality of internal improvements carried on by the national government is no longer discussed in Congress. By common consent the question of principle is disregarded, and each state and section of the country eagerly seeks to obtain as much as possible for itself, without much thought of possible consequences in centralizing the power of the government. The real justification of the internal improvement measures is that they are essential to the carrying out of some of the express powers of government. Many of the improvements are necessary incidents of the regulation of commerce; while the right to establish post roads and the military necessities of the government have been invoked as a warrant for others.

§ 95. **Measures based on the general welfare clause.** — The attempt has frequently been made to justify internal improvement bills under the general welfare clause of the Constitution, a use of that clause which several of the veto messages have justly treated as unwarranted.[1] In spite of executive warnings, however, Congress, becoming gradually aware of the great possibilities of this indefinite clause, has passed acts for the relief of unfortunate people. Such was the act for the benefit of the San Domingo refugees, and the act for the relief of sufferers from flood, which could be justified only under the general welfare clause. In the internal improvement bills, the principle was put forward as a collateral reason for the constitutionality of the measures. In the bills just referred to, and in the Texas Seed bill, the general welfare clause is put forward as the sole constitutional justification for the proposed legislation. The practice is in substance an addition to the express powers of the government of the United States, and is open to grave objection. It is at this point in our system of government that the greatest watchfulness is necessary, lest a generous impulse open the door to the passage of bills attacking private rights instead of remedying private misfortunes. The danger of centralization is perhaps a distant and imaginary one, but the dangers of waste, of extravagance, of discriminations between citizens, and of accustoming the people to depend upon the government, are certainly near and real.

§ 96. **Texas Seed Bill.** — Against this dangerous tendency President Cleveland set himself in his veto of the bill authorizing a special distribution of seeds in the drought-stricken counties of Texas.[2] The President vetoed the measure on the ground that there was no warrant for such an appropriation in the Constitution; that the relief of individual suffering which is not properly related to the public service and benefit is not the duty of the national government. He argued, further, that not only is such aid not justified by the Constitution, but that it would tend to weaken the sturdiness of our national character and the thoughtfulness of the people for each other. The President closed by pointing out that if Congressmen wished to aid the Texans, they could do so very easily and in an entirely constitutional way by transferring to the representatives of the drought-stricken districts their orders upon the Commissioner of Agriculture for seeds.

[1] *Ante*, § 84.   [2] Appendix A, No. 262.

When the veto message came up in the House, Mr. Lapham, who introduced the bill, spoke briefly in opposition to the message.[1] He referred to similar acts passed in 1875 and 1883, and said that if it was constitutional for the Department of Agriculture to distribute seeds at all, it certainly was justified in this case. This argument overlooks the fact that, by the bill, the Department of Agriculture was not to perform its regular work, but to act as the agent of the government in distributing the special appropriation made to relieve the sufferers in Texas. The veto was, however, effective in checking the proposed legislation; and it lays down a principle which, if observed, must be of permanent value to the country. The government is too busy and too remote to examine into or to relieve cases of individual distress; and the States which leave the work of charity to the general government must expect that government also to assume powers which the States would gladly retain.

§ 97. **War powers.** — A few bills have been vetoed which had reference to the exercise of the war power of Congress. None of these bills were general in their scope, and all of them failed of executive approval solely on the ground of their inexpediency; no constitutional questions were touched upon.

The first military bill which failed of approval was vetoed February 28, 1797. It was entitled, "An act to ascertain and fix the military establishment of the United States."[2]

The President refused his assent because the bill was drawn in a careless manner, and because the soldiers whom the bill proposed to muster out were needed by the government. When the message was read in the House, one or two speakers thought that the President's objections were not well taken.[3] The debate was, however, short, and it is evident from the vote, that the great majority agreed with the President.

July 2, 1862, President Lincoln vetoed a bill entitled, "An act to provide additional medical officers of the volunteer service.[4] The President refused to sign the bill because he had already approved one for the same purpose.

July 14, 1870, President Grant vetoed an act which provided

---

[1] Congressional Record, 49 Cong., 2 sess., 1875.
[2] Appendix A, No. 21.
[3] Annals of Congress, 4 Cong., 2 sess., 2331.
[4] Appendix A, No. 51.

for the payment of bounties to men in the first and second regiments of Florida Cavalry and in the first Alabama Cavalry.[1] The men in these regiments or their heirs had already received or were receiving their bounties. The bill altered the amount of the bounties in many cases, and also the order in which the heirs of the soldiers should inherit the bounties: it would therefore be exceedingly difficult, and in many cases unjust, to apply the act; and the President vetoed it.[2]

January 15, 1877, President Grant protested against a joint resolution authorizing the Secretary of War to supply the Reform School in the District of Columbia with blankets, on the ground that the act would deprive the army of blankets which could not be spared.[3] The protest was not sent with the resolution, as is generally the case, but was sent to Congress in the manner of a veto message, the President retaining the resolution. Later, the President signed it, and it became law.

The pension and relief vetoes are at the same time military and financial. They have been sufficiently considered in the earlier pages of this work.[4]

§ 98. **General effect of the veto on the exercise of the powers of government.** — Before concluding this part of our subject, a few vetoes must be mentioned which do not fit into any of the preceding classes, and which are not of sufficient importance to warrant separation into additional classes. The bills were all either needless or improperly drawn. The first of these vetoes was interposed by President Lincoln to prevent the passage of a bill which was not drawn in a satisfactory manner.[5] July 20, 1876, President Grant vetoed a bill amending the post-office statutes on the ground that the bill as drawn would not accomplish its purpose.[6] April 30, 1886, President Cleveland vetoed a bill which attempted to extend to the city of Omaha privileges which it already possessed under a prior act.[7] July 30, 1886, President Cleveland vetoed a bill providing for a bridge across an arm of Lake Champlain, on the ground that a bill for the purpose had

---

[1] Appendix A, No. 75.
[2] For the text of the act, see Senate Journal, 41 Cong., 2 sess., 1080.
[3] Appendix B, No. 9.
[4] *Ante*, §§ 68, 81.
[5] Appendix A, No. 52.   [6] Ibid., No. 105.
[7] Ibid., No. 136.

already been approved.[1] August 14, 1888, President Cleveland vetoed a joint resolution authorizing the printing of additional United States maps of the edition of 1886,[2] on the ground that the map for 1887, which was a better and cheaper map than the one for 1886, was all ready for publication.

All the vetoes affecting the powers of government have now been considered. It is difficult to summarize their combined effect, because of the variety of subjects considered. In regard to the exercise of governmental authority over individuals, the President's power has usually been employed for the protection of individual rights. In territorial affairs the veto for a long time checked the policy of rapid disposition of the public lands, and attempted to check the unwise admission of unripe States. In finance the veto has been used, — with the exception, perhaps, of Jackson's and Tyler's bank vetoes, and the French spoliation vetoes, — to protect the funds of the government, to secure a sound currency, and to prevent extravagant expenditures. Almost the only application of the veto to commercial powers has been in internal improvement legislation; and here, though finally overcome by the continued policy of Congress, the Presidents long set themselves against this somewhat doubtful use of the powers of government. One courageous stand has been taken against the extension of the general welfare principle. The war powers had their great development, during the Civil War, with no executive interference.

In so far as these diverse effects can be summed up in a word, it may be said that the veto has been used to prevent Congress from unduly extending its authority; that in almost all cases it has been used wisely; and that it has failed only in those cases in which Congress has been supported by a strong public opinion, or in which the majority of the people took no interest.

[1] Appendix A, No. 236.   [2] Ibid., No. 392.

CHAPTER V.

CONSTITUTIONAL PROCEDURE AS TO VETOES.

§ 99. The action of the President.
  § 100. Is the exercise of the veto a legislative power?
  § 101. Constitutionality of pocket vetoes. The legal ten days.
  § 102. May a bill be vetoed without stating reasons?
  § 103. May a bill be signed after the adjournment of Congress?
  § 104. May a President refuse to carry out an act?
  § 105. The President's right of protest.
  § 106. Is the signature of the President essential to constitutional amendments?
§ 107. The action of Congress.
  § 108. Has the Executive a right to recall a veto?
  § 109. What is a two-thirds majority?
  § 110. Has the Speaker a right to vote on reconsideration?
  § 111. Second reconsideration of a veto.
  § 112. Failure to enter the veto message in the journal.
  § 113. Frequent neglect of reconsideration.
§ 114. Comparative unimportance of constitutional details.

§ 99. **The action of the President.** — The veto power has been in operation in the government of the United States for more than a hundred years; and in that time many interesting questions of procedure as to the acceptance and disallowance of bills have arisen and have been settled. In the present chapter the more important of these questions will be discussed. For convenience those questions which have arisen in regard to procedure between the time when the President receives the bill and the time when he returns it to Congress with his objections have been grouped together;[1] while those questions which relate to procedure after Congress has received the message, are placed in a separate group.

After the passage of bills they are enrolled, formally engrossed and compared, signed by the speaker of the House and the President of the Senate, and finally presented to the President of the United States by the committee on enrolled bills of that branch of Congress in which the bill originated.[2]

---
[1] For the practice in the States, see Appendix E, Nos. 1-10.
[2] McDonald, Manual of the Senate (1886), 262.

§ 100. **Is the exercise of the veto a legislative power?** — The first question which naturally suggests itself is as to the nature of the veto power. Dr. Von Holst [1] maintains that the veto is in no sense a part of the legislative power, since "all" legislative power is vested in Congress. Mr. Bryce in his recent work seems hardly consistent on this point. In one place he speaks of the President as not at all a part of the legislature; [2] while in another place he speaks of the President's veto power as a legislative function.[3] Mr. Bryce expressly says that by granting the President the veto the Federal Convention made him "a distinct branch of the legislature, but for negative purposes only. Thus the executive was strengthened, not as an executive, but by being made a part of the legislature." [4]

The latter view is in itself the more reasonable, and better harmonizes with the known deviations in the Constitution from the strict principle of separation of powers. Thus the Senate, in impeachments, is a judicial and not a legislative body. In like manner the President acts as a part of the law-making power when he approves or disapproves an act. This conclusion is strengthened by an examination of the growth of the veto. It has been pointed out in an earlier portion of this work [5] that the veto in the Federal Constitution was derived from the State Constitutions, — a view which is supported by the Federalist itself.[6] The power in the States was derived in a somewhat modified form from the Colonial systems and from the institutions of the mother country; while in England the power was a remnant of the once important legislative power of the kings.[7]

Thus it appears as a matter of historical development as well as of theory that the veto is a legislative power. It therefore seems a reasonable explanation of the declaration that "all legislative power is vested in Congress," to say that the general statement is limited by the particular power given to the President in a later part of the same instrument.

---

[1] Constitutional Law of the United States, 112.
[2] The American Commonwealth (Am. edition), I, 52.
[3] Ibid., I, 220.
[4] Cooley also calls the veto a legislative power. Principles of Constitutional Law, 50.
[5] *Ante*, §§ 8, 10.
[6] The Federalist (Dawson's ed.), No. LXVIII.
[7] *Ante*, § 5.

§ 101. **Constitutionality of pocket vetoes. The legal ten days.**
— The Constitution provides that no bill shall become a law which is presented to the President within ten days of the end of a session of Congress, unless it be signed and returned to Congress before adjournment. The provision is plain, and it is surprising that the constitutionality of these "pocket vetoes" has ever been questioned. In 1833, however, Henry Clay assailed President Jackson's pocket veto of the bill for the distribution of the proceeds of the public land, on the ground that it was unconstitutional.[1] Clay maintained that the constitutional provision only applied to bills presented to the President within ten days of the adjournment of the first or of an extra session of Congress. In other words, Clay held that the President might withhold his signature where the day of the adjournment was fixed by simple joint resolution, but not otherwise. This reasoning is wholly unsound. It is unsupported by the Constitution, and too comprehensive as a matter of principle; for if the rule which Clay contended for should be adopted it would destroy the veto power; Congress could prevent the President from vetoing a bill by presenting it to him so late in the final session that he could not veto it and still send his message to Congress before adjournment. In fact, the bill concerning which Clay complained passed the House but two days before the expiration of that session. No case, therefore, could better illustrate the weakness of Clay's argument, or bring out more clearly the great usefulness of the pocket veto. How freely the pocket veto has been employed may be seen from an examination of the statistics. Many Presidents have left bills to perish for lack of their signature, including Presidents who had vetoed no bills directly.[2]

Another very interesting question relative to pocket vetoes is that of the length of time during which an act may be held by the President unsigned before it becomes law. In the appendix will be found numerous cases in which a veto message was returned from eleven to twenty-four days after the last action of either House. The Constitution distinctly provides, "if any bill shall not be returned by the President within ten days (Sundays excepted) after it shall have been presented to him, the same shall become a law in like manner as if he had signed it." The explana-

[1] Appendix A, No. 17; Debates of Congress, Vol. X, Part I, 14–18.
[2] Cf. Appendix D. For State practice, see Appendix E, Nos. 22–26.

tion of the discrepancy is simple. In the first place, Sundays are not considered a legal part of the ten days, so that the twelfth day after submission to the President may legally be the tenth. In the second place, the day of reception is not included.[1] In the third place, the bill is frequently not presented to the President until some days after passing, through the final stages of legislation. It may therefore be set down as certain that all bills which pass the second House in which they are considered as late as February 20 in the odd years will fail without a veto, unless signed by the President; and bills passed between the 18th and 20th may fail.

§ 102. **May a bill be vetoed without stating reasons?** — All of the presidential vetoes have been accompanied by the reasons for the refusal to sign. Indeed it is difficult to see how any other plan could be followed, since the Constitution requires that if the President fails to approve a bill he shall return it, with his objections, to that House in which it shall have originated.[2] Furthermore, it is maintained in a pamphlet by Mr. J. H. Benton, Jr.,[3] that the objections assigned must be objections to the intrinsic merits of the bill. He quotes at length from the proceedings of the Federal Convention, from the Federalist, and from the writings of Madison and Hamilton, to show that the President's authority was similar to that of the Council of Revision in the State of New York, and that this Council had power to state objections only to the intrinsic merits of the bills brought before it. This restriction would narrow the plain wording of the Constitution by an appeal to the practice of a body unknown to the Constitution, and equally unknown to English parliamentary practice. The Constitution sets no limit upon the nature of the objections stated by the President, nor is it generally assumed that there are any limits.[4] If there be none, the President has a constitutional right to veto a bill simply because undue influence had been used in securing its passage, or for any other reason that seems good to him, even though his objections may have no reference to the contents of the measure.

---

[1] Story, Commentaries. (Cooley's ed.) § 891, notes. For States, see Appendix E, Nos. 27–36.

[2] *Ante*, § 11. In Georgia no veto message is required. Appendix E, No. 5.

[3] Benton, The Veto Power in the United States, 35.

[4] Von Holst, Constitutional Law, 113, note; Cooley, Principles of Constitutional Law, 50.

§ 103. **May a bill be signed after the adjournment of Congress?**
— There is nothing in the Constitution to prevent the President from signing a bill after the adjournment of Congress. The only provision is in regard to bills which the President leaves unsigned; these cannot become law if Congress, by its adjournment, cuts short the ten days allowed the executive for the consideration of bills. Nor is there any consideration of parliamentary law which demands that Congress should be in session when a bill is signed. Congressional jurisdiction over a bill ceases when it is sent to the President for his signature, and there is no legal method of recovering possession of the subject other than by a subsequent act of repeal passed under the usual forms. The act is not even returned to Congress, but is deposited by the President in the State Department.[1]

The interests of good government seem to demand that the President should have the power to distribute over the succeeding ten days the immense responsibility of signing the bills with which he is inundated during the last hours of Congress. At present he must either sign or "pocket veto" a multitude of bills with scarce a glance at them; and to refuse his signature when detailed examination is impossible means to cut off essential appropriations, or to defeat measures of great public importance. Should the President be given the additional time, his functions would be performed more carefully, and Congress would perhaps hesitate to pour upon him such a mass of crude legislation.

In one important instance the right of a President to sign a bill after the adjournment of Congress has been distinctly recognized. March 3, 1863, Congress passed an act providing for the collection of abandoned property, and the prevention of frauds in insurrectionary districts of the United States.[2] March 12, 1863, President Lincoln signed the bill. In 1883, in a case in the Court of Claims,[3] the validity of the act was questioned, but the Court said that the Supreme Court had passed on cases under this act as if it had been valid law, and that Congress had recognized the validity of the act by amending it July 4, 1864, and speaking of it as the act of *March 12*, 1863. The particular case under consideration was, however, decided on another point, without a judicial determination of the validity of the act.

[1] Revised Statutes, § 204.
[2] Congressional Globe, Part II, 37 Cong., 3 sess., 1543.
[3] 18 Court of Claims, 700.

In at least three of the States of the Union, New York, Georgia, and Illinois, amendments to the State Constitution have been passed authorizing the governor to sign bills after the adjournment of the legislature; but in all three States it had previously been held by the courts that, under constitutional provisions copied word for word from the Constitution of the United States, the power of the governor to sign bills within ten days of the time they are presented to him does not cease with the adjournment of the legislature.[1] The Illinois case is, perhaps, the most important, because it was carried to the Supreme Court of the United States. Chief Justice Waite in delivering the opinion said: "The question to consider is whether a bill passed by both Houses of the Legislature, and presented to the governor before the Legislature adjourns, becomes a law when signed by the governor after the session of the Legislature has terminated by adjournment, but signed within ten days of the time it is presented to him. We see nothing in the Constitution of Illinois, express or implied, to forbid it, and in our judgment from every view of the case we think he can."[2]

After these decisions it seems hardly probable that the Supreme Court would hesitate to declare valid an act approved by the President of the United States under similar circumstances.

§ 104. **May a President refuse to carry out an act?** — August 14, 1876, President Grant, in signing a river and harbor bill, protested against certain provisions in the measure, and declared it to be his intention not to carry out these provisions.[3] This was a novel and a clearly unconstitutional way of defeating the will of Congress.[4] The President's purpose could be justified only in regard to such acts as merely authorize the President or his secretaries to take certain action. But even in those cases where the President is commanded to carry out the legislative will there seems to be no way in which he can be compelled to obey the command. He is one of the co-ordinate branches of the government, and it is a well-established principle that the President in his official capacity is

---

[1] 21 N. Y. 317; 30 Barb. 304; 41 Ga. 157. For the provisions of State Constitutions, see Appendix E, Nos. 37–43.

[2] 103 U. S. 423. [3] Appendix B, No. 7.

[4] No President has so strenuously stood out against the policy of Congress as Andrew Johnson. But even President Johnson declared himself constitutionally bound to carry out the details of the Reconstruction Acts passed over his veto.

not amenable to the Supreme Court, nor can he be reached by Congress except through the cumbrous and well-nigh impracticable machinery of impeachment. Practically then, the President is independent in his particular sphere as chief executive officer of the nation; and if he refuse to carry out the provisions of a law which is entrusted to him for enforcement, there is no method of compelling him to act. Such refusal is, however, only suspensive and not absolute, since the effect ceases with the close of the President's term of office.

§ 105. **The President's right of protest.** — In Appendix B will be found a list of Presidential protests against various acts and resolutions of Congress. They cover a long period of time and a great variety of subjects. The first one — President Jackson's protest against the Senate resolution of censure — is the longest, and perhaps the most important.[1]

The Senate maintained that for the President to send to the Senate a protest against any of its acts,[2] was an infringement of its rights. The objection seems well taken. To be sure, the Constitution is silent on the point, but each of the two Houses of Congress may pass resolutions which do not require the signature of the President, and are entirely free from his veto. In such cases a Presidential protest is both undignified and unjustifiable. In this particular instance, the Senate had put itself in the wrong by an equally unwarranted criticism of the President's action.

A somewhat different and a larger question is whether the President may constitutionally protest against joint resolutions and bills of Congress, without a formal veto. The Constitution does not in terms give or withhold such a right, but it does subject joint resolutions and bills alike to the veto. The veto power, by reasonable implication, includes the lesser power of objecting while signing. It may, therefore, be laid down as a principle, that a protest is constitutional wherever a veto would be constitutional.

§ 106. **Is the signature of the President essential to constitutional amendments?** — When the Thirteenth Amendment to the Constitution was presented to the President after its passage by Congress, he signed it and notified Congress to that effect.[3] The Senate immediately adopted a resolution declaring that the Presi-

---

[1] Appendix B, No. 1.
[2] Debates of Congress, XII, 363.
[3] Congressional Globe, 38 Cong., 2 sess., 588.

dent's signature to the amendment was unnecessary. In this the Senate was undoubtedly correct. In the first place, the President's power to approve a bill seems bestowed rather as incident of his power to veto; when it would be impossible for him successfully to veto a measure, the necessity for his signature no longer exists. A resolution to amend the Constitution must already have received a two-thirds vote of each branch of the Legislature. Such a resolution is therefore beyond the reach of the veto and consequently beyond the necessity for Presidential approval.

About thirteen hundred amendments to the Constitution have been introduced into Congress since 1789.[1] Of these but nineteen have received the approval of both Houses of Congress. The practice of the government has been almost uniformly that suggested by the Senate. President Buchanan did indeed sign the Corwin Amendment in 1861;[2] this, however, is the only case out of the number, except that already mentioned, in which a presidential signature has been affixed.

§ 107. **The action of Congress.** — Should a bill be approved, or should Congress have adjourned before the expiration of the ten days, no further action of Congress upon that bill is possible. In case of an ordinary veto, however, the revisionary power of Congress at once comes into effect, and it is the questions arising out of this second consideration of vetoed bills to which the remainder of this chapter will be devoted.[3]

Vetoes are transmitted to that House of Congress in which originated the bill which has failed of executive approval; and are carried to that House by the President's private secretary.

§ 108. **Has the Executive a right to recall a veto?** — August 15, 1876, President Grant vetoed a bill providing for the sale of certain Indian lands.[4] The veto was sent to the Senate, but before that body had acted upon it, a message was received from the President saying that his veto of the bill was premature, and requesting that the bill be returned to him in order that he might sign it. An interesting discussion immediately arose as to the power of the President to recall a veto message which had been received by

---

[1] Stated by Mr. H. V. Ames from his researches in the Journals of Congress.
[2] Nicolay and Hay in the Century, New Series, xiii, 73.
[3] For action of State legislatures, see Appendix E, Nos. 11-17.
[4] Appendix A, No. 108.

Congress.[1] It was generally held that the President had no such power, and that the only effect, and in fact the intended effect, of the President's second message was to destroy the persuasive force of the first message. The bill was accordingly passed over the veto in both Houses by large majorities.

The question seems to have been decided correctly; for surely the President could have no more right to recall a veto message which had been delivered to Congress, than a branch of that body would have to reconsider a vote on the passage of a bill after presentation to the President. Moreover, if a President could recall a veto, he would inevitably be subjected to a very heavy pressure, from which he is now relieved by the fact that vetoes are often sent in before persons interested in the bill have time to remonstrate.

The President was evidently satisfied with the result of his message, for on January 12, 1877, he requested that a bill vetoed on August 15, 1876, be returned in order that he might sign it.[2] It is not possible to suppose in this case that the message was anything more than a request to Congress to pass the bill over the veto. For reasons not evident upon the face of the matter, the bill was not passed over the veto, or even reconsidered.

The action on the part of Congress in the second case was commendable, since the dangers just referred to as attendant upon a power in the executive to recall veto messages would not be obviated under a procedure whereby the President could practically nullify his veto by a message to Congress.

§ 109. **What is a two-thirds majority?** — The veto message once before the House, the next question is, what constitutes the constitutional two-thirds majority necessary to enact a bill over the veto? Upon this question the proceedings of the Federal Convention throw a great deal of light. In all the early stages of the discussion, it was provided that a bill must receive a vote of "*two-thirds of each branch of the national legislature.*"[3] This phrase could only mean two-thirds of all the members in each branch of Congress. When the resolution was taken up by the

---

[1] Congressional Record, 44 Cong., 1 sess., 5664. The Confederate Congress occasionally recalled a bill after sending it to President Davis; some confusion was caused, but there was no objection.

[2] Appendix A, No. 109.

[3] Elliot, Debates V, 349, 376; *ante*, § 10.

Committee of Detail the wording was changed, so that a bill to become a law in spite of the veto must be passed by two-thirds of each House.[1] This change in the wording is significant, for in the Constitution the word house is in such connection used as synonymous with quorum.[2]

Nevertheless, the question continued occasionally to be debated until 1856. On May 19 of that year President Pierce vetoed an internal improvement bill.[3] When the veto came up for reconsideration in the Senate, the thirty-one votes cast in favor of passing the bill, over the President's objections, made two-thirds of the members present, but not two-thirds of the total number of Senators. The President of the Senate, however, declared the bill passed. An appeal from the decision was not sustained by the Senate.[4] This decision has ever since been accepted as a precedent.[5]

§ 110. **Has the Speaker a right to vote on reconsideration?** — March 3, 1817, the House of Representatives considered President Madison's veto of the "bonus bill."[6] When the vote was taken, the Speaker, Henry Clay, claimed and exercised the right to vote on the ground that the occasion "differed from every other question before the House."[7] At the present time it is the custom for the Speaker to vote in all cases where the Constitution requires a two-thirds vote. The rules of the House are, however, silent on the point, merely providing that the Speaker must vote whenever his vote would be decisive, or when the vote is to be by ballot.[8] There appears to be nothing in the position of the Speaker of the House of Representatives which deprives him of a vote upon such questions; and it is doubtful whether any rule of the House could withdraw the right.

§ 111. **Second reconsideration of a veto.** — The question whether a house after taking a vote upon a vetoed bill and failing to pass it over a veto, may a second time bring it to a vote, is not one touched upon directly by the Constitution; it is a question of which the solution has been left wholly to the discretion of Congress.

[1] Elliot, Debates, V, 378, 431, 536.
[2] Ibid., V, 406, 407; cf. Constitution, Art. 1, Sec. 5.
[3] Appendix A, No. 38.   [4] Senate Journal, 34 Cong., 1 and 2 sess., 419.
[5] Rules of House of Representatives, 49 Cong., 2 sess., 473.
[6] Appendix A, No. 8.   [7] Annals of Congress, 14 Cong., 2 sess., 1062.
[8] Rules of the House of Representatives, 49 Cong., 2 sess., 236.

At the close of President Pierce's administration five bills were passed over the veto; and in the case of each of the last two the first vote in the Senate on reconsideration was not sufficient to pass the bill; afterwards the vote was reconsidered and the necessary two-thirds majority obtained.[1] In the second case, the Senate had not only failed to pass the bill, but had by message informed the House of that fact; and before they reconsidered the vote they requested the return of the message. The House complied, and the vote was duly reconsidered. The action of the Senate met with much objection. Senator Bayard held that by "reconsideration" in the case of a veto the Constitution meant a single vote, and that since the Senate had voted upon the bill and failed to pass it, it was dead, and could not again be considered.[2] Senator Stewart on the other hand claimed that by "reconsider" the Constitution meant that Congress could open the whole question and treat it just as in the original discussion, except that a two-thirds vote was necessary to carry it.[3] Similar ground was taken by Senator Seward, who maintained that until a bill had gone beyond the control of the Senate it could be reconsidered indefinitely.[4] This was the view also of 'the President of the Senate, who ruled that the case came under the general practice of the Senate, by which every question that has been decided may be reconsidered. An appeal was taken, but the ruling was sustained by the decisive vote of 32 to 9.[5]

The House of Representatives settled the question at a much earlier date and in exactly the opposite way. When Tyler's veto of June 11, 1844, came up in the House, the bill was reconsidered and lost.[6] Later on in the same session, an attempt was made to reconsider this vote, but the Speaker ruled that this could not be done, and the ruling was sustained by the House by a vote of 97 to 85.[7]

In both these cases the objection made was parliamentary rather than constitutional: it evidently rests within the discretion of each House either to permit or to forbid the second reconsideration for itself; but neither House can impose its principle upon the other.

[1] Appendix A, Nos. 41, 42.
[2] Congressional Globe, 34 Cong., 1 sess., 2205.
[3] Ibid. [4] Ibid., 2206.
[5] Congressional Globe, 34 Cong., 1 sess., 2206.
[6] Appendix A, No. 29.
[7] Congressional Globe, 28 Cong., 1 sess., 675.

§ 112. **Failure to enter the veto message in the journal.** — The Constitution strictly provides that the veto message shall be entered at large upon the Journal of the House in which it originated. In one instance this duty apparently has been omitted.[1] President Hayes' veto of June 15, 1880,[2] does not appear in the Senate Journals. The receipt of the message is recorded for the last day of the session, but a careful search has failed to discover the message itself. The failure in this case seems due to the negligence of one of the Houses. The omission of the constitutional requirement, however, cannot vitiate the veto. The action of the President was complete, and was acknowledged by the Senate.

On the other hand, although the provision for the entry of the President's objections is plainly intended to preserve a permanent record, yet, in this, as in other directory parts of the Constitution, there is no process by which Congress can be compelled to perform its duty.

§ 113. **Frequent neglect of reconsideration.** — The same principle applies to the last constitutional point which remains to be noted. During the early history of the government, Congress was very particular to comply with the constitutional provision requiring that a bill should be reconsidered after its veto. Indeed it was not until President Lincoln's administration that the first failure occurred.[3] From that time on, however, the constitutional duty of Congress in this particular has been less and less observed, and in President Cleveland's administration, as well as in President Grant's, it was the exception, and not the rule, to reconsider a vetoed bill. The complete change in procedure in these two administrations may be accounted for in part by the great number of vetoes by these two Presidents.

A wider reason, perhaps including that just stated, is the great pressure of business upon Congress. It is difficult to secure time for the reconsideration of a bill unless it can probably command a two-thirds majority in both Houses. Even where the success of a bill is certain, it is often impossible to secure the attention of Congress.

---

[1] President Jackson, in 1837, signed a veto message dated "March 3, 11.45 P.M." Congress was to expire in a few minutes and instead of sending the message to the Senate for entry in the Journals, he deposited it in the Department of State. Appendix A, No. 21. For State practice, see Appendix E, Nos. 18–21.

[2] Appendix A, No. 127.   [3] Ibid., No. 50.

§ 114. **Comparative unimportance of constitutional details.** — From the discussion in this chapter it is apparent that, although the veto power has been many times employed to uphold constitutional principles, few and unimportant questions have arisen as to its nature and the method of its operation. For this apparent paradox two reasons may be assigned. In the first place, the power is very accurately and carefully defined by the Constitution, thus leaving little room for controversy. A more important reason, however, is that the veto is not a substantive power, but, in the legal sense, an adjective power, a modifying influence, which changes with every change in administration.

The effect of the veto depends upon the substantive power to which it may for the time be linked, and of which the exercise may be forwarded or prevented by the exercise of this form of presidential discretion. Attacks upon the veto have therefore occurred rather as attacks upon the substantive powers accompanying it. It is only these latter powers, as for example the power to make internal improvements, which present tangible and continuing principles which can be attacked or defended for themselves. For these reasons, the veto power has never aroused that determined hostility to its existence or mode of operation which has generally preceded and caused modifications of the other powers of government.

For the very reason that the veto power is used as a means to an end, the temporary contentions over the manner of its use have been more frequent and more violent; and, in the next chapter, we shall pass to the discussion of the veto as a political engine.

CHAPTER VI.

POLITICAL DEVELOPMENT OF THE VETO POWER.

§ 115. Reasons for chronological treatment.
§ 116. Statistics of vetoes.
§ 117. Personal element in the veto.
    § 118. Presidents who vetoed no bills.
    § 119. Presidents who vetoed few bills.
    § 120. Presidents who vetoed many bills.
§ 121. Reasons expressed for vetoes.
    § 122. The constitution and expediency.
    § 123. Cause of the increasing use of expediency as a reason for vetoes.
§ 124. Effect of the veto on parties.
§ 125. Effect of the veto on legislation.
    § 126. Prevention of unwise measures.
    § 127. Prevention of unwise lines of policy.
    § 128. Indirect influence of the veto on legislation.
    § 129. Vetoes which have failed of their object.
§ 130. Popular objections to the veto.
§ 131. Proposed constitutional amendments.
    § 132. Attempts to destroy the power.
    § 133. Attempts to diminish the power.
    § 134. Attempts to enlarge the power.
§ 135. The veto power in 1789 and in 1889.

§ 115. **Reasons for chronological treatment.** — The history of the veto power could be obviously incomplete without some general view of its political growth and tendencies. The main body of the work has been devoted to the study in its details of the effect of the veto on the form, distribution, and exercise of the various powers of the government. In thus grouping the vetoes about great lines of legislation, there is danger of losing sight of the veto as a political power.

§ 116. **Statistics of vetoes.** — A glance at Appendix A will suggest several generalizations as to the number of vetoes and their classification according to their general character and recapture by Congress.

Of the four hundred and thirty-three vetoes enumerated, it is important to observe that only twenty-nine bear the double star, indicating that the bills eventually passed over the veto.[1] Favorable as this showing is to the power of the veto, it is an underestimate; fifteen of the bills, or more than half, were passed over the veto in the administration of President Johnson, when the relations between the executive and Congress were so abnormal that no important inference can be drawn from them as to the effectiveness of the veto. It is often stated that Johnson was the first President whose veto was overridden. The statement is incorrect; one bill was passed over the veto in President Tyler's administration and five in President Pierce's.[2]

In eleven cases bills were passed over the veto in one of the Houses of Congress, but were either not reconsidered or failed upon reconsideration in the other House.[3] Seven of these instances occurred in the administration of President Cleveland. And in each of the seven cases the House which passed the bill over the veto was the Senate. This fact is partly accounted for by the fact that the President was not a member of the party having a majority in the Senate. But as the bills thus passed were, with two exceptions, for the erection of public buildings, party considerations had probably little weight.[4]

Although so few bills have been passed over the veto even by a single House, it was the universal custom down to President Lincoln's administration to take a formal vote on the question of reconsideration; a proceeding which, at the beginning of the government, was little more than a form. Three hundred and eighty-four bills have failed of executive approval since 1861, and of these bills only sixty-three were reconsidered. This would indicate that reconsideration is no longer insisted upon for form's sake, and is only resorted to when it is expected that the bill can be passed over the veto by at least one of the two Houses.[5]

It remains to consider the number of "pocket vetoes"; the failures to sign bills for which a President has sent an official statement of reasons at a later session of Congress. There have been sixteen of them. The practice began in President Madison's

---

[1] Appendix A, Nos. 30, 38, 39, 40, 41, 42, 54, 57, 59, 61, 62, 63, 64, 65, 66, 67, 68, 69, 70, 71, 73, 83, 98, 103, 108, 117, 131, 221, 234.

[2] By the Confederate Congress the veto of President Davis was once overridden. Appendix C, No. 34; cf. Nos. 9, 11.

[3] Appendix A, Nos. 74, 78, 111, 132, 134, 156, 157, 273, 277, 407, 429.

[4] Several of the Confederate vetoes met with like treatment. Appendix C, Nos. 23, 33, 35, 38.   [5] *Ante*, § 113.

administration, and continued down to 1865. Since President Lincoln's administration no "pocket vetoes" have occurred. This does not mean that all the bills presented have been signed within ten days of the close of the sessions of Congress. On the contrary, it is true that more bills than ever fail in this way. What the apparent disuse of the pocket veto indicates is that a failure to sign has ceased to be a matter of sufficient importance to attract the attention of Congress.[1]

§ 117. **Personal element in the veto.** — The question of the distribution of vetoes among the various Presidents is quite as important as their total number, and it is noticeable that many circumstances apart from the intrinsic merits of the legislation presented to them have influenced the Presidents in their determination either to use or not to use the veto. There are personal elements, depending upon the individual characteristics of the various Presidents and their relations with the different Congresses, which have had as much to do with the exercise of the veto power as has the character of the proposed legislation.

§ 118. **Presidents who vetoed no bills.** — Seven Presidents have omitted to exercise the veto power.[2] In the cases of the first four the failure was due in part no doubt to the fact that, during their terms of office, they had to do with Congresses which were almost continuously in political agreement with them. In the case of Jefferson the character of the man was an additional cause for the disuse of the veto; not only was he solidly supported by Congress, but he also implicitly believed that "the people" were always right, and on this account did not use the "royal prerogative." Even the bitter personal humiliation of the repeal of the embargo was endured without a suggestion of a veto. Van Buren's peculiar caution must also have had much to do with his acceptance of legislation. An astute politician, heir to a well-defined policy,

---

[1] The attempt has been made to prepare a table which would show the precise numbers of bills which failed under the ten-day rule for want of the President's signature. The journals are so confused that it has been impossible to complete it for this work. But President Grant suffered a large number of bills to fail in this way; and a large number became acts without his signature.

In the Southern Confederacy there were no "pocket vetoes"; but President Davis twice sent notice to Congress that he had left bills unsigned, and had not time to state his reasons. Appendix C, Nos. 5, 17.

[2] John Adams, Jefferson, John Quincy Adams, Van Buren, W. H. Harrison, Taylor, Garfield.

and well supported by his party, his conciliatory character was averse to the use of a weapon so keen as the veto.

There was nothing in the character of W. H. Harrison, Taylor, or Garfield to suggest a like restraint; but the death of each of these Presidents shortly after entering upon the duties of office took away the opportunity. It is almost certain that President Taylor would have vetoed the compromise of 1850 had he lived.[1]

§ 119. **Presidents who vetoed few bills.** — Turning now to those Presidents who did veto bills, we distinguish two classes. In the first we find those Presidents who vetoed few bills and whose exercise of the power seems incidental rather than the result of any fixed policy. In the second we find those who have exercised the veto freely and with some definite policy in view. Nine Presidents belong in the first group.[2]

The personal element had practically no influence in the vetoes of Washington, Madison, and Monroe, but when we come to Tyler we find a man who was largely influenced by private motives.[3] Confidence in his own judgment, resentment at the dictation of the Whigs, and the hope of a renomination controlled him in his use of the veto. The bitter hostility of Congress did much to irritate him. Under these circumstances it is small wonder that the merits of the various bills found little place in the real reasons for Tyler's vetoes; and that his exercise of the power was scarcely more than an incident in his wrangle with Congress. Polk, Pierce, Buchanan, and Lincoln always had majorities of their own party in both Houses, except for the defection of the House, 1859-1861. Each vetoed a few bills simply because they disapproved of the legislation; they were apparently unaffected by any motives of a personal nature.

§ 120. **Presidents who vetoed many bills.** — Five Presidents have each vetoed twelve or more bills;[4] and in each instance either the personal characteristics of the President or his peculiar relations with Congress are largely responsible for the vigorous use of the veto.

No administration was more thoroughly affected by the personal characteristics of its chief executive than that of President Jack-

---

[1] Von Holst, Constitutional History, III, 541.
[2] Washington, Madison, Monroe, Tyler, Polk, Pierce, Buchanan, Lincoln, Arthur.
[3] Von Holst, Constitutional History of the United States, II, 425, 455, 457.
[4] Jackson, Johnson, Grant, Hayes, Cleveland.

son; and his intense personality and enjoyment of a conflict were nowhere more prominent than in the vetoes; they were imbued with prejudices, yet were based upon a certain rugged persistence of honest conviction. President Johnson's vetoes were largely the result of his contest with Congress over reconstruction, — a struggle which his own foolishness and obstinacy did much to bring about.

President Grant was the first occupant of the chair to make a systematic and determined use of his share in legislation. Against more than a hundred and thirty bills he made the silent protest of permitting them to become law without his signature.[1] Between one and two hundred bills were killed under the ten-day rule by withholding his signature, and his vetoes, forty-three in number, are more numerous than those of any other President except Cleveland. He was influenced to make this extensive use of his power by a strong determination to check the indiscriminate granting of relief to persons who claimed to have suffered unjustly in the Civil War. Here again we see that a vigorous use of the veto depended not so much upon the character of the legislation as upon the peculiar sense of duty of the President.

In President Hayes' exercise of the veto power the personal element is almost wholly lacking. He displayed commendable determination in vetoing the appropriation bills to which riders had been attached;[2] but it was due rather to a desire to hand down the prerogatives of the President unimpaired than to any personal feeling.

President Cleveland has far outstripped all his predecessors in his use of the veto. Three hundred and one of the four hundred and thirty-three vetoes, or more than two-thirds of all, bear his signature. His administration is too recent, and the question is perhaps too closely connected with present politics for a perfectly impartial view. There are, however, several reasons in the circumstances of the administration which account in part for the sweeping use of the veto power. In the first place, the mass of legislation thrown upon the President for consideration by far exceeded anything previously known. Grant, in his two terms, signed 2885 bills; Cleveland, in his one term, was called upon to consider nearly four thousand bills, of which he signed 3146, and vetoed 301. No

---

[1] Appendix D.   [2] *Ante*, § 35.

man could accept this mass of legislation unquestioned, and the very number of bills suggested the hurry at the Capitol, and pointed to crude and undigested legislation. The number of private bills, which always receive least attention and are subject to least examination by Congress, had increased in greater proportion than legislation in general. As had been the case in Grant's administration, the nature of the bills showered upon the President, quite as much as their number, called for numerous vetoes. The precedent set by Grant was followed. But the underlying cause was in the personal qualities of the President, — his freedom from pledges, his rigorous independence of judgment, and determination to prevent a wasteful expenditure. The inexpediency of the measures was no greater than those of a similar nature which had been approved in large numbers by previous Presidents; but the determination of the executive to stop the indiscriminate granting of money was stronger, and it was this additional factor which accounts for most of President Cleveland's vetoes.

§ 121. **Reasons expressed for vetoes.** — In the search for the causes of the exercise of the veto power, lying in the minds of the successive Presidents, the primary or expressed reasons must not be omitted. A long succession of messages has set forth a great variety of objections to proposed bills, but they may all be reduced to one of two heads, — constitutionality and expediency. The alternative of the two classes of reasons marks the development of new conceptions of the veto and therefore forms the subject of the succeeding paragraphs.

§ 122. **The Constitution and expediency.** — President Washington based his first veto upon constitutional grounds.[1] This precedent was followed closely by the earlier Presidents. Down through Jackson's administration twenty-one bills were vetoed, and only five or six were based upon other than constitutional grounds. Some of them, as, for example, Madison's last veto and Monroe's Cumberland Road veto,[2] were not so much vetoes of measures as general expositions of the Constitution. From Jackson's administration to the Civil War vetoes on grounds of expediency became more frequent, but they were still in a decided minority. Since the war constitutional arguments in a veto message have been almost unknown.

---

[1] Appendix A, No. 1.   [2] Ibid., No. 9.

The series of vetoes based on expediency began almost as soon as did that of vetoes based on constitutional grounds, for Washington's second veto was of this character.[1] Such objections were, however, uncommon down to the Civil War, but they passed unquestioned in almost all cases. Since 1865 the great increase in the number of these vetoes has caused members of Congress to question their validity. President Cleveland's last veto message was objected to by Senator Sherman on this ground.[2] The Senator declared that the President should only make use of his revisionary power when the defence of the Constitution demanded it. This question has been sufficiently discussed already. It is a well-settled principle that a President is the sole judge of the nature of the reasons which shall be assigned for a veto.

§ 123. **Cause of the increasing use of expediency as a reason for vetoes.** — For the change in the character of the objections stated by Presidents there must be a reason. It is not that Presidents have become wiser or more dictatorial, nor because the proper function of the veto has altered. It is due rather to the "adjective" character of the veto. The scope of national legislation has changed, and the basis of the veto has of necessity become altered to correspond. For the first seventy years of national life the most important questions with which Congress had to deal were constitutional. There were wide differences of opinion as to the proper settlement of great fundamental lines of policy, and the veto was frequently brought into use as an additional factor on one side or the other. Objections on grounds of expediency were often made by Washington, Madison, and almost all of their successors down to the Civil War, but the quantity of legislation was smaller, and it was better digested before presentation to the President; therefore vetoes on other than constitutional grounds were rare.

After the war the nature of the questions before Congress changed. The result of that struggle was to leave permanently in the hands of the general government powers up to that time disputed. Questions as to the administration of the government then became important, and the veto accordingly became a weapon of expediency. This change was felt, if not understood, by Senator Vest when, in the debate on the veto of the Direct Tax bill,[3] he

[1] Appendix A, No. 2. Many of the Confederate vetoes are based on expediency; Appendix C.
[2] Congressional Record, 50 Cong., 2 sess., 2612, 2613.   [3] Appendix A, No. 433.

said, "It has come to this point in our country, that the man who attempts to question anything under a constitutional grant of power is looked upon as an effete and worn-out fossil who lives in ancient history, and is unfit for the active life of to-day."[1] It is indeed true that the era of great constitutional debates has passed. No Hayne attacks or Webster defends the great principles of the Constitution, and the character of the arguments in veto messages is a reflex of the character of the debates which preceded them.

§ 124. **Effect of the veto on parties.** — Whatever the ground upon which vetoes have from time to time been based, they have had singularly little influence upon the history or development of parties. In a government in which legislative power is so developed, it is impossible to make the use of the veto a party principle. Where the minority in either House agrees with the President, they may urge him to veto measures passed by the majority; but every presidential election breaks up existing combinations. On the other hand, the use of the veto by a President has seldom strengthened his authority as a party leader, and has frequently weakened his influence on his party. Madison's and Monroe's elaborate vetoes were both swept aside by their own parties. Jackson's vetoes were a very important element in the building up of the Democratic party, because they forced politicians to side with him or against him; and they had great effect in fixing the later tenets of that party, especially in questions of the bank and currency. But Jackson used the veto, as he used appointments, as a temporary means to an end: his Democratic successors could not make the veto venerated, and Polk was the first President to suffer the mortification of seeing a veto overruled by Congress.

That the veto is in itself not a consolidating agent is seen plainly in the case of Tyler. Armed with that weapon he was able to paralyze the Whig party; but he could make no headway either in winning the Democrats or in creating a personal following. He exasperated and injured the Whigs; but they elected their candidate in 1848. Johnson's experience was much the same, except that a two-thirds majority stood ready to overrule him. His vetoes, therefore, strengthened his enemies. Grant used the veto frequently and wisely, but neither sought nor gained party advantage from it. It was much the same with Cleveland: it is

---

[1] Congressional Record, 50 Cong., 2 sess., 2612.

impossible to say whether he strengthened his hold upon his party or the popularity of his party in the country, by his fearless use of the veto. The veto is a negative power, not popular or unpopular in itself; and since a veto always confronts a majority in both Houses, the presumption is that its use is an opposition to party.

§ 125. **Effect of the veto on legislation.** — Turning from this question we come to the more practical question of the effects of the vetoes. Whatever the reasons in the minds of Presidents, the expectations of the framers of the Constitution have been realized only if the veto has been so used as to favor good legislation.

§ 126. **Prevention of unwise measures.** — In many instances the veto has been used to prevent the passage of isolated measures which were not connected with any general line of policy, but which were evidently ill-considered or unwise. In this category should be placed President Washington's second veto,[1] and President Madison's naturalization veto,[2] and also two of Lincoln's vetoes;[3] the bills checked by the latter were unwise, however, simply in the sense of being inefficient. The two bills for enabling a New York mining company to get control of land in Montana were for a fraudulent purpose, and were wisely vetoed by President Johnson.[4] President Grant's refusal to sign the inflation bill is a striking instance of the usefulness of the veto.[5] The bill was in no sense corrupt, but it was the result of a craze caused by the panic of 1873, and would have done great mischief to the business interests of the country if it had been allowed to succeed. President Hayes's veto of the Chinese bill[6] is a case in which the veto was used to protect the diplomatic interests of the nation from a heedless attack of Congress. The government cannot be said to have had any policy in regard to its treatment of the Indians. Bills have been passed having no connection with each other, and whose only object was to satisfy the unjust claims of western constituents. In many instances, particularly in President Cleveland's administration, these unjust bills have been prevented from becoming law by the exercise of the veto.[7]

[1] Appendix A, No. 2.
[2] Ibid., No. 6.
[3] Ibid., Nos. 51, 52.
[4] Appendix A, Nos. 56, 58.
[5] Ibid., No. 92.
[6] Ibid., No. 119.
[7] See *ante*, § 41; Appendix A, No. 393.

Many other illustrations might be given of the use of the veto to prevent the enactment of unwise laws. All of Grant's pension vetoes, and many of Cleveland's, were based on the technical defects or unnecessary character of the bills. This was also true of the veto of many relief bills, and of Cleveland's veto of the act "for the promotion of anatomical science."[1]

To the numerous vetoes mentioned in this paragraph no just exception can be taken: few or none of them encountered a two-thirds vote in either House, and they go far toward proving the indispensable character of the power we are studying.

§ 127. **Prevention of unwise lines of policy.** — In several instances the veto has been used not merely to prevent the enactment of a single unwise law, but to stop the execution of an unwise policy by Congress. The most striking example was the bank controversy. The scheme of a United States Bank had been recognized by the Supreme Court, approved by Madison, had been in full operation for twenty years, and was thought well of by the people; yet the vetoes of Jackson and Tyler destroyed the plan beyond the hope of reconstruction.[2]

It can hardly be said that it is the policy of Congress to encroach on the executive. There is, however, and always has been, a tendency of which Congress is perhaps unconscious, — a political attraction of gravitation, which causes the legislative department to seize power whenever possible. The tendency, if it cannot be dignified by the name of policy, has many times been checked by the use of the veto.[3] A recent instance is President Hayes's refusal to sign bills which were framed with the intention of compelling the President to approve measures which if presented by themselves would not have been approved. The struggle was severe and protracted, but the President won, thus restoring to the executive power what had been usurped by Congress many years before.[4]

President Cleveland's refusal to approve the Texas Seed bill is a more recent illustration. The unfortunate tendency of the bill, and the policy of the government in this particular, have already been discussed.[5] It is enough here to point out that the attempt has been checked by the veto. It must, however, be admitted that the check is probably merely temporary, and that similar demands

[1] Appendix A, No. 135. [2] *Ante*, §§ 57–59. [3] *Ante*, §§ 21–36.
[4] *Ante*, § 35. [5] *Ante*, §§ 95, 96.

are likely to be made until, like the sentiment in favor of internal improvements, they shall have become too strong to be questioned.

§ 128. **Indirect influence of the veto on legislation.** — It is not easy to specify instances in which the veto has affected legislation indirectly, for such an effect must almost necessarily be of a kind that would not ordinarily appear in the records. It is, however, known that the Compromise of 1850 was delayed by the knowledge of the fact that President Taylor would probably veto it if Congress passed it. Again, President Cleveland's pension vetoes not only killed the vetoed bills, but prevented the passage of similar bills. At the present moment [1] the fear of the veto is an argument against extreme silver legislation.

There have even been cases in which both Houses have been driven by a flurry of popular feeling to agree to measures in the hope that the President would, by his veto, prevent the act from passing. A veto is like a decision of a court, an announcement to all concerned that future cases of the same kind will by that court be treated in the same manner.

§ 129. **Vetoes which have failed of their object.** — Many times, however, the veto has not succeeded either in killing a particular bill or in checking legislation. Twenty-nine bills have been passed over the veto, and in many cases they were of great importance; the reconstruction bills vetoed by President Johnson, and the Bland silver bill which President Hayes refused to sign [2] are striking examples. In these instances Congress carried out its purposes by overriding the veto. There are other cases even more important in which Congress has in the end maintained its policy notwithstanding the vetoes. Very few internal improvement vetoes, and no public land vetoes, have been overridden; but the policy of the government in these two respects has been determined in opposition to the President's will. The weak point in the veto power is that it cannot, or at least does not, stand in the way of a strong and continuous public sentiment. A temporary agitation, a craze like the greenback movement, may be successfully resisted, but no President can permanently stay legislation like the internal improvements. The veto is but an appeal to the sober second thought of the nation, and when that second thought is like the first the appeal can accomplish nothing.

[1] 1890.   [2] Appendix A, No. 117.

This seeming weakness in the veto is not a defect. The theory of our government is that in the long run the people are right. The veto would be a hindrance if it could permanently check the strong underlying tendencies in the public mind. And in any case, in a government founded on nearly universal suffrage, a positive check to popular measures is not what is wanted. The most that can safely be done is to hinder the enactment of propositions until the people can determine whether they are really in earnest in their demands; and this delay the veto power is most admirably constructed to accomplish.

§ 130. **Popular objections to the veto.** — Popular objections to the veto power date back to a very early time in our national history. In 1818 a resolution found its way into Congress calling for a total abolition of the veto power.[1] The ground for the resolution was the undue power which, it was asserted, the President possessed. A second era of objection to the veto dates from about 1833. From this time until well down to 1850 the President's right to refuse his signature to bills was vigorously attacked. It was contended that since the veto was almost never overridden it was absolute, and therefore contrary to the intention of the founders of the Constitution and the genius of our institutions.[2] Again, it was urged that the veto had been given to the executive to strengthen an otherwise weak position, but that the President was now fortified by the patronage he controlled, and hence no longer needed the veto.[3] Again, it was claimed that the veto had been granted to the President to be used only in defence of the Constitution: he had used it for other purposes, and therefore it should be taken from him.[4] On the other hand, there were objections to the use of the veto to defend the Constitution, on the ground that the Supreme Court had been established to settle constitutional points.[5] The great objection to the veto at this time, however, was that it took a two-thirds majority of each branch of Congress to override the President's will. This was said to be an infringement of the right of the majority to govern, and wholly anti-republican.[6]

---

[1] Ex. Papers, 15 Cong., 1 sess., Vol. VIII, No. 200.
[2] House Reports, 27 Cong., 2 sess., Vol. V, No. 1104.
[3] Democratic Review, XXIV, 19.
[4] American Whig Review, X, 121.
[5] Democratic Review, XXIV, 20.
[6] American Whig Review, X, 113.

The outcry against the "monarchical" character of the veto subsided rapidly after Tyler's administration; and the veto power was accepted as it stood until President Hayes's administration. The struggle at that time over riders upon appropriation bills gave rise to a new agitation, this time for the extension of the veto power. The power was declared incomplete because the President could not refuse his assent to particular items in the appropriation bills presented to him without destroying the bill.[1] This was the difficulty into which President Hayes was thrown. Complaint has also been made within recent years because two-thirds of the members present and voting, instead of two-thirds of the total number of members in each branch, can pass a bill over the veto.

§ 131. **Proposed constitutional amendments.** — The objections to the veto power referred to in the last paragraph are readily arranged in three well-defined groups: first, scattering complaints against the whole power and a desire to do away with it; secondly, in the forties, a specific outcry because the veto defeated the will of the majority; lastly, fault has been found within recent years because the veto was not powerful enough. The propositions to amend the veto power may be divided into corresponding classes.

§ 132. **Attempts to destroy the power.** — Only one positive attempt entirely to do away with the veto has been found. In 1818 a resolution was introduced into the House by Mr. Lewis, proposing that in the future "the President of the United States shall not have the power of approving or disapproving any bill or bills, or joint resolutions passed by the Senate and House of Representatives."[2] The resolve was read and ordered to lie on the table.[3]

§ 133. **Attempts to diminish the power.** — Propositions to amend the Constitution so as to diminish the veto power began in President Jackson's administration. Hostility to Jackson was the first principle of the early Whigs, and this hostility was increased, if not occasioned, by the President's frequent use of the veto. In 1833 Senator Kent introduced a resolution providing for an amendment to the Constitution so that the majority vote of all the members of each House, instead of two-thirds of those present, should

---

[1] For provisions in State Constitutions on this subject, see Appendix E, Nos. 8, 9. The President of the Southern Confederacy had this power, but no case of its exercise has been found: Appendix C.   [2] Ex. Papers, 15 Cong., 1 sess., Vol. VIII.

[3] House Journal, 15 Cong., 1 sess., 478, 479.

pass a bill over the veto.[1] This resolution was read a second time and laid on the table.[2] Eleven other propositions of exactly similar nature have since been offered either in the Senate or House,[3] but in no case was the resolution passed by the House in which it was presented.

The reasons for these resolutions have already been referred to in stating the popular objections to the veto. They are compactly stated by Mr. Kent in a speech in support of the resolution introduced in 1835. His arguments for the proposed change were, in the first place, the fact that the veto power as then exercised tended to unite the legislative and executive branches, a union which was contrary to the fundamental principles of our government. In the second place, he argued that the veto had been granted to the executive only as a means of defence, and that recent Presidents had exceeded their authority. Lastly, Mr. Kent maintained that the executive was exceedingly apt to encroach upon the other branches of government, and that therefore the power of that department should be curtailed.[4] The occasion for these propositions was the activity of Jackson and Tyler, and the bitter sense of unexpected defeat at the hands of the executive, felt at that time by the Whig party. It is extremely fortunate that the attempts did not succeed, for success would have meant the practical destruction of the veto, and the complete control of affairs by the majority in Congress. The rights of the minority and of the executive, as well as the interests of the nation, would have lost an important safeguard.

§ 134. **Attempts to enlarge the power.** — President Hayes, after his struggle with Congress over the attaching of riders to appropriation bills, recommended that the executive be given the power to approve or veto the separate items of an appropriation bill. This recommendation was taken up and acted upon, and from that time to the present there has been a constant agitation for an increase of the range of the veto. Twenty-four resolutions authorizing amendments to the Constitution have been offered in Congress, each one of which embodied President Hayes's suggestion.[5]

This measure if adopted not only would increase the power of the veto, but also would practically destroy the only power which

---

[1] Senate Journal, 23 Cong., 1 sess., 65.   [2] Ibid., 74.
[3] 1835, 1836, 1838, 1841(2), 1842(3), 1849, 1850, 1884.
[4] Debates of Congress, Vol. XI, 540.
[5] 1876, 1879, 1882(4), 1883(9), 1884, 1885, 1886(4), 1888(3).

Congress now has over the President, apart from impeachment. For, as a recent writer has observed,[1] the only coercion which Congress can make use of against the President, except by impeachment, is by tacking measures distasteful to the President to general appropriation bills, hoping in this way to compel him to assent to measures which, if presented on their own merits, would surely be vetoed. This power of coercion would be removed by the contemplated amendment.

The amendment would moreover almost certainly check extravagant legislation. A President would have every incentive to use the new power. Even if he cared not to check extravagance as a matter of principle, he very often would be called upon to do it as a matter of party policy, and the exercise of the power from whatever motive would be of advantage to the country. The very least that could be said is that the change would not increase the expenditure of the government, and in all probability it would diminish it.

Three attempts have been made to extend the power of the veto by making a two-thirds majority of all the members of each branch of Congress necessary to pass a bill over the veto.[2] The cause of the resolutions is apparent. August 1, 1882, President Arthur vetoed a river and harbor bill. August 2 it was passed over the veto in each House of Congress by a vote of less than two-thirds of the total membership of that House.[3] August 4 the resolution to amend the Constitution was introduced by Mr. Hutchins of New York, the same State from which the President came. The resolution in 1883 was introduced by the same man, and the one in 1884 by another representative from the State of New York. The resolutions seem, therefore, very much like expressions of executive displeasure at the failure of the veto, just as in earlier times the resolutions to diminish the veto power were expressions of congressional displeasure at the success of that power.

§ 135. **The veto power in 1789 and in 1889.** — The true character and the development of the veto power may best be understood by a comparison of the veto as the framers of the Constitution evidently intended it, with the veto as exercised a century later.

[1] Bryce, American Commonwealth, I, 207-211.
[2] 1882, 1883, 1884.
[3] Appendix A, No. 131.

When the Constitution was founded, the great fear in men's minds was that of executive usurpation. But the experience of the Continental Congress, of the Confederation, and of the States had also shown to what lengths an unchecked legislature can go. Hence, men like Hamilton [1] pointed out the tendency of the legislative department to encroach on the executive, and the necessity of a veto, absolute or qualified. They had also clearly in mind the prevention of hasty and imprudent legislation.[1] Hamilton early expresses this fear in the Federalist: "It establishes a salutary check upon the legislative body calculated to guard the community against the effects of faction, precipitancy, or of any impulse unfriendly to the public good, which may happen to influence a majority of that body." [2]

The actual use of the veto power is an interesting commentary upon the expectations of those who established it. No idea was apparently entertained that the veto would ever be necessary to prevent Congress from unconstitutionally enlarging its powers, except in the direction of encroachments upon the executive; yet the most important class of constitutional vetoes have been for this unanticipated purpose. In the category we find Washington's first veto,[3] the long series of internal improvement vetoes,[4] the public land vetoes,[5] the veto of the Texas Seed bill,[6] and others.

More numerous than the vetoes just referred to, if not more important, are those based upon grounds of expediency. This series, like the last, began in President Washington's administration, and has been increasing in numbers and importance ever since. Prominent in the group are the pension and relief vetoes.[7]

Last of all we come to the vetoes which Hamilton mentioned first: those for the protection of the executive.[8] These vetoes have been of great service, but their practical importance is much less than that of either of the preceding classes, and they are fewer in number.

The veto power then has not followed the course marked out for it by the Federal Convention, but has worked out for itself a path different both in direction and extent from that prophesied. The change is no proof of weakness in the veto, but rather shows

---

[1] Madison, Works, IV, 369.
[2] Federalist, No. 73.
[3] Ante, § 14.
[4] Ante, §§ 83-94.
[5] Ante, §§ 46-49.
[6] Ante, §§ 95, 96.
[7] Ante, §§ 65-81.
[8] Ante, § 22-36.

its vigor. The power can be adapted to the changing needs of the nation, without losing its efficacy. Indeed, the difference between the veto in 1789 and in 1889 is not a difference in nature but in exercise. Then it was used sparingly and in a cumbrous manner as a weapon of constitutional warfare; to-day it is used frequently and easily as a means of preventing mistakes in the administration of the business of the government. This latter use is likely to become of increasing value as time goes on, for: "As the business of the country increases, as legislation piles its bills still higher, and as the whole social and political network grows more complicated in its demands and conflict of interests and its multiplicity of interferences, more and more will be the necessity of cutting Gordian knots with the swift, sharp edge of a single blow, and of having an executive brave enough to take the responsibility of interposing his veto."

APPENDIX A.

A CHRONOLOGICAL LIST OF ALL BILLS VETOED
FROM APRIL 6, 1789, TO MARCH 4, 1889,
TOGETHER WITH A BRIEF LEGISLATIVE HISTORY OF EACH BILL.

Explanation of Signs and Abbreviations.

A single star (*) placed before the number of the veto indicates that the bill passed one of the houses of Congress over the veto.

A double star (**) placed before the number of the veto indicates that the bill passed both houses of Congress over the veto, and thus became a law without the President's signature.

A dagger (†) placed before the number of the veto indicates that the bill was disposed of by a "pocket veto."

The dates which precede the words "in the," in the history of the bill, indicate the day on which the bill was introduced into one of the houses of Congress, and the day on which it passed that house; *e. g.*, the first dates in the history of the first bill mean that on Feb. 7, 1792, the bill was introduced into the House of Representatives, and that on Feb. 21 it passed the House of Representatives.

The letter P placed after a page of the Senate Journal indicates that on that page is recorded the passage by the Senate of the bill under consideration.

The letter P placed after a page of the House Journal indicates that on that page is recorded the passage by the House of the bill under consideration.

The letter R after a page of the Senate Journal indicates that on that page is recorded the reconsideration of the bill under consideration.

The letter R after a page of the House Journal indicates that on that page is recorded the reconsideration of the bill under consideration.

The sign O after a page indicates that on that page will be found the text of the veto.

In references to the journals and in the numbers of the bills, *sess.* stands for session, and *Cong.* for Congress. Thus in the first veto, *1 sess. 2 Cong.* means first session of the second Congress.

After the title of each veto the paragraphs of the text in which that veto is discussed will be placed, enclosed in brackets, thus: [§ 1].

Texts of the Vetoes.

Reference (by the sign O) is in this Appendix invariably made to the Journals, because they are official, and are the only source in which all the messages appear. Nearly all the messages down to Aug. 4, 1886, will be found in the Senate Miscellaneous Documents, No. 53, of the 2 sess. of the 49 Cong. Most of the messages down to 1854 can be found in the Statesman's Manual. Lastly, a large proportion of the messages will be found, under the date of the message, in the records of Congressional debates; viz.: Annals of Congress (1789-1824); Debates in Congress (1825-1837); Congressional Globe (1833-1873); Congressional Record (1873-1889).

PRESIDENT WASHINGTON (1789-1797).—[2 VETOES.]

1. Apportionment of representatives. [§§ 14, 121.]

H. R. 163, 1 sess. 2 Cong. "An act for an apportionment of Representatives among the several States, according to the first enumeration."

1792. Feb. 7 to Feb. 21, in the House.—— Feb. 21 to Mar. 12, in the Senate.

Apr. 5, vetoed.—— Apr. 6, reconsidered by the House; vote, 28–33.

House Journal, vol. I., 1 and 2 Cong. pp. 503, 507, 509, 510, 511, 516 P, 535, 538, 540, 543, 544, 545, 549, 551, 563 O, 565 R.—— *Senate Journal, vol. I., 1 sess. 2 Cong.* pp. 394, 396, 404, 405, 406, 408, 409 P, 415, 416, 422.

2. Reduction of the army. [§§ 97, 121.]

H. R. 219, 2 sess. 4 Cong. "An act to alter and amend an act entitled 'An act to ascertain and fix the military establishment of the United States.'"

1797. Jan. 30 to Feb. 8, in the House.—— Feb. 9 to Feb. 20, in the Senate.

Feb. 28, vetoed.—— Mar. 1, reconsidered by the House; vote, 55–36.

House Journal, vol. II., 3 and 4 Cong. pp. 666, 679, 683, 685 P, 708, 709, 714, 726 O, 728 R.—— *Senate Journal, vol. II., 2 sess. 4 Cong.* pp. 321, 326, 327, 328 P, 329, 330, 339 O.

PRESIDENT MADISON (1809-1817).—[6 VETOES.]

3. Incorporating church in Alexandria. [§ 39.]

H. R. 155, 3 sess. 11 Cong. "An act incorporating the Protestant-Episcopal Church in the town of Alexandria, in the District of Columbia."

1810. Dec. 30 to 1811, Jan. 28, in the House.—— 1811, Jan. 28 to Feb. 8, in the Senate.

1811. Feb. 21, vetoed.—— Feb. 23, reconsidered by the House; vote, 29–74.

House Journal, vol. VII., 11 Cong. pp. 457, 463, 504, 506 P, 538, 547, 554, 566 O, 569, 570 R.—— *Senate Journal, vol. IV., 3 sess. 11 Cong.* pp. 552, 553, 559, 561, 565, 566 P, 570, 573, 582.

4. Land-grant for church in Mississippi. [§§ 39, 46.]

H. R. 170, 3 sess. 11 Cong. "An act for the relief of Richard Tervin, William Coleman, Edwin Lewis, Samuel Mims, Joseph Wilson, and the Baptist Church at Salem Meeting-House, in the Mississippi Territory."

1811. Jan. 7 to Feb. 6, in the House.—— Feb. 6 to Feb. 20, in the Senate.

Feb. 28, vetoed.—— Mar. 2, reconsidered by the House; vote, 33–55.

House Journal, vol. VII., 11 Cong. pp. 475, 533, 534 P, 564, 566, 574, 602 O, 608 R.—— *Senate Journal, vol. IV., 3 sess. 11 Cong.* pp. 563, 564, 569, 576, 577 P, 579, 583, 593.

5. Trials in district courts. [§ 15.]

H. R. 81, 1 sess. 12 Cong. "An act providing for the trial of causes pending in the respective District Courts of the United States, in the case of the absence or disability of the judges thereof."

1812. Mar. 4 to Mar. 10, in the House.—— Mar. 10 to Mar. 18, in the Senate.

Apr. 3, vetoed.—— Apr. 8, reconsidered by the House; vote, 26–70.

House Journal, vol. VIII., 12 Cong. pp. 219, 235, 240, 241 P, 255, 258, 259, 260, 261, 262, 264, 274 O, 279, 281 R.—— *Senate Journal, vol. V., 1 sess. 12 Cong.* pp. 72, 74, 76, 78, 79 P, 82, 83, 99, 100.

† 6. Naturalization. [§ 40.]

H. R. 170, 1 sess. 12 Cong. "An act supplementary to the acts heretofore passed on the subject of an uniform rule of naturalization."

1792-1830]   Washington's to Jackson's Administration.   143

1812.   June 29 to July 2, in the House. —— July 2 to July 4, in the Senate.
   Nov. 6, veto message signed.
   House Journal, vol. VIII., 12 Cong.   pp. 403, 413, 414 P, 421, 429, 544 O. —— *Senate Journal, vol. V., 1 sess. 12 Cong.*   pp. 178, 179, 181, 182 P, 183, 184.

7. Incorporating national bank. [§ 56.]
   S. 67, *3 sess. 13 Cong.*   "An act to incorporate the subscribers to the Bank of the United States of America."
   1814.   Dec. 2 to Dec. 9, in the Senate. —— Dec. 9 to 1815, Jan. 7, in the House.
   1815.   Jan. 30, vetoed. —— Feb. 2, reconsidered by the Senate; vote, 15-19.
   Senate Journal, vol. V., 3 sess. 13 Cong.   pp. 565, 566, 567, 568, 569, 570, 571 P, 597-603, 606-610, 614, 620 O, 622, 631 R. —— *House Journal, 3 sess. 13 Cong.*   pp. 294, 295, 330, 389, 392, 394, 403, 414, 419, 434, 440, 450, 476, 484 P, 526, 531, 546, 553, 604.

8. Internal improvements (Bonus Bill). [§§ 84-110.]
   H. R. 29, *2 sess. 14 Cong.*   "An act to set apart and pledge certain funds for internal improvements."
   1816.   Dec. 23 to 1817, Feb. 8, in the House. —— 1817, Feb. 10 to Feb. 28, in the Senate.
   1817.   Mar. 3, vetoed. —— Mar. 3, reconsidered by the House; vote, 61-63.
   House Journal, 2 sess. 14 Cong.   pp. 98, 341, 345, 351, 369 P, 492, 504, 519, 534 O R. —— *Senate Journal, 2 sess, 14 Cong.*   pp. 216, 223, 239, 284, 308, 311, 320, 339, 340, 341 P, 356, 374, 375, 393, 405-409 O.

PRESIDENT MONROE (1817-1825). — [1 VETO.]

9. Internal improvements (Cumberland Road). [§§ 85, 121.]
   H. R. 50, *1 sess. 17 Cong.*   "An act for the preservation and repair of the Cumberland Road."
   1822.   Jan. 21 to Apr. 29, in the House. —— Apr. 29 to May 3, in the Senate.
   May 4, vetoed. —— May 6, reconsidered by the House; vote, 68-72.
   House Journal, 1 sess. 17 Cong.   pp. 169, 469, 491, 495, 496, 513 P, 549, 553, 560 O, 578 R. —— *Senate Journal, 1 sess. 17 Cong.*   pp. 316, 317, 318, 324, 331 P, 333, 335, 337, 338.

PRESIDENT JACKSON (1829-1837). — [12 VETOES.]

10. Internal improvements (Maysville Road). [§ 86.]
   H. R. 285, *1 sess. 21 Cong.*   "An act to authorize a subscription of stock in the Maysville, Washington, Paris, and Lexington Turnpike Road Company."
   1830.   Feb. 24 to Apr. 29, in the House. —— Apr. 29 to May 15, in the Senate.
   May 27, vetoed. —— May 28, reconsidered by the House; vote, 96-92.
   House Journal, 1 sess. 21 Cong.   pp. 333, 571, 581, 585 P, 664, 674, 733 O, 761 R. —— *Senate Journal, 1 sess. 21 Cong.*   pp. 274, 276, 281, 285, 304, 306 P, 311, 313, 316, 340.

11. Internal improvements (turnpike stock). [§ 86.]
   S. 27, *1 sess. 21 Cong.*   "An act to authorize a subscription of stock in the Washington Turnpike Road Company."
   1829.   Dec. 30 to 1830, May 13, in the Senate. —— May 13 to May 29, in the House.
   1830.   May 31, vetoed. —— May 31, reconsidered by the Senate; vote, 21-17.
   Senate Journal, 1 sess. 21 Cong.   pp. 55, 58, 256, 295, 298 P, 356, 357, 360, 360 O, 382 R. —— *House Journal, 1 sess. 21 Cong.*   pp. 646, 650, 654, 786, 801, 804 P, 807, 809, 812.

† 12. **Internal improvements (light-houses and beacons).** [§ 86.]

H. R. *304, 1 sess. 21 Cong.* "An act for making appropriations for building light-houses, light-boats, beacons, and monuments, placing buoys, and for improving harbors and directing surveys."

1830. Feb. 27 to Apr. 7, in the House.—— Apr. 7 to May 13, in the Senate.

Dec. 6, veto message signed.

House Journal, 1 sess. 21 Cong. pp. 348, 445, 510, 513 P, 646, 649, 668, 786, 790, 801, 806.—— *Senate Journal, 1 sess. 21 Cong.* pp. 231, 252, 269, 287, 297, 299 P, 354. —— *House Journal, 2 sess. 21 Cong.* p. 15 O.

† 13. **Internal improvements (canal stock).** [§ 86.]

S. *74, 1 sess. 21 Cong.* "An act to authorize a subscription for stock in the Louisville and Portland Canal Company."

1830. Jan. 26 to Mar. 15, in the Senate.—— Mar. 15 to May 29, in the House.

Dec. 6, veto message signed.

Senate Journal, 1 sess. 21 Cong. pp. 102, 117, 119, 184, 187 P, 356, 357, 360, 383. —— *House Journal, 1 sess. 21 Cong.* pp. 419, 420, 786, 799, 803 P, 807, 809.—— *Senate Journal, 2 sess. 21 Cong.* p. 13 O.

14. **Extension of charter of the U. S. Bank.** [§§ 19, 57.]

S. *147, 1 sess. 22 Cong.* "An act to modify and continue the act entitled 'An act to incorporate the subscribers to the Bank of the United States.'"

1832. Mar. 13 to June 11, in the Senate.—— June 11 to July 3, in the House.

July 10, vetoed.—— July 13, reconsidered by Senate; vote, 22-19.

Senate Journal, 1 sess. 22 Cong. pp. 183, 296, 297, 302, 305, 308, 310, 314, 318, 324, 327, 329, 333, 339, 341, 344, 345 P, 394, 397, 401, 433 O, 451, 456, 463 R.—— *House Journal, 1 sess. 22 Cong.* pp. 871, 874, 879, 1035, 1044, 1066, 1074 P, 1076, 1082, 1097, 1162.

† 15. **Interest on State claims.** [§ 54.]

S. *5, 1 sess. 22 Cong.* "An act providing for the final settlement of the claims of States for interest on advances to the United States made during the last war."

1831. Dec. 19 to 1832, Jan. 5, in the Senate.—— 1832, Jan. 5 to July 14, in the House.

1832. Dec. 6, veto message signed.

Senate Journal, 1 sess. 22 Cong. pp. 30, 54, 59, 62 P, 480, 482.—— *House Journal, 1 sess. 22 Cong.* pp. 156, 180, 237, 1166, 1174 P, 1180, 1186.—— *Senate Journal, 2 sess. 22 Cong.* p. 19 O.

† 16. **River and Harbor Bill.** [§ 86.]

H. R. *516, 1 sess. 22 Cong.* "An act for the improvement of certain harbors and the navigation of certain rivers."

1832. Mar. 29 to June 5, in the House.—— June 6 to July 5, in the Senate.

Dec. 6, veto message signed.

House Journal, 1 sess. 22 Cong. pp. 551, 791, 802, 827, 837, 848, 850, 852 P, 1092, 1099, 1152, 1153, 1157, 1165, 1183.—— *Senate Journal, 1 sess. 22 Cong.* pp. 331, 368, 393, 399, 404 P, 456, 460, 468, 469, 481.—— *House Journal, 2 sess. 22 Cong.* p. 24 O.

† 17. **Proceeds of land sales (Clay's bill).** [§§ 46, 101.]

S. *6, 2 sess. 22 Cong.* "An act to appropriate for a limited time the proceeds of the sales of the public lands of the United States and for granting lands to certain States."

1832. Dec. 11 to 1833, Jan. 25, in the Senate.—— 1833, Jan. 25 to Mar. 1, in the House.

1833. Dec. 4, veto message signed.

Senate Journal, 2 sess. 22 Cong. pp. 26, 53, 54, 63, 70, 73, 76, 80, 85, 104, 107, 109, 111, 114, 119, 123, 125, 137, 138 P, 229, 230, 236.——*House Journal*, 2 sess. 22 Cong. pp. 239, 459, 460 P, 461, 462, 470.——*Senate Journal*, 1 sess. 23 Cong. pp. 21 O, 50, 240.

† **18. Internal improvements (Wabash River).** [§ 86.]
S. 97, *1 sess. 23 Cong.* "An act to improve the navigation of the Wabash River."
1834. Feb. 18 to June 26, in the Senate.—— June 26 to June 28, in the House.
Dec. 1, veto message signed.
Senate Journal, 1 sess. 23 Cong. pp. 146, 182, 357 P, 358, 382, 385, 387, 415.——*House Journal*, 1 sess. 23 Cong. pp. 845, 853, 887, 888 P, 893, 901, 930.——*Senate Journal*, 2 sess. 23 Cong. p. 23 O.

19. Compromising claims against the Two Sicilies. [§ 21.]
S. *160, 2 sess. 23 Cong.* "An act to authorize the Secretary of the Treasury to compromise the Claims allowed by the Commissioners under the Treaty with the King of the Two Sicilies, concluded October 14, 1832."
1835. Feb. 12 to Feb. 27, in the Senate.—— Feb. 27 to Feb. 28, in the House.
Mar. 3, vetoed.—— Mar. 3, reconsidered by the Senate; laid on the table.
Senate Journal, 2 sess. 23 Cong. pp. 156, 199 P, 203, 215, 217, 222, 233 O R.——*House Journal*, 2 sess. 23 Cong. pp. 476, 481 P, 503, 514.

20. Regulation for congressional sessions. [§ 14.]
S. *141, 1 sess. 24 Cong.* "An act to appoint a day for the annual meeting of Congress."
1836. Feb. 16 to June 2, in the Senate.—— June 3, in the House.
June 9, vetoed.—— June 27, reconsidered by the Senate; vote, 16–23.
Senate Journal, 1 sess. 24 Cong. pp. 165, 393, 400 P, 401, 403, 406, 415, 421 O, 467, 486 R.——*House Journal*, 1 sess. 24 Cong. pp. 928, 931 P, 938, 970, 1108.

† **21. Funds receivable for United States revenues.** [§ 60.]
S. *144, 2 sess. 24 Cong.* "An act designating and limiting the funds receivable for the revenues of the United States."
1837. Jan. 18 to Feb. 10, in the Senate.—— Feb. 10 to Mar. 1, in the House.
Mar. 3, 11.45 P.M., veto message signed.[1]
Senate Journal, 2 sess. 24 Cong. pp. 133, 144, 165, 169, 173, 177, 235 P, 309, 313, 326.——*House Journal*, 2 sess. 24 Cong. pp. 368, 420, 510, 556, 558 P, 567, 580.

PRESIDENT TYLER (1841-1845).—[9 VETOES.]

22. Incorporating the Fiscal Bank. [§§ 58, 124, 128.]
S. *5, 1 sess. 27 Cong.* "An act to incorporate the subscribers to the Fiscal Bank of the United States."
1841. June 21 to July 28, in the Senate.—— July 28 to Aug. 6, in the House.
Aug. 16, vetoed.—— Aug. 19, reconsidered by the Senate; vote, 25–24.
Senate Journal, 1 sess. 27 Cong. pp. 51, 60, 65, 68, 70, 71, 73, 74, 76, 78, 81, 84, 86, 88, 100, 102, 104, 114, 116, 122, 125 P, 143, 144, 145, 165 O, 173, 178 R.——*House Journal*, 1 sess. 27 Cong. pp. 288, 307, 311, 314, 318, 322, 323, 324 P, 326, 387.

23. Incorporating the Fiscal Corporation. [§ 58.]
H. R. *14, 1 sess. 27 Cong.* "An act to provide for the better collection, safe keeping and disbursement of the public revenue, by means of a corporation styled the Fiscal Corporation of the United States."

---

[1] This message was never sent to Congress, but was deposited in the Department of State. See Senate Miscellaneous Documents, No. 53, p. 151, 49 Cong. 2 Sess.

1841. July 21 to Aug. 23, in the House.—— Aug. 24 to Sept. 3, in the Senate.

Sept. 9, vetoed.—— Sept. 10, reconsidered by the House; vote, 103–80.

House Journal, 1 sess. 27 Cong. pp. 267, 394, 404, 405, 409 P, 410, 459, 460, 485 O, 497 R.—— *Senate Journal, 1 sess. 27 Cong.* pp. 212, 220, 228, 232, 234 P, 236, 255.

24. First Whig tariff bill. [§§ 46, 53.]

H. R. 480, 2 sess. 27 Cong. "An act to extend for a limited period the present laws for laying and collecting duties on imports."

1842. June 9 to June 15, in the House.—— June 15 to June 24, in the Senate.

June 29, vetoed.—— July 4, reconsidered by the House; vote, 42–144.

House Journal, 2 sess. 27 Cong. pp. 936, 943, 967, 969, 972, 974 P, 1014, 1016, 1023, 1025, 1032 O, 1043, 1045, 1047, 1050 R.—— *Senate Journal, 2 sess. 27 Cong.* pp. 400, 402, 407, 417, 426, 428 P, 430, 431, 453.

25. Second Whig tariff bill. [§§ 46, 53.]

H. R. 472, 2 sess. 27 Cong. "An act to provide revenue from imports, and to change and modify existing laws imposing duties on imports, and for other purposes."

1842. June 3 to July 16, in the House.—— July 18 to Aug. 5, in the Senate.

Aug. 9, vetoed.—— Aug. 17, reconsidered by the House; vote, 126–76.

House Journal, 2 sess. 27 Cong. pp. 911, 933, 939, 995, 998, 1000, 1003, 1004, 1056, 1057, 1061, 1062, 1067, 1069, 1070, 1073, 1078–1110, 1110 P, 1225, 1226, 1228, 1242 O, 1252, 1261, 1296, 1327 R, 1343.—— *Senate Journal, 2 sess. 27 Cong.* pp. 472, 48/, 503, 508, 511, 513, 515, 520, 526, 528, 531, 537, 544 P, 545, 547, 549.

† 26. Proceeds of public land sales. [§ 46.]

H. R. 604, 2 sess. 27 Cong. "An act to repeal the proviso of the sixth section of the act entitled 'An act to appropriate the proceeds of the sales of the public lands and to grant pre-emption rights.'"

1842. Aug. 25 to Aug. 26, in the House.—— Aug. 26 to Aug. 29, in the Senate.

Dec. 14, veto message signed.

House Journal, 2 sess. 27 Cong. pp. 1409, 1420, 1422, 1423 P, 1444, 1450, 1468.—— *Senate Journal, 2 sess. 27 Cong.* pp. 613, 626, 631 P, 640, 645.—— *House Journal, 3 sess. 27 Cong.* p. 57 O.

† 27. Testimony in contested elections. [§ 15.]

H. R. 210, 2 sess. 27 Cong. "An act regulating the taking of testimony in cases of contested elections, and for other purposes."

1842. Feb. 21 to Aug. 8, in the House.—— Aug. 9 to Aug. 29, in the Senate.

Dec. 14, veto message signed.

House Journal, 2 sess. 27 Cong. pp. 418, 693, 1217, 1227, 1232, 1233 P, 1444, 1446, 1452, 1453, 1458, 1464, 1471, 1478.—— *Senate Journal, 2 sess. 27 Cong.* pp. 557, 561, 585, 597, 603, 626, 632 P, 637, 638, 640, 642, 647, 648.—— *House Journal, 3 sess. 27 Cong.* p. 57 O.

† 28. Payment of Cherokee certificates. [§ 41.]

H. R. 37, 3 sess. 27 Cong. Resolution "directing payment of the certificates or awards issued by the commissioners, under the treaty with the Cherokee Indians."

1843. Feb. 9 to Feb. 25, in the House.—— Feb. 25 to Mar. 2, in the Senate.

Dec. 18, veto message signed.

House Journal, 3 sess. 27 Cong. pp. 339, 457, 462 P, 542, 553, 557.—— *Senate Journal, 3 sess. 27 Cong.* pp. 222, 229, 261, 275 P, 284, 295.—— *House Journal, 1 sess. 28 Cong.* p. 69 O.

29. Rivers and harbors. [§ 87.]

H. R. 203, 1 sess. 28 Cong. "An act making appropriation for certain harbors and rivers."

1844. Mar. 8 to May 16, in the House.—— May 17 to June 1, in the Senate.

June 11, vetoed.—— June 11, reconsidered by the House; vote, 104–84.

House Journal, 1 sess. 28 Cong. pp. 542, 751, 752, 770, 772, 842, 934, 935, 936, 937, 938 P, 1001, 1002, 1081 O, 1083 R, 1084, 1085, 1086, 1093, 1097.—— *Senate Journal, 1 sess. 28 Cong.* pp. 286, 287, 294, 317 P, 321, 324, 327, 347.

** **30. Revenue cutters and steamers.** [§§ 21, 129.]

S. 66, 2 sess. 28 Cong. "An act relating to revenue cutters and steamers."

1845. Jan. 6 to Feb. 4, in the Senate.—— Feb. 4 to Feb. 7, in the House.

Feb. 20, vetoed.—— Mar. 3, reconsidered by the Senate; passed over the veto, 41 to 1.—— Mar. 3, by the House; passed over the veto, 127 to 30.

Senate Journal, 2 sess. 28 Cong. pp. 73, 78, 124, 133 P, 145, 149, 157, 193 O, 194, 197, 203, 256 R, 262.—— *House Journal, 2 sess. 28 Cong.* pp. 324, 326, 339 P, 348, 568 R.

PRESIDENT POLK (1845-1849).—[3 VETOES.]

31. Rivers and harbors. [§ 88.]

H. R. 18, 1 sess. 29 Cong. "An act making appropriations for the improvement of certain harbors and rivers."

1845. Dec. 31 to 1846, Mar. 20, in the House.—— 1846, Mar. 23 to July 24, in the Senate.

1846. Aug. 3, vetoed.—— Aug. 4, reconsidered by the House; vote, 97–91.

House Journal, 1 sess. 29 Cong. pp. 180, 408, 409, 448, 460, 464, 492, 493, 500, 503, 504, 508, 514, 516, 518, 522, 525, 531, 536, 537, 538, 539–566, 566 P, 1146, 1150, 1154, 1209 O, 1217 R, 1218.—— *Senate Journal, 1 sess. 29 Cong.* pp. 208, 309, 426, 429, 440 P, 444, 446, 447, 480.

32. French spoliation claims. [§ 64.]

S. 68, 1 sess. 29 Cong. "An act to provide for the ascertainment and satisfaction of claims of American citizens for spoliations committed by the French prior to the thirty-first day of July, 1801."

1846. Feb. 2 to June 8, in the Senate.—— June 8 to Aug. 4, in the House.

Aug. 8, vetoed.—— Aug. 10, reconsidered by the Senate; vote, 27–15.

Senate Journal, 1 sess. 29 Cong. pp. 128, 258, 261, 277, 302, 305, 308, 316, 330, 334 P, 480, 482, 489, 490, 513 O, 520 R.—— *House Journal, 1 sess. 29 Cong.* pp. 924, 932, 1071, 1185, 1208, 1219, 1221, 1223 P, 1225, 1242, 1248, 1308.

† **33. Internal improvements.** [§ 88.]

H. R. 84, 1 sess. 29 Cong. "An act to provide for continuing certain works in the Territory of Wisconsin, and for other purposes."

1846. Jan. 9 to 1847, Feb. 20, in the House.—— 1847, Feb. 22 to Mar. 3, in the Senate.

1847. Dec. 15, veto message signed.

House Journal, 1 sess. 29 Cong. pp. 216, 608.—— *House Journal, 2 sess. 29 Cong.* pp. 377, 378, 394, 395 P, 505, 506, 509.—— *Senate Journal, 2 sess. 29 Cong.* pp. 218, 221, 223, 269 P, 274, 287.—— *House Journal, 1 sess. 30 Cong.* pp. 82 O, 101, 534, 560.

PRESIDENT PIERCE (1853-1857).—[9 VETOES.]

34. Land grants for indigent insane. [§ 47.]

S. 44, 1 sess. 33 Cong. "An act making a grant of public lands to the several States for the benefit of indigent insane persons."

148 | *List of Vetoes.* [APP. A

1853. Dec. 21 to 1854, Mar. 8, in the Senate. —— 1854, Mar. 8 to Apr. 19, in the House.
1854. May 3, vetoed. —— July 6, reconsidered by the Senate; vote, 21–26.

Senate Journal, 1 sess. 33 Cong. pp. 58, 121, 171, 202, 203, 224, 227, 230, 241, 243 P, 334, 340, 343, 348, 361 O, 372, 374, 390, 393, 395, 397, 420, 423, 431, 444, 447, 450, 453, 454, 476, 477, 478 R, 479. —— *House Journal, 1 sess. 33 Cong.* pp. 467, 576, 665–670 P, 694, 1105.

35. Internal improvements (completion). [§ 89.]

H. R. 392, 1 sess. 33 Cong. "An act making appropriation for the repair, preservation and completion of certain public works heretofore commenced under the authority of law."

1854. June 10 to July 13, in the House. —— July 13 to Aug. 1, in the Senate.
Aug. 4, vetoed.[1] —— Dec. 6, reconsidered by the House; vote, 95–80.

House Journal, 1 sess. 33 Cong. pp. 979, 1125, 1126, 1130, 1131, 1133–1136, 1136 P, 1247, 1262, 1263, 1284, 1311, 1313–1318, 1323–1325, 1327, 1334, 1337, 1340 O. —— *Senate Journal, 1 sess. 33 Cong.* pp. 501, 502, 555, 592, 593, 599, 600, 601, 609–611, 615–618, 618 P, 666, 667, 678, 679, 684, 686. —— *House Journal, 2 sess. 33 Cong.* pp. 8, 9, 49 R, 50, 124. —— *Senate Journal, 2 sess. 33 Cong.* pp. 36, 79, 91.

36. French spoliation claims. [§ 64.]

H. R. 117, 1 sess. 33 Cong. "An act to provide for the ascertainment of claims of American citizens for spoliations committed by the French prior to the thirty-first of July, one thousand eight hundred and one."

1854. Jan. 4 to 1855, Jan. 27, in the House. —— 1855, Jan. 29 to Feb. 6, in the Senate.
1855. Feb. 17, vetoed. —— Feb. 19, reconsidered by the House; vote, 113–86.

House Journal, 1 sess. 33 Cong. pp. 163, 164. —— *House Journal, 2 sess. 33 Cong.* pp. 237, 239, 240, 243, 250, 252, 253 P, 335, 341, 352, 397 O, 413 R, 414, 415. —— *Senate Journal, 2 sess. 33 Cong.* pp. 168, 174, 180, 181, 198, 204, 205 P, 222, 226, 232, 292.

37. Subsidy for ocean mails. [§ 82.]

H. R. 595, 2 sess. 33 Cong. "An act making appropriations for the transportation of the United States mail, by ocean steamers and otherwise, during the fiscal years ending the 30th day of June, 1855, and the 30th of June, 1856."

1854. Dec. 22 to 1855, Feb. 17, in the House. —— 1855, Feb. 17 to Feb. 28, in the Senate.

1855. Mar. 3, vetoed. —— Mar. 3, reconsidered by the House; vote, 79–99.

House Journal, 2 sess. 33 Cong. pp. 102, 383, 384, 387, 388, 389, 391–396, 396 P, 497, 506, 509, 540 O, 541, 542, 543, 544, 545, 546 R, 547. —— *Senate Journal, 2 sess. 33 Cong.* pp. 282, 290, 314, 335, 336, 342, 343, 344 P, 345, 353, 357, 382.

** 38. Internal improvements (Mississippi River). [§§ 89, 109.]

S. 14, 1 and 2 sess. 34 Cong. "An act to remove obstructions to navigation in the mouth of the Mississippi River at the Southwest Pass and Pass à l'Outre."

1856. Feb. 4 to Mar. 17, in the Senate. —— Mar. 20 to May 12, in the House.
May 19, vetoed. —— July 7, reconsidered by the Senate; passed over the veto, 31 to 12. —— July 8, by the House; passed over the veto, 143–55.

Senate Journal, 1 and 2 sess. 34 Cong. pp. 85, 93, 187 P, 321, 322, 323, 340 O, 341, 348, 359, 362, 365, 402, 418 R, 419, 431, 432, 433. —— *House Journal, 1 and 2 sess. 34 Cong.* pp. 703, 779, 908, 959, 960 P, 964, 987, 1174, 1175, 1176 R.

---

[1] Dec. 30, 1854, the President gave his reasons for this veto at considerable length. See Senate Miscellaneous Documents, No. 53, p. 221, 49 Cong. 2 sess.

1854-1859]   Pierce's and Buchanan's Administrations.   149

** 39. Internal improvements (Saint Clair Flats). [§ 89.]
S. 1, 1 and 2 sess. 34 Cong. "An act making an appropriation for deepening the channel over the Saint Clair Flats, in the State of Michigan."
1856. Feb. 4 to Mar. 17, in the Senate.—— Mar. 20 to May 5, in the House.
May 19, vetoed.—— July 7, reconsidered by the Senate; passed over the veto, 28 to 8.—— July 8, by the House; passed over the veto, 139 to 55.
Senate Journal, 1 and 2 sess. 34 Cong. pp. 83, 84, 91, 186 P, 304, 305, 310, 311, 341 O, 342, 420 R, 431, 432, 433.—— *House Journal, 1 and 2 sess. 34 Cong.* pp. 703, 779, 923, 924 P, 933, 987, 1174, 1176 R.

** 40. Internal improvements (Saint Mary's River). [§ 89.]
S. 2, 1 and 2 sess. 34 Cong. "An act making an appropriation for deepening the channel over the flats of the Saint Mary's River in the State of Michigan."
1856. Feb. 4 to Mar. 17, in the Senate.—— Mar. 20 to May 12, in the House.
May 22, vetoed.—— July 7, reconsidered by the Senate; passed over the veto, 28 to 10.—— July 8, by the House; passed over the veto, 136 to 54.
Senate Journal, 1 and 2 sess. 34 Cong. pp. 84, 91, 186 P, 321-323, 351 O, 352, 419 R, 432, 433.—— *House Journal, 1 and 2 sess. 34 Cong.* pp. 703, 779, 957 P, 964, 987, 1174, 1177 R.

** 41. Internal improvements (Des Moines Rapids). [§§ 89, 111.]
H. R. 12, 1 and 2 sess. 34 Cong. "An act for continuing the improvement of the Des Moines Rapids in the Mississippi River."
1856. Feb. 18 to July 28, in the House.—— July 28 to July 31, in the Senate.
Aug. 11, vetoed.—— Aug. 11, reconsidered by the House; passed over the veto, 130 to 54.—— Aug. 16, by the Senate; passed over the veto, 30 to 14.
House Journal, 1 and 2 sess. 34 Cong. pp. 555, 556, 871, 1292, 1293, 1294 P, 1333, 1334, 1420 O R, 1421, 1505.—— *Senate Journal, 1 and 2 sess. 34 Cong.* pp. 485, 486, 491, 492, 501 P, 508, 509, 512, 559, 560, 585, 597, 620 R, 621.

** 42. Internal improvements (Patapsco River). [§§ 89, 111.]
S. 53, 1 and 2 sess. 34 Cong. "An act for the improvement of the navigation of the Patapsco River, and to render the Port of Baltimore accessible to the war steamers of the United States."
1856. Feb. 6 to Mar. 17, in the Senate.—— Mar. 20 to Aug. 4, in the House.
Aug. 14, vetoed.—— Aug. 16, reconsidered by the Senate; passed over the veto, 31 to 14.—— Aug. 16, by the House; passed over the veto, 127 to 47.
Senate Journal, 1 and 2 sess. 34 Cong. pp. 94, 187 P, 514, 521, 524, 527, 608 O, 609, 615, 621, 622 R, 626, 629.—— *House Journal, 1 and 2 sess. 34 Cong.* pp. 703, 843, 874, 1355, 1356 P, 1373, 1377, 1488, 1492, 1493, 1499 R, 1500.

PRESIDENT BUCHANAN (1857-1861).—[7 VETOES.]

† 43. Overland mail. [§ 21.]
H. R. 37, 1 sess. 35 Cong. "A joint resolution in regard to the carrying of the United States mails from Saint Joseph, Missouri, to Placerville, California."
1858. June 10, in the House.—— June 10 to June 12, in the Senate.
1859. Jan. 7, veto message signed.
House Journal, 1 sess. 35 Cong. pp. 1071 P, 1127, 1147.—— *Senate Journal, 1 sess. 35 Cong.* pp. 660, 669, 698, 704 P, 705, 707, 708, 710.—— *House Journal, 2 sess. 35 Cong.* p. 151 O.

44. Land grants for agricultural colleges. [§ 47.]
H. R. 2, 2 sess. 35 Cong. "An act donating public lands to the several States and

Territories which may provide colleges for the benefit of agriculture and the mechanic arts."

1857. Dec. 14 to 1858, Apr. 22, in the House.——1858, Apr. 22 to 1859, Feb. 7, in the Senate.

1859. Feb. 24, vetoed.——Feb. 26, reconsidered by the House; vote, 105-96.

House Journal, 1 sess. 35 Cong. pp. 67, 68, 73, 74, 77, 629, 632, 653, 654, 655, 667-672, 672 P.—— *Senate Journal, 1 sess. 35 Cong.* pp. 371, 376, 422, 483, 484.—— *House Journal, 2 sess. 35 Cong.* pp. 359, 425-428, 433, 437, 501 O, 508 R.—— *Senate Journal, 2 sess. 35 Cong.* pp. 57, 61, 90, 244-246, 251, 256, 257, 258, 259, 260, 278 P, 326, 327, 332.

† 45. **Internal improvements (Saint Clair Flats).** [§ 90.]

S. 321, 1 sess. 35 Cong. "An act making an appropriation for deepening the channel over the Saint Clair Flats, in the State of Michigan."

1858. May 10 to Dec. 21, in the Senate.—— Dec. 22 to 1859, Mar. 2, in the House.

1860. Feb. 1, veto message signed.

Senate Journal, 1 sess. 35 Cong. p. 428.—— *Senate Journal, 2 sess. 35 Cong.* pp. 82 P, 428, 431, 434, 439.—— *House Journal, 2 sess. 35 Cong.* pp. 107, 219, 547, 548, 549 P, 559, 563.—— *Senate Journal, 1 sess. 36 Cong.* pp. 114 O, 121, 128.

† 46. **Internal improvements (Mississippi River).** [§ 90.]

S. Res. 87, 2 sess. 35 Cong. "Joint resolution in relation to removal of obstructions to navigation in the mouth of the Mississippi River."

1859. Mar. 2, in the Senate.—— Mar. 2, in the House.

1860. Feb. 6, veto message signed.

Senate Journal, 2 sess. 35 Cong. pp. 423 P, 428, 431, 434, 439.—— *House Journal, 2 sess. 35 Cong.* pp. 540, 546 P, 559, 563.—— *Senate Journal, 1 sess. 36 Cong.* p. 129 O.

47. **Relief of A. Edwards and Co.** [§ 66.]

S. 29, 1 sess. 36 Cong. "An act for the relief of Arthur Edwards and his associates."

1860. Jan. 3 to Mar. 30, in the Senate.—— Apr. 2 to Apr. 9, in the House.

Apr. 17, vetoed.——June 7, reconsidered by the Senate; vote, 22-30.

Senate Journal, 1 sess. 36 Cong. pp. 57, 114, 325 P, 374, 376, 377, 380, 406 O, 453, 580 R, 581.—— *House Journal, 1 sess. 36 Cong.* pp. 645, 670, 671, 692, 693, 694 P, 703.

48. **Homestead Act.** [§ 47.]

S. 416, 1 sess. 36 Cong. "An act to secure homesteads to actual settlers on the public domain, and for other purposes."

1860. Apr. 17 to May 10, in the Senate.—— May 11 to May 21, in the House.

June 22, vetoed.——June 23, reconsidered by the Senate; vote, 28-18.

Senate Journal, 1 sess. 36 Cong. pp. 407, 410, 412, 414, 415, 444, 445, 446, 447, 448, 449, 450, 454, 456, 457, 458 P, 487, 533, 538, 539, 615, 620, 623, 656, 657, 667, 669, 710, 711, 716, 719, 723, 747 O, 753, 756 R, 757.—— *House Journal, 1 sess. 36 Cong.* pp. 823, 884-888, 888 P, 950, 958, 1056, 1092, 1096, 1154, 1155-1157, 1158, 1163.

49. **Relief of Hockaday and Leggit.** [§ 66.]

H. R. 915, 2 sess. 36 Cong. "An act for the relief of Hockaday and Leggit."

1861. Jan. 7, in the House.—— Jan. 10 to Jan. 11, in the Senate.

Jan. 25, vetoed.—— Jan. 26, reconsidered by the House; vote, 81-67.

House Journal, 2 sess. 36 Cong. pp. 148 P, 175, 179, 227 O, 228 R, 229.—— *Senate Journal, 2 sess. 36 Cong.* pp. 86, 89 P, 94, 105.

PRESIDENT LINCOLN (1861-1865).—[3 VETOES.]

50. Bank notes in the District of Columbia. [§ 60.]

S. *193*, *2 sess. 37 Cong.* "An act to repeal that part of an act of Congress which prohibits the circulation of bank notes of a less denomination than five dollars in the District of Columbia."

1862. Feb. 11 to Apr. 4, in the Senate.—— Apr. 7 to June 11, in the House.

June 23, vetoed.

Senate Journal, 2 sess. 37 Cong. pp. 191, 373 P, 638, 641, 645, 650, 705 O, 734.—— *House Journal, 2 sess. 37 Cong.* pp. 511, 524, 525, 841 P, 860, 864.

51. Medical officers for the army. [§§ 97, 126.]

S. *343*, *2 sess. 37 Cong.* "An act to provide for additional medical officers of the volunteer service."

1862. June 9 to June 11, in the Senate.—— June 12 to June 13, in the House.

July 2, vetoed.—— July 2, reconsidered by the Senate; vote, 0–37.

Senate Journal, 2 sess. 37 Cong. pp. 620, 623, 633 P, 650, 658, 663, 706, 713, 714, 746 O R.—— *House Journal, 2 sess. 37 Cong.* pp. 844, 857 P, 876, 881, 928, 950.

† 52. Correction of clerical errors. [§§ 98, 126.]

H. Res. *123*, *1 sess. 38 Cong.* "Joint resolution to correct certain clerical errors in the internal revenue act."

1864. July 2, in the House.—— July 4, in the Senate.

1865. Jan. 5, veto message signed.

House Journal, 1 sess. 38 Cong. p. 1031 P.—— *Senate Journal, 1 sess. 38 Cong.* p. 751 P.—— *House Journal, 2 sess. 38 Cong.* p. 80 O.

PRESIDENT JOHNSON (1865-1869).—[21 VETOES.]

53. Freedmen's Bureau. [§ 34.]

S. *60*, *1 sess. 39 Cong.* "An act to establish a Bureau for the relief of Freedmen and Refugees."

1866. Jan. 5 to Jan. 25, in the Senate.—— Jan. 25 to Feb. 6, in the House.

Feb. 19, vetoed.—— Feb. 20, reconsidered by the Senate; vote, 30–18.

Senate Journal, 1 sess. 39 Cong. pp. 62, 72, 77, 78, 86, 88, 92, 94, 95, 97, 98, 99, 100, 103, 104, 105, 106, 109 P, 110, 112, 140, 145, 147, 152, 153, 168 O, 173–176, 179 R.—— *House Journal, 1 sess. 39 Cong.* pp. 188, 189, 207, 213, 218, 225, 233, 235, 240 P, 255, 256, 266, 268.

** 54. Civil Rights Act. [§§ 34, 42.]

S. *61*, *1 sess. 39 Cong.* "An act to protect all persons in the United States in their civil rights, and furnish the means of their vindication."

1866. Jan. 5 to Feb. 2, in the Senate.—— Feb. 3 to Mar. 13, in the House.

Mar. 27, vetoed.—— Apr. 6, reconsidered by the Senate; passed over the veto, 33 to 15.—— Apr. 9, by the House; passed over the veto, 122 to 41.

Senate Journal, 1 sess. 39 Cong. pp. 62, 72, 78, 110, 112, 117, 120, 125, 127, 128, 131, 132 P, 229, 231, 236, 237, 240, 241, 279 O, 285, 306, 313, 317 R, 324.—— *House Journal, 1 sess. 39 Cong.* pp. 225, 232, 240, 345, 352, 372, 377, 380, 382, 396, 397 P, 409, 414, 521, 526, 528 R.

55. Admission of Colorado. [§ 50.]

S. *74*, *1 sess. 39 Cong.* "An act for the admission of the State of Colorado into the Union."

1866. Jan. 12 to Apr. 25, in the Senate. —— Apr. 26 to May 3, in the House.
May 15, vetoed.

Senate Journal, 1 sess. 39 Cong. pp. 76, 90, 212, 225, 227, 229, 230, 233, 352, 358, 370, 372, 373 P, 374, 398, 403, 405, 430 O, 432, 433. —— *House Journal, 1 sess. 39 Cong.* pp. 622, 657, 661 P, 668, 672.

56. Public lands (Montana Iron Company). [§§ 48, 126.]

S. 203, 1 sess. 39 Cong. "An act to enable the New York and Montana Iron Mining and Manufacturing Company to purchase a certain amount of the public lands not now in the market."

1866. Mar. 15 to May 1, in the Senate. —— May 1 to June 5, in the House.
June 15, vetoed.

Senate Journal, 1 sess. 39 Cong. pp. 235, 371, 377, 379, 388 P, 492, 494, 495, 531 O, 535, 536, 537. —— *House Journal, 1 sess. 39 Cong.* pp. 645, 698, 702, 794 P, 799, 824.

** 57. Continuation of Freedmen's Bureau. [§ 34.]

H. R. 613, 1 sess. 39 Cong. "An act to continue in force, and to amend 'An act to establish a Bureau for the relief of Freedmen and Refugees, and for other purposes.'"

1866. May 22 to May 29, in the House. —— May 30 to June 26, in the Senate.
July 16, vetoed. —— July 16, reconsidered by the House; passed over the veto, 103 to 33. —— July 16, by the Senate; passed over the veto, 33 to 12.

House Journal, 1 sess. 39 Cong. pp. 737, 741, 744, 746, 770–773 P, 915, 924, 936, 943, 947, 951, 958, 1024 O, 1028, 1030, 1039 R, 1050. —— *Senate Journal, 1 sess. 39 Cong.* pp. 476, 506, 527, 575, 576 P, 590, 594, 595, 600, 601, 608, 610, 660, 661 R.

58. Surveying district of Montana. [§§ 48, 126.]

H. R. 466, 1 sess. 39 Cong. "An act erecting the Territory of Montana into a surveying district, and for other purposes."

1866. Apr. 9 to May 24, in the House. —— May 24 to July 16, in the Senate.
July 28, vetoed.

House Journal, 1 sess. 39 Cong. pp. 525, 743 P, 1028, 1044, 1051, 1065, 1196 O, 1197, 1198. —— *Senate Journal, 1 sess. 39 Cong.* pp. 463, 465, 481, 656 P, 657, 679, 681, 686.

** 59. Suffrage in the District of Columbia. [§ 34.]

S. 1, 1 sess. 39 Cong. "An act to regulate the elective franchise in the District of Columbia."

1865. Dec. 4 to 1866, Dec. 13, in the Senate. —— 1866, Dec. 14, in the House.
1867. Jan. 5, vetoed. —— Jan. 7, reconsidered by the Senate; passed over the veto, 29 to 10. —— Jan. 8, by the House; passed over the veto, 112–38.

Senate Journal, 1 sess. 39 Cong. pp. 5, 26, 53, 70, 76, 82, 86, 582, 584. —— *Senate Journal, 2 sess. 39 Cong.* pp. 28, 29, 31, 32, 35, 36 P, 38, 42, 43, 56, 64 O, 74, 77 R. —— *House Journal, 2 sess. 39 Cong.* pp. 75, 77 P, 86, 108, 131, 132, 133 R.

60. Admission of Colorado. [§ 50.]

S. 462, 2 sess. 39 Cong. "An act to admit the State of Colorado into the Union."

1866. Dec. 10 to 1867, Jan. 9, in the Senate. —— 1867, Jan. 10 to Jan. 15, in the House.
1867. Jan. 29, vetoed. —— Mar. 1, reconsidered by the Senate; vote, 29–19.

Senate Journal, 2 sess. 39 Cong. pp. 27, 30, 83, 84 P, 104, 106, 107, 110, 154, 157 O, 162 R, 395, 396. —— *House Journal, 2 sess. 39 Cong.* pp. 145, 174, 175, 176 P, 177, 180, 181, 183.

** 61. Admission of Nebraska. [§ 50.]

S. 456, 2 sess. 39 Cong. "An act for the admission of the State of Nebraska into the Union."

1866. Dec. 5 to 1867, Jan. 9, in the Senate. —— 1867, Jan. 9 to Jan. 15, in the House.
1867. Jan. 29, vetoed. —— Feb. 8, reconsidered by the Senate; passed over the veto, 31 to 9. —— Feb. 9, by the House; passed over the veto, 103-55.
Senate Journal, 2 sess. 39 Cong. pp. 19, 22, 26, 39, 43, 46, 50, 51, 53, 56, 74, 75, 78, 81, 82, 83 P, 84, 101, 105, 106, 107, 110, 163 O, 166 R, 228, 235. —— *House Journal, 2 sess. 39 Cong.* pp. 142, 148, 149, 158, 170, 172, 174 P, 180, 181, 183, 353, 354 R.

** 62. Tenure of Office Act. [§§ 28, 34.]
S. 453, 2 sess. 39 Cong. "An act to regulate the tenure of certain civil offices."
1866. Dec. 3 to 1867, Jan. 18, in the Senate. —— 1867, Jan. 19 to Feb. 2, in the House.
1867. Mar. 2, vetoed. —— Mar. 2, reconsidered by the Senate; passed over the veto, 35 to 11. —— Mar. 2, by the House; passed over the veto, 138 to 40.
Senate Journal, 2 sess. 39 Cong. pp. 6, 22, 26, 59, 74, 87, 91, 92, 93, 98, 101, 107, 111, 115, 116 P, 198, 216, 266, 267, 302, 303, 304, 306, 307, 315, 412 O, 416, 417, 418, 419 R, 423. —— *House Journal, 2 sess. 39 Cong.* pp. 195, 196, 299, 305, 306, 307, 308, 310, 311, 312 P, 344, 379, 389, 421, 424, 425, 426, 438, 578, 580 R.

** 63. Reconstruction Act. [§ 34.]
H. R. 1143, 2 sess. 39 Cong. "An act to provide for the more efficient government of the rebel States."
1867. Feb. 6 to Feb. 13, in the House. —— Feb. 13 to Feb. 16, in the Senate.
Mar. 2, vetoed. —— Mar. 2, reconsidered by the House; passed over the veto, 138 to 51. —— Mar. 2, by the Senate; passed over the veto, 38 to 10.
House Journal, 2 sess. 39 Cong. pp. 345, 349, 352, 353, 363, 370, 371, 372, 373, 374, 375, 376 P, 413, 418, 419, 420, 421, 422, 423, 424, 433, 435, 436, 442, 443, 444, 457, 471, 562, 563 O, 563-575 R, 583. —— *Senate Journal, 2 sess. 39 Cong.* pp. 257, 258, 266, 275, 278-281, 286-294 P, 306, 316, 317, 319, 320, 325, 331, 419, 420, 424 R.

** 64. Supplemental Reconstruction Act. [§ 34.]
H. R. 33, 1 sess. 40 Cong. "An act supplementary to an act entitled 'An act to provide for the more efficient government of the rebel States.'"
1867. Mar. 11, in the House. —— Mar. 12 to Mar. 16, in the Senate.
Mar. 23, vetoed. —— Mar. 23, reconsidered by the House; passed over the veto, 114 to 25. —— Mar. 23, by the Senate; passed over the veto, 40 to 7.
House Journal, 1 sess. 40 Cong. pp. 35, 36 P, 37, 53, 58, 65, 66, 68, 69, 70, 72, 80, 98 O, 99, 100, 101, 102 R. —— *Senate Journal, 1 sess. 40 Cong.* pp. 31, 32, 34, 40, 41, 45, 46, 49, 50, 51, 52, 53, 54, 55 P, 59, 60, 64, 66, 67, 68, 73, 87, 88 R.

** 65. Supplemental Reconstruction Act. [§ 34.]
H. R. 123, 1 sess. 40 Cong. "An act supplementary to an act entitled 'An act to provide for the more efficient government of the rebel States,' passed on the second day of March, 1867, and an act supplementary thereto, passed on the twenty-third day of March, 1867."
1867. July 8 to July 9, in the House. —— July 9 to July 11, in the Senate.
July 19, vetoed. —— July 19, reconsidered by the House; passed over the veto, 109 to 25. —— July 19, by the Senate; passed over the veto, 30 to 6.
House Journal, 1 sess. 40 Cong. pp. 175, 176 P, 190, 194, 199, 202, 206, 207, 210, 214, 215, 230, 232 O, 233, 234, 235, 236, 237, 238, 239 R, 243, 244. —— *Senate Journal, 1 sess. 40 Cong.* pp. 141, 148, 149 P, 151, 152, 153, 155, 158, 159, 169, 170-177 R.

** 66. Joint resolution on reconstruction. [§ 34.]
H. Res. 71, 1 sess. 40 Cong. "Joint resolution to carry into effect the several acts providing for the more efficient government of the rebel States."

1867. July 13, in the House. —— July 13 to July 15, in the Senate.
 July 19, vetoed. —— July 19, reconsidered by the House; passed over the veto, 99 to 22. —— July 19, by the Senate; passed over the veto, 32 to 4.
House Journal, 1 sess. 40 Cong. pp. 208 P, 213, 214, 215, 240 O R, 243, 244. —— *Senate Journal, 1 sess. 40 Cong.* pp. 155, 156 P, 158, 159, 170, 178 R.

** 67. Amending Judiciary Act. [§ 34.]
S. 213, 2 sess. 40 Cong. "An act to amend an act entitled 'An act to amend the Judiciary Act, passed the twenty-fourth of September, seventeen hundred and eighty-nine.'"
1868. Jan. 6 to Mar. 11, in the Senate. —— Mar. 11 to Mar. 12, in the House.
 Mar. 25, vetoed. —— Mar. 26, reconsidered by the Senate; passed over the veto, 33 to 9. —— Mar. 27, by the House; passed over the veto, 115 to 34.
Senate Journal, 2 sess. 40 Cong. pp. 73, 292, 293 P, 300, 304, 308, 347 O, 348, 349, 350, 352 R, 355. —— *House Journal, 2 sess. 40 Cong.* pp. 506, 512, 513 P, 516, 582, 584 R.

** 68. Admission of Arkansas. [§ 34.]
H. R. 1039, 2 sess. 40 Cong. "An act to admit the State of Arkansas to representation in Congress."
1868. May 7 to May 8, in the House. —— May 12 to June 1, in the Senate.
 June 20, vetoed. —— June 20, reconsidered by the House; passed over the veto, 111 to 31. —— June 22, by the Senate; passed over the veto, 30 to 7.
House Journal, 2 sess. 40 Cong. pp. 661, 663, 664 P, 788, 800, 804, 809, 814, 819, 829, 898, 900 O, 903 R, 915. —— *Senate Journal, 2 sess. 40 Cong.* pp. 392, 398, 399, 424, 428, 430, 431, 434, 435, 438, 439, 440 P, 453, 454, 457, 462, 463, 525, 526, 527, 528, 532 R, 533.

** 69. Admission of Southern States. [§ 34.]
H. R. 1058, 2 sess. 40 Cong. "An act to admit the States of North Carolina, South Carolina, Louisiana, Georgia, Alabama, and Florida to representation in Congress."
1868. May 11 to May 14, in the House. —— May 16 to June 10, in the Senate.
 June 25, vetoed. —— June 25, reconsidered by the House; passed over the veto, 108 to 32. —— June 25, by the Senate; passed over the veto, 35 to 8.
House Journal, 2 sess. 40 Cong. pp. 676, 683, 686, 687, 688, 689 P, 838, 839, 841, 848, 853, 931 O, 932 R. —— *Senate Journal, 2 sess. 40 Cong.* pp. 399, 400, 442, 456, 458, 467, 471, 472, 473, 474 P, 480, 543, 544 R.

** 70. Exclusion of electoral votes of unreconstructed States. [§ 34.]
S. Res. 139, 2 sess. 40 Cong. "A resolution excluding from the electoral college the votes of States lately in rebellion which shall not have been reorganized."
1868. June 2 to July 10, in the Senate. —— July 11 to July 20, in the House.
 July 20, vetoed. —— July 20, reconsidered by the Senate; passed over the veto, 45 to 8. —— July 20, by the House; passed over the veto, 134 to 36.
Senate Journal, 2 sess. 40 Cong. pp. 443, 558, 568, 578, 581, 614, 616, 621, 622, 623, 624, 625 P, 637, 644, 699 O, 700, 701, 702 R, 703. —— *House Journal, 2 sess. 40 Cong.* pp. 1040, 1044, 1046 P, 1116, 1118 R.

** 71. Discontinuance of Freedmen's Bureau. [§ 34.]
S. 567, 2 sess. 40 Cong. "An act relating to the Freedmen's Bureau, and providing for its discontinuance."
1868. June 24 to July 11, in the Senate. —— July 11 to July 13, in the House.
 July 25, vetoed. —— July 25, reconsidered by the Senate; passed over the veto, 42 to 5. —— July 25, by the House; passed over the veto, 115 to 23.

Senate Journal, 2 sess. 40 Cong. pp. 539, 558, 634, 635 P, 644, 654, 659, 671, 759 O, 760 R. —— *House Journal, 2 sess. 40 Cong.* pp. 1043, 1057 P, 1074, 1086, 1194 R.

72. Trustees of colored schools in the District of Columbia. [§ 34.]

S. 609, 2 sess. 40 Cong. "An act transferring the duties of trustees of colored schools of Washington and Georgetown."

1868. July 10, in the Senate. —— July 10 to 1869, Feb. 5, in the House.
1869. Feb. 13, vetoed.

Senate Journal, 2 sess. 40 Cong. pp. 617 P. —— *House Journal, 2 sess. 40 Cong.* pp. 1026, 1199, 1200. —— *Senate Journal, 3 sess. 40 Cong.* pp. 211, 220, 257 O, 258. —— *House Journal, 3 sess. 40 Cong.* pp. 286 P, 292.

** 73. Tariff on copper. [§ 53.]

H. R. 1460, 2 sess. 40 Cong. "An act regulating the duties on imported copper and copper ores."

1868. July 25 to Dec. 8, in the House. —— Dec. 9 to 1869, Jan. 19, in the Senate.
1869. Feb. 22, vetoed. —— Feb. 23, reconsidered by the House; passed over the veto, 115 to 56. —— Feb. 24, by the Senate; passed over the veto, 38 to 12.

House Journal, 2 sess. 40 Cong. pp. 1206, 1213, 1221. —— *House Journal, 3 sess. 40 Cong.* pp. 17, 19, 20 P, 184, 257, 299, 304, 418, 422 O, 423 R, 440. —— *Senate Journal, 3 sess. 40 Cong.* pp. 11, 16, 49, 108, 114, 115, 119, 120, 121 P, 220, 221, 326, 338 R, 340.

PRESIDENT GRANT (1869-1877).—[43 VETOES.]

* 74. Relief of Rollin White. [§ 69.]

S. 273, 1 sess. 41 Cong. "An act for the relief of Rollin White."

1869. Apr. 9, in the Senate. —— Apr. 9, in the House.
1870. Jan. 11, vetoed. —— May 31, reconsidered by the Senate; passed over the veto, 41 to 13. —— June 22, by the House; vote, 12-168.

Senate Journal, 1 sess. 41 Cong. pp. 149, 155 P, 163. —— *House Journal, 1 sess. 41 Cong.* pp. 216, 237 P, 238. —— *Senate Journal, 2 sess. 41 Cong.* pp. 31, 82 O, 157, 288, 735 R, 874. —— *House Journal, 2 sess. 41 Cong.* pp. 886, 1069 R.

75. Southern Union troops. [§ 97.]

S. 476, 2 sess. 41 Cong. "An act to fix the status of certain federal soldiers enlisting in the Union army from the States of Alabama and Florida."

1870. Feb. 1 to Mar. 10, in the Senate. —— Mar. 11 to July 8, in the House.
July 14, vetoed.

Senate Journal, 2 sess. 41 Cong. pp. 171, 352 P, 1003, 1009, 1021, 1078 O, 1080. —— *House Journal, 2 sess. 41 Cong.* pp. 456, 701, 1177 P, 1182.

76. Relief of Charles Cooper and others. [§ 66.]

H. R. 1395, 2 sess. 41 Cong. "An act for the relief of Charles Cooper, Goshorn A. Jones, Jerome Rowley, William Hannegan, and John Hannegan."

1870. Mar. 1 to Apr. 9, in the House. —— Apr. 11 to June 13, in the Senate.
1871. Jan. 4, vetoed.

House Journal, 2 sess. 41 Cong. pp. 392, 596 P, 987, 1072, 1107, 1108, 1112. —— *Senate Journal, 2 sess. 41 Cong.* pp. 479, 482, 739, 794 P, 911, 912. —— *House Journal, 3 sess. 41 Cong.* pp. 101 O, 108.

77. Relief of naval contractors. [§ 66.]

S. R. 92, 2 sess. 41 Cong. "A resolution for the relief of certain contractors for the construction of vessels of war and steam machinery."

1870. Jan. 10 to July 8, in the Senate. —— July 9 to 1871, Jan. 30, in the House.

1871. Feb. 7, vetoed. —— Feb. 16, reconsidered by the Senate; vote, 30-20.

Senate Journal, 2 sess. 41 Cong. pp. 76, 136, 141, 640, 1001 P. —— *House Journal, 2 sess. 41 Cong.* pp. 1187, 1293. —— *Senate Journal, 3 sess. 41 Cong.* pp. 192, 196, 212, 236 O, 237, 299 R. —— *House Journal, 3 sess. 41 Cong.* pp. 238 P, 248.

* **78. Relief of estate of Dr. John F. Hanks.** [§ 69.]

H. R. 1550, 2 sess. 42 Cong. "An act for the relief of the estate of Dr. John F. Hanks."
1872. Feb. 16, in the House. —— Feb. 19 to Mar. 14, in the Senate.

Apr. 1, vetoed. —— 1873, Jan. 18, reconsidered by the House; passed over the veto, 126 to 17.

House Journal, 2 sess. 42 Cong. pp. 354 P, 503, 513, 603 O. —— *Senate Journal, 2 sess. 42 Cong.* pp. 255, 376 P, 384. —— *House Journal, 3 sess. 42 Cong.* pp. 202 R, 203. —— *Senate Journal, 3 sess. 42 Cong.* pp. 179, 182 R.

79. Relief of J. T. Johnson. [§ 69.]

H. R. 1867, 2 sess. 42 Cong. "An act for the relief of James T. Johnson."
1872. Mar. 8, in the House. —— Mar. 8 to Mar. 19, in the Senate.

Apr. 1, vetoed.

House Journal, 2 sess. 42 Cong. pp. 470 P, 537, 549, 599, 616, 649 O. —— *Senate Journal, 2 sess. 42 Cong.* pp. 349, 367, 396 P, 410.

80. Relief of children of J. W. Baker. [§ 66.]

H. R. 2041, 2 sess. 42 Cong. "An act for the relief of the children of John W. Baker, deceased."
1872. Mar. 19, in the House. —— Mar. 20 to Mar. 28, in the Senate.

Apr. 10, vetoed.

House Journal, 2 sess. 42 Cong. pp. 537 P, 602, 618, 639, 681 O. —— *Senate Journal, 2 sess. 42 Cong.* pp. 402, 403, 453 P, 478.

81. Pension to Abigail Ryan. [§ 72.]

S. 805, 2 sess. 42 Cong. "An act granting a pension to Abigail Ryan."
1872. Mar. 14, in the Senate. Mar. 14 to Apr. 4, in the House.

Apr. 15, vetoed.

Senate Journal, 2 sess. 42 Cong. pp. 377 P, 494, 501, 514, 546 O, 819. —— *House Journal, 2 sess. 42 Cong.* pp. 504, 513, 629 P, 640.

82. Pension to R. B. Crawford. [§ 72.]

H. R. 622, 2 sess. 42 Cong. "An act granting a pension to Richard B. Crawford."
1871. Dec. 15, in the House. —— Dec. 18 to 1872, Mar. 22, in the Senate.
1872. Apr. 22, vetoed.

House Journal, 2 sess. 42 Cong. pp. 74 P, 557, 618, 632, 663, 665, 685, 722, 728 O. —— *Senate Journal, 2 sess. 42 Cong.* pp. 54, 413 P, 477, 484, 527, 528, 543.

** **83. Pension to M. A. Montgomery.** [§ 72.]

S. 955, 2 sess. 42 Cong. "An act granting a pension to Mary Ann Montgomery."
1872. Apr. 11, in the Senate. —— Apr. 11 to Apr. 24, in the House.

May 14, vetoed. —— May 17, reconsidered by the Senate; passed over the veto, 44 to 1. —— June 7, by the House; passed over the veto, 101 to 44.

Senate Journal, 2 sess. 42 Cong. pp. 536 P, 604, 606, 691, 710, 712, 736 O, 772 R, 981. —— *House Journal, 2 sess. 42 Cong.* pp. 671, 727, 748 P, 831, 835, 887, 1060 R.

84. Relief of J. M. Best. [§ 70.]

S. 105, 2 sess. 42 Cong. "An act for the relief of J. Milton Best."
1871. Dec. 14 to 1872, Apr. 8, in the Senate. —— 1872, Apr. 9 to May 18, in the House.

1872. June 1, vetoed.

Senate Journal, 2 sess. 42 Cong. pp. 47, 509 P, 787, 792, 796, 927 O, 928, 929. —— *House Journal, 2 sess. 42 Cong.* pp. 660, 809, 893, 894 P, 914.

85. Relief of T. B. Wallace. [§ 70.]

S. *569, 2 sess. 42 Cong.* " An act for the relief of Thomas B. Wallace, of Lexington, in the State of Missouri."

1872. Feb. 1 to May 13, in the Senate. —— May 13 to May 24, in the House. June 7, vetoed.

Senate Journal, 2 sess. 42 Cong. pp. 184, 525, 618, 726 P, 840, 846, 849, 864, 985 O, 986. —— *House Journal, 2 sess. 42 Cong.* pp. 856, 859, 958, 975 P, 986.

86. Relief of Edmund Jussen. [§ 66.]

H. R. 2291, 2 sess. 42 Cong. " An act for the relief of Edmund Jussen."

1872. Apr. 15 to May 18, in the House. —— May 20 to Dec. 11, in the Senate.
1873. Jan. 6, vetoed.

House Journal, 2 sess. 42 Cong. pp. 691, 893 P. —— *Senate Journal, 2 sess. 42 Cong.* pp. 790, 792. —— *House Journal, 3 sess. 42 Cong.* pp. 63, 130 O. —— *Senate Journal, 3 sess. 42 Cong.* pp. 53 P, 67.

87. New trials in Court of Claims. [§ 15.]

H. R. 630, 2 sess. 42 Cong. " An act in relation to new trials in the Court of Claims."
1871. Dec. 18 to 1872, May 14, in the Honse. —— 1872, May 15 to 1873, Jaq. 9, in the Senate.
1873. Jan. 22, vetoed.

House Journal, 2 sess. 42 Cong. pp. 80, 865 P. —— *Senate Journal, 2 sess. 42 Cong.* pp. 749, 754, 816. —— *House Journal, 3 sess. 42 Cong.* pp. 144, 149, 229 O. —— *Senate Journal, 3 sess. 42 Cong.* pp. 124 P, 131.

88. Relief of East Tennessee University. [§ 70.]

S. *490, 2 sess. 42 Cong.* " An act for the relief of the East Tennessee University."
1872. Jan. 17 to Apr. 9, in the Senate. —— Apr. 10 to 1873, Jan. 18, in the House.
1873. Jan. 29, vetoed.

Senate Journal, 2 sess. 42 Cong. pp. 121, 122, 518 P. —— *House Journal, 2 sess. 42 Cong.* pp. 665, 837. —— *Senate Journal, 3 sess. 42 Cong.* pp. 174, 179, 185, 251 O, 252, 262. —— *House Journal, 3 sess. 42 Cong.* pp. 200 P, 219.

89. Relief of James A. McCullah. [§ 66.]

H. R. 2852, 2 sess. 42 Cong. " An act for the relief of James A. McCullah, late collector of the fifth district of Missouri."
1872. May 20, in the House. —— May 20 to 1873, Jan. 24, in the Senate.
1873. Feb. 8, vetoed.

House Journal, 2 sess. 42 Cong. p. 915 P. —— *Senate Journal, 2 sess. 42 Cong.* p. 794. —— *House Journal, 3 sess. 42 Cong.* pp. 240, 262, 362 O. —— *Senate Journal, 3 sess. 42 Cong.* pp. 143, 211 P, 216, 222.

90. Relief for owners of salt works destroyed by war. [§ 70.]

S. 161, 2 sess. 42 Cong. " An act for the relief of those suffering from the destruction of salt works near Manchester, Kentucky."
1872. Feb. 23 to Apr. 8, in the Senate. —— 1873, Jan. 18, in the House.
1873. Feb. 11, vetoed.

Senate Journal, 2 sess. 42 Cong. pp. 274, 511 P. —— *Senate Journal, 3 sess. 42 Cong.* pp. 174, 179, 185, 228, 234, 331 O, 332, 334. —— *House Journal, 3 sess. 42 Cong.* pp. 200 P, 201, 219, 268.

91. Relief of W. H. Denniston. [§ 70.]

H. R. 1224, 1 sess. 43 Cong. "An act for the relief of William H. Denniston, late an acting second lieutenant, Seventieth New York Volunteers."

1874. Jan. 16, in the House. —— Jan. 19 to Mar. 27, in the Senate.
Apr. 10, vetoed.

House Journal, 1 sess. 43 Cong. pp. 247, 250 P, 675, 688, 785, 798, 799 O. —— *Senate Journal, 1 sess. 43 Cong.* pp. 158, 159, 259, 389 P, 400, 405, 462.

92. Inflation of currency. [§§ 61, 126.]

S. 617, 1 sess. 43 Cong. "An act to fix the amount of United States notes and the circulation of national banks, and for other purposes."

1874. Mar. 23 to Apr. 6, in the Senate. —— Apr. 7 to Apr. 14, in the House.
Apr. 22, vetoed. —— Apr. 28, reconsidered by the Senate; vote, 34–30.

Senate Journal, 1 sess. 43 Cong. pp. 369, 376, 379, 383, 384, 390, 395, 396, 397, 398, 401, 402, 403, 404, 405, 408, 409, 413, 414, 415, 416, 417, 420, 427, 428, 429, 430, 431, 432, 433, 434 P, 464, 466, 467, 485 O, 504, 505 R, 510. —— *House Journal, 1 sess. 43 Cong.* pp. 734, 745, 800, 801 P, 810.

93. Relief of Spencer and Mead. [§ 66.]

H. R. 1331, 1 sess. 43 Cong. "An act for the relief of Jacob Spencer and James R. Mead for supplies furnished the Kansas tribe of Indians."

1874. Jan. 19 to Feb. 27, in the House. —— Mar. 2 to Apr. 29 in the Senate.
May 12, vetoed.

House Journal, 1 sess. 43 Cong. pp. 260, 415, 526, 528 P, 848, 880, 885, 918, 962, 965 O. —— *Senate Journal, 1 sess. 43 Cong.* pp. 307, 308, 338, 508 P, 519, 563.

94. Relief of A. Burtch. [§ 67.]

H. R. 4462, 2 sess. 43 Cong. "An act for the relief of Alexander Burtch."

1875. Jan. 22, in the House. —— Jan. 22 to Jan. 25, in the Senate.
Jan. 30, vetoed.

House Journal, 2 sess. 43 Cong. pp. 234 P, 249, 259, 270, 380 O, 386 O. —— *Senate Journal, 2 sess. 43 Cong.* pp. 151, 158 P, 168.

95. Pension to Lewis Hinely. [§ 72.]

H. R. 2352, 1 sess. 43 Cong. "An act granting a pension to Lewis Hinely."

1874. Mar. 6 to Apr. 3, in the House. —— Apr. 6 to 1875, Feb. 3, in the Senate.
1875. Feb. 12, vetoed.

House Journal, 1 sess. 43 Cong. pp. 571, 712, 713 P. —— *Senate Journal, 1 sess. 43 Cong.* pp. 426, 437. —— *House Journal, 2 sess. 43 Cong.* pp. 387, 395, 437, 448, 476 O. —— *Senate Journal, 2 sess. 43 Cong.* pp. 156, 199 P, 210, 221.

96. Custody of Indian trust funds. [§ 41.]

H. R. 1561, 1 sess. 44 Cong. "An act transferring the custody of certain Indian trust funds from the Secretary of the Interior to the Treasurer of the United States."

1876. Jan. 25, in the House. —— Jan. 25 to Jan. 26, in the Senate.
Feb. 3, vetoed.

House Journal, 1 sess. 44 Cong. pp. 264, 265 P, 275, 278, 330 O. —— *Senate Journal, 1 sess. 44 Cong.* pp. 137, 143 P, 146, 150.

97. Relief of James A. Hill. [§ 67.]

H. R. 83, 1 sess. 44 Cong. "An act for the relief of James A. Hill, of Lewis County, Missouri."

1875. Dec. 14 to 1876, Feb. 4, in the House. —— 1876, Feb. 7 to Mar. 14, in the Senate.
1876. Mar. 27, vetoed.

House Journal, 1 sess. 44 Cong. pp. 45, 283, 336 P, 589, 597, 675 O, 692. —— *Senate Journal, 1 sess. 44 Cong.* pp. 175, 176, 277, 308 P, 324.

** 98. Relief of G. B. Tyler and E. H. Luckett. [§ 66.]
S. 489, 1 sess. 44 Cong. "An act for the relief of G. B. Tyler and E. H. Luckett, assignees of William T. Cheatham."
1876. Feb. 24, in the Senate. —— Feb. 25 to Mar. 17, in the House.
   Mar. 31, vetoed. —— May 20, reconsidered by the Senate; passed over the veto, 46 to 0. —— May 26, by the House; passed over the veto, 181 to 14.
Senate Journal, 1 sess. 44 Cong. pp. 231 P, 322, 329, 331, 343, 390 O, 391, 392, 440, 516 R, 533. —— *House Journal, 1 sess. 44 Cong.* pp. 462, 483, 606 P, 627, 991, 993, 1014 R.

99. Reduction of President's salary. [§ 33.]
S. 172, 1 sess. 44 Cong. "An act fixing the salary of the President of the United States."
1876. Jan. 6 to Mar. 14, in the Senate. —— Apr. 3 to Apr. 6, in the House.
   Apr. 18, vetoed.
Senate Journal, 1 sess. 44 Cong. pp. 76, 243, 309 P, 379, 400, 403, 410, 425, 438 O, 524. —— *House Journal, 1 sess. 44 Cong.* pp. 733, 749, 754 P, 760.

100. Recording in the District of Columbia. [§ 15.]
H. R. 1922, 1 sess. 44 Cong. "An act providing for the recording of deeds, mortgages, and other conveyances affecting real estate in the District of Columbia."
1876. Feb. 7 to Mar. 20, in the House. —— Mar. 21 to Apr. 13, in the Senate.
   May 26, vetoed.
House Journal, 1 sess. 44 Cong. pp. 349, 623 P, 804, 816, 957, 962, 1011 O. —— *Senate Journal, 1 sess. 44 Cong.* pp. 329, 331, 412, 426, 427 P, 504, 507, 508.

101. Relief of M. W. Brock. [§ 66.]
S. 165, 1 sess. 44 Cong. "An act for the relief of Michael W. Brock of Meigs County, Tennessee, late a private in Company D, Tenth Tennessee Volunteers."
1876. Jan. 5 to Feb. 14, in the Senate. —— Feb. 15 to May 26, in the House.
   June 9, vetoed.
Senate Journal, 1 sess. 44 Cong. pp. 73, 182, 196 P, 197, 533, 546, 549, 557, 584 O, 585, 606. —— *House Journal, 1 sess. 44 Cong.* pp. 399, 444, 843, 1017 P, 1045.

102. Internal improvements (appropriations for salaries). [§ 91.]
S. 692, 1 sess. 44 Cong. "An act to amend chapter one hundred and sixty-six of the laws of the second session of the Forty-third Congress."
1876. Apr. 3, in the Senate. —— Apr. 4 to June 10, in the House.
   June 30, vetoed.
Senate Journal, 1 sess. 44 Cong. pp. 378 P, 582, 593, 595, 614, 665 O, 666, 667. —— *House Journal, 1 sess. 44 Cong.* pp. 743, 749, 1087 P, 1117.

** 103. Relief of Nelson Tiffany. [§ 67.]
H. R. 1337, 1 sess. 44 Cong. "An act for the relief of Nelson Tiffany."
1876. Jan. 18 to Apr. 29, in the House. —— May 1 to June 29, in the Senate.
   July 11, vetoed. —— July 28, reconsidered by the House; passed over the veto, 178 to 1. —— July 31, by the Senate; passed over the veto, 40 to 0.
House Journal, 1 sess. 44 Cong. pp. 221, 889 P, 1186, 1195, 1225, 1254 O, 1311, 1314, 1340, 1345 R, 1361. —— *Senate Journal, 1 sess. 44 Cong.* pp. 473, 474, 597, 649 P, 653, 657, 763, 768 R, 769.

104. Pension to E. J. Blumer. [§ 72.]

H. R. *11, 1 sess. 44 Cong.* "An act granting a pension to Eliza Jane Blumer."
1875. Dec. 14 to 1876, Mar. 3, in the House.—— 1876, Mar. 6 to June 29, in the Senate.
1876. July 13, vetoed.
House Journal, 1 sess. 44 Cong. pp. 39, 460, 508, 509 P, 1185, 1195, 1224, 1263 O.
—— *Senate Journal, 1 sess. 44 Cong.* pp. 275, 281, 398, 645 P, 653, 657.

105. Post-office statutes. [§ 98.]

H. R. *2684, 1 sess. 44 Cong.* "An act to amend sections 3946, 3951, and 3954 of the Revised Statutes."
1876. Mar. 15 to June 8, in the House.—— June 9 to July 5, in the Senate.
July 20, vetoed.
House Journal, 1 sess. 44 Cong. pp. 595, 1068 P, 1213, 1260, 1270, 1275, 1308 O.
—— *Senate Journal, 1 sess. 44 Cong.* pp. 577, 581, 641, 677 P, 701, 709, 712.

106. Restoration of Capt. E. S. Meyer. [§ 68.]

H. R. *36, 1 sess. 44 Cong.* "An act to restore the name of Edward S. Meyer to the active list of the Army."
1875. Dec. 14 to 1876, July 12, in the House.—— 1876, July 13 to July 28, in the Senate.
1876. Aug. 14, vetoed.
House Journal, 1 sess. 44 Cong. pp. 41, 1255 P, 1343, 1362, 1368, 1370, 1498 O.——
Senate Journal, 1 sess. 44 Cong. pp. 703, 708, 761 P, 776, 777.

107. Paving Pennsylvania Avenue. [§ 45.]

H. R. *4085, 1 sess. 44 Cong.* "An act to repeal section five of 'An act authorizing the repavement of Pennsylvania Avenue,' approved July 19, 1876."
1876. Aug. 8, in the House.—— Aug. 8 to Aug. 14, in the Senate.
Aug. 15, vetoed.
House Journal, 1 sess. 44 Cong. pp. 1405 P, 1478, 1481, 1499 O, 1517.—— *Senate Journal, 1 sess. 44 Cong.* pp. 808, 814, 817, 868 P, 869, 872, 874.

** 108. Sale of Indian lands. [§ 41.]

S. *779, 1 sess. 44 Cong.* "An act to provide for the sale of a portion of the reservation of the Confederated Otoe and Missouria, and the Sacs and Foxes of the Missouri tribes of Indians in the States of Kansas and Nebraska."
1876. Apr. 26 to June 1, in the Senate.—— June 1 to July 12, in the House.
Aug. 15, vetoed.—— Aug. 15, reconsidered by the Senate; passed over the veto, 36 to 0.—— Aug. 15, by the House; passed over the veto, 120 to 18.
Senate Journal, 1 sess. 44 Cong. pp. 460, 542 P, 703, 704, 717, 808, 811, 819, 829, 864, 883 O, 885 R, 892, 893.—— *House Journal, 1 sess. 44 Cong.* pp. 1042, 1048, 1254 P, 1270, 1281, 1310, 1312, 1404, 1413, 1425, 1511 R.

109. Relief of Major J. T. Turner. [§§ 70, 108.]

S. *561, 1 sess. 44 Cong.* "An act for the relief of Major Junius T. Turner."
1876. Mar. 6 to Mar. 15, in the Senate.—— Mar. 15 to Aug. 10, in the House.
Aug. 15, vetoed.
Senate Journal, 1 sess. 44 Cong. pp. 277, 312 P, 816, 827, 829, 864, 885 O, 886.——
House Journal, 1 sess. 44 Cong. pp. 595, 598, 1424 P, 1438, 1515.—— *Senate Journal, 2 sess. 44 Cong.* pp. 103, 232.

110. Homestead entries. [§ 48.]

H. R. *2041, 1 sess. 44 Cong.* "An act to amend section 2291 of the Revised Statutes of the United States, in relation to proof required in homestead entries."

1876. Feb. 14 to Mar. 7, in the House.—— Mar. 8 to Aug. 9, in the Senate.
1877. Jan. 15, vetoed.
House Journal, 1 sess. 44 Cong. pp. 387, 526 P, 1413.—— *Senate Journal, 1 sess. 44 Cong.* pp. 288, 290, 480, 810 P. —— *House Journal, 2 sess. 44 Cong.* pp. 156, 159, 164, 200, 249 O. —— *Senate Journal, 2 sess. 44 Cong.* pp. 81, 85.

*111. District of Columbia police. [§ 45.]

H. R. 4350, 2 sess. 44 Cong. "An act to abolish the Board of Commissioners of the Metropolitan Police of the District of Columbia, and to transfer its duties to the Commissioners of the District of Columbia."
1877. Jan. 8, in the House.—— Jan. 8 to Jan. 9, in the Senate.
Jan. 23, vetoed.—— Jan. 30, reconsidered by the House; passed over the veto, 159 to 78.—— Feb. 6, by the Senate; vote, 33–22.
House Journal, 2 sess. 44 Cong. pp. 177 P, 187, 195, 216, 326 O, R, 396. —— *Senate Journal, 2 sess. 44 Cong.* pp. 87, 92 P, 95, 96, 178, 179, 197, 205 R.

112. Diplomatic congratulations. [§ 24.]

H. Res. 171 and 172, 2 sess. 44 Cong. "Joint resolution relating to congratulations from the Argentine Republic," and "Joint resolution in reference to congratulations from the Republic of Pretoria, South Africa."
1876. Dec. 15, in the House.—— Dec. 15 to 1877, Jan. 11, in the Senate.
1877. Jan. 26, vetoed.
House Journal, 2 sess. 44 Cong. pp. 82 P, 206, 218, 241, 328 O. —— *Senate Journal, 2 sess. 44 Cong.* pp. 52, 98 P, 108.

113. Muster of D. H. Kelly. [§ 69.]

S. 685, 1 sess. 44 Cong. "An act to place the name of Daniel H. Kelly upon the muster roll of Company F, Second Tennessee Infantry."
1876. Apr. 3 to June 8, in the Senate.—— June 8 to 1877, Jan. 16, in the House.
1877. Jan. 26, vetoed.
Senate Journal, 1 sess. 44 Cong. pp. 377, 575 P. —— *House Journal, 1 sess. 44 Cong.* pp. 1070, 1092.—— *Senate Journal, 2 sess. 44 Cong.* pp. 114, 137, 138, 151, 158 O, 159. —— *House Journal, 2 sess. 44 Cong.* pp. 238 P, 255.

114. Desertion of Alfred Rowland. [§ 67.]

H. R. 3367, 1 sess. 44 Cong. "An act to remove the charge of desertion from the military record of Alfred Rowland."
1876. May 4 to June 30, in the House.—— July 1 to 1877, Jan. 30, in the Senate.
1877. Feb. 14, vetoed.
House Journal, 1 sess. 44 Cong. pp. 915, 1191 P. —— *Senate Journal, 1 sess. 44 Cong.* pp. 661, 667.—— *House Journal, 2 sess. 44 Cong.* pp. 340, 358, 382, 438 O. —— *Senate Journal, 2 sess. 44 Cong.* pp. 110, 172, 173 P, 190.

115. Advertising of Executive Departments. [§ 21.]

H. R. 3156, 1 sess. 44 Cong. "An act to perfect the revision of the Statutes of the United States."
1876. Apr. 19 to June 1, in the House.—— June 2 to 1877, Jan. 12, in the Senate.
1877. Feb. 14, vetoed.
House Journal, 1 sess. 44 Cong. pp. 823, 933, 1003, 1037, 1039 P. —— *Senate Journal, 1 sess. 44 Cong.* pp. 546, 550.—— *House Journal, 2 sess. 44 Cong.* pp. 233, 235, 269, 292, 294, 340, 346, 363, 382, 451 O. —— *Senate Journal, 2 sess. 44 Cong.* pp. 92, 96, 99, 102 P, 149, 151, 170, 193, 194.

116. Relief of Edward A. Leland. [§ 70.]

S. *691, 1 sess. 44 Cong.* "An act for the relief of Edward A. Leland."
1876. Apr. 3 to Aug. 15, in the Senate.—— Aug. 15 to 1877, Feb. 16, in the House.
1877. Feb. 28, vetoed.

Senate Journal, 1 sess. 44 Cong. pp. 378, 692, 881 P.—— *House Journal, 1 sess. 44 Cong.* p. 1509.—— *Senate Journal, 2 sess. 44 Cong.* pp. 256, 307, 340, 366 O, 367, 368.—— *House Journal, 2 sess. 44 Cong.* pp. 157, 460 P, 517.

PRESIDENT HAYES (1877-1881).—[12 VETOES.]

** 117. Standard silver dollar. [§§ 62, 129.]

H. R. 1093, 1 sess. 45 Cong. "An act to authorize the coinage of the silver dollar and to restore its legal tender character."
1877. Nov. 5, in the House.—— Nov. 6 to 1878, Feb. 15, in the Senate.
1878. Feb. 28, vetoed.—— Feb. 28, reconsidered by the House; passed over the veto, 196 to 73.—— Feb. 28, by the Senate; passed over the veto, 46 to 19.

House Journal, 1 sess. 45 Cong. p. 144 P.—— *Senate Journal, 1 sess. 45 Cong.* pp. 46, 78.—— *House Journal, 2 sess. 45 Cong.* pp. 458, 468, 485, 517, 546 O, 550 R, 555.—— *Senate Journal, 2 sess. 45 Cong.* pp. 31, 130, 136, 140, 141, 142, 145, 148, 156, 165, 169, 172, 176, 182, 187, 188, 193, 196, 200, 201, 202, 203, 204, 205, 206, 207, 208, 209 P, 231, 250, 252 R.

118. Special term of courts in Mississippi. [§ 15.]

H. R. 3072, 2 sess. 45 Cong. "An act to authorize a special term of the Circuit Court of the United States for the southern district of Mississippi, to be held at Scranton, in Jackson County."
1878. Feb. 5, in the House.—— Feb. 6 to Feb. 28, in the Senate.
Mar. 6, vetoed.

House Journal, 2 sess. 45 Cong. pp. 368, 369 P, 555, 563, 585, 600 O.—— *Senate Journal, 2 sess. 45 Cong.* pp. 168, 169, 185, 246, 249, 250, 252 P, 253, 260.

119. Restricting Chinese immigration. [§§ 43, 126.]

H. R. 2423, 2 sess. 45 Cong. "An act to restrict the immigration of Chinese to the United States."
1878. Jan. 14 to 1879, Jan. 28, in the House.—— 1879, Jan. 29 to Feb. 15, in the Senate.
1879. Mar. 1, vetoed.—— Mar. 1, reconsidered by the House; vote, 110–96.

House Journal, 2 sess. 45 Cong. p. 190.—— *House Journal, 3 sess. 45 Cong.* pp. 176, 297, 298 P, 456, 500, 517, 535, 603 O, 608, 609 R, 610.—— *Senate Journal, 3 sess. 45 Cong.* pp. 184, 185, 232, 266, 271, 276, 282, 283, 284, 285 P, 353, 355.

120. Army appropriations. [§ 35.]

H. R. 1, 1 sess. 46 Cong. "An act making appropriation for the support of the Army, for the fiscal year ending June thirtieth, eighteen hundred and eighty, and for other purposes."
1879. Mar. 27 to Apr. 5, in the House.—— Apr. 7 to Apr. 25, in the Senate.
Apr. 29, vetoed.—— May 1, reconsidered by the House; vote, 121–110.

House Journal, 1 sess. 46 Cong. pp. 31, 33, 34, 36, 38, 40, 41, 42, 43, 44, 45, 46 P, 198, 208 O, 221 R, 222.—— *Senate Journal, 1 sess. 46 Cong.* pp. 67, 68, 74, 75, 76, 77, 79, 80, 83, 85, 86, 88, 90, 93, 95, 97, 98, 99, 100, 103, 104, 105, 106 P, 107.

121. Interference at elections. [§ 34.]

H. R. 1382, 1 sess. 46 Cong. "An act to prohibit military interference at elections."

1879. May 5 to May 6, in the House.——May 6 to May 9, in the Senate.
1879. **May 12,** vetoed.——May 13, reconsidered by the House; vote, 128–97.
House Journal, 1 sess. 46 Cong. pp. 232, 259, 260, 261, 262, 263 P, 277, 278, 291 O, 295, 297, 298 R, 481, 539.——*Senate Journal, 1 sess. 46 Cong.* pp. 125, 127, 131, 133, 135, 136 P, 138.

122. Civil appropriations. [§ 35.]
H. R. 2, 1 sess. 46 Cong. "An act making appropriations for the legislative, executive, and judicial expenses of the government for the fiscal year ending June thirtieth, eighteen hundred and eighty, and for other purposes."
1879. Apr. 1 to Apr. 26, in the House.——Apr. 28 to May 20, in the Senate.
May 29, vetoed.——May 29, reconsidered by the House; vote, 114–93.
House Journal, 1 sess. 46 Cong. pp. 35, 49, 58, 59, 66, 82, 88, 92, 93, 94, 98, 106, 176, 186, 187, 192, 194, 195, 198, 200 P, 202, 341, 360, 389, 404, 410 O, 414 R, 415.—— *Senate Journal, 1 sess. 46 Cong.* pp. 111, 123, 137, 138, 140, 142, 145, 147, 149, 150, 151, 152, 153, 154, 155, 156, 157 P, 158, 165.

123. Payment of marshals. [§ 35.]
H. R. 2252, 1 sess. 46 Cong. "An act making appropriations for certain judicial expenses."
1879. June 9 to June 10, in the House.——June 11 to June 16, in the Senate.
June 23, vetoed.——June 23, reconsidered by the House; vote, 102–78.
House Journal, 1 sess. 46 Cong. pp. 469, 474, 475 P, 514, 518, 526, 527, 528, 529, 540, 549 O, 553 R.——*Senate Journal, 1 sess. 46 Cong.* pp. 199, 200, 201, 208, 211, 212, 216 P, 223, 224, 225, 241, 249, 250, 251.

124. Relief of Major Collins. [§ 69.]
S. 595, 1 sess. 46 Cong. "An act to amend an act for the relief of Joseph C. Collins, approved March third, eighteen hundred and seventy-nine."
1879. May 14 to May 27, in the Senate.——May 28 to June 12, in the House.
June 27, vetoed.
Senate Journal, 1 sess. 46 Cong. pp. 144, 168 P, 204, 210, 222, 274 O, 275.——*House Journal, 1 sess. 46 Cong.* pp. 406, 487, 488 P, 505.

125. Payment of marshals. [§ 35.]
H. R. 2382, 1 sess. 46 Cong. "An act making appropriations to pay fees of United States marshals and their general deputies."
1879. June 26 to June 27, in the House.——June 27 to June 28, in the Senate.
June 30, vetoed.——June 30, reconsidered by the House; vote, 85–63.
House Journal, 1 sess. 46 Cong. pp. 567, 574, 575 P, 585, 588, 591 O, 592 R, 594.
——*Senate Journal, 1 sess. 46 Cong.* pp. 271, 275, 278 P, 279, 280.

126. Payment of marshals. [§ 35.]
H. R. 4924, 2 sess. 46 Cong. "An act making appropriations to supply certain deficiencies in the appropriations for the service of the government for the fiscal year ending June thirtieth, eighteen hundred and eighty, and for other purposes."
1880. Mar. 12 to Mar. 19, in the House.——Mar. 22 to Apr. 1, in the Senate.
May 4, vetoed.
House Journal, 2 sess. 46 Cong. pp. 769, 770, 798, 803, 809, 816, 820 P, 935, 937, 957, 1047, 1048, 1064, 1075, 1088, 1089, 1095, 1117, 1143, 1154, 1170, 1174 O.—— *Senate Journal, 2 sess. 46 Cong.* pp. 360, 361, 377, 384, 389, 390, 395 P, 473, 477, 478, 483, 492, 494, 495, 504, 505.

127. Payment of marshals.[1] [§§ 34, 112.]

S. *1726, 2 sess. 46 Cong.* "An act regulating the pay and appointment of deputy marshals."

1880. May 6 to May 21, in the Senate. —— May 21 to   , in the House. June 15, vetoed.

Senate Journal, 2 sess. 46 Cong. pp. 519, 558, 573, 574, 575, 576, 585, 587 P, 588, 589, 724, 737, 742, 745, 748, 759. —— *House Journal, 2 sess. 46 Cong.* pp. 1304, 1403, 1451, 1460, 1486, 1491.

128. Refunding the national debt. [§ 59.]

H. R. 4592, 2 sess. 46 Cong. "An act to facilitate the refunding of the national debt."

1880. Feb. 18 to 1881, Jan. 19, in the House. —— 1881, Jan. 20 to Feb. 18, in the Senate.

1881. Mar. 3, vetoed.

House Journal, 2 sess. 46 Cong. pp. 520, 680, 822, 1277, 1278. —— *House Journal, 3 sess. 46 Cong.* pp. 37, 68, 71, 84, 114, 118, 129, 139, 164, 169, 179, 180, 199, 200, 201, 204, 212 P, 446, 558, 560, 569, 580, 585 O. —— *Senate Journal, 3 sess. 46 Cong.* pp. 142, 143, 204, 256, 261, 267, 273, 274, 275, 276, 277, 281, 282, 283 P, 367, 369.

PRESIDENT ARTHUR (1881-1885).—[4 VETOES.]

129. Chinese immigration. [§ 43.]

S. *71, 1 sess. 47 Cong.* "An act to execute certain treaty stipulations relating to Chinese."

1881. Dec. 5 to 1882, Mar. 9, in the Senate. —— 1882, Mar. 10 to Mar. 23, in the House.

1882. Apr. 4, vetoed. —— Apr. 5, reconsidered by the Senate; vote, 29-21.

Senate Journal, 1 sess. 47 Cong. pp. 35, 222, 357, 363, 367, 373, 381, 385, 390, 395, 396, 397 P, 466, 473, 477, 526 O, 527-534, 540, 541 R. —— *House Journal, 1 sess. 47 Cong.* pp. 783, 784, 816, 824, 845, 849, 881, 882, 883, 886, 887, 888, 889 P, 890, 900.

130. Passengers by sea. [§ 82.]

H. R. 2744, 1 sess. 47 Cong. "An act to regulate the carriage of passengers by sea."

1882. Jan. 9 to Apr. 18, in the House. —— Apr. 19 to June 19, in the Senate.

July 1, vetoed.

House Journal, 1 sess. 47 Cong. pp. 241, 1065 P, 1502, 1518, 1525, 1575 O, 1804. —— *Senate Journal, 1 sess. 47 Cong.* pp. 602, 802, 845 P, 859.

** 131. Rivers and harbors. [§ 92.]

H. R. 6242, 1 sess. 47 Cong. "An act making appropriations for the construction, repair, and preservation of certain works on rivers and harbors, and for other purposes."

1882. June 1 to June 17, in the House. —— June 19 to July 12, in the Senate.

Aug. 1, vetoed. —— Aug. 2, reconsidered by the House; passed over the veto, 122 to 59. —— Aug. 2, by the Senate; passed over the veto, 41 to 16.

House Journal, 1 sess. 47 Cong. pp. 1389, 1422, 1477, 1479, 1484, 1489, 1490 P, 1491, 1625, 1634, 1653, 1654, 1655, 1665, 1681, 1689, 1697, 1729, 1734, 1753, 1762, 1788 O, 1792 R, 1804, 1808. —— *Senate Journal, 1 sess. 47 Cong.* pp. 844, 916, 927, 928, 931, 937, 938, 939, 946, 947, 951-953, 956, 957 P, 958, 939, 971, 973, 980, 992, 993, 994, 1016, 1023, 1028, 1058, 1059, 1060, 1061 R.

---

[1] For the text of the veto see Senate Miscellaneous Documents, No. 53, p. 438, 49 Cong. 2 sess.

1880-1886]   Hayes's to Cleveland's Administration.   165

*132. Relief of Fitz-John Porter. [§§ 29, 68.]
H. R. 1015, 1 sess. 48 Cong. "An act for the relief of Fitz-John Porter."
1883. Dec. 11 to 1884, Feb. 1, in the House.——1884, Feb. 4 to Mar. 13, in the Senate.
1884. July 2, vetoed.——July 2, reconsidered by the House; passed over the veto, 168 to 78.——July 3, by the Senate; vote, 27–27.
House Journal, 1 sess. 48 Cong. pp. 97, 253, 310, 349, 350, 413, 414, 470, 471 P, 822, 1207, 1222, 1462, 1466, 1481, 1638 O, 1640 R, 1648.——Senate Journal, 1 sess. 48 Cong. pp. 252, 254, 352, 420, 422, 423 P, 620, 622, 635, 771, 776, 778, 779, 792, 798, 897, 899 R.

PRESIDENT CLEVELAND (1885-1889).—[301 VETOES.]

133. Relief of J. H. McBlair. [§ 66.]
S. 193, 1 sess. 49 Cong. "An act for the relief of John Hollins McBlair."
1885. Dec. 8, to 1886, Jan. 13, in the Senate.——1886, Jan. 14 to Feb. 19, in the House.
1886. Mar. 10, vetoed.
Senate Journal, 1 sess. 49 Cong. pp. 55, 161, 170 P, 322, 333, 342, 404 O, 406.——House Journal, 1 sess. 49 Cong. pp. 363, 370, 423, 633, 713 P, 740.

*134. Settlers' titles to Des Moines River lands. [§ 48.]
S. 150, 1 sess. 49 Cong. "An act to quiet the title of settlers on the Des Moines River lands in the State of Iowa, and for other purposes."
1885. Dec. 8 to 1886, Feb. 11, in the Senate.——1886, Feb. 12 to Feb. 24, in the House.
1886. Mar. 11, vetoed.——June 29, reconsidered by the Senate; passed over the veto, 34 to 15.——July 1, by the House; vote, 161–93.
Senate Journal, 1 sess. 49 Cong. pp. 53, 179, 280 P, 333, 335, 339, 367, 412 O, 415, 1009, 1016 R, 1036.——House Journal, 1 sess. 49 Cong. pp. 628, 640, 740 P, 754, 2046, 2059 O, 2061 R, 2062, 2063.

135. Bodies for dissection. [§§ 45, 126.]
S. 349, 1 sess. 49 Cong. "An act for the promotion of anatomical science, and to prevent the desecration of graves."
1885. Dec. 16 to 1886, Feb. 17, in the Senate.——1886, Feb. 18 to Apr. 12, in the House.
1886. Apr. 26, vetoed.——Apr. 30, reconsidered by the Senate; vote, 6–48.
Senate Journal, 1 sess. 49 Cong. pp. 72, 203, 246, 302 P, 554, 558, 559, 562, 632 O, 634, 660 R.——House Journal, 1 sess. 49 Cong. pp. 701, 836, 1238 P, 1245.

136. Omaha a port of delivery. [§ 98.]
S. 141, 1 sess. 49 Cong. "An act to extend the provisions of the act of June tenth, eighteen hundred and eighty, entitled, 'An act to amend the statutes in relation to the mediate transportation of dutiable goods, and for other purposes,' to the port of Omaha, in the State of Nebraska."
1885. Dec. 8 to 1886, Jan. 7, in the Senate.——1886, Jan. 11 to Apr. 15, in the House.
1886. Apr. 30, vetoed.
Senate Journal, 1 sess. 49 Cong. pp. 53, 142 P, 566, 593, 618, 661 O, 662, 663.——House Journal, 1 sess. 49 Cong. pp. 317, 350, 827, 1265 P, 1316.

137. Pension to Abigail Smith. [§ 72.]
H. R. 3019, 1 sess. 49 Cong. "An act to increase the pension of Abigail Smith."
1886. Jan. 7 to Feb. 12, in the House.——Feb. 15 to Apr. 21, in the Senate.
May 8, vetoed.
House Journal, 1 sess. 49 Cong. pp. 297, 561, 635, 636 P, 1340, 1371, 1547 O.——Senate Journal, 1 sess. 49 Cong. pp. 287, 565, 601 P, 623, 627.

138. Pension to Andrew J. Hill. [§ 73.]
H. R. *1471, 1 sess. 49 Cong.* "An act increasing the pension of Andrew J. Hill."
1886. Jan. 5 to Feb. 12, in the House. —— Feb. 15 to Apr. 21, in the Senate.
    May 8, vetoed.
House Journal, 1 sess. 49 Cong. pp. 215, 553, 635, 636 P, 1339, 1370, 1548 O. —— *Senate Journal, 1 sess. 49 Cong.* pp. 287, 499, 599 P, 623, 626.

139. Springfield a port of delivery. [§ 82.]
S. *1397, 1 sess. 49 Cong.* "An act to establish a port of delivery at Springfield, in the State of Massachusetts."
1886. Feb. 5 to Apr. 21, in the Senate. —— Apr. 22 to Apr. 28, in the House.
    May 17, vetoed.
Senate Journal, 1 sess. 49 Cong. pp. 251, 278, 609 P, 647, 669, 685, 743 O, 744. —— *House Journal, 1 sess. 49 Cong.* pp. 1330, 1352, 1406, 1423 P, 1440.

140. Pension to Louis Melcher. [§ 74.]
S. *2186, 1 sess. 49 Cong.* "An act granting a pension to Louis Melcher."
1886. Apr. 20 to Apr. 21, in the Senate. —— Apr. 22 to May 7, in the House.
    May 24, vetoed.
Senate Journal, 1 sess. 49 Cong. pp. 581, 603 P, 702, 716, 732, 784 O, 785, 822, 1080, 1138. —— *House Journal, 1 sess. 49 Cong.* pp. 1338, 1355, 1448, 1540, 1543 P, 1589.

141. Pension to Edward Ayres. [§ 74.]
S. *363, 1 sess. 49 Cong.* "An act granting a pension to Edward Ayres."
1885. Dec. 10 to 1886, Apr. 21, in the Senate. —— 1886, Apr. 22 to May 7, in the House.
1886. May 24, vetoed.
Senate Journal, 1 sess. 49 Cong. pp. 72, 582, 603 P, 701, 716, 717, 731, 787 O, 788, 823, 1080, 1138. —— *House Journal, 1 sess. 49 Cong.* pp. 1335, 1352, 1447, 1540, 1543 P, 1588.

142. Pension to J. C. Chandler. [§ 74.]
S. *1630, 1 sess. 49 Cong.* "An act granting a pension to James C. Chandler."
1886. Feb. 24 to Apr. 21, in the Senate. —— Apr. 22 to May 7, in the House.
    May 24, vetoed.
Senate Journal, 1 sess. 49 Cong. pp. 331, 519, 597 P, 702, 716, 717, 732, 786 O, 787, 823, 1080, 1190. —— *House Journal, 1 sess. 49 Cong.* pp. 1337, 1354, 1447, 1540, 1543 P, 1588.

143. Pension to D. B. Branch. [§ 74.]
S. *857, 1 sess. 49 Cong.* "An act granting a pension to Dudley B. Branch."
1886. Jan. 5 to Apr. 21, in the Senate. —— Apr. 22 to May 7, in the House.
    May 24, vetoed.
Senate Journal, 1 sess. 49 Cong. pp. 130, 518, 597 P, 701, 716, 717, 731, 783 O, 784, 1080, 1190. —— *House Journal, 1 sess. 49 Cong.* pp. 1335, 1353, 1447, 1540, 1543 P, 1588.

144. Pension to J. D. Ham. [§ 74.]
S. *1998, 1 sess. 49 Cong.* "An act for the relief of John D. Ham."
1886. Mar. 29 to Apr. 21, in the Senate. —— Apr. 22 to May 7, in the House.
    May 25, vetoed.
Senate Journal, 1 sess. 49 Cong. pp. 487, 490, 595 P, 702, 716, 717, 732, 805 O, 806, 1080, 1138. —— *House Journal, 1 sess. 49 Cong.* pp. 1337, 1355, 1448, 1540, 1543 P, 1588.

145. Pension to D. W. Hamilton. [§ 74.]
S. 1290, 1 sess. 49 Cong. "An act granting a pension to David W. Hamilton."
1886. Jan. 29 to Apr. 21, in the Senate.——Apr. 22 to May 7, in the House.
May 25, vetoed.
Senate Journal, 1 sess. 49 Cong. pp. 224, 565, 603 P, 701, 716, 717, 732, 803 O, 805, 1080, 1138.——*House Journal, 1 sess. 49 Cong.* pp. 1336, 1354, 1447, 1540, 1543 P, 1588.

146. Pension to Mrs. A. C. Owen. [§ 74.]
S. 1850, 1 sess. 49 Cong. "An act granting a pension to Mrs. Annie C. Owen."
1886. Mar. 11 to Apr. 21, in the Senate.——Apr. 22 to May 14, in the House.
May 28, vetoed.
Senate Journal, 1 sess. 49 Cong. pp. 411, 552, 603 P, 741, 760, 761, 768, 823 O, 824, 1184.——*House Journal, 1 sess. 49 Cong.* pp. 1337, 1536, 1610, 1611 P, 1653.

147. Pension to J. D. Haworth. [§ 74.]
S. 1253, 1 sess. 49 Cong. "An act granting a pension to J. D. Haworth."
1886. Jan. 27 to Apr. 21, in the Senate.——Apr. 22 to May 14, in the House.
May 28, vetoed.
Senate Journal, 1 sess. 49 Cong. pp. 213, 583, 604 P, 741, 760, 761, 768, 824 O, 825, 1080, 1138.——*House Journal, 1 sess. 49 Cong.* pp. 1336, 1353, 1535, 1610, 1611 P, 1653.

148. Pension to Mrs. R. Eldridge. [§ 74.]
H. R. 2145, 1 sess. 49 Cong. "An act for the relief of Rebecca Eldridge."
1886. Jan. 6 to Feb. 12, in the House.——Feb. 15 to Apr. 21, in the Senate.
May 28, vetoed.
House Journal, 1 sess. 49 Cong. pp. 254, 567, 634, 636 P, 1338, 1351, 1410, 1541, 1542, 1607, 1747 O.——*Senate Journal, 1 sess. 49 Cong.* pp. 287, 288, 565, 605 P, 702, 742.

149. Pension to Mrs. E. C. Bangham. [§ 74.]
H. R. 1582, 1 sess. 49 Cong. "An act for the relief of Eleanor C. Bangham."
1886. Jan. 5 to Jan. 29, in the House.——Feb. 1 to Apr. 21, in the Senate.
May 28, vetoed.
House Journal, 1 sess. 49 Cong. pp. 221, 425, 506, 507 P, 1338, 1351, 1406, 1541, 1542, 1607, 1747 O.——*Senate Journal, 1 sess. 49 Cong.* pp. 229, 230, 479, 600 P, 702, 742.

150. Pension to S. W. Harden. [§ 74.]
H. R. 1406, 1 sess. 49 Cong. "An act granting a pension to Simmons W. Harden."
1886. Jan. 5 to Feb. 12, in the House.——Feb. 15 to Apr. 21, in the Senate.
May 28, vetoed.
House Journal, 1 sess. 49 Cong. pp. 212, 567, 634, 636 P, 1338, 1351, 1406, 1541, 1542, 1607, 1748 O, 2147.——*Senate Journal, 1 sess. 49 Cong.* pp. 287, 288, 498, 600 P, 702, 742.

151. Pension to M. Romahn. [§ 74.]
S. 1441, 1 sess. 49 Cong. "An act granting a pension to M. Romahn."
1886. Feb. 9 to Apr. 21, in the Senate.——Apr. 22 to May 14, in the House.
June 1, vetoed.
Senate Journal, 1 sess. 49 Cong. pp. 268, 560, 606 P, 741, 760, 761, 768, 833 O, 834, 1080, 1138. *House Journal, 1 sess. 49 Cong.* pp. 1337, 1354, 1451, 1610, 1611 P, 1653.

168 . *List of Vetoes.* [APP. A

152. Pension to J. S. Williams. [§ 74.]
S. 789, 1 sess. 49 Cong. "An act granting a pension to John S. Williams."
1885. Dec. 21 to 1886, Apr. 21, in the Senate.——1886, Apr. 22 to May 21, in the House.
1886. June 2, vetoed.—— Aug. 4, reconsidered by the Senate; vote, 19–15.
Senate Journal, 1 sess. 49 Cong. pp. 118, 491, 597 P, 782, 807, 808, 813, 845 O, 846, 1080, 1138, 1281 R.—— *House Journal, 1 sess. 49 Cong.* pp. 1335, 1353, 1449, 1678, 1679 P, 1719.

153. Pension to J. E. O'Shea. [§§ 74, 79.]
S. 327, 1 sess. 49 Cong. "An act granting a pension to James E. O'Shea."
1885. Dec. 9 to 1886, Apr. 21, in the Senate.——1886, Apr. 22 to May 21, in the House.
1886. June 2, vetoed.
Senate Journal, 1 sess. 49 Cong. pp. 67, 582, 603 P, 782, 807, 808, 813, 846 O, 847, 1080, 1138.—— *House Journal, 1 sess. 49 Cong.* pp. 1335, 1352, 1607, 1678, 1679 P, 1719.

154. Pension to A. F. Stevens. [§ 74.]
S. 1726, 1 sess. 49 Cong. "An act granting a pension to Augustus Field Stevens."
1886. Mar. 2 to Apr. 21, in the Senate.—— Apr. 22 to May 21, in the House.
June 2, vetoed.
Senate Journal, 1 sess. 49 Cong. pp. 360, 583, 604 P, 782, 807, 808, 813, 847 O, 848, 1080, 1139.—— *House Journal, 1 sess. 49 Cong.* pp. 1337, 1354, 1578, 1679 P, 1719.

155. Pension to Mrs. M. D. Marchand. [§ 74.]
S. 226, 1 sess. 49 Cong. "An act granting a pension to Margaret D. Marchand."
1885. Dec. 9 to 1886, Mar. 19, in the Senate.——1886, Mar. 19 to May 28, in the House.
1886. June 19, vetoed.
Senate Journal, 1 sess. 49 Cong. pp. 63, 358, 453 P, 830, 851, 852, 890, 954 O, 955, 979, 1075, 1279.—— *House Journal, 1 sess. 49 Cong.* pp. 988, 1027, 1707, 1749, 1750 P, 1793.

* **156. Pension to T. S. Hopkins.** [§ 76.]
S. 183, 1 sess. 49 Cong. "An act for the relief of Thomas S. Hopkins, late of Company C, Sixteenth Maine Volunteers."
1885. Dec. 8 to 1886, Apr. 21, in the Senate.——1886, Apr. 22 to May 28, in the House.
1886. June 19, vetoed.—— 1887, Feb. 23, reconsidered by the Senate; passed over the veto, 55 to 7.—— Mar. 3, by the House; vote, 153–95.
Senate Journal, 1 sess. 49 Cong. pp. 54, 475, 595 P, 830, 851, 852, 890, 955 O, 956, 979, 1185.—— *House Journal, 1 sess. 49 Cong.* pp. 1335, 1352, 1673, 1749, 1750 P, 1793.
—— *Senate Journal, 2 sess. 49 Cong.* p. 414 R.—— *House Journal, 2 sess. 49 Cong.* pp. 726, 826 R.

* **157. Public building at Sioux City.** [§ 93.]
S. 763, 1 sess. 49 Cong. "An act for the erection of a public building at Sioux City, Iowa."
1885. Dec. 21 to 1886, Feb. 9, in the Senate.——1886, Feb. 11 to June 5, in the House.
1886. June 19, vetoed.——1887, Mar. 3, reconsidered by the Senate; passed over the veto, 38 to 19.—— Mar. 3, by the House; vote, 109–72.
Senate Journal, 1 sess. 49 Cong. pp. 117, 218, 271 P, 855, 856, 879, 887, 898, 959 O, 960.—— *House Journal, 1 sess. 49 Cong.* pp. 615, 628, 885, 1799 P, 1820, 1837.——
Senate Journal, 2 sess. 49 Cong. p. 562 R.—— *House Journal, 2 sess. 49 Cong.* pp. 842, 853 R.

158. Public building at Zanesville. [§ 93.]

S. 206, 1 sess. 49 Cong. "An act to provide for the erection of a public building in the city of Zanesville, Ohio."

1885. Dec. 8 to 1886, Feb. 9, in the Senate. —— 1886, Feb. 11 to June 5, in the House.
1886. June 19, vetoed.

Senate Journal, 1 sess. 49 Cong. pp. 55, 246, 271 P, 855, 856, 879, 887, 898, 957 O, 959. —— *House Journal, 1 sess. 49 Cong.* pp. 614, 627, 681, 1799 P, 1820, 1837.

159. Pension to J. Hunter. [§ 74.]

H. 1990, 1 sess. 49 Cong. "An act granting a pension to John Hunter."
1886. Jan. 6 to Mar. 12, in the House. —— Mar. 15 to May 26, in the Senate.
June 19, vetoed.

House Journal, 1 sess. 49 Cong. pp. 247, 814, 916, 917 P, 1725, 1756, 1856, 1955 O. —— *Senate Journal, 1 sess. 49 Cong.* pp. 424, 425, 677, 810, 811 P, 831, 832.

160. Pension to John Taylor. [§ 73.]

H. R. 3826, 1 sess. 49 Cong. "An act for the relief of John Taylor."
1886. Jan. 11 to Mar. 5, in the House. —— Mar. 8 to May 26, in the Senate.
June 19, vetoed.

House Journal, 1 sess. 49 Cong. pp. 345, 743, 851, 852 P, 1725, 1756, 1856, 1953 O. —— *Senate Journal, 1 sess. 49 Cong.* pp. 393, 396, 692, 811 P, 831, 832.

161. Pension to C. W. Tiller. [§ 75.]

H. R. 4002, 1 sess. 49 Cong. "An act granting a pension to Carter W. Tiller."
1886. Jan. 18 to Mar. 5, in the House. —— Mar. 8 to May 26, in the Senate.
June 19, vetoed. —— 1887, Feb. 2, reconsidered by the House; vote, 136-115.

House Journal, 1 sess. 49 Cong. pp. 394, 742, 850, 851 P, 1725, 1756, 1856, 1953 O, 2079, 2102, 2146, 2222. —— *Senate Journal, 1 sess. 49 Cong.* pp. 393, 396, 692, 811 P, 831, 832. —— *House Journal, 2 sess. 49 Cong.* pp. 467, 468 R, 469, 470.

162. Pension to Joel D. Monroe. [§ 74.]

H. R. 4058, 1 sess. 49 Cong. "An act for the relief of Joel D. Monroe."
1886. Jan. 18 to Mar. 5, in the House. —— Mar. 8 to May 26, in the Senate.
June 19, vetoed.

House Journal, 1 sess. 49 Cong. pp. 397, 742, 850, 851 P, 1725, 1756, 1856, 1953 O, 2397. —— *Senate Journal, 1 sess. 49 Cong.* pp. 393, 396, 678, 810, 811 P, 831, 832.

163. Pension to F. J. Leese. [§ 74.]

H. R. 3624, 1 sess. 49 Cong. "An act granting a pension to Frederick J. Leese."
1886. Jan. 11 to Mar. 19, in the House. —— Mar. 22 to May 26, in the Senate.
June 21, vetoed.

House Journal, 1 sess. 49 Cong. pp. 337, 911, 991, 992 P, 1725, 1756, 1856, 1955 O. —— *Senate Journal, 1 sess. 49 Cong.* pp. 458, 459, 678, 810, 811 P, 831, 832.

164. Pension to H. Hipple, Jr. [§ 74.]

H. R. 6897, 1 sess. 49 Cong. "An act granting a pension to Henry Hipple, Jr."
1886. Mar. 16 to Apr. 9, in the House. —— Apr. 12 to May 26, in the Senate.
June 21, vetoed.

House Journal, 1 sess. 49 Cong. pp. 943, 1172, 1206 P, 1726, 1756, 1856, 1954 O. —— *Senate Journal, 1 sess. 49 Cong.* pp. 544, 678, 810, 811 P, 831, 832.

165. Pension to John W. Farris. [§ 73.]

H. R. 6136, 1 sess. 49 Cong. "An act granting an increase of pension to John W. Farris."

1886. Mar. 1 to Apr. 9, in the House. —— Apr. 12 to May 26, in the Senate.

June 21, vetoed. —— 1887, Feb. 22, reconsidered by the House; vote, 131–74.

House Journal, 1 sess. 49 Cong. pp. 791, 1170, 1206 P, 1726, 1756, 1954 O, 2225, 2393, 2409. —— *Senate Journal, 1 sess. 49 Cong.* pp. 544, 675, 810 P, 831, 832. —— *House Journal, 2 sess. 49 Cong.* pp. 682 R, 683.

166. Pension to E. P. Hensley. [§ 74.]

H. R. 1707, 1 sess. 49 Cong. "An act granting a pension to Elijah P. Hensley."

1886. Jan. 5 to Mar. 19, in the House. —— Mar. 22 to May 26, in the Senate.

June 21, vetoed.

House Journal, 1 sess. 49 Cong. pp. 227, 846, 991, 992 P, 1725, 1756, 1856, 1955 O. —— *Senate Journal, 1 sess. 49 Cong.* pp. 458, 459, 686, 810 P, 831, 832.

167. Pension to Mrs. E. Luce. [§ 74.]

H. R. 5997, 1 sess. 49 Cong. "An act granting a pension to Elizabeth Luce."

1886. Mar. 1 to Mar. 26, in the House. —— Mar. 29 to May 26, in the Senate.

June 19, vetoed. —— July 26, reconsidered by the House; vote, 116–124.

House Journal, 1 sess. 49 Cong. pp. 786, 962, 1066, 1067 P, 1726, 1756, 1856, 1956 O, 2163, 2222 R. —— *Senate Journal, 1 sess. 49 Cong.* pp. 488, 692, 811 P, 831, 832.

168. Pension to Mrs. E. S. De Krafft. [§ 71.]

S. 2223, 1 sess. 49 Cong. "An act granting a pension to Elizabeth S. De Krafft."

1886. Apr. 21, in the Senate. —— Apr. 22 to May 28, in the House.

June 21, vetoed.

Senate Journal, 1 sess. 49 Cong. pp. 591, 604 P, 830, 851, 852, 890, 952 O, 954, 979, 1080, 1138. —— *House Journal, 1 sess. 49 Cong.* pp. 1338, 1355, 1698, 1749, 1750 P, 1793.

169. Pension to Mrs. C. R. Schenck. [§ 74.]

S. 1584, 1 sess. 49 Cong. "An act for the relief of Cornelia R. Schenck."

1886. Feb. 18 to Apr. 21, in the Senate. —— Apr. 22 to May 28, in the House.

June 21, vetoed.

Senate Journal, 1 sess. 49 Cong. pp. 311, 582, 603 P, 830, 851, 852, 890, 956 O, 957, 979, 1080, 1138. —— *House Journal, 1 sess. 49 Cong.* pp. 1337, 1354, 1448, 1749, 1750 P, 1793.

170. Pension to Alfred Denny. [§ 74.]

S. 1192, 1 sess. 49 Cong. "An act granting a pension to Alfred Denny."

1886. Jan. 21 to Apr. 21, in the Senate. —— Apr. 22 to June 4, in the House.

June 22, vetoed.

Senate Journal, 1 sess. 49 Cong. pp. 197, 560, 605 P, 855, 879, 887, 898, 974 O, 975, 1080, 1138. —— *House Journal, 1 sess. 49 Cong.* pp. 1336, 1353, 1451, 1797 P, 1837.

171. Pension to W. H. Beck. [§ 74.]

S. 1400, 1 sess. 49 Cong. "An act granting a pension to William H. Beck."

1886. Feb. 5 to Apr. 21, in the Senate. —— Apr. 22 to June 4, in the House.

June 22, vetoed.

Senate Journal, 1 sess. 49 Cong. pp. 251, 582, 603 P, 855, 879, 887, 898, 976 O, 977, 1080, 1138. —— *House Journal, 1 sess. 49 Cong.* pp. 1337, 1354, 1449, 1797 P, 1838.

172. Pension to Mrs. M. J. Nottage. [§ 74.]

S. 2005, 1 sess. 49 Cong. "An act granting a pension to Mary J. Nottage."

1886. Mar. 30 to Apr. 21, in the Senate. —— Apr. 22 to June 4, in the House.

June 22, vetoed. —— Aug. 3, reconsidered by the Senate; vote, 26–19.

Senate Journal, 1 sess. 49 Cong. pp. 493, 539, 597 P, 855, 879, 887, 898, 973 O, 974, 1023, 1080, 1127, 1211, 1264 R. —— *House Journal, 1 sess. 49 Cong.* pp. 1337, 1355, 1452, 1797 P, 1838.

173. Pension to Mrs. M. Parsons. [§ 74.]
S. 342, 1 sess. 49 Cong. "An act granting a pension to Marrilla Parsons, of Detroit, Michigan."
1885. Dec. 10 to 1886, Apr. 21, in the Senate. —— 1886, Apr. 22 to June 4, in the House.
1886. June 22, vetoed.
Senate Journal, 1 sess. 49 Cong. pp. 72, 584, 604 P, 855, 879, 887, 898, 971 O, 972, 1185. —— *House Journal, 1 sess. 49 Cong.* pp. 1335, 1352, 1448, 1797 P, 1837.

174. Pension to Mrs. H. Welch. [§ 74.]
S. 1383, 1 sess. 49 Cong. "An act granting a pension to Harriet Welch."
1886. Feb. 4 to Apr. 21, in the Senate. —— Apr. 22 to June 4, in the House.
June 22, vetoed.
Senate Journal, 1 sess. 49 Cong. pp. 248, 491, 595 P, 855, 879, 887, 898, 975 O, 976, 1080, 1138. —— *House Journal, 1 sess. 49 Cong.* pp. 1336, 1354, 1448, 1797 P, 1837.

175. Pension to J. Butler. [§ 74.]
S. 2025, 1 sess. 49 Cong. "An act granting a pension to James Butler."
1886. Apr. 1 to Apr. 21, in the Senate. —— Apr. 22 to June 4, in the House.
June 22, vetoed.
Senate Journal, 1 sess. 49 Cong. pp. 505, 565, 603 P, 855, 879, 887, 898, 972 O, 973, 1080, 1138. —— *House Journal, 1 sess. 49 Cong.* pp. 1337, 1355, 1451, 1797 P, 1838.

176. Pension to Robert Holsey. [§ 74.]
S. 1288, 1 sess. 49 Cong. "An act granting a pension to Robert Holsey."
1886. Jan. 29 to Apr. 21, in the Senate. —— Apr. 22 to June 4, in the House.
June 22, vetoed.
Senate Journal, 1 sess. 49 Cong. pp. 224, 583, 604 P, 855, 879, 887, 898, 977 O, 978, 1080, 1138. —— *House Journal, 1 sess. 49 Cong.* pp. 1336, 1354, 1449, 1797 P, 1837.

177. Pension to William Bishop. [§§ 74, 79.]
H. R. 6688, 1 sess. 49 Cong. "An act for the relief of William Bishop."
1886. Mar. 16 to Apr. 23, in the House. —— Apr. 26 to May 24, in the Senate.
June 23, vetoed.
House Journal, 1 sess. 49 Cong. pp. 934, 1313, 1361, 1362 P, 1710, 1731, 2004 O. —— *Senate Journal, 1 sess. 49 Cong.* pp. 635, 636, 675, 793 P, 816, 817.

178. Pension to J. Steward. [§ 71.]
H. R. 7979, 1 sess. 49 Cong. "An act granting a pension to Jackson Steward."
1886. Apr. 19 to May 14, in the House. —— May 17 to June 5, in the Senate.
June 23, vetoed.
House Journal, 1 sess. 49 Cong. pp. 1292, 1449, 1611, 1612 P, 1824, 1846, 2005 O. —— *Senate Journal, 1 sess. 49 Cong.* pp. 746, 796, 861 P, 891, 896.

179. Pension to Mrs. M. A. Van Etten. [§§ 74, 79.]
H. R. 6170, 1 sess. 49 Cong. "An act granting a pension to Mary A. Van Etten."
1886. Mar. 1 to May 14, in the House. —— May 17 to June 5, in the Senate.
June 23, vetoed.
House Journal, 1 sess. 49 Cong. pp. 793, 1453, 1611, 1612 P, 1823, 1845, 1997 O. —— *Senate Journal, 1 sess. 49 Cong.* pp. 746, 829, 861 P, 891, 895.

180. Pension to Mrs. A. E. Travers. [§ 74.]
H. R. 6753, 1 sess. 49 Cong. "An act granting a pension to Mrs. Alice E. Travers."
1886. Mar. 16 to May 7, in the House.——May 10 to June 5, in the Senate.
June 23, vetoed.
House Journal, 1 sess. 49 Cong. pp. 937, 1448, 1541, 1542 P, 1823, 1845, 1997 O.
——*Senate Journal, 1 sess. 49 Cong.* pp. 700, 759, 860 P, 891, 896.

181. Pension to Philip Arner. [§ 74.]
H. R. 6266, 1 sess. 49 Cong. "An act granting a pension to Philip Arner."
1886. Mar. 1 to Apr. 9, in the House.——Apr. 12 to June 5, in the Senate.
June 23, vetoed.
House Journal, 1 sess. 49 Cong. pp. 797, 1171, 1205, 1206 P, 1823, 1845, 1997 O.
——*Senate Journal, 1 sess. 49 Cong.* pp. 544, 760, 860 P, 891, 895.

182. Pension to J. D. Cotton. [§ 75.]
H. R. 6117, 1 sess. 49 Cong. "An act granting a pension to James D. Cotton."
1886. Mar. 1 to Apr. 23, in the House.——Apr. 26 to June 5, in the Senate.
June 23, vetoed.
House Journal, 1 sess. 49 Cong. pp. 791, 1261, 1361, 1362 P, 1823, 1845, 1998 O.
——*Senate Journal, 1 sess. 49 Cong.* pp. 635, 636, 715, 859 P, 891, 895.

183. Pension to Mrs. M. A. Miller. [§ 74.]
H. R. 1816, 1 sess. 49 Cong. "An act granting a pension to Mary Ann Miller."
1886. Jan. 6 to Mar. 12, in the House.——Mar. 15 to May 24, in the Senate.
June 23, vetoed.
House Journal, 1 sess. 49 Cong. pp. 240, 812, 917 P, 1710, 1731, 1998 O.——*Senate Journal, 1 sess. 49 Cong.* pp. 424, 425, 675, 793 P, 816, 817.

184. Pension to Mrs. M. Anderson. [§ 74.]
H. R. 7436, 1 sess. 49 Cong. "An act to grant a pension to Mary Anderson."
1886. Mar. 29 to May 7, in the House.——May 10 to June 5, in the Senate.
June 23, vetoed.——July 30, reconsidered by the House; vote, 120–95.
House Journal, 1 sess. 49 Cong. pp. 1086, 1448, 1541, 1542 P, 1824, 1846, 1998 O, 2328, 2390, 2409 R.——*Senate Journal, 1 sess. 49 Cong.* pp. 700, 759, 860 P, 891, 896.

185. Pension to D. T. Elderkin. [§ 74.]
H. R. 5995, 1 sess. 49 Cong. "An act granting a pension to David T. Elderkin."
1886. Mar. 1 to Mar. 26, in the House.——Mar. 29 to May 24, in the Senate.
June 23, vetoed.
House Journal, 1 sess. 49 Cong. pp. 786, 962, 1066, 1067 P, 1710, 1731, 1999 O, 2225, 2409.——*Senate Journal, 1 sess. 49 Cong.* pp. 488, 675, 793 P, 816, 817.

186. Pension to G. W. Guyse. [§ 74.]
H. R. 3205, 1 sess. 49 Cong. "An act granting a pension to George W. Guyse."
1886. Jan. 11 to Feb. 19, in the House.——Feb. 23 to May 24, in the Senate.
June 23, vetoed.
House Journal, 1 sess. 49 Cong. pp. 319, 620, 715, 716 P, 1710, 1731, 2000 O.——*Senate Journal, 1 sess. 49 Cong.* pp. 323, 324, 646, 793 P, 816, 817.

187. Pension to S. Miller. [§ 74.]
H. R. 7401, 1 sess. 49 Cong. "An act granting a pension to Samuel Miller."
1886. Mar. 29 to May 7, in the House.——May 10 to June 5, in the Senate.
June 23, vetoed.

House Journal, 1 sess. 49 Cong. pp. 1085, 1410, 1541, 1542 P, 1824, 1846, 2000 O.
—— *Senate Journal, 1 sess. 49 Cong.* pp. 700, 766, 861 P, 891, 896.

188. Pension to G. C. Hawley. [§ 74.]

H. R. 424, 1 sess. 49 Cong. "An act to pension Giles C. Hawley."
1885. Dec. 21 to 1886, Feb. 26, in the House.—— 1886, Mar. 1 to May 24, in the Senate.
1886. June 23, vetoed.
House Journal, 1 sess. 49 Cong. pp. 157, 553, 767 P, 1710, 1731, 2000 O.—— *Senate Journal, 1 sess. 49 Cong.* pp. 347, 675, 793 P, 816, 817.

189. Pension to Charles Schuler. [§ 71.]

H. R. 7298, 1 sess. 49 Cong. "An act for the relief of Charles Schuler."
1886. Mar. 29 to Apr. 23, in the House.—— Apr. 26 to May 24, in the Senate.
June 23, vetoed.
House Journal, 1 sess. 49 Cong. pp. 1080, 1261, 1361, 1362 P, 1710, 1731, 2001 O.
—— *Senate Journal, 1 sess. 49 Cong.* pp. 636, 675, 793 P, 816, 817.

190. Pension to Mrs. M. S. Woodson. [§ 74.]

H. R. 7073, 1 sess. 49 Cong. "An act granting a pension to Mary S. Woodson."
1886. Mar. 22 to Apr. 23, in the House.—— Apr. 26 to June 5, in the Senate.
June 23, vetoed.
House Journal, 1 sess. 49 Cong. pp. 1013, 1261, 1361, 1362 P, 1823, 1845, 2001 O.
—— *Senate Journal, 1 sess. 49 Cong.* pp. 635, 636, 723, 859 P, 891, 896.

191. Pension to A. J. Wilson. [§ 74.]

H. R. 7108, 1 sess. 49 Cong. "An act granting a pension to Andrew J. Wilson."
1886. Mar. 22 to Apr. 9, in the House.—— Apr. 12 to June 5, in the Senate.
June 23, vetoed.—— July 29, reconsidered by the House; vote, 106-86.
House Journal, 1 sess. 49 Cong. pp. 1015, 1174, 1206 P, 1823, 1845, 2001 O, 2079, 2392, 2400 R.—— *Senate Journal, 1 sess. 49 Cong.* pp. 544, 707, 859 P, 891, 896.

192. Pension to C. West. [§ 74.]

H. R. 7222, 1 sess. 49 Cong. "An act granting a pension to Callie West."
1886. Mar. 28 to Apr. 23, in the House.—— Apr. 26 to June 5, in the Senate.
June 23, vetoed.
House Journal, 1 sess. 49 Cong. pp. 1077, 1361, 1362 P, 1824, 1845, 2002 O.——
Senate Journal, 1 sess. 49 Cong. pp. 636, 723, 859 P, 891, 896.

193. Pension to Julia Connelly. [§ 74.]

H. R. 6257, 1 sess. 49 Cong. "An act for the relief of Julia Connelly."
1886. Mar. 1 to Apr. 2, in the House.—— Apr. 5 to June 5, in the Senate.
June 23, vetoed.
House Journal, 1 sess. 49 Cong. pp. 797, 1033, 1132, 1133 P, 1823, 1845, 2002 O.
—— *Senate Journal, 1 sess. 49 Cong.* pp. 512, 513, 796, 861 P, 891, 895.

194. Pension to B. Schultz. [§ 71.]

H. R. 6774, 1 sess. 49 Cong. "An act granting a pension to Bruno Schultz."
1886. Mar. 16 to Apr. 23, in the House.—— Apr. 26 to June 5, in the Senate.
June 23, vetoed.
House Journal, 1 sess. 49 Cong. pp. 938, 1311, 1361, 1362 P, 1823, 1845, 2002 O,
—— *Senate Journal, 1 sess. 49 Cong.* pp. 635, 636, 715, 859 P, 891, 896.

195. Pension to Mrs. L. C. Beezely. [§ 74.]

H. R. 576, 1 sess. 49 Cong. "An act for the relief of Louisa C. Beezely."

1885. Dec. 21 to 1886, Apr. 23 (?), in the House.——1886, Apr. 26 to June 5, in the Senate.
1886. June 23, vetoed.
House Journal, 1 sess. 49 Cong. pp. 164, 1260, 1360, 1362 P, 1821, 1844, 2002 O.
——*Senate Journal, 1 sess. 49 Cong.* pp. 635, 636, 707, 858 P, 891, 895.

196. Pension to Mrs. Maria Hunter. [§ 71.]
H. R. 7167, 1 sess. 49 Cong. "An act for the relief of Mrs. Maria Hunter."
1886. Mar. 22 to Apr. 9, in the House.——Apr. 12 to May 24, in the Senate. June 23, vetoed.——July 30, reconsidered by the House; vote, 111–108.
House Journal, 1 sess. 49 Cong. pp. 1017, 1173, 1206 P, 1710, 1716, 1736, 2007 O, 2193, 2222, 2395, 2407 R.——*Senate Journal, 1 sess. 49 Cong.* pp. 544, 647, 790 P, 816, 817.

197. Pension to Mrs. S. Harbaugh. [§ 74.]
H. R. 6895, 1 sess. 49 Cong. "An act granting a pension to Sarah Harbaugh."
1886. Mar. 16 to May 7, in the House.——May 10 to June 5, in the Senate. June 23, vetoed.
House Journal, 1 sess. 49 Cong. pp. 943, 1358, 1541, 1542 P, 1823, 1845, 2008 O.
——*Senate Journal, 1 sess. 49 Cong.* pp. 700, 766, 861 P, 891, 896.

198. Pension to Mrs. Anna A. Probert. [§ 74.]
H. R. 7703, 1 sess. 49 Cong. "An act granting a pension to Anna A. Probert."
1886. Apr. 12 to May 14, in the House.——May 17 to June 5, in the Senate. June 23, vetoed.
House Journal, 1 sess. 49 Cong. pp. 1227, 1449, 1611, 1612 P, 1824, 1846, 2003 O.
——*Senate Journal, 1 sess. 49 Cong.* pp. 745, 746, 806, 861 P, 891, 896.

199. Pension to Mrs. M. McIlwain. [§ 74.]
H. R. 7162, 1 sess. 49 Cong. "An act granting a pension to Martha McIlwain."
1886. Mar. 22 to May 14, in the House.——May 17 to June 5, in the Senate. June 23, vetoed.
House Journal, 1 sess. 49 Cong. pp. 1017, 1535, 1611, 1612 P, 1823, 1845, 2003 O.
——*Senate Journal, 1 sess. 49 Cong.* pp. 746, 806, 861 P, 891, 896.

200. Pension to Clark Boon. [§ 74.]
H. R. 7931, 1 sess. 49 Cong. "An act increasing the pension of Clark Boon."
1886. Apr. 19 to May 14, in the House.——May 17 to June 5, in the Senate. June 23, vetoed.
House Journal, 1 sess. 49 Cong. pp. 1290, 1451, 1611, 1612 P, 1824, 1846, 2004 O.
——*Senate Journal, 1 sess. 49 Cong.* pp. 746, 806, 861 P, 891, 896.

201. Pension to James H. Darling. [§ 74.]
H. R. 7257, 1 sess. 49 Cong. "An act granting a pension to James H. Darling."
1886. Mar. 29 to May 7, in the House.——May 10 to June 5, in the Senate. June 23, vetoed.
House Journal, 1 sess. 49 Cong. pp. 1079, 1357, 1541, 1542 P, 1824, 1846, 2004 O, 2399.——*Senate Journal, 1 sess. 49 Cong.* pp. 700, 759, 860 P, 891, 896.

202. Pension to Charles A. Chase. [§ 74.]
H. R. 6372, 1 sess. 49 Cong. "An act to pension Charles A. Chase."
1886. Mar. 1 to Apr. 16, in the House.——Apr. 19 to June 5, in the Senate. June 23, vetoed.

203. Pension to H. Tillman. [§ 73.]

H. R. 7614, 1 sess. 49 Cong. "An act granting an increase of pension to Hezekiah Tillman."

1886. Apr. 5 to Apr. 23, in the House.——Apr. 26 to June 5, in the Senate. June 23, vetoed.

House Journal, 1 sess. 49 Cong. pp. 1151, 1311, 1362, 1363 P, 1824, 1846, 2006 O. —— *Senate Journal, 1 sess. 49 Cong.* pp. 636, 723, 859 P, 891, 896.

204. Pension to W. H. Starr. [§ 71.]

H. R. 6718, 1 sess. 49 Cong. "An act granting a pension to William H. Starr."

1886. Mar. 16 to Apr. 23, in the House.——Apr. 26 to June 5, in the Senate. June 23, vetoed.

House Journal, 1 sess. 49 Cong. pp. 935, 1271, 1361, 1362 P, 1823, 1845, 2006 O. —— *Senate Journal, 1 sess. 49 Cong.* pp. 635, 636, 723, 859 P, 891, 896.

205. Pension to Mrs. M. Norman. [§ 74.]

H. R. 6192, 1 sess. 49 Cong. "An act granting a pension to Mary Norman."

1886. Mar. 1 to Apr. 2, in the House.——Apr. 5 to May 24, in the Senate. June 23, vetoed.

House Journal, 1 sess. 49 Cong. pp. 794, 963, 1133 P, 1710, 1731, 2006 O, 2147, 2407. —— *Senate Journal, 1 sess. 49 Cong.* pp. 512, 513, 676, 793 P, 816, 817.

206. Pension to Joseph Tuttle. [§ 75.]

H. R. 7109, 1 sess. 49 Cong. "An act granting a pension to Joseph Tuttle."

1886. Mar. 22 to Apr. 9, in the House.——Apr. 12 to June 5, in the Senate. June 23, vetoed.

House Journal, 1 sess. 49 Cong. pp. 1015, 1174, 1206 P, 1823, 1845, 1999 O. —— *Senate Journal, 1 sess. 49 Cong.* pp. 544, 707, 859 P, 891, 896.

207. Pension to J. S. Kirkpatrick. [§ 74.]

S. 1797, 1 sess. 49 Cong. "An act granting a pension to John S. Kirkpatrick."

1886. Mar. 8 to Apr. 21, in the Senate.——Apr. 22 to June 12, in the House. June 29, vetoed.

Senate Journal, 1 sess. 49 Cong. pp. 394, 583, 604 P, 903, 941, 966, 1024 O, 1025, 1165.——*House Journal, 1 sess. 49 Cong.* pp. 1337, 1354, 1604, 1870, 1871 P, 1914.

208. Pension to N. Parker. [§ 72.]

S. 1077, 1 sess. 49 Cong. "An act granting a pension to Newcomb Parker."

1886. Jan. 14 to Apr. 21, in the Senate.——Apr. 22 to June 12, in the House. June 29, vetoed.

Senate Journal, 1 sess. 49 Cong. pp. 173, 565, 603 P, 903, 941, 966, 1025 O, 1026, 1165.——*House Journal, 1 sess. 49 Cong.* pp. 1336, 1353, 1578, 1870, 1871 P, 1914.

209. Pension to W. Boone. [§ 74.]

H. R. 473, 1 sess. 49 Cong. "An act granting a pension to William Boone."

1885. Dec. 21 to 1886, Mar. 12, in the House.——1886, Mar. 15 to May 21, in the Senate. 1886. July 2, vetoed.

House Journal, 1 sess. 49 Cong. pp. 160, 812, 917 P, 1683, 1720, 2085 O. —— *Senate Journal, 1 sess. 49 Cong.* pp. 424, 425, 638, 778 P, 809, 810.

210. Pension to M. L. Bundy. [§ 66.]

S. 365, 1 sess. 49 Cong. "An act for the relief of Martin L. Bundy."

1885. Dec. 10 to 1886, May 17, in the Senate.—— 1886, May 18 to June 16, in the House.
1886. July 3, vetoed.
Senate Journal, 1 sess. 49 Cong. pp. 72, 321, 747 P, 918, 966, 981, 1053 O, 1054.
—— *House Journal, 1 sess. 49 Cong.* pp. 1651, 1656, 1894, 1903, 1904 P, 1961.

211. Pension to A. F. Loomis. [§ 72.]

H. R. 7018, 1 sess. 49 Cong. "An act granting a pension to Aretus F. Loomis."
1886. Mar. 22 to Apr. 16, in the House.—— Apr. 19 to June 17, in the Senate.
July 5, vetoed.
House Journal, 1 sess. 49 Cong. pp. 1011, 1200, 1277 P, 1919, 1935, 2111 O.——
Senate Journal, 1 sess. 49 Cong. pp. 577, 578, 913, 927 P, 949, 950.

212. Pension to H. L. Kyler. [§ 74.]

H. R. 1818, 1 sess. 49 Cong. "An act granting a pension to H. L. Kyler."
1886. Jan. 6 to Apr. 16, in the House.—— Apr. 19 to June 5, in the Senate.
July 5, vetoed.
House Journal, 1 sess. 49 Cong. pp. 240, 1098, 1276, 1277 P, 1821, 1841, 2111 O.
—— *Senate Journal, 1 sess. 49 Cong.* pp. 577, 578, 715, 859 P, 879, 888.

213. Pension to James T. Irwin. [§ 74.]

H. R. 3640, 1 sess. 49 Cong. "An act granting a pension to James T. Irwin."
1886. Jan. 11 to May 7, in the House.—— May 10 to June 5, in the Senate.
July 5, vetoed.
House Journal, 1 sess. 49 Cong. pp. 337, 1410, 1541, 1542 P, 1821, 1842, 2134 O.——
Senate Journal, 1 sess. 49 Cong. pp. 699, 700, 759, 860 P, 879, 888.

214. Pension to Mrs. R. V. Rowley. [§ 74.]

H. R. 5306, 1 sess. 49 Cong. "An act granting a pension to Roxana V. Rowley."
1886. Feb. 8 to Mar. 19, in the House.—— Mar. 22 to June 5, in the Senate.
July 5, vetoed.
House Journal, 1 sess. 49 Cong. pp. 582, 846, 992, 993 P, 1822, 1842, 2135 O.——
Senate Journal, 1 sess. 49 Cong. pp. 459, 796, 861 P, 879, 888.

215. Pension to Mrs. M. A. Jacoby. [§ 74.]

H. R. 5021, 1 sess. 49 Cong. "An act granting a pension to Margaret A. Jacoby."
1886. Feb. 1 to Mar. 19, in the House.—— Mar. 22 to June 5, in the Senate.
July 5, vetoed.
House Journal, 1 sess. 49 Cong. pp. 523, 847, 991, 992 P, 1822, 1842, 2136 O.——
Senate Journal, 1 sess. 49 Cong. pp. 459, 796, 861 P, 879, 888.

216. Pension to A. Morehead. [§ 74.]

H. R. 3304, 1 sess. 49 Cong. "An act to restore the name of Abner Morehead to the pension-roll."
1886. Jan. 11 to May 7, in the House.—— May 10 to June 5, in the Senate.
July 5, vetoed.
House Journal, 1 sess. 49 Cong. pp. 323, 1447, 1541, 1542 P, 1821, 1842, 2137 O.
—— *Senate Journal, 1 sess. 49 Cong.* pp. 699, 700, 759, 860 P, 879, 888.

217. Pension to E. McKay. [§ 74.]

H. R. 4782, 1 sess. 49 Cong. "An act granting a pension to Elizabeth McKay."
1886. Jan. 26 to Apr. 2, in the House.—— Apr. 5 to June 5, in the Senate.
July 5, vetoed.
House Journal, 1 sess. 49 Cong. pp. 474, 1034, 1132, 1133 P, 1820, 1832, 1842, 2138 O.—— *Senate Journal, 1 sess. 49 Cong.* pp. 511, 513, 708, 862 P, 871, 879, 889.

218. Pension to William Dermody. [§ 74.]
H. R. 1505, 1 sess. 49 Cong. "An act granting a pension to William Dermody."
1886. Jan. 5 to Feb. 19, in the House.—— Feb. 23 to June 5, in the Senate.
July 5, vetoed.
House Journal, 1 sess. 49 Cong. pp. 217, 619, 715, 716 P, 1821, 1841, 2138 O.——
Senate Journal, 1 sess. 49 Cong. pp. 323, 324, 796, 861 P, 879, 887.

219. Pension to W. H. Nevil. [§ 71.]
H. R. 3623, 1 sess. 49 Cong. "An act granting a pension to William H. Nevil."
1886. Jan. 11 to Mar. 26, in the House.—— Mar. 29 to June 5, in the Senate.
July 5, vetoed.
House Journal, 1 sess. 49 Cong. pp. 337, 911, 1066, 1067 P, 1821, 1842, 2139 O.——
Senate Journal, 1 sess. 49 Cong. pp. 488, 706, 858 P, 879, 888.

220. Pension to F. Deming. [§ 74.]
H. R. 2971, 1 sess. 49 Cong. "An act granting a pension to Francis Deming."
1886. Jan. 7 to Apr. 9, in the House.—— Apr. 12 to June 5, in the Senate.
July 5, vetoed.
House Journal, 1 sess. 49 Cong. pp. 295, 1172, 1205, 1206 P, 1821, 1837, 2141 O.
—— *Senate Journal, 1 sess. 49 Cong.* pp. 544, 752, 860 P, 879, 887.

** **221. Pension to J. Romiser.** [§ 74.]
H. R. 1059, 1 sess. 49 Cong. "An act to grant a pension to Joseph Romiser."
1886. Jan. 5 to May 21, in the House.—— May 24 to June 17, in the Senate.
July 5, vetoed.—— July 16, reconsidered by the House; passed over the veto, 175 to 38.—— Aug. 3, by the Senate; passed over the veto, 50 to 0.
House Journal, 1 sess. 49 Cong. pp. 197, 1454, 1679 P, 1919, 1935, 2143 O. 2192, 2229 R, 2230, 2529.—— *Senate Journal, 1 sess. 49 Cong.* pp. 783, 792, 906, 927 P, 949, 950, 1128, 1129, 1139, 1265 R.

222. Pension to James Carroll. [§ 74.]
H. R. 4642, 1 sess. 49 Cong. "An act granting a pension to James Carroll."
1886. Jan. 26 to Mar. 5, in the House.—— Mar. 8 to June 5, in the Senate.
July 6, vetoed.
House Journal, 1 sess. 49 Cong. pp. 468, 850, 851 P, 1822, 1842, 2139 O.——
Senate Journal, 1 sess. 49 Cong. pp. 394, 396, 705, 858 P, 879, 888.

223. Pension to L. W. Scanland. [§ 74.]
H. R. 3043, 1 sess. 49 Cong. "An act granting a pension to Lewis W. Scanland."
1886. Jan. 7 to Apr. 23, in the House.—— Apr. 26 to June 5, in the Senate.
July 6, vetoed.
House Journal, 1 sess. 49 Cong. pp. 298, 1313, 1361, 1363 P, 1821, 1841, 2140 O.
—— *Senate Journal, 1 sess. 49 Cong.* pp. 635, 636, 723, 859 P, 879, 888.

224. Pension to Maria Cunningham. [§ 74.]
H. R. 5414, 1 sess. 49 Cong. "An act granting a pension to Maria Cunningham."
1886. Feb. 8 to May 7, in the House.—— May 10 to June 5, in the Senate.
July 6, vetoed.
House Journal, 1 sess. 49 Cong. pp. 586, 1358, 1541, 1542 P, 1822, 1842, 2137 O.
—— *Senate Journal, 1 sess. 49 Cong.* pp. 700, 759, 860 P, 879, 888.

225. Pension to R. H. Stapleton. [§ 74.]
H. R. 4797, 1 sess. 49 Cong. "An act granting a pension to Robert H. Stapleton."
1886. Jan. 26 to Apr. 16, in the House.—— Apr. 19 to June 5, in the Senate.

1886. July 6, vetoed.
House Journal, 1 sess. 49 Cong. pp. 475, 963, 1276, 1277 P, 1822, 1842, 2136 O. —— *Senate Journal, 1 sess. 49 Cong.* pp. 577, 578, 706, 858 P, 879, 888.

226. **Pension to Mrs. M. Karstetter.** [§ 74.]
H. R. 2043, 1 sess. 49 Cong. "An act to place Mary Karstetter on the pension-roll."
1886. Jan. 6 to Apr. 9, in the House. —— Apr. 12 to June 17, in the Senate.
July 6, vetoed.
House Journal, 1 sess. 49 Cong. pp. 249, 1171, 1206 P, 1919, 1935, 2135 O. —— *Senate Journal, 1 sess. 49 Cong.* pp. 544, 752, 920 P, 949, 950.

227. **Public Building at Duluth.** [§ 93.]
H. R. 5550, 1 sess. 49 Cong. "An act to provide for the erection of a public building at Duluth, Minnesota."
1886. Feb. 11 to Apr. 5, in the House. —— Apr. 6 to June 17, in the Senate.
July 6, vetoed.
House Journal, 1 sess. 49 Cong. pp. 617, 1159 P, 1919, 1935, 2140 O. —— *Senate Journal, 1 sess. 49 Cong.* pp. 517, 877, 927 P, 949, 950.

228. **Pension to Mrs. F. E. Evans.** [§ 74.]
H. R. 4426, 1 sess. 49 Cong. "An act granting a pension to Fannie E. Evans."
1886. Jan. 26 to Feb. 26, in the House. —— Mar. 1 to June 5, in the Senate.
July 6, vetoed.
House Journal, 1 sess. 49 Cong. pp. 458, 691, 767 P, 1822, 1842, 2134 O. —— *Senate Journal, 1 sess. 49 Cong.* pp. 347, 752, 860 P, 879, 888.

229. **Pension to Mrs. S. A. Bradley.** [§ 74.]
H. R. 5394, 1 sess. 49 Cong. "An act granting a pension to Sally Ann Bradley."
1886. Feb. 8 to Mar. 12, in the House. —— Mar. 15 to June 5, in the Senate.
July 6, vetoed. —— 1887, Mar. 3, reconsidered by the House; vote, 123–122.
House Journal, 1 sess. 49 Cong. pp. 585, 812, 917 P, 1822, 1842, 2121 O, 2295, 2388, —— *Senate Journal, 1 sess. 49 Cong.* pp. 425, 705, 858 P, 879, 888. —— *House Journal, 2 sess. 49 Cong.* pp. 640, 641, 832 R.

230. **Pension to Mrs. C. McCarty.** [§ 74.]
H. R. 5603, 1 sess. 49 Cong. "An act granting a pension to Mrs. Catherine McCarty."
1886. Feb. 15 to Mar. 5, in the House. —— Mar. 8 to June 5, in the Senate.
July 6, vetoed. —— July 16, reconsidered in the House; vote, 124–97.
House Journal, 1 sess. 49 Cong. pp. 659, 763, 851, 852 P, 1822, 1843, 2116 O, 2117, 2163, 2225, 2228 R. —— *Senate Journal, 1 sess. 49 Cong.* pp. 394, 396, 705, 858 P, 879, 889.

231. **Pension to E. M. Harrington.** [§ 74.]
H. R. 6648, 1 sess. 49 Cong. "An act for the relief of Edward M. Harrington."
1886. Mar. 8 to Apr. 2, in the House. —— Apr. 5 to June 5, in the Senate.
July 6, vetoed.
House Journal, 1 sess. 49 Cong. pp. 872, 1033, 1132, 1133 P, 1821, 1832, 1843, 2111 O. —— *Senate Journal, 1 sess. 49 Cong.* pp. 512, 513, 708, 857 P, 871, 879, 889.

232. **Right of way to railroads in Northern Montana.** [§ 41.]
S. 2281, 1 sess. 49 Cong. "An act granting to railroads the right of way through the Indian reservation in Northern Montana."
1886. Apr. 29 to June 17, in the Senate. —— June 18 to June 22, in the House.
July 7, vetoed.

Senate Journal, 1 sess. 49 Cong. pp. 653, 766, 919 P, 964, 981, 1003, 1059 O, 1062, 1127.—— *House Journal, 1 sess. 49 Cong.* pp. 1917, 1927, 1961 P, 1987.

233. Pension to Daniel H. Ross. [§ 71.]

H. R. 524, 1 sess. 49 Cong. "An act granting a pension to Daniel H. Ross."
1885. Dec. 21 to 1886, Mar. 5, in the House. —— 1886, Mar. 8 to June 5, in the Senate.
1886. July 9, vetoed.
House Journal, 1 sess. 49 Cong. pp. 162, 762, 850, 851 P, 1820, 1832, 1866, 2018, 2023, 2161 O. —— *Senate Journal, 1 sess. 49 Cong.* pp. 393, 396, 707, 857 P, 1004, 1005.

** 234. Public building at Dayton, Ohio. [§ 93.]

S. 856, 1 sess. 49 Cong. "An act to provide for the erection of a public building in the city of Dayton, Ohio."
1886. Jan. 5 to Feb. 9, in the Senate. —— Feb. 11 to June 19, in the House.
   July 9, vetoed. —— 1887, Mar. 3, reconsidered by the Senate; passed over the veto, 39 to 18. —— Mar. 3, by the House; passed over the veto, 133 to 64.
Senate Journal, 1 sess. 49 Cong. pp. 130, 246, 271 P, 947, 950, 990, 991, 1003, 1082 O, 1083. —— *House Journal, 1 sess. 49 Cong.* pp. 615, 628, 1930 P, 1951, 1994. —— *Senate Journal, 2 sess. 49 Cong.* pp. 561 R, 580. —— *House Journal, 2 sess. 49 Cong.* pp. 842, 851 R, 852.

235. Public building at Asheville, N. C. [§ 93.]

H. R. 5546, 1 sess, 49 Cong. "An act for the erection of a public building at Asheville, North Carolina."
1886. Feb. 11 to Mar. 4, in the House. —— Mar. 4 to June 17, in the Senate.
   July 10, vetoed.
House Journal, 1 sess. 49 Cong. pp. 616, 836, 837 P, 1919, 1992, 2178 O. —— *Senate Journal, 1 sess. 49 Cong.* pp. 377, 380, 877, 927 P, 990, 991.

236. Bridge across Lake Champlain. [§ 98.]

S. 63, 1 sess. 49 Cong. "An act to authorize the construction of a highway bridge across that part of the waters of Lake Champlain lying between the towns of North Hero and Alburgh in the State of Vermont."
1885. Dec. 8 to 1886, Apr. 21, in the Senate. —— 1886, Apr. 22 to July 20, in the House.
1886. July 30, vetoed.
Senate Journal, 1 sess. 49 Cong. pp. 49, 336, 610 P, 1146, 1156, 1160, 1205 O, 1206. —— *House Journal, 1 sess. 49 Cong.* pp. 1329, 1351, 1646, 2280 P, 2308.

237. Public building at Springfield, Mo. [§ 93.]

H. R. 1391, 1 sess. 49 Cong. "An act to provide for the erection of a public building at Springfield, Missouri."
1886. Jan. 5 to June 7, in the House. —— June 8 to July 22, in the Senate.
   July 30, vetoed.
House Journal, 1 sess. 49 Cong. pp. 212, 681, 1828 P, 2308, 2317, 2456 O. —— *Senate Journal, 1 sess. 49 Cong.* pp. 871, 876, 1001, 1152 P, 1157.

238. Pension to W. H. Weaver. [§ 74.]

S. 1421, 1 sess. 49 Cong. "An act granting a pension to William H. Weaver."
1886. Feb. 8 to May 24, in the Senate. —— May 25 to July 23, in the House.
   July 31, vetoed.
Senate Journal, 1 sess. 49 Cong. pp. 260, 639, 789 P, 1161, 1177, 1178, 1179, 1226 O, 1228. —— *House Journal, 1 sess. 49 Cong.* pp. 1711, 1717, 1742, 2155, 2231, 2324 P, 2344.

239. Pension to Mrs. M. J. Hagerman. [§ 74.]
S. 2160, 1 sess. 49 Cong. "An act granting a pension to Mary J. Hagerman."
1886. Apr. 16 to May 24, in the Senate.—— May 25 to July 16, in the House. July 31, vetoed.
Senate Journal, 1 sess. 49 Cong. pp. 570, 639, 789 P, 1128, 1145, 1147, 1228 O, 1229. —— *House Journal, 1 sess. 49 Cong.* pp. 1711, 1718, 1743, 2155, 2231 P, 2277.

240. Pension to Mrs. J. Dow. [§ 74.]
H. R. 3363, 1 sess. 49 Cong. "An act granting a pension to Jeannette Dow."
1886. Jan. 11 to May 28, in the House.—— June 1 to July 16, in the Senate. July 31, vetoed.
House Journal, 1 sess. 49 Cong. pp. 326, 1673, 1749, 1750 P, 2228, 2248, 2475 O.
—— *Senate Journal, 1 sess. 49 Cong.* pp. 830, 832, 962, 1121 P, 1130.

241. Pension to Mrs. R. Barnes. [§ 74.]
H. R. 9106, 1 sess. 49 Cong. "An act granting a pension to Rachel Barnes."
1886. May 24 to June 18, in the House.—— June 21 to July 22, in the Senate. July 31, vetoed.
House Journal, 1 sess. 49 Cong. pp. 1699, 1921, 1922 P, 2308, 2317, 2482 O. ——
Senate Journal, 1 sess. 49 Cong. pp. 949, 984, 1152 P, 1157.

242. Pension to Duncan Forbes. [§ 73.]
H. R. 8336, 1 sess. 49 Cong. "An act granting an increase of pension to Duncan Forbes."
1886. May 1 to May 14, in the House.—— May 17 to July 22, in the Senate. July 31, vetoed.
House Journal, 1 sess. 49 Cong. pp. 1454, 1611, 1612 P, 2308, 2317, 2482 O. ——
Senate Journal, 1 sess. 49 Cong. pp. 746, 1002, 1152 P, 1157.

243. Pension to Mrs. A. Kinney. [§ 74.]
H. R. 5389, 1 sess. 49 Cong. "An act granting a pension to Ann Kinney."
1886. Feb. 8 to June 12, in the House.—— June 15 to July 26, in the Senate. Aug. 4, vetoed.
House Journal, 1 sess. 49 Cong. pp. 585, 1522, 1871, 1872 P, 2356, 2378, 2541, O.
—— *Senate Journal, 1 sess. 49 Cong.* pp. 907, 908, 1137, 1180 P, 1188, 1193.

244. Pension to A. Points. [§ 74.]
H. R. 8556, 1 sess. 49 Cong. "An act granting a pension to Abraham Points."
1886. May 3 to May 28, in the House.—— June 1 to July 26, in the Senate. Aug. 4, vetoed.
House Journal, 1 sess. 49 Cong. pp. 1478, 1673, 1749, 1750 P, 2357, 2379, 2540 O.
—— *Senate Journal, 1 sess. 49 Cong.* pp. 830, 832, 1151, 1181 P, 1189, 1194.

245. Pension to G. W. Cutler. [§ 74.]
H. R. 3551, 1 sess. 49 Cong. "An act granting a pension to George W. Cutler, late a private in Company B, Ninth New Hampshire Volunteers."
1886. Jan. 11 to May 21, in the House.—— May 24 to July 26, in the Senate. Aug. 4, vetoed.
House Journal, 1 sess. 49 Cong. pp. 334, 1605, 1678, 1679 P, 2356, 2378, 2541 O. ——
Senate Journal, 1 sess. 49 Cong. pp. 783, 792, 1158, 1181 P, 1188, 1193.

246. Pension to Susan Hawes. [§ 74.]
H. R. 7234, 1 sess. 49 Cong. "An act granting a pension to Susan Hawes."
1886. Mar. 29 to June 12, in the House.—— June 15 to July 26, in the Senate.

1886. Aug. 4, vetoed.
House Journal, 1 sess. 49 Cong. pp. 1078, 1577, 1871 P, 2356, 2379, 2542 O.—— *Senate Journal, 1 sess. 49 Cong.* pp. 908, 1151, 1181 P, 1189, 1194.

247. Pension to A. C. Richardson. [§ 75.]
H. R. 1584, 1 sess. 49 Cong. "An act for the relief of Mrs. Aurelia C. Richardson."
1886. Jan. 5 to May 28, in the House.—— June 1 to July 26, in the Senate.
Aug. 4, vetoed.
House Journal, 1 sess. 49 Cong. pp. 221, 1674, 1749, 1750 P, 2356, 2379, 2543 O. —— *Senate Journal, 1 sess. 49 Cong.* pp. 830, 832, 1095, 1180 P, 1189, 1193.

248. Pension to W. Dickens. [§ 72.]
S. 2269, 1 sess. 49 Cong. "An act granting a pension to William Dickens."
1886. Apr. 28 to May 26, in the Senate.—— May 26 to Dec. 18, in the House.
1887. Jan. 19, vetoed.
Senate Journal, 1 sess. 49 Cong. pp. 648, 676, 811 P.—— *House Journal, 1 sess. 49 Cong.* pp. 1726, 1730, 1893.—— *Senate Journal, 2 sess. 49 Cong.* pp. 90, 116, 117, 121, 176 O.—— *House Journal, 2 sess. 49 Cong.* pp. 121, 122 P.

249. Pension to B. Obekiah. [§ 72.]
S. 2173, 1 sess. 49 Cong. "An act granting a pension to Benjamin Obekiah."
1886. Apr. 19 to Apr. 21, in the Senate.—— Apr. 22 to 1887, Jan. 7, in the House.
1887. Jan. 27, vetoed.
Senate Journal, 1 sess. 49 Cong. pp. 578, 584, 604 P.—— *House Journal, 1 sess. 49 Cong.* pp. 1337, 1355, 1900.—— *Senate Journal, 2 sess. 49 Cong.* pp. 126, 148, 152, 161, 224 O, 225, 230.—— *House Journal, 2 sess. 49 Cong.* pp. 188 P, 248.

250. Relief of H. K. Belding. [§ 66.]
S. 127, 1 sess. 49 Cong. "An act for the relief of H. K. Belding."
1885. Dec. 8 to 1886, May 18, in the Senate.—— May 18 to 1887, Jan. 7, in the House.
1887. Jan. 27, vetoed.
Senate Journal, 1 sess. 49 Cong. pp. 52, 330, 756 P.—— *House Journal, 1 sess. 49 Cong.* pp. 1653, 1656, 2013.—— *Senate Journal, 2 sess. 49 Cong.* pp. 120, 148, 152, 161, 225 O, 227.—— *House Journal, 2 sess. 49 Cong.* pp. 182 P, 247.

251. Pension to Margaret Dunlap. [§ 74.]
S. 2167, 1 sess. 49 Cong. "An act granting a pension to Mrs. Margaret Dunlap."
1886. Apr. 16 to June 5, in the Senate.—— June 7 to 1887, Jan. 14, in the House.
1887. Jan. 31, vetoed.
Senate Journal, 1 sess. 49 Cong. pp. 571, 706, 861 P.—— *House Journal, 1 sess. 49 Cong.* pp. 1824, 1833, 1968.—— *Senate Journal, 2 sess. 49 Cong.* pp. 158, 172, 173, 177, 241 O, 242.—— *House Journal, 2 sess. 49 Cong.* pp. 262, 263 P, 310.

252. Pension to A. Falconer. [§ 74.]
H. R. 6443, 1 sess. 49 Cong. "An act granting a pension to Alexander Falconer."
1886. Mar. 8 to May 21, in the House.—— May 24 to 1887, Jan. 17, in the Senate.
1887. Feb. 3, vetoed.
House Journal, 1 sess. 49 Cong. pp. 863, 1504, 1678, 1679 P.—— *Senate Journal, 1 sess. 49 Cong.* pp. 783, 793, 1185.—— *House Journal, 2 sess. 49 Cong.* pp. 304, 325, 485 O.—— *Senate Journal, 2 sess. 49 Cong.* pp. 159 P, 178, 184.

253. Pension to W. Lynch. [§ 74.]
H. R. 6132, 1 sess. 49 Cong. "An act granting a pension to William Lynch."
1886. Mar. 1 to June 18, in the House.—— June 21 to 1887, Jan. 17, in the Senate.

1887. Feb. 3, vetoed.
House Journal, 1 sess. 49 Cong. pp. 791, 1649, 1921 P. —— *Senate Journal, 1 sess. 49 Cong.* pp. 948, 949, 1185. —— *House Journal, 2 sess. 49 Cong.* pp. 304, 325, 486 O. —— *Senate Journal, 2 sess. 49 Cong.* pp. 159 P, 178, 184.

254. Pension to R. K. Bennett. [§ 74.]

H. R. 7698, 1 sess. 49 Cong. "An act granting a pension to Robert K. Bennett." 1886. Apr. 12 to June 18, in the House. —— June 21 to 1887, Jan. 17, in the Senate. 1887. Feb. 4, vetoed.
House Journal, 1 sess. 49 Cong. pp. 1227, 1672, 1921 P. —— *Senate Journal, 1 sess. 49 Cong.* pp. 949, 1197. —— *House Journal, 2 sess. 49 Cong.* pp. 304, 325, 502 O. —— *Senate Journal, 2 sess. 49 Cong.* pp. 159 P, 178, 184.

255. Pension to Franklin Sweet. [§ 72.]

H. R. 7540, 1 sess. 49 Cong. "An act to increase the pension of Franklin Sweet." 1886. Apr. 5 to Dec. 18, in the House. —— Dec. 20 to 1887, Jan. 17, in the Senate. 1887. Feb. 4, vetoed.
House Journal, 1 sess. 49 Cong. pp. 1148, 1892. —— *House Journal, 2 sess. 49 Cong.* pp. 121, 122, 124 P, 304, 325, 501 O. —— *Senate Journal, 2 sess. 49 Cong.* pp. 90, 91, 132, 159 P, 178, 184.

256. Pension to A. P. Griggs. [§ 74.]

H. R. 8834, 1 sess. 49 Cong. "An act granting a pension to Abraham P. Griggs." 1886. May 17 to June 18, in the House. —— June 21 to 1887, Jan. 17, in the Senate. 1887. Feb. 4, vetoed.
House Journal, 1 sess. 49 Cong. pp. 1628, 1706, 1921 P. —— *Senate Journal, 1 sess. 49 Cong.* pp. 949, 1213. —— *House Journal, 2 sess. 49 Cong.* pp. 304, 326, 501 O. —— *Senate Journal, 2 sess. 49 Cong.* pp. 159 P, 179, 184.

257. Pension to C. Stone. [§ 74.]

H. R. 927, 1 sess. 49 Cong. "An act granting a pension to Cudbert Stone." 1885. Dec. 21 to 1886, Feb. 26, in the House. —— 1886, Mar. 1 to 1887, Jan. 17, in the Senate.
1887. Feb. 4, vetoed.
House Journal, 1 sess. 49 Cong. pp. 178, 682, 767 P. —— *Senate Journal, 1 sess. 49 Cong.* p. 347. —— *House Journal, 2 sess. 49 Cong.* pp. 304, 325, 500 O. —— *Senate Journal, 2 sess. 49 Cong.* pp. 132, 159 P, 178, 184.

258. Pension to Jesse Campbell. [§ 72.]

H. R. 8150, 1 sess. 49 Cong. "An act granting a pension to Jesse Campbell." 1886. Apr. 26 to July 9, in the House. —— July 10 to 1887, Jan. 17, in the Senate. 1887. Feb. 4, vetoed.
House Journal, 1 sess. 49 Cong. pp. 1384, 1743, 2081, 2154 P. —— *Senate Journal, 1 sess. 49 Cong.* pp. 1079, 1083, 1184. —— *House Journal, 2 sess. 49 Cong.* pp. 304, 325, 502 O. —— *Senate Journal, 2 sess. 49 Cong.* pp. 159 P, 179, 184.

259. Pension to Catharine Sattler. [§ 74.]

H. R. 6832, 1 sess. 49 Cong. "An act granting a pension to Mrs. Catharine Sattler." 1886. Mar. 16 to June 12, in the House. —— June 15 to 1887, Jan. 17, in the Senate. 1887. Feb. 4, vetoed.
House Journal, 1 sess. 49 Cong. pp. 940, 1453, 1871 P. —— *Senate Journal, 1 sess. 49 Cong.* pp. 908, 1213. —— *House Journal, 2 sess. 49 Cong.* pp. 304, 325, 503 O. —— *Senate Journal, 2 sess. 49 Cong.* pp. 159 P, 178, 184.

260. Pension to J. R. Baylor. [§ 74.]

H. R. 6825, 1 sess. 49 Cong. "An act granting a pension to James R. Baylor."
1886. Mar. 6 to June 12, in the House.—— June 15 to 1887, Jan. 17, in the Senate.
1887. Feb. 4, vetoed.

House Journal, 1 sess. 49 Cong. pp. 940, 1605, 1871, 1872 P.—— *Senate Journal, 1 sess. 49 Cong.* pp. 908, 1185.—— *House Journal, 2 sess. 49 Cong.* pp. 304, 325, 504 O.—— *Senate Journal, 2 sess. 49 Cong.* pp. 159 P, 178, 184.

261. Dependent Pension Bill. [§ 77.]

H. R. 10457, 2 sess. 49 Cong. "An act for the relief of dependent parents and honorably discharged soldiers and sailors who are now disabled and dependent upon their own labor for support."
1887. Jan. 10 to Jan. 17, in the House.—— Jan. 18 to Jan. 27, in the Senate.
Feb. 11, vetoed.—— Feb. 24, reconsidered by the House; vote, 175–125.

House Journal, 2 sess. 49 Cong. pp. 202, 293, 294 P, 402, 410, 415, 421, 664, 719, 720, 567 O, 664, 719 R, 720.—— *Senate Journal, 2 sess. 49 Cong.* pp. 166, 168, 170, 218 P, 219, 222, 227, 235.

262. Texas seed bill. [§ 96.]

H. R. 10203, 2 sess. 49 Cong. "An act to enable the Commissioner of Agriculture to make a special distribution of seeds in the drought-stricken counties of Texas, and making an appropriation therefor."
1886. Dec. 13 to 1887, Jan. 29, in the House.—— 1887, Jan. 29 to Feb. 2, in the Senate.
1887. Feb. 16, vetoed.—— Feb. 17, reconsidered by the House; vote, 83–159.

House Journal, 2 sess. 49 Cong. pp. 81, 328, 417 P, 467, 479, 634 O, 635 R.—— *Senate Journal, 2 sess. 49 Cong.* pp. 231, 248 P, 259.

263. Pension to Charlotte O'Neal. [§ 74.]

S. 859, 1 sess. 49 Cong. "An act granting a pension to Charlotte O'Neal."
1886. Jan. 5 to May 24, in the Senate.—— May 25 to 1887, Feb. 4, in the House.
1887. Feb. 19, vetoed.

Senate Journal, 1 sess. 49 Cong. pp. 130, 646, 789 P.—— *House Journal, 1 sess. 49 Cong.* pp. 1711, 1716.—— *Senate Journal, 2 sess. 49 Cong.* pp. 276, 287, 288, 303, 381 O, 382.—— *House Journal, 2 sess. 49 Cong.* pp. 470, 497, 498 P, 530.

264. Pension to John Reed. [§ 75.]

S. 1626, 1 sess. 49 Cong. "An act granting a pension to John Reed, senior."
1886. Feb. 24 to May 24, in the Senate.—— May 25 to 1887, Feb. 4, in the House.
1887. Feb. 19, vetoed.

Senate Journal, 1 sess. 49 Cong. pp. 331, 639, 789 P.—— *House Journal, 1 sess. 49 Cong.* pp. 1711, 1717, 1891.—— *Senate Journal, 2 sess. 49 Cong.* pp. 276, 287, 288, 303, 382 O, 384.—— *House Journal, 2 sess. 49 Cong.* pp. 497, 498 P, 530.

265. Pension to Rachel Ann Pierpont. [§ 72.]

S. 2452, 1 sess. 49 Cong. "An act granting a pension to Rachel Ann Pierpont."
1886. May 18 to June 5, in the Senate.—— June 7 to 1887, Feb. 4, in the House.
1887. Feb. 21, vetoed.

Senate Journal, 1 sess. 49 Cong. pp. 752, 862 P.—— *House Journal, 1 sess. 49 Cong.* pp. 1825, 1833, 1891.—— *Senate Journal, 2 sess. 49 Cong.* pp. 275, 287, 288, 303, 392 O, 393.—— *House Journal, 2 sess. 49 Cong.* pp. 497, 498 P, 530.

266. Pension to Jacob Smith. [§ 72.]

S. 2111, 1 sess. 49 Cong. "An act granting a pension to Jacob Smith."
1886. Apr. 12 to May 24, in the Senate.—— May 25 to 1887, Feb. 4, in the House.

1887. Feb. 21, vetoed.

Senate Journal, 1 sess. 49 Cong. pp. 547, 676, 789 P. —— *House Journal, 1 sess. 49 Cong.* pp. 1711, 1718. —— *Senate Journal, 2 sess. 49 Cong.* pp. 276, 287, 288, 303, 393 O, 394. —— *House Journal, 2 sess. 49 Cong.* pp. 337, 497, 498 P, 530.

267. Pension to J. D. Fincher. [§ 74.]

S. 1768, 1 sess. 49 Cong. "An act granting a pension to John D. Fincher."

1886. Mar. 3 to June 18, in the Senate. —— June 21 to 1887, Feb. 4, in the House.

1887. Feb. 21, vetoed.

Senate Journal, 1 sess. 49 Cong. pp. 371, 639, 939 P. —— *House Journal, 1 sess. 49 Cong.* pp. 1937, 1959, 2012. —— *Senate Journal, 2 sess. 49 Cong.* pp. 276, 287, 288, 303, 394 O, 395. —— *House Journal, 2 sess. 49 Cong.* pp. 497, 498 P, 530.

268. Pension to Margaret R. Jones. [§ 73.]

H. R. 10082, 2 sess. 49 Cong. "An act to increase the pension of Margaret R. Jones."

1886. Dec. 13 to 1887, Jan. 21, in the House. —— 1887, Jan. 24 to Feb. 5, in the Senate.

1887. Feb. 23, vetoed.

House Journal, 2 sess. 49 Cong. pp. 75, 256, 341 P, 515, 538, 713 O. —— *Senate Journal, 2 sess. 49 Cong.* pp. 190, 191, 244, 275 P, 296, 300.

269. Pension to A. McRobertson. [§ 73.]

H. R. 7327, 1 sess. 49 Cong. "An act granting a pension to Anthony McRobertson."

1886. Mar. 29 to June 18, in the House. —— June 21 to 1887, Feb. 5, in the Senate.

1887. Feb. 23, vetoed.

House Journal, 1 sess. 49 Cong. pp. 1082, 1672, 1921 P. —— *Senate Journal, 1 sess. 49 Cong.* pp. 948, 949. —— *House Journal, 2 sess. 49 Cong.* pp. 514, 537, 712 O. —— *Senate Journal, 2 sess. 49 Cong.* pp. 244, 275 P, 296, 299.

270. Pension to L. Burritt. [§ 73.]

H. R. 8002, 1 sess. 49 Cong. "An act to increase the pension of Loren Burritt."

1886. Apr. 19 to May 8, in the House. —— May 10 to 1887, Feb. 5, in the Senate.

1887. Feb. 23, vetoed.

House Journal, 1 sess. 49 Cong. pp. 1293, 1410, 1541, 1542, 1546, 1547 P. —— *Senate Journal, 1 sess. 49 Cong.* p. 700. —— *House Journal, 2 sess. 49 Cong.* pp. 514, 537, 713 O. —— *Senate Journal, 2 sess. 49 Cong.* pp. 201, 275 P, 296, 299.

271. Relief of W. H. Morhiser. [§ 66.]

H. R. 5877, 1 sess. 49 Cong. "An act for the relief of William H. Morhiser."

1886. Feb. 19 to June 16, in the House. —— June 18 to 1887, Feb. 7, in the Senate.

1887. Feb. 23, vetoed.

House Journal, 1 sess. 49 Cong. pp. 712, 1903, 1904 P. —— *Senate Journal, 1 sess. 49 Cong.* pp. 936, 1094. —— *House Journal, 2 sess. 49 Cong.* pp. 531, 548, 713 O. —— *Senate Journal, 2 sess. 49 Cong.* pp. 283 P, 305, 306.

272. Relief of John How. [§ 66.]

H. R. 7648, 1 sess. 49 Cong. "An act for the relief of the estate of the late John How, Indian agent, and his sureties."

1886. Apr. 9 to Dec. 15, in the House. —— Dec. 15 to 1887, Feb. 8, in the Senate.

1887. Feb. 24, vetoed.

House Journal, 1 sess. 49 Cong. p. 1202. —— *House Journal, 2 sess. 49 Cong.* pp. 99 P, 540, 562, 725 O. —— *Senate Journal, 2 sess. 49 Cong.* pp. 72, 73, 143, 293 P, 311, 312.

* 273. Public building at Lynn, Mass. [§ 93.]

S. 1162, 1 sess. 49 Cong. "An act for the erection of a post-office building at Lynn, Massachusetts."

1886. Jan. 20 to July 22, in the Senate.——July 22 to 1887, Feb. 10, in the House.
1887. Feb. 25, vetoed.——Mar. 3, reconsidered by the Senate; passed over the veto, 37 to 15.
Senate Journal, 1 sess. 49 Cong. pp. 192, 1002, 1152 P.——*House Journal, 1 sess. 49 Cong.* pp. 2308, 2311.——*Senate Journal, 2 sess. 49 Cong.* pp. 307, 328, 331, 437 O, 438, 563 R.——*House Journal, 2 sess. 49 Cong.* pp. 95, 552 P, 590, 842.

274. Pension to Mrs. Sarah Hamilton. [§ 74.]

S. *2045, 1 sess. 49 Cong.* "An act granting a pension to Mrs. Sarah Hamilton."
1886. Apr. 5 to May 26, in the Senate.——May 26 to 1887, Feb. 11, in the House.
1887. Feb. 26, vetoed.
Senate Journal, 1 sess. 49 Cong. pp. 513, 676, 811 P.——*House Journal, 1 sess. 49 Cong.* pp. 1726, 1730, 2239.——*Senate Journal, 2 sess. 49 Cong.* pp. 320, 330, 334, 339, 448 O, 449.——*House Journal, 2 sess. 49 Cong.* pp. 574, 575 P, 591.

275. Pension to Anna Wright. [§ 72.]

S. *2210, 1 sess. 49 Cong.* "An act granting a pension to Anna Wright."
1886. Apr. 21 to June 5, in the Senate.——June 7 to 1887, Feb. 11, in the House.
1887. Feb. 26, vetoed.
Senate Journal, 1 sess. 49 Cong. pp. 592, 705, 861 P.——*House Journal, 1 sess. 49 Cong.* pp. 1824, 1833.——*Senate Journal, 2 sess. 49 Cong.* pp. 320, 330, 334, 339, 449 O, 450.——*House Journal, 2 sess. 49 Cong.* pp. 490, 574, 575 P, 591.

276. Public building at Portsmouth, Ohio. [§ 93.]

H. R. *6976, 1 sess. 49 Cong.* "An act to erect a public building at Portsmouth, Ohio."
1886. Mar. 17 to 1887, Feb. 10, in the House.——Feb. 11 to Feb. 12, in the Senate.
1887. Feb. 26, vetoed.
House Journal, 1 sess. 49 Cong. p. 962.——*House Journal, 2 sess. 49 Cong.* pp. 558 P, 580, 610, 757 O.——*Senate Journal, 2 sess. 49 Cong.* pp. 310, 311, 323 P, 334.

*277. Public building at La Fayette, Ind. [§ 93.]

S. *531, 1 sess. 49 Cong.* "An act to provide for the erection of a public building at La Fayette, Indiana."
1885. Dec. 14 to 1886, May 14, in the Senate.——1886, May 15 to 1887, Feb. 10, in the House.
1887. Feb. 28, vetoed.——Mar. 3, reconsidered by the Senate; passed over the veto, 38 to 18.
Senate Journal, 1 sess. 49 Cong. pp. 84, 368, 736 P.——*House Journal, 1 sess. 49 Cong.* pp. 1616, 1645.——*Senate Journal, 2 sess. 49 Cong.* pp. 307, 322, 343, 349, 356, 480 O, 482, 562 R.——*House Journal, 2 sess. 49 Cong.* pp. 433, 552 P, 591, 842, 859, 866, 868, 873, 874.

278. Relief of Nathaniel McKay. [§ 66.]

H. R. *2477, 1 sess. 50 Cong.* "An act for the relief of Nathaniel McKay and the executors of Donald McKay."
1888. Jan. 4 to Feb. 10, in the House.——Feb. 20 to Mar. 20, in the Senate. Apr. 4, vetoed.
House Journal, 1 sess. 50 Cong. pp. 147, 391, 748 P, 1274, 1295, 1451 O.——*Senate Journal, 1 sess. 50 Cong.* pp. 344, 345, 505 P, 523, 525.

279. Pension to Laura A. Wright. [§ 74.]

H. R. *445, 1 sess. 50 Cong.* "An act granting a pension to Laura A. Wright."
1887. Dec. 21 to 1888, Mar. 2, in the House.——Mar. 5 to Mar. 31, in the Senate.
1888. Apr. 16, vetoed.

186   *List of Vetoes.*   [APP. A

House Journal, *1 sess. 50 Cong.* pp. 88, 516, 1018 P, 1410, 1651 O. —— *Senate Journal*, *1 sess. 50 Cong.* pp. 416, 418, 459, 579 P, 598, 603.

280. Pension to Betsey Mansfield. [§§ 75, 79.]
S. 809, 1 sess. 50 Cong. "An act granting a pension to Betsey Mansfield."
1887. Dec. 15 to 1888, Feb. 16, in the Senate. —— 1888, Feb. 17 to Mar. 30, in the House.
1888. Apr. 16, vetoed.
Senate Journal, *1 sess. 50 Cong.* pp. 74, 275, 332 P, 568, 598, 603, 610, 665 O, 666, 1026, 1053. —— *House Journal*, *1 sess. 50 Cong.* pp. 833, 874, 971, 1380 P, 1444.

281. Pension to Hannah R. Langdon. [§§ 74, 79.]
S. 549, 1 sess. 50 Cong. "An act granting a pension to Hannah R. Langdon."
1887. Dec. 12 to 1888, Feb. 16, in the Senate. —— 1888, Feb. 17 to Mar. 30, in the House.
1888. Apr. 16, vetoed.
Senate Journal, *1 sess. 50 Cong.* pp. 48, 204, 331 P, 568, 582, 598, 603, 610, 666 O, 668, 1026, 1053. —— *House Journal*, *1 sess. 50 Cong.* pp. 833, 874, 970, 1381 P, 1443, 1444.

282. Relief of Major Daniel N. Bash. [§ 66.]
S. 258, 1 sess. 50 Cong. "An act for the relief of Major Daniel N. Bash, paymaster United States Army."
1887. Dec. 12 to 1888, Mar. 21, in the Senate. —— 1888, Mar. 22 to Apr. 3, in the House.
1888. Apr. 18, vetoed.
Senate Journal, *1 sess. 50 Cong.* pp. 36, 258, 515 P, 597, 628, 629, 633, 686 O, 690. —— *House Journal*, *1 sess. 50 Cong.* pp. 1293, 1305, 1335, 1438 P.

283. Pension to William H. Brokenshaw. [§ 74.]
H. R. 418, 1 sess. 50 Cong. "An act granting a pension to William H. Brokenshaw."
1887. Dec. 21 to 1888, Mar. 2, in the House. —— 1888, Mar. 5 to Apr. 6, in the Senate.
1888. Apr. 21, vetoed.
House Journal, *1 sess. 50 Cong.* pp. 87, 614, 1018 P, 1516, 1727 O. —— *Senate Journal*, *1 sess. 50 Cong.* pp. 416, 418, 500, 616 P, 646, 647.

284. Pension to Hannah C. De Witt. [§ 72.]
H. R. 823, 1 sess. 50 Cong. "An act granting a pension to Hannah C. De Witt."
1887. Dec. 22 to 1888,[1] , in the House. —— 1888, Mar. 5 to Apr. 6, in the Senate.
1888. Apr. 21, vetoed.
House Journal, *1 sess. 50 Cong.* pp. 109, 615, 1018, 1019, 1727 O. —— *Senate Journal*, *1 sess. 50 Cong.* pp. 416, 418, 547, 617 P, 646, 647.

285. Pension to Morris T. Mantor. [§ 74.]
H. R. 4633, 1 sess. 50 Cong. "An act granting a pension to Morris T. Mantor."
1888. Jan. 10 to Mar. 16, in the House. —— Mar. 19 to Apr. 6, in the Senate.
Apr. 21, vetoed.
House Journal, *1 sess. 50 Cong.* pp. 327, 883, 1202, 1203 P, 1517, 1728 O. —— *Senate Journal*, *1 sess. 50 Cong.* pp. 489, 490, 512, 617 P, 646, 647.

286. Pension to William H. Brimmer. [§ 74.]
H. R. 5247, 1 sess. 50 Cong. "An act granting a pension to William H. Brimmer."
1888. Jan. 15 to Mar. 9, in the House. —— Mar. 12 to Apr. 6, in the Senate.
Apr. 24, vetoed.

---

[1] No further account of the bill appears in the House Journal until the message vetoing the bill is read. Reference is, however, made in the index to S. 451 which passed both houses and was approved Mar. 10, 1888, which granted a pension to the same person.

House Journal, 1 sess. 50 Cong. pp. 398, 1074, 1110 P, 1517, 1744 O. —— *Senate Journal, 1 sess. 50 Cong.* pp. 453, 454, 471, 616 P, 646, 647.

287. Pension to William P. Witt. [§ 74.]

H. R. 6908, *1 sess. 50 Cong.* "An act granting a pension to William P. Witt."
1888. Feb. 8 to Mar. 9, in the House. —— Mar. 12 to Apr. 6, in the Senate. Apr. 24, vetoed.
House Journal, 1 sess. 50 Cong. pp. 711, 1073, 1110 P, 1517, 1742 O. —— *Senate Journal, 1 sess. 50 Cong.* pp. 453, 454, 548, 617 P, 646, 647.

288. Pension to Chloe Quiggle. [§ 74.]

H. R. 4550, *1 sess. 50 Cong.* "An act granting a pension to Chloe Quiggle, widow of Philip Quiggle."
1888. Jan. 10 to Mar. 16, in the House. —— Mar. 19 to Apr. 6, in the Senate. Apr. 24, vetoed.
House Journal, 1 sess. 50 Cong. pp. 324, 884, 1202, 1203 P, 1517, 1743 O. —— *Senate Journal, 1 sess. 50 Cong.* pp. 489, 490, 591, 617 P, 646, 647.

289. Pension to William Sackman, Sr. [§§ 74, 79.]

S. 465, *1 sess. 50 Cong.* "An act granting a pension to William Sackman, senior."
1887. Dec. 12 to 1888, Feb. 16, in the Senate. —— 1888, Feb. 17 to Apr. 13, in the House. 1888. Apr. 30, vetoed.
Senate Journal, 1 sess. 50 Cong. pp. 44, 165, 331 P, 660, 682, 684, 695, 743 O, 745, 1025, 1026, 1053. —— *House Journal, 1 sess. 50 Cong.* pp. 833, 874, 1257, 1620 P, 1669.

290. Pension to Mary Sullivan. [§ 72.]

S. 838, *1 sess. 50 Cong.* "An act granting a pension to Mary Sullivan."
1887. Dec. 15 to 1888, Feb. 16, in the Senate, —— 1888, Feb. 17 to Apr. 13, in the House. 1888. Apr. 30, vetoed.
Senate Journal, 1 sess. 50 Cong. pp. 75, 240, 331 P, 660, 682, 685, 695, 745 O, 746, 1026, 1053. —— *House Journal, 1 sess. 50 Cong.* pp. 833, 875, 1072, 1618, 1619 P, 1669.

291. Relief of H. B. Wilson. [§ 66.]

H. R. 19, *1 sess. 50 Cong.* "An act for the relief of H. B. Wilson, administrator of the estate of William Tinder, deceased."
1887. Dec. 21 to 1888, Jan. 31, in the House. —— 1888, Jan. 31 to Feb. 13, in the Senate. 1888. May 1, vetoed.
House Journal, 1 sess. 50 Cong. pp. 72, 440, 620 P, 772, 1800 O. —— *Senate Journal, 1 sess. 50 Cong.* pp. 247, 248, 282, 305 P, 719, 720.

292. Relief of Emily G. Mills. [§§ 74, 79.]

H. R. 4534, *1 sess. 50 Cong.* "An act for the relief of Emily G. Mills."
1888. Jan. 10 to Mar. 16, in the House. —— Mar. 19 to Apr. 17, in the Senate. May 3, vetoed.
House Journal, 1 sess. 50 Cong. pp. 324, 884, 1202, 1203 P, 1678, 1811 O. —— *Senate Journal, 1 sess. 50 Cong.* pp. 489, 490, 635, 678 P, 719, 720.

293. Sale of Indian Lands. [§ 41.]

H. R. 1406, *1 sess. 50 Cong.* "An act to provide for the sale of certain New York Indian lands in Kansas."
1888. Jan. 4 to Jan. 26, in the House. —— Jan. 30 to Apr. 23, in the Senate. May 7, vetoed.
House Journal, 1 sess. 50 Cong. pp. 195, 386, 553, 556 P, 1726, 1846 O. —— *Senate Journal, 1 sess. 50 Cong.* pp. 227, 228, 441, 468, 520, 705 P, 721, 722.

294. Public building at Allentown, Penn. [§ 93.]
H. R. 4357, 1 sess. 50 Cong. "An act to erect a public building at Allentown, Pennsylvania."
1888. Jan. 10 to Feb. 23, in the House.—— Feb. 24 to Apr. 24, in the Senate.
May 9, vetoed.
House Journal, 1 sess. 50 Cong. pp. 341, 785, 904 P, 1753, 1862 O, 2065.—— *Senate Journal, 1 sess. 50 Cong.* pp. 371, 673, 716 P, 736, 737.

295. Relief of Georgia A. Stricklett. [§ 74.]
H. R. 7715, 1 sess. 50 Cong. "An act for the relief of Georgia A. Stricklett."
1888. Feb. 25 to Apr. 13, in the House.—— Apr. 16 to Apr. 24, in the Senate.
May 10, vetoed.
House Journal, 1 sess. 50 Cong. pp. 924, 1253, 1619 P, 1753, 1873 O.—— *Senate Journal, 1 sess. 50 Cong.* pp. 661, 692, 716 P, 736, 737.

296. Pension to Mrs. Theodora M. Piatt. [§ 74.]
H. R. 2282, 1 sess. 50 Cong. "An act to pension Mrs. Theodora M. Piatt."
1888. Jan. 4 to Apr. 13, in the House.—— Apr. 16 to May 2, in the Senate.
May 18, vetoed.
House Journal, 1 sess. 50 Cong. pp. 140, 1194, 1619 P, 1813, 1942 O.—— *Senate Journal, 1 sess. 50 Cong.* pp. 661, 710, 758 P, 772, 773.

297. Pension to Nancy F. Jennings. [§ 74.]
H. R. 5545, 1 sess. 50 Cong. "An act granting a pension to Nancy F. Jennings."
1888. Jan. 20 to Apr. 13, in the House.—— Apr. 16 to May 2, in the Senate.
May 18, vetoed.
House Journal, 1 sess. 50 Cong. pp. 473, 1071, 1619 P, 1814, 1943 O.—— *Senate Journal, 1 sess. 50 Cong.* pp. 661, 710, 757 P, 772, 773.

298. Use of Castle Island, Boston Harbor. [§ 48.]
H. Res. 56, 1 sess. 50 Cong. A joint resolution "authorizing the use and improvement of Castle Island, in Boston Harbor."
1888. Jan. 10 to Feb. 28, in the House.—— Feb. 29 to May 1, in the Senate.
May 18, vetoed.
House Journal, 1 sess. 50 Cong. pp. 324, 881, 978 P, 1802, 1947 O.—— *Senate Journal, 1 sess. 50 Cong.* pp. 397, 401, 693, 750 P, 765, 766, 768.

299. Relief of L. J. Worden. [§ 66.]
S. 1064, 1 sess. 50 Cong. "An act for the relief of L. J. Worden."
1887. Dec. 21 to 1888, Apr. 26, in the Senate.—— 1888, Apr. 27 to May 2, in the House.
1888. May 18, vetoed.
Senate Journal, 1 sess. 50 Cong. pp. 101, 486, 730 P, 753, 779, 782, 787, 856 O, 858.
—— *House Journal, 1 sess. 50 Cong.* pp. 1771, 1801 P, 1843.

300. Pension to Sally A. Randall. [§ 74.]
H. R. 88, 1 sess. 50 Cong. "An act granting a pension to Sally A. Randall."
1887. Dec. 21 to 1888, Apr. 20, in the House.—— 1888, Apr. 23 to May 2, in the Senate.
1888. May 19, vetoed.
House Journal, 1 sess. 50 Cong. pp. 74, 1075, 1702 P, 1813, 1944 O.—— *Senate Journal, 1 sess. 50 Cong.* pp. 703, 718, 758 P, 772, 773.

301. Pension to William H. Hester. [§ 74.]
H. R. 8164, 1 sess. 50 Cong. "An act granting a pension to William H. Hester."

1886. Mar. 6 to Apr. 13, in the House.—— Apr. 16 to May 2, in the Senate.
May 19, vetoed.
House Journal, 1 sess. 50 Cong. pp. 1054, 1341, 1619 P, 1814, 1934, 1945 O.——
Senate Journal, 1 sess. 50 Cong. pp. 661, 710, 758 P, 772, 773.

302. Pension to Royal J. Hiar. [§ 74.]
H. R. 879, 1 sess. 50 Cong. "An act granting a pension to Royal J. Hiar."
1887. Dec. 22 to 1888, Apr. 13, in the House.—— 1888, Apr. 16 to May 2, in the Senate.
1888. May 19, vetoed.
House Journal, 1 sess. 50 Cong. pp. 111, 1071, 1619 P, 1813, 1944 O.—— *Senate Journal, 1 sess. 50 Cong.* pp. 661, 700, 757 P, 772, 773.

303. Pension to Cyrenius G. Stryker. [§ 74.]
H. R. 5234, 1 sess. 50 Cong. "An act granting a pension to Cyrenius G. Stryker."
1888. Jan. 16 to Apr. 20, in the House.—— Apr. 23 to May 2, in the Senate.
May 19, vetoed.
House Journal, 1 sess. 50 Cong. pp. 397, 1152, 1702 P, 1813, 1946 O.—— *Senate Journal, 1 sess. 50 Cong.* pp. 703, 718, 758 P, 772, 773.

304. Pension to Ellen Shea. [§ 74.]
H. R. 3579, 1 sess. 50 Cong. "An act granting a pension to Ellen Shea."
1888. Jan. 9 to Apr. 13, in the House.—— Apr. 16 to May 2, in the Senate.
May 19, vetoed.
House Journal, 1 sess. 50 Cong. pp. 262, 1072, 1619 P, 1813, 1946 O.—— *Senate Journal, 1 sess. 50 Cong.* pp. 661, 710, 757 P, 772, 773.

305. Relief of Sarah E. McCaleb. [§ 74.]
H. R. 6609, 1 sess. 50 Cong. "An act for the relief of Sarah E. McCaleb."
1888. Feb. 4 to Apr. 13, in the House.—— Apr. 16 to May 2, in the Senate.
May 19, vetoed.
House Journal 1 sess. 50 Cong. pp. 656, 1072, 1619 P, 1814, 1947 O.——*Senate Journal, 1 sess. 50 Cong.* pp. 661, 710, 758 P, 771, 772, 773.

306. Pension to Farnaren Ball. [§ 74.]
H. R. 4580, 1 sess. 50 Cong. "An act granting a pension to Farnaren Ball."
1888. Jan. 10 to Apr. 13, in the House.—— Apr. 16 to May 2, in the Senate.
May 19, vetoed.
House Journal, 1 sess. 50 Cong. pp. 325, 1074, 1618, 1619 P, 1813, 1947 O.——
Senate Journal, 1 sess. 50 Cong. pp. 661, 710, 758 P, 772, 773.

307. Relief of J. E. Pilcher. [§ 69.]
H. R. 339, 1 sess. 50 Cong. "An act for the relief of J. E. Pilcher."
1887. Dec. 21 to 1888, Jan. 25, in the House.—— 1888, Jan. 25 to May 10, in the Senate.
1888. May 26, vetoed.
House Journal, 1 sess. 50 Cong. pp. 84, 543 P, 1870, 2016 O.—— *Senate Journal, 1 sess. 50 Cong.* pp. 213, 792, 804 P, 812, 813, 817.

308. Public building at Youngstown, Ohio. [§ 93.]
S. 347, 1 sess. 50 Cong. "An act to provide for the erection of a public building in the city of Youngstown, Ohio."
1887. Dec. 12 to 1888, Apr. 30, in the Senate.—— 1888, Apr. 30 to May 11, in the House.
1888. May 28, vetoed.
Senate Journal, 1 sess. 50 Cong. pp. 39, 487, 740 P, 811, 813, 839, 840, 847, 886 O, 887.—— *House Journal, 1 sess. 50 Cong.* pp. 1786, 1791, 1855, 1876 P, 1923.

309. Pension to Anna Mertz. [§§ 74, 79.]
S. *1237, 1 sess. 50 Cong.* "An act granting a pension to Anna Mertz."
1888. Jan. 9 to Mar. 31, in the Senate.——Apr. 2 to May 11, in the House.
   May 28, vetoed.
Senate Journal, 1 sess. 50 Cong. pp. 129, 424, 572 P, 811, 839, 840, 847, 887 O, 888, 1026, 1053.——*House Journal, 1 sess. 50 Cong.* pp. 1411, 1426, 1628, 1881 P, 1924.

310. Pension to David A. Servis. [§§ 74, 79.]
S. *820, 1 sess. 50 Cong.* "An act granting a pension to David A. Servis."
1887. Dec. 15 to 1888, Feb. 16, in the Senate.——1888, Feb. 17 to May 11, in the House.
1888. May 28, vetoed.
Senate Journal, 1 sess. 50 Cong. pp. 74, 240, 331 P, 810, 839, 840, 847, 889 O, 890, 1026, 1053.——*House Journal, 1 sess. 50 Cong.* pp. 833, 875, 1255, 1879, 1881 P, 1923.

311. Relief of Elisha Griswold. [§ 74.]
S. *835, 1 sess. 50 Cong.* "An act for the relief of Elisha Griswold."
1887. Dec. 15 to 1888, Feb. 16, in the Senate.——1888, Feb. 17 to May 11, in the House.
1888. May 28, vetoed.
Senate Journal, 1 sess. 50 Cong. pp. 74, 312, 332 P, 810, 839, 840, 847, 890 O, 891.——*House Journal, 1 sess. 50 Cong.* pp. 833, 875, 1879, 1881 P, 1923.

312. Public building at Columbus, Ga. [§ 93.]
H. R. *1275, 1 sess. 50 Cong.* "An act for the erection of a public building at Columbus, Georgia, and appropriating money therefor."
1888. Jan. 4 to Feb. 28, in the House.——Feb. 29 to May 15, in the Senate.
   May 29, vetoed.
House Journal, 1 sess. 50 Cong. pp. 187, 805, 975, 976 P, 1909, 2025 O.——*Senate Journal, 1 sess. 50 Cong.* pp. 397, 401, 774, 825 P, 846, 851.

313. Public building at Bar Harbor, Me. [§ 93.]
H. R. *4467, 1 sess. 50 Cong.* "An act for the erection of a public building at Bar Harbor, in Maine."
1888. Jan. 10 to Feb. 28, in the House.——Feb. 29 to May 22, in the Senate.
   June 5, vetoed.
House Journal, 1 sess. 50 Cong. pp. 348, 804, 975 P, 1968, 2069 O.——*Senate Journal, 1 sess. 50 Cong.* pp. 397, 401, 785, 862 P, 873.

314. Government land purchase at Council Bluffs. [§ 93.]
H. R. *1394, 1 sess. 50 Cong.* "An act authorizing the Secretary of the Treasury to purchase additional ground for the accommodation of Government offices in Council Bluffs, Iowa."
1888. Jan. 4 to Feb. 23, in the House.——Feb. 24 to May 22, in the Senate.
   June 5, vetoed.
House Journal, 1 sess. 50 Cong. pp. 194, 786, 903, 905 P, 1979, 2070 O.——*Senate Journal, 1 sess. 50 Cong.* pp. 370, 371, 774, 867 P, 873.

315. Pension to Johanna Loewinger. [§§ 74, 79.]
S. *739, 1 sess. 50 Cong.* "An act granting a pension to Johanna Loewinger."
1887. Dec. 14 to 1888, Feb. 16, in the Senate.——1888, Feb. 17 to May 18, in the House.
1888. June 5, vetoed.
Senate Journal, 1 sess. 50 Cong. pp. 67, 276, 334 P, 846, 873, 874, 927 O, 928, 1026, 1053.——*House Journal, 1 sess. 50 Cong.* pp. 833, 874, 1930 P, 1985.

316. Relief of John H. Marion. [§ 66.]
S. *1772, 1 sess. 50 Cong.* "An act for the relief of John H. Marion."
1888. Jan. 30 to Mar. 31, in the Senate.—— Apr. 2 to May 28, in the House.
June 12, vetoed.
Senate Journal, 1 sess. 50 Cong. pp. 234, 432, 577 P, 891, 909, 913, 961 O, 962.——
House Journal, 1 sess. 50 Cong. pp. 1414, 1430, 2012 P, 2039.

317. Pension to Stephen Schiedel. [§ 74.]
S. *1017, 1 sess. 50 Cong.* "An act granting a pension to Stephen Schiedel."
1887. Dec. 20 to 1888, Mar. 31, in the Senate.—— 1888, Apr. 2 to May 25, in the House.
1888. June 12, vetoed.
Senate Journal, 1 sess. 50 Cong. pp. 96, 388, 571 P, 881, 896, 898, 960 O, 961.——
House Journal, 1 sess. 50 Cong. pp. 1411, 1426, 1611, 1996 P, 2017.

318. Relief of Elijah Martin. [§ 72.]
H. R. *5522, 1 sess. 50 Cong.* "An act for the relief of Elijah Martin."
1888. Jan. 20 to Apr. 20, in the House.—— Apr. 23 to June 4, in the Senate.
June 18, vetoed.
House Journal, 1 sess. 50 Cong. pp. 473, 1075, 1702 P, 2068, 2156 O.—— *Senate Journal, 1 sess. 50 Cong.* pp. 703, 783, 917 P, 940, 941, 942.

319. Pension to Dolly Blazer. [§ 74.]
H. R. *3959, 1 sess. 50 Cong.* "An act granting a pension to Dolly Blazer."
1888. Jan. 9 to Apr. 27, in the House.—— Apr. 30 to June 4, in the Senate.
June 18, vetoed.
House Journal, 1 sess. 50 Cong. pp. 276, 1155, 1773 P, 2068, 2156 O.—— *Senate Journal, 1 sess. 50 Cong.* pp. 735, 736, 784, 917 P, 940, 941, 942.

320. Pension to Elizabeth Burr. [§ 74.]
H. R. *488, 1 sess. 50 Cong.* "An act granting a pension to Elizabeth Burr."
1887. Dec. 21 to 1888, Apr. 27, in the House.—— 1888, Apr. 30 to June 4, in the Senate.
1888. June 19, vetoed.
House Journal, 1 sess. 50 Cong. pp. 89, 1155, 1773 P, 2068, 2164 O.—— *Senate Journal, 1 sess. 50 Cong.* pp. 735, 736, 784, 917 P, 940, 941, 942.

321. Pension to Virtue Smith. [§ 74.]
S. *1957, 1 sess. 50 Cong.* "An act granting a pension to Virtue Smith."
1888. Feb. 13 to Mar. 31, in the Senate.—— Apr. 2 to June 1, in the House.
June 19, vetoed.
Senate Journal, 1 sess. 50 Cong. pp. 303, 388, 570 P, 911, 940, 941, 942, 945, 993 O, 994.—— *House Journal, 1 sess. 50 Cong.* pp. 1412, 1427, 1611, 2040 P, 2086.

322. Pension to Mary F. Harkins. [§ 74.]
H. R. *3016, 1 sess. 50 Cong.* "An act granting a pension to Mary F. Harkins."
1888. Jan. 4 to May 11, in the House.—— May 14 to June 6, in the Senate.
June 22, vetoed.
House Journal, 1 sess. 50 Cong. pp. 168, 1339, 1880 P, 2087, 2193 O.—— *Senate Journal, 1 sess. 50 Cong.* pp. 811, 813, 923, 936 P, 945, 953, 954.

323. Pension to Mary Minor Hoxey. [§ 73.]
H. R. *600, 1 sess. 50 Cong.* "An act increasing the pension of Mary Minor Hoxey."
1887. Dec. 21 to 1888, Apr. 27, in the House.—— 1888, Apr. 30 to June 6, in the Senate.

1888. June 22, vetoed.
House Journal, 1 sess. 50 Cong. pp. 93, 1257, 1773 P, 2087, 2193 O.—— *Senate Journal, 1 sess. 50 Cong.* pp. 735, 736, 876, 935 P, 945, 953, 954.

324. Relief of Lieut. James G. W. Hardy. [§ 74.]
H. R. 8281, 1 sess. 50 Cong. "An act for the relief of Lieutenant James G. W. Hardy."
1888. Mar. 9 to May 11, in the House.—— May 14 to June 6, in the Senate.
June 22, vetoed.
House Journal, 1 sess. 50 Cong. pp. 1095, 1608, 1880 P, 2088, 2194 O.—— *Senate Journal, 1 sess. 50 Cong.* pp. 812, 813, 892, 935 P, 945, 954.

325. Pension to Ellen Sexton. [§ 74.]
H. R. 8174, 1 sess. 50 Cong. "An act granting a pension to Ellen Sexton."
1888. Mar. 6 to May 11, in the House.—— May 14 to June 6, in the Senate.
June 22, vetoed.
House Journal, 1 sess. 50 Cong. pp. 1054, 1880 P, 2088, 2194 O.—— *Senate Journal, 1 sess. 50 Cong.* pp. 812, 813, 876, 935 P, 945, 954.

326. Pension to Charles Glamann. [§ 74.]
H. R. 2215, 1 sess. 50 Cong. "An act granting a pension to Charles Glamann."
1888. Jan. 4 to May 11, in the House.—— May 14 to June 6, in the Senate.
June 22, vetoed.
House Journal, 1 sess. 50 Cong. pp. 137, 1260, 1880 P, 2087, 2194 O.—— *Senate Journal, 1 sess. 50 Cong.* pp. 811, 813, 923, 936 P, 945, 953, 954.

327. Pension to the widow of John A. Turley. [§ 74.]
S. 845, 1 sess. 50 Cong. "An act granting a pension to the widow of John A. Turley."
1887. Dec. 15 to 1888, Feb. 16, in the Senate.—— 1888, Feb. 17 to June 8, in the House.
1888. June 26, vetoed.
Senate Journal, 1 sess. 50 Cong. pp. 75, 312, 332 P, 945, 974, 975, 977, 1018 O, 1077.—— *House Journal, 1 sess. 50 Cong.* pp. 833, 875, 1662, 2102, 2103 P, 2135.

328. Relief of Joel B. Morton. [§ 76.]
S. 432, 1 sess. 50 Cong. "An act for the relief of Joel B. Morton."
1887. Dec. 12 to 1888, Mar. 31, in the Senate.—— 1888, Apr. 2 to June 15, in the House.
1888. July 5, vetoed.
Senate Journal, 1 sess. 50 Cong. pp. 43, 389, 576 P, 980, 1006, 1011, 1017, 1057 O, 1058.—— *House Journal, 1 sess. 50 Cong.* pp. 1411, 1425, 1697, 2142, 2143 P, 2201.

329. Pension to Polly H. Smith. [§ 74.]
S. 43, 1 sess. 50 Cong. "An act granting a pension to Polly H. Smith."
1887. Dec. 12 to 1888, Feb. 16, in the Senate.—— 1888, Feb. 17 to June 15, in the House.
1888. July 5, vetoed.
Senate Journal, 1 sess. 50 Cong. pp. 28, 333 P, 980, 1006, 1011, 1017, 1059 O.—— *House Journal, 1 sess. 50 Cong.* pp. 832, 872, 1028, 2142, 2143 P, 2201.

330. Pension to Mary Ann Dougherty. [§ 76.]
S. 1547, 1 sess. 50 Cong. "An act granting a pension to Mary Ann Dougherty."
1888. Jan. 19 to Mar. 31, in the Senate.—— Apr. 2 to June 15, in the House.
July 5, vetoed.
Senate Journal, 1 sess. 50 Cong. pp. 187, 440, 577 P, 980, 1006, 1012, 1017, 1060 O, 1062.—— *House Journal, 1 sess. 50 Cong.* pp. 1412, 1427, 1662, 2142, 2143 P, 2201.

331. Pension to Julia Welch. [§ 74.]

H. R. 8291, 1 sess. 50 Cong. "An act granting a pension to Julia Welch."

1888. Mar. 9 to May 25, in the House.—— May 28 to June 20, in the Senate. July 5, vetoed.

House Journal, 1 sess. 50 Cong. pp. 1095, 1252, 1996 P, 2168, 2280 O.—— *Senate Journal, 1 sess. 50 Cong.* pp. 882, 885, 978, 995 P, 1007, 1011.

332. Pension to Mary Ann Lang. [§ 74.]

H. R. 7907, 1 sess. 50 Cong. "An act granting a pension to Mary Ann Lang."

1888. Feb. 29 to May 18, in the House.—— May 21 to June 20, in the Senate. July 5, vetoed.

House Journal, 1 sess. 50 Cong. pp. 978, 1609, 1931 P, 2168, 2281 O.—— *Senate Journal, 1 sess. 50 Cong.* pp. 846, 847, 948, 994 P, 1007, 1011.

333. Pension to William M. Campbell, Jr. [§ 74.]

H. R. 9184, 1 sess. 50 Cong. "An act granting a pension to William M. Campbell, junior."

1888. Apr. 3 to June 8, in the House.—— June 11 to June 20, in the Senate. July 6, vetoed.

House Journal, 1 sess. 50 Cong. pp. 1418, 1661, 2103 P, 2168, 2292 O.—— *Senate Journal, 1 sess. 50 Cong.* pp. 946, 947, 971, 995 P, 1007, 1011.

334. Pension to Harriet E. Cooper. [§ 74.]

H. R. 8807, 1 sess. 50 Cong. "An act granting a pension to Harriet E. Cooper."

1888. Mar. 23 to June 8, in the House.—— June 11 to June 20, in the Senate. July 6, vetoed.

House Journal, 1 sess. 50 Cong. pp. 1297, 1627, 2103 P, 2168, 2293 O.—— *Senate Journal, 1 sess. 50 Cong.* pp. 946, 947, 971, 995 P, 1007, 1011.

335. Relief of Van Buren Brown. [§ 74.]

H. R. 6431, 1 sess. 50 Cong. "An act for the relief of Van Buren Brown."

1888. Jan. 31 to June 8, in the House.—— June 11 to June 20, in the Senate. July 6, vetoed.

House Journal, 1 sess. 50 Cong. pp. 604, 1613, 2103 P, 2168, 2293 O.—— *Senate Journal, 1 sess. 50 Cong.* pp. 946, 947, 964, 995 P, 1007, 1010.

336. Pension to Nathaniel D. Chase. [§ 74.]

H. R. 367, 1 sess. 50 Cong. "An act granting a pension to Nathaniel D. Chase."

1887. Dec. 21 to 1888, June 8, in the House.—— 1888, June 11 to June 20, in the Senate.

1888. July 6, vetoed.

House Journal, 1 sess. 50 Cong. pp. 85, 1612, 2103 P, 2167, 2293 O.—— *Senate Journal, 1 sess. 50 Cong.* pp. 946, 947, 971, 995 P, 1006, 1010.

337. Relief of Mary Fitzmorris. [§ 72.]

H. R. 9520, 1 sess. 50 Cong. "An act for the relief of Mary Fitzmorris."

1888. Apr. 17 to June 22, in the House.—— June 25 to June 30, in the Senate. July 16, vetoed.

House Journal, 1 sess. 50 Cong. pp. 1653, 2192 P, 2254, 2366 O.—— *Senate Journal, 1 sess. 50 Cong.* pp. 1006, 1008, 1020, 1041 P, 1055, 1057.

338. Pension to Tobias Baney. [§ 74.]

S. 121, 1 sess. 50 Cong. "An act granting a pension to Tobias Baney."

1887. Dec. 12 to 1888, Feb. 16, in the Senate.—— 1888, Feb. 17 to June 29, in the House.

1888. July 16, vetoed.
Senate Journal, 1 sess. 50 Cong. pp. 30, 313, 332 P, 1037, 1055, 1056, 1067, 1113 O, 1114. —— House Journal, 1 sess. 50 Cong. pp. 832, 873, 2079, 2243, 2244 P, 2272.

339. Pension to Amanda F. Deck. [§ 74.]
S. 470, 1 sess. 50 Cong. "An act granting a pension to Amanda F. Deck."
1887. Dec. 12 to 1888, Mar. 29, in the Senate. —— 1888, Mar. 30 to June 29, in the House.
1888. July 16, vetoed.
Senate Journal, 1 sess. 50 Cong. pp. 44, 350, 559 P, 1036, 1055, 1056, 1067, 1114 O, 1115. —— House Journal, 1 sess. 50 Cong. pp. 1378, 1387, 1610, 2243, 2244 P, 2272.

340. Pension to John F. Ballier. [§ 72.]
S. 1613, 1 sess. 50 Cong. "An act granting an increase of pension to John F. Ballier."
1888. Jan. 24 to Feb. 16, in the Senate. —— Feb. 17 to June 29, in the House.
July 17, vetoed.
Senate Journal, 1 sess. 50 Cong. pp. 204, 331 P, 1036, 1055, 1056, 1068, 1124 O, 1125. —— House Journal, 1 sess. 50 Cong. pp. 834, 876, 2079, 2243, 2244 P, 2273.

341. Pension to Thomas Shannon. [§ 74.]
H. R. 5913, 1 sess. 50 Cong. "An act granting a pension to Thomas Shannon."
1888. Jan. 24 to June 15, in the House. —— June 18 to June 30, in the Senate.
July 17, vetoed.
House Journal, 1 sess. 50 Cong. pp. 518, 1664, 2143 P, 2253, 2376 O. —— Senate Journal, 1 sess. 50 Cong. pp. 981, 982, 1020, 1041 P, 1055, 1057.

342. Pension to Woodford M. Houchin. [§ 74.]
H. R. 9174, 1 sess. 50 Cong. "An act granting a pension to Woodford M. Houchin."
1888. Apr. 3 to June 15, in the House. —— June 18 to June 30, in the Senate.
July 17, vetoed.
House Journal, 1 sess. 50 Cong. pp. 1417, 1769, 2143 P, 2254, 2377 O. —— Senate Journal, 1 sess. 50 Cong. pp. 981, 982, 991, 1040 P, 1055, 1057.

343. Pension to Theresa Herbst. [§ 76.]
H. R. 8078, 1 sess. 50 Cong. "An act granting a pension to Theresa Herbst, widow of John Herbst, late private Company G, One hundred and fortieth Regiment of New York Volunteers."
1888. Mar. 5 to June 15, in the House. —— June 18 to June 30, in the Senate.
July 17, vetoed.
House Journal, 1 sess. 50 Cong. pp. 1032, 2143 P, 2253, 2377 O. —— Senate Journal, 1 sess. 50 Cong. pp. 981, 982, 1020, 1041 P, 1055, 1057.

344. Pension to Bridget Foley. [§ 74.]
S. 1447, 1 sess. 50 Cong. "An act granting a pension to Bridget Foley."
1888. Jan. 16 to Mar. 31, in the Senate. —— Apr. 2 to July 13, in the House.
July 26, vetoed.
Senate Journal, 1 sess. 50 Cong. pp. 159, 458, 578 P, 1110, 1125, 1126, 1128, 1186 O, 1187. —— House Journal, 1 sess. 50 Cong. pp. 1412, 1427, 1662, 2345 P, 2379.

345. Right of way for a railroad through Indian Lands. [§ 41.]
S. 2644, 1 sess. 50 Cong. "An act granting the right of way to the Fort Smith, Paris, and Dardanelle Railway Company, to construct and operate a railroad, telegraph, and telephone line from Fort Smith, Arkansas, through the Indian Territory, to or near Baxter Springs, in the State of Kansas."

1888. Apr. 9 to May 2, in the Senate.——May 4 to July 10, in the House. July 26, vetoed.
Senate Journal, 1 sess. 50 Cong. pp. 627, 726, 760 P, 1091, 1093, 1102, 1103, 1105, 1187 O, 1193.——*House Journal, 1 sess. 50 Cong.* pp. 1825, 2311 P, 2334, 2341.

346. Relief of P. A. Leatherbury. [§ 66.]
H. R. 3008, 1 sess. 50 Cong. "An act for the relief of P. A. Leatherbury."
1888. Jan. 4 to May 2, in the House.——May 3 to July 19, in the Senate.
Aug. 3, vetoed.
House Journal, 1 sess. 50 Cong. pp. 167, 701, 1804 P, 2413, 2542 O.——*Senate Journal, 1 sess. 50 Cong.* pp. 762, 763, 928, 1134 P, 1143.

347. Land grant to Tacoma, W. T. [§ 48.]
S. 1870, 1 sess. 50 Cong. "An act granting the use of certain lands in Pierce County, Washington Territory, to the city of Tacoma, for the purpose of a public park."
1888. Feb. 6 to Mar. 31, in the Senate.——Apr. 2 to July 24, in the House.
Aug. 7, vetoed.
Senate Journal, 1 sess. 50 Cong. pp. 270, 451, 581 P, 1172, 1181, 1182, 1193, 1251 O, 1253, 1322.——*House Journal, 1 sess. 50 Cong.* pp. 1414, 1430, 1689, 2454 P, 2470.

348. Pension to Mrs. Anna Butterfield. [§ 74.]
H. R. 8761, 1 sess. 50 Cong. "An act granting a pension to Mrs. Anna Butterfield."
1888. Mar. 21 to June 1, in the House.——June 4 to July 25, in the Senate.
Aug. 9, vetoed.
House Journal, 1 sess. 50 Cong. pp. 1263, 1612, 2041 P, 2473, 2560 O.——*Senate Journal, 1 sess. 50 Cong.* pp. 912, 915, 1052, 1176 P, 1211, 1213.

349. Pension to Eliza Smith. [§ 74.]
H. R. 2140, 1 sess. 50 Cong. "An act granting a pension to Eliza Smith."
1888. Jan. 4 to June 29, in the House.——June 30 to July 25, in the Senate.
Aug. 9, vetoed.
House Journal, 1 sess. 50 Cong. pp. 134, 2160, 2243 P, 2472, 2561 O.——*Senate Journal, 1 sess. 50 Cong.* pp. 1037, 1106, 1176 P, 1211, 1212.

350. Pension to Stephen A. Seavey. [§ 74.]
H. R. 7510, 1 sess. 50 Cong. "An act granting a pension to Stephen A. Seavey."
1888. Feb. 20 to July 13, in the House.——July 16 to July 25, in the Senate.
Aug. 9, vetoed.
House Journal, 1 sess. 50 Cong. pp. 843, 1338, 2345 P, 2473, 2562 O.——*Senate Journal, 1 sess. 50 Cong.* pp. 1110, 1111, 1142, 1177 P, 1203, 1204.

351. Pension to Sarah A. Corson. [§ 74.]
H. R. 6307, 1 sess. 50 Cong. "An act granting a pension to Sarah A. Corson."
1888. Jan. 30 to June 29, in the House.——June 30 to July 25, in the Senate.
Aug. 9, vetoed.
House Journal, 1 sess. 50 Cong. pp. 577, 2123, 2244 P, 2473, 2562 O.——*Senate Journal, 1 sess. 50 Cong.* pp. 1037, 1090, 1176 P, 1211, 1212.

352. Pension to Manuel Garcia. [§ 74.]
H. R. 3521, 1 sess. 50 Cong. "An act granting a pension to Manuel Garcia."
1888. Jan. 9 to June 29, in the House.——June 30 to July 25, in the Senate.
Aug. 9, vetoed.
House Journal, 1 sess. 50 Cong. pp. 260, 2123, 2243 P, 2472, 2563 O.——*Senate Journal, 1 sess. 50 Cong.* pp. 1037, 1053, 1176 P, 1211, 1212.

353. Pension to Rachel Barnes. [§ 74.]

H. R. 149, 1 sess. 50 Cong. "An act granting a pension to Rachel Barnes."

1887. Dec. 21 to 1888, June 29, in the House. —— 1888, June 30 to July 25, in the Senate.

1888. Aug. 10, vetoed.

House Journal, 1 sess. 50 Cong. pp. 77, 1736, 2243 P, 2472, 2572 O. —— *Senate Journal, 1 sess. 50 Cong.* pp. 1037, 1053, 1176 P, 1211, 1212.

354. Pension to Sallie T. Ward. [§ 74.]

H. R. 8574, 1 sess. 50 Cong. "An act granting a pension to Sallie T. Ward, widow of the late W. T. Ward."

1888. Mar. 16 to July 13, in the House. —— July 16 to July 25, in the Senate.

Aug. 10, vetoed.

House Journal, 1 sess. 50 Cong. pp. 1187, 1340, 2345 P, 2473, 2572 O. —— *Senate Journal, 1 sess. 50 Cong.* pp. 1110, 1111, 1138, 1177 P, 1211, 1213.

355. Pension to George W. Pitner. [§ 74.]

H. R. 490, 1 sess. 50 Cong. "An act granting a pension to George W. Pitner."

1887. Dec. 21 to 1888, June 29, in the House. —— 1888, June 30 to July 25, in the Senate.

1888. Aug. 10, vetoed.

House Journal, 1 sess. 50 Cong. pp. 89, 2244 P, 2472, 2573 O. —— *Senate Journal, 1 sess. 50 Cong.* pp. 1037, 1090, 1176 P, 1211, 1212.

356. Pension to Lydia A. Heiny. [§ 74.]

H. R. 9034, 1 sess. 50 Cong. "An act granting a pension to Lydia A. Heiny."

1888. Mar. 30 to June 29, in the House. —— June 30 to July 25, in the Senate.

Aug. 10, vetoed.

House Journal, 1 sess. 50 Cong. pp. 1367, 1894, 2243 P, 2473, 2574 O. —— *Senate Journal, 1 sess. 50 Cong.* pp. 1037, 1106, 1176 P, 1211, 1213.

357. Pension to William P. Riddle. [§ 76.]

H. R. 9183, 1 sess. 50 Cong. "An act granting a pension to William P. Riddle."

1888. Apr. 3 to June 29, in the House. —— June 30 to July 25, in the Senate.

Aug. 10, vetoed.

House Journal, 1 sess. 50 Cong. pp. 1418, 2161, 2244 P, 2473, 2575 O. —— *Senate Journal, 1 sess. 50 Cong.* pp. 1037, 1053, 1176 P, 1211, 1213.

358. Pension to Bernard Carlin. [§ 72.]

H. R. 2233, 1 sess. 50 Cong. "An act granting a pension to Bernard Carlin."

1888. Jan. 4 to June 8, in the House. —— June 11 to July 25, in the Senate.

Aug. 10, vetoed.

House Journal, 1 sess. 50 Cong. pp. 138, 1696, 2104 P, 2472, 2576 O. —— *Senate Journal, 1 sess. 50 Cong.* pp. 946, 1036, 1175 P, 1211, 1212.

359. Relief of Edson Saxberry. [§ 74.]

H. R. 6193, 1 sess. 50 Cong. "An act for the relief of Edson Saxberry."

1888. Jan. 30 to June 29, in the House. —— June 30 to July 25, in the Senate.

Aug. 10, vetoed.

House Journal, 1 sess. 50 Cong. pp. 573, 2196, 2243 P, 2473, 2576 O. —— *Senate Journal, 1 sess. 50 Cong.* pp. 1037, 1079, 1176 P, 1211, 1212.

360. Pension to Mrs. Caroline G. Seyfforth. [§ 74.]

H. R. 9126, 1 sess. 50 Cong. "An act granting a pension to Mrs. Caroline G. Seyfforth."

1888. Apr. 2 to June 30, in the House. —— June 30 to July 25, in the Senate.
Aug 10, vetoed.

House Journal, 1 sess. 50 Cong. pp. 1393, 2161, 2244 P, 2473, 2575 O. —— *Senate Journal, 1 sess. 50 Cong.* pp. 1037, 1052, 1176 P, 1211, 1213.

361. Pension to James C. White. [§ 76.]

H. R. 9344, 1 sess. 50 Cong. "An act granting a pension to James C. White."

1888. Apr. 4 to June 29, in the House. —— June 30 to July 25, in the Senate.
Aug. 10, vetoed.

House Journal, 1 sess. 50 Cong. pp. 1582, 2160, 2243 P, 2473, 2574 O. —— *Senate Journal, 1 sess. 50 Cong.* pp. 1037, 1053, 1176 P, 1211, 1213.

362. Additional copies of the U. S. map for 1886. [§ 98.]

S. Res. 17, 1 sess. 50 Cong. Joint resolution providing for the printing of additional copies of the United States map of the edition of 1886, prepared by the Commissioner of Public Lands.

1887. Dec. 15 to 1888, Feb. 7, in the Senate. —— 1888, Feb. 14 to July 28, in the House.
1888. Aug. 14, vetoed.

Senate Journal, 1 sess. 50 Cong. pp. 76, 277 P, 1206, 1232, 1235, 1284 O, 1285. —— *House Journal, 1 sess. 50 Cong.* pp. 792, 2494 P.

363. Pension to Mary Curtin. [§ 74.]

S. 2653, 1 sess. 50 Cong. "An act granting a pension to Mary Curtin."

1888. Apr. 10 to Apr. 17, in the Senate. —— Apr. 18 to July 27, in the House.
Aug. 14, vetoed.

Senate Journal, 1 sess. 50 Cong. pp. 635, 679 P, 1202, 1223, 1230, 1233, 1285 O, 1286. —— *House Journal, 1 sess. 50 Cong.* pp. 1677, 1687, 1895, 2487, 2488 P, 2516.

364. Pension to the widow of John Leary. [§ 74.]

S. 1076, 1 sess. 50 Cong. "An act granting a pension to the widow of John Leary, deceased."

1887. Dec. 22 to 1888, May 2, in the Senate. —— 1888, May 3 to July 27, in the House.
1888. Aug. 14, vetoed.

Senate Journal, 1 sess. 50 Cong. pp. 105, 390, 671, 756 P, 1202, 1223, 1229, 1233, 1286 O, 1288. —— *House Journal, 1 sess. 50 Cong.* pp. 1814, 1821, 1898, 2487, 2488 P, 2517.

365. Pension to Benjamin A. Burtram. [§ 74.]

S. 1762, 1 sess. 50 Cong. "An act granting a pension to Benjamin A. Burtram."

1888. Jan. 30 to Apr. 6, in the Senate. —— Apr. 4 to July 27, in the House.
Aug. 14, vetoed.

Senate Journal, 1 sess. 50 Cong. pp. 233, 548, 615 P, 1202, 1223, 1229, 1233, 1288 O, 1289. —— *House Journal, 1 sess. 50 Cong.* pp. 1518, 1599, 1895, 2487, 2488 P, 2516.

366. Relief of P. E. Parker. [§ 66.]

S. 3038, 1 sess. 50 Cong. "An act for the relief of P. E. Parker."

1888. May 28 to Aug. 1, in the Senate. —— Aug. 1 to Aug. 2, in the House.
Aug. 22, vetoed.

Senate Journal, 1 sess. 50 Cong. pp. 882, 1108, 1222 P, 1232, 1264, 1265, 1269, 1326 O, 1328. —— *House Journal, 1 sess. 50 Cong.* pp. 2518, 2521 P, 2564.

367. Pension to James E. Kabler. [§ 74.]

S. 2616, 1 sess. 50 Cong. "An act granting a pension to James E. Kabler."

1888. Apr. 6 to May 2, in the Senate. —— May 3 to Aug. 3, in the House.

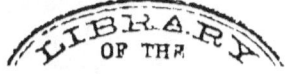

1888. Aug. 22, vetoed.
Senate Journal, 1 sess. 50 Cong. pp. 613, 709, 756 P, 1245, 1264, 1265, 1269, 1328 O, 1329.——*House Journal, 1 sess. 50 Cong.* pp. 1815, 1822, 1965, 2534, 2535 P, 2564.

368. Pension to Sarah C. Anderson. [§ 74.]
S. 2370, 1 sess. 50 Cong. "An act granting a pension to Sarah C. Anderson and children under sixteen years of age."
1888. Mar. 14 to May 2, in the Senate.——May 3 to Aug. 3, in the House.
Aug. 22, vetoed.
Senate Journal, 1 sess. 50 Cong. pp. 466, 671, 756 P, 1244, 1264, 1265, 1269, 1329 O, 1330.——*House Journal, 1 sess. 50 Cong.* pp. 1815, 1822, 1978, 2534, 2535 P, 2564.

369. Pension to David H. Lutman. [§ 74.]
S. 2206, 1 sess. 50 Cong. "An act granting a pension to David H. Lutman."
1888. Mar. 1 to Apr. 6, in the Senate.——Apr. 4 to Aug. 3, in the House.
Aug. 22, vetoed.
Senate Journal, 1 sess. 50 Cong. pp. 406, 499, 615 P, 1244, 1264, 1265, 1269, 1330 O, 1331.——*House Journal, 1 sess. 50 Cong.* pp. 1518, 1600, 1898, 2534, 2535 P, 2564.

370. Pension to Mrs. Margaret B. Todd. [§ 74.]
S. 645, 1 sess. 50 Cong. "An act granting a pension to Mrs. Margaret B. Todd."
1887. Dec. 13 to 1888, Apr. 6, in the Senate.——1888, Apr. 4 to Aug. 3, in the House.
1888. Aug. 22, vetoed.
Senate Journal, 1 sess. 50 Cong. pp. 61, 585, 616 P, 1244, 1264, 1265, 1268, 1331 O, 1332.——*House Journal, 1 sess. 50 Cong.* pp. 1517, 1599, 2286, 2535, 2536 P, 2563.

371. Pension to John W. Reynolds. [§ 74.]
S. 1542, 1 sess. 50 Cong. "An act granting a pension to John W. Reynolds."
1888. Jan. 19 to Mar. 31, in the Senate.——Apr. 2 to Aug. 3, in the House.
Aug. 22, vetoed.
Senate Journal, 1 sess. 50 Cong. pp. 187, 425, 577, 578 P, 1244, 1264, 1265, 1269, 1332 O, 1333.——*House Journal, 1 sess. 50 Cong.* pp. 1412, 1427, 1978, 2534, 2535 P, 2563.

372. Relief of W. S. Carpenter. [§ 66.]
H. R. 2088, 1 sess. 50 Cong. "An act for the relief of W. S. Carpenter."
1888. Jan. 4 to May 15, in the House.——May 16 to Aug. 7, in the Senate.
Aug. 22, vetoed.
House Journal, 1 sess. 50 Cong. pp. 132, 1258, 1910 P, 2551, 2642 O.——*Senate Journal, 1 sess. 50 Cong.* pp. 830, 831, 964, 1250 P, 1261, 1262.

373. Relief of Clement A. Lounsberry. [§ 70.]
H. R. 2524, 1 sess. 50 Cong. "An act for the relief of Clement A. Lounsberry."
1888. Jan. 4 to May 17, in the House.——May 21 to Aug. 10, in the Senate.
Aug. 27, vetoed.
House Journal, 1 sess. 50 Cong. pp. 149, 1665, 1924 P, 2584, 2683 O.——*Senate Journal, 1 sess. 50 Cong.* pp. 846, 1127, 1271 P, 1281, 1282.

374. Public building at Sioux City, Iowa. [§ 93.]
S. 288, 1 sess. 50 Cong. "An act for the erection of a public building at Sioux City, Iowa."
1887. Dec. 12 to 1888, Mar. 29, in the Senate.——1888, Mar. 30 to July 30, in the House.
1888. Aug. 27, vetoed.

Senate Journal, 1 sess. 50 Cong. pp. 37, 360, 561 P, 1210, 1214, 1232, 1264, 1270, 1290, 1291, 1303, 1354 O, 1356.——*House Journal, 1 sess. 50 Cong.* pp. 1379, 1388, 1660, 2500 P, 2514, 2564, 2567, 2597.

375. Pension to John S. Bryant. [§ 74.]
H. R. 5155, 1 sess. 50 Cong. "An act granting a pension to John S. Bryant."
1888. Jan. 16 to July 20, in the House.——July 23 to Aug. 15, in the Senate.
   Sept. 1, vetoed.
House Journal, 1 sess. 50 Cong. pp. 394, 1795, 2419 P, 2599, 2712 O.——*Senate Journal, 1 sess. 50 Cong.* pp. 1150, 1169, 1294 P, 1303, 1306.

376. Pension to Edwin J. Godfrey. [§ 74.]
H. R. 9363, 1 sess. 50 Cong. "An act granting a pension to Edwin J. Godfrey."
1888. Apr. 13 to July 20, in the House.——July 23 to Aug. 15, in the Senate.
   Sept. 1, vetoed.
House Journal, 1 sess. 50 Cong. pp. 1589, 1735, 2419 P, 2599, 2712 O.——*Senate Journal, 1 sess. 50 Cong.* pp. 1150, 1169, 1294 P, 1303, 1306.

377. Pension to Russell L. Doane. [§ 74.]
H. R. 2507, 1 sess. 50 Cong. "An act granting a pension to Russell L. Doane, of Peck, Sanilac County, Michigan."
1888. Jan. 4 to July 27, in the House.——July 28 to Aug. 21, in the Senate.
   Sept. 6, vetoed.
House Journal, 1 sess. 50 Cong. pp. 148, 1896, 2487 P, 2637, 2736 O.——*Senate Journal, 1 sess. 50 Cong.* pp. 1206, 1207, 1220, 1316 P, 1342, 1343.

378. Pension to John Dean. [§ 74.]
H. R. 9372, 1 sess. 50 Cong. "An act granting a pension to John Dean."
1888. Apr. 13 to Aug. 10, in the House.——Aug. 13 to Aug. 21, in the Senate.
   Sept. 7, vetoed.
House Journal, 1 sess. 50 Cong. pp. 1590, 2216, 2579 P, 2638, 2740 O.——*Senate Journal, 1 sess. 50 Cong.* pp. 1274, 1279, 1301, 1317 P, 1342, 1344.

379. Pension to C. T. Maphet. [§ 74.]
H. R. 217, 1 sess. 50 Cong. "An act granting a pension to C. T. Maphet."
1887. Dec. 21 to 1888, July 6, in the House.——1888, July 9 to Aug. 21, in the Senate.
1888. Sept. 7, vetoed.
House Journal, 1 sess. 50 Cong. pp. 79, 2184, 2290 P, 2637, 2741 O.——*Senate Journal, 1 sess. 50 Cong.* pp. 1074, 1247, 1317 P, 1342, 1343.

380. Pension to Charles Walster. [§ 74.]
H. R. 5503, 1 sess. 50 Cong. "An act granting a pension to Charles Walster."
1888. Jan. 19 to Aug. 3, in the House.——Aug. 6 to Aug. 21, in the Senate.
   Sept. 7, vetoed.
House Journal, 1 sess. 50 Cong. pp. 465, 2160, 2536 P, 2637, 2741 O.——*Senate Journal, 1 sess. 50 Cong.* pp. 1245, 1263, 1317 P, 1342, 1344.

381. Pension to Catherine Bussey. [§ 74.]
H. R. 333, 1 sess. 50 Cong. "An act granting a pension to Catherine Bussey."
1887. Dec. 21 to 1888, July 27, in the House.——1888, July 28 to Aug. 21, in the Senate.
1888. Sept. 7, vetoed.
House Journal, 1 sess. 50 Cong. pp. 83, 2487 P, 2637, 2741 O.——*Senate Journal, 1 sess. 50 Cong.* pp. 1206, 1207, 1247, 1317 P, 1342, 1343.

382. Pension to Mrs. Jane Potts. [§ 74.]
H. R. 5525, 1 sess. 50 Cong. "An act granting a pension to Mrs. Jane Potts."
1888. Jan. 20 to Aug. 10, in the House. —— Aug. 13 to Aug. 21, in the Senate.
Sept. 7, vetoed.
House Journal, 1 sess. 50 Cong. pp. 473, 2417, 2579 P, 2637, 2742 O. —— *Senate Journal, 1 sess. 50 Cong.* pp. 1274, 1279, 1301, 1317 P, 1342, 1344.

383. Pension to Mrs. Catherine Reed. [§ 74.]
H. R. 7717, 1 sess. 50 Cong. "An act granting a pension to Mrs. Catherine Reed."
1888. Feb. 25 to July 27, in the House. —— July 28 to Aug. 21, in the Senate.
Sept. 7, vetoed.
House Journal, 1 sess. 50 Cong. pp. 924, 2487, 2488 P, 2637, 2742, 2743 O. —— *Senate Journal, 1 sess. 50 Cong.* pp. 1206, 1207, 1220, 1316 P, 1342, 1344.

384. Pension to Jacob Newhard. [§ 74.]
H. R. 4855, 1 sess. 50 Cong. "An act granting a pension to Jacob Newhard."
1888. Jan. 13 to Aug. 3, in the House. —— Aug. 6 to Aug. 21, in the Senate.
Sept. 7, vetoed.
House Journal, 1 sess. 50 Cong. pp. 379, 2535, 2536 P, 2637, 2743 O. —— *Senate Journal, 1 sess. 50 Cong.* pp. 1245, 1277, 1317 P, 1342, 1344.

385. Pension to Jesse M. Stilwell. [§ 74.]
H. R. 6371, 1 sess. 50 Cong. "An act granting a pension to Jesse M. Stilwell."
1888. Jan. 31 to July 20, in the House. —— July 23 to Aug. 21, in the Senate.
Sept. 13, vetoed.
House Journal, 1 sess. 50 Cong. pp. 601, 2065, 2419 P, 2639, 2776 O. —— *Senate Journal, 1 sess. 50 Cong.* pp. 1150, 1255, 1316 P, 1325, 1362.

386. Land grant to Kansas. [§ 48.]
H. Res. 14, 1 sess. 50 Cong. "Joint resolution to authorize the Secretary of the Interior to certify lands to the State of Kansas for the benefit of agriculture and the mechanic arts."
1888. Jan. 4 to July 24, in the House. —— July 26 to Aug. 31, in the Senate.
Sept. 24, vetoed.
House Journal, 1 sess. 50 Cong. pp. 197, 2455 P, 2709, 2828 O. —— *Senate Journal, 1 sess. 50 Cong.* pp. 1181, 1185, 1216, 1371 P, 1377.

387. Sale of military reservation in Kansas. [§ 48.]
H. R. 8310, 1 sess. 50 Cong. "An act to provide for the disposal of the Fort Wallace military reservation in Kansas."
1888. Mar. 10 to July 24, in the House. —— July 26 to Aug. 1, in the Senate.
Sept. 24, vetoed.
House Journal, 1 sess. 50 Cong. pp. 1117, 2456 P, 2518, 2830 O. —— *Senate Journal, 1 sess. 50 Cong.* pp. 1181, 1185, 1216, 1224 P, 1238, 1366, 1367, 1380, 1381.

388. Relief of Laura E. Maddox. [§ 66.]
S. 2201, 1 sess. 50 Cong. "An act for the relief of Laura E. Maddox, widow and executrix, and Robert Morrison, executor of Joseph H. Maddox, deceased."
1888. Mar. 1 to May 31, in the Senate. —— May 31 to Sept. 21, in the House.
Oct. 10, vetoed.
Senate Journal, 1 sess. 50 Cong. pp. 405, 903 P, 1448, 1467, 1471, 1484, 1534 O, 1537. —— *House Journal, 1 sess. 50 Cong.* pp. 2029, 2034, 2816, 2817, 2841.

389. Pension to Sarah A. Woodbridge. [§ 76.]
S. 3276, 1 sess. 50 Cong. "An act granting restoration of pension to Sarah A. Woodbridge."

1888. July 9 to Aug. 23, in the Senate.——Aug. 24 to Sept. 21, in the House.
Oct. 12, vetoed.

Senate Journal, 1 sess. 50 Cong. pp. 1071, 1162, 1273, 1322, 1334 P, 1448, 1467, 1471, 1484, 1546 O, 1547.——*House Journal, 1 sess. 50 Cong.* pp. 2661, 2664, 2725, 2818 P, 2842.

390. Relief of James M. Wilbur. [§ 66.]

S. 1044, 1 sess. 50 Cong. "An act authorizing the Secretary of the Treasury to state and settle the account of James M. Wilbur with the United States, and to pay said Wilbur such sum of money as may be found due him thereon."

1887. Dec. 21 to 1888, Mar. 21, in the Senate.——1888, Mar. 22 to Sept. 21, in the House.
1888. Oct. 12, vetoed.

Senate Journal, 1 sess. 50 Cong. pp. 100, 251, 515 P, 1448, 1467, 1471, 1484, 1550 O, 1553.——*House Journal, 1 sess. 50 Cong.* pp. 1294, 1694, 2450, 2816, 2817 P, 2841.

391. Pension to Mary K. Richards. [§ 72.]

S. 3306, 1 sess. 50 Cong. "An act granting a pension to Mary K. Richards."

1888. July 11 to Aug. 21, in the Senate.——Aug. 22 to Sept. 28, in the House.
Oct. 15, vetoed.

Senate Journal, 1 sess. 50 Cong. pp. 1092, 1301, 1315 P, 1480, 1499, 1500, 1507, 1548 O.——*House Journal, 1 sess. 50 Cong.* pp. 2636, 2645, 2778, 2856 P, 2878.

392. Pension to William S. Bradshaw. [§ 74.]

S. 3208, 1 sess. 50 Cong. "An act granting a pension to William S. Bradshaw."

1888. June 25 to Aug. 21, in the Senate.——Aug. 22 to Sept. 28, in the House.
Oct. 15, vetoed.

Senate Journal, 1 sess. 50 Cong. pp. 1002, 1280, 1315 P, 1480, 1499, 1500, 1507, 1548 O, 1550.——*House Journal, 1 sess. 50 Cong.* pp. 2636, 2645, 2739, 2856 P, 2878.

393. Pension to Mary Woodworth. [§ 74.]

H. R. 7657, 1 sess. 50 Cong. "An act granting a pension to Mary Woodworth, widow of Ebenezer F. Woodworth."

1888. Feb. 24 to Aug. 24, in the House.——Aug. 27 to Sept. 25, in the Senate.
Oct. 16, vetoed.

House Journal, 1 sess. 50 Cong. pp. 906, 2307, 2661 P, 2845, 2935 O.——*Senate Journal, 1 sess. 50 Cong.* pp. 1352, 1353, 1385, 1458 P, 1499, 1501.

394. Pension to Mrs. Sophia Vogelsang. [§ 74.]

H. R. 10661, 1 sess. 50 Cong. "An act granting a pension to Mrs. Sophia Vogelsang."

1888. June 30 to Sept. 7, in the House.——Sept. 10 to Sept. 25, in the Senate.
Oct. 16, vetoed.

House Journal, 1 sess. 50 Cong. pp. 2244, 2491, 2746 P, 2845, 2933 O.——*Senate Journal, 1 sess. 50 Cong.* pp. 1399, 1415, 1459 P, 1499, 1502.

395. Pension to John Robeson. [§ 74.]

H. R. 6201, 1 sess. 50 Cong. "An act granting a pension to John Robeson."

1888. Jan. 30 to Aug. 24, in the House.——Aug. 27 to Sept. 25, in the Senate.
Oct. 16, vetoed.

House Journal, 1 sess. 50 Cong. pp. 573, 2661 P, 2844, 2932 O.——*Senate Journal, 1 sess. 50 Cong.* pp. 1352, 1353, 1385, 1458 P, 1499, 1501.

396. Pension to Peter Liner. [§ 74.]

H. R. 9106, 1 sess. 50 Cong. "An act granting a pension to Peter Liner."

1888. Apr. 2 to Sept. 7, in the House.——Sept. 10 to Sept. 25, in the Senate.
Oct. 16, vetoed.

House Journal, 1 sess. 50 Cong. pp. 1392, 2552, 2746 P, 2845, 2933 O. —— *Senate Journal, 1 sess. 50 Cong.* pp. 1399, 1400, 1414, 1459 P, 1499, 1501.

397. Pension to William S. Latham. [§ 76.]
H. R. 10563, 1 sess. 50 Cong. "An act granting a pension to William S. Latham."
1888. June 18 to Aug. 24, in the House. —— Aug. 27 to Sept. 25, in the Senate.
Oct. 16, vetoed.
House Journal, 1 sess. 50 Cong. pp. 2148, 2286, 2663 P, 2845, 2934 O. —— *Senate Journal, 1 sess. 50 Cong.* pp. 1352, 1353, 1389, 1458 P, 1499, 1502.

398. Pension to Lydia A. Eaton. [§ 74.]
H. R. 2472, 1 sess. 50 Cong. "An act granting a pension to Lydia A. Eaton."
1888. Jan. 4 to Sept. 7, in the House. —— Sept. 10 to Sept. 25, in the Senate.
Oct. 17, vetoed.
House Journal, 1 sess. 50 Cong. pp. 147, 2131, 2746 P, 2844, 2937 O. —— *Senate Journal, 1 sess. 50 Cong.* pp. 1399, 1400, 1415, 1459 P, 1499, 1500.

399. Pension to John Dauper. [§ 74.]
H. R. 10342, 1 sess. 50 Cong. "An act granting a pension to John Dauper."
1888. June 4 to Aug. 24, in the House. —— Aug. 27 to Sept. 25, in the Senate.
Oct. 17, vetoed.
House Journal, 1 sess. 50 Cong. pp. 2048, 2492, 2662 P, 2845, 2937 O. —— *Senate Journal, 1 sess. 50 Cong.* pp. 1352, 1353, 1389, 1458 P, 1499, 1502.

400. Pension to Ester Gaven. [§ 72.]
H. R. 11005, 1 sess. 50 Cong. "An act granting a pension to Ester Gaven."
1888. July 26 to Sept. 7, in the House. —— Sept. 10 to Sept. 25, in the Senate.
Oct. 17, vetoed.
House Journal, 1 sess. 50 Cong. pp. 2466, 2666, 2746 P, 2846, 2938 O. —— *Senate Journal, 1 sess. 50 Cong.* pp. 1399, 1400, 1414, 1459 P, 1499, 1502.

401. Pension to Mary Hooper. [§ 74.]
H. R. 10504, 1 sess. 50 Cong. "An act granting a pension to Mary Hooper."
1888. June 13 to Aug. 31, in the House. —— Sept. 3 to Sept. 25, in the Senate.
Oct. 17, vetoed.
House Journal, 1 sess. 50 Cong. pp. 2129, 2659, 2703 P, 2845, 2938 O. —— *Senate Journal, 1 sess. 50 Cong.* pp. 1373, 1374, 1400, 1458 P, 1499, 1502.

402. Pension to Ellen Kelly. [§ 74.]
H. R. 4820, 1 sess. 50 Cong. "An act granting a pension to Ellen Kelly."
1888. Jan. 13 to Aug. 31, in the House. —— Sept. 3 to Sept. 25, in the Senate.
Oct. 17, vetoed.
House Journal, 1 sess. 50 Cong. pp. 378, 2659, 2702 P, 2844, 2936 O. —— *Senate Journal, 1 sess. 50 Cong.* pp. 1373, 1374, 1405, 1458 P, 1499, 1501.

403. Pension to Elizabeth Heckler. [§ 74.]
H. R. 11222, 1 sess. 50 Cong. "An act granting a pension to Elizabeth Heckler."
1888. Aug. 20 to Sept. 7, in the House. —— Sept. 10 to Sept. 25, in the Senate.
Oct. 17, vetoed.
House Journal, 1 sess. 50 Cong. pp. 2624, 2708, 2746 P, 2846, 2936 O. —— *Senate Journal, 1 sess. 50 Cong.* pp. 1399, 1400, 1414, 1459 P, 1499, 1502.

404. Pension to Mary A. Carr. [§ 74.]
H. R. 4102, 1 sess. 50 Cong. "An act granting a pension to Mary A. Carr."
1888. Jan. 9 to Mar. 9, in the House. —— Mar. 12 to Sept. 25, in the Senate.

1888. Oct. 17, vetoed.
House Journal, 1 sess. 50. Cong. pp. 281, 882, 1110 P, 2844, 2937 O. —— *Senate Journal,* 1 sess. 50 Cong. pp. 453, 1356, 1457 P, 1499, 1501.

405. Pension to Eliza S. Glass. [§ 74.]
H. R. 11332, 1 sess. 50 Cong. "An act granting a pension to Eliza S. Glass."
1888. Sept. 1 to Sept. 14, in the House. —— Sept. 17 to Sept. 25, in the Senate. Oct. 17, vetoed.
House Journal, 1 sess. 50 Cong. pp. 2704, 2756, 2784 P, 2846, 2935 O. —— *Senate Journal,* 1 sess. 50 Cong. pp. 1428, 1429, 1443, 1459 P, 1499, 1502.

406. Relief of C. B. Wilson. [§ 70.]
H. R. 5080, 1 sess. 50 Cong. "An act for the relief of C. B. Wilson."
1888. Jan. 16 to May 14, in the House. —— May 15 to Dec. 12, in the Senate. Dec. 19, vetoed.
House Journal, 1 sess. 50 Cong. pp. 392, 789, 1902 P. —— *Senate Journal,* 1 sess. 50 Cong. pp. 824, 1209. —— *House Journal,* 2 sess. 50 Cong. pp. 78, 81, 89, 114, 118 O. —— *Senate Journal,* 2 sess. 50 Cong. pp. 57 P, 58.

407. Relief of Michael Piggott. [§ 66.]
H. R. 8469, 1 sess. 50 Cong. "An act for the relief of Michael Piggott."
1888. Mar. 13 to Sept. 14, in the House. —— Sept. 17 to Dec. 21, in the Senate.
1889. Jan. 16, vetoed.
House Journal, 1 sess. 50 Cong. pp. 1158, 2781, 2782 P. —— *Senate Journal,* 1 sess. 50 Cong. pp. 1428, 1429, 1473. —— *House Journal,* 2 sess. 50 Cong. pp. 135, 140, 155, 258 O. —— *Senate Journal,* 2 sess. 50 Cong. pp. 98 P, 106, 107.

408. Pension to Thomas Walsh. [§ 74.]
H. R. 7, 1 sess. 50 Cong. "An act granting a pension to Thomas B. Walsh."
1887. Dec. 21 to 1888, Sept. 28, in the House. —— 1888, Oct. 1 to Dec. 20, in the Senate.
1889. Jan. 16, vetoed.
House Journal, 1 sess. 50 Cong. pp. 71, 2160, 2856 P. —— *Senate Journal,* 1 sess. 50 Cong. pp. 1480, 1481, 1504. —— *House Journal,* 2 sess. 50 Cong. pp. 127, 140, 256 O. —— *Senate Journal,* 2 sess. 50 Cong. pp. 91 P, 106, 107.

409. Pension to Charles E. Scott. [§ 74.]
H. R. 4887, 1 sess. 50 Cong. "An act granting a pension to Charles E. Scott."
1888. Jan. 13 to Oct. 5, in the House. —— Oct. 8 to Dec. 20, in the Senate.
1889. Jan. 16, vetoed.
House Journal, 1 sess. 50 Cong. pp. 381, 2778, 2892, 2893 P. —— *Senate Journal,* 1 sess. 50 Cong. pp. 1512, 1517, 1545. —— *House Journal,* 2 sess. 50 Cong. pp. 127, 140, 155, 257 O. —— *Senate Journal,* 2 sess. 50 Cong. pp. 92 P, 106, 107.

410. Pension to Eli J. Yamgheim. [§ 74.]
H. R. 2236, 1 sess. 50 Cong. "An act granting a pension to Eli J. Yamgheim."
1888. Jan. 4 to Oct. 5, in the House. —— Oct. 8 to Dec. 20, in the Senate.
1889. Jan. 16, vetoed.
House Journal, 1 sess. 50 Cong. pp. 138, 2779, 2892, 2893 P. —— *Senate Journal,* 1 sess. 50 Cong. pp. 1516, 1517, 1545. —— *House Journal,* 2 sess. 50 Cong. pp. 127, 140, 155, 257 O. —— *Senate Journal,* 2 sess. 50 Cong. pp. 92 P, 106, 107.

* 411. Relief of W. R. Wheaton and C. H. Chamberlain. [§ 66.]
S. 3646, 2 sess. 50 Cong. "An act for the relief of William R. Wheaton and Charles H. Chamberlain, of California."

1888. Dec. 4 to Dec. 20, in the Senate. —— Dec. 21 to 1889, Jan. 3, in the House.
1889. Jan. 17, vetoed. —— Feb. 26, reconsidered in the Senate; passed over the veto, 35 to 8.
Senate Journal, 2 sess. 50 Cong. pp. 32, 45, 92 P, 106, 113, 115, 169 O, 171, 406 R. —— *House Journal, 2 sess. 50 Cong.* pp. 127, 139 P, 154, 640.

412. Pension to Mary I. Drake. [§ 74.]
H. R. 9173, 1 sess. 50 Cong. "An act granting a pension to Mary I. Drake."
1888. Apr. 3 to Sept. 28, in the House. —— Oct. 1 to Dec. 20, in the Senate.
1889. Jan. 18, vetoed.
House Journal, 1 sess. 50 Cong. pp. 1417, 2161, 2856 P. —— *Senate Journal, 1 sess. 50 Cong.* pp. 1481, 1503. —— *House Journal, 2 sess. 50 Cong.* pp. 127, 146, 174, 299, 303 O. —— *Senate Journal, 2 sess. 50 Cong.* pp. 91 P, 111, 114.

413. Pension to Mrs. Catherine Baberick. [§ 74.]
H. R. 9252, 1 sess. 50 Cong. "An act granting a pension to Mrs. Catherine Baberick, of Watertown."
1888. Apr. 4 to Sept. 21, in the House. —— Sept. 24 to Dec. 20, in the Senate.
1889. Jan. 18, vetoed.
House Journal, 1 sess. 50 Cong. pp. 1492, 2739, 2818 P. —— *Senate Journal, 1 sess. 50 Cong.* pp. 1449, 1453, 1485. —— *House Journal, 2 sess. 50 Cong.* pp. 127, 146, 174, 299, 304 O. —— *Senate Journal, 2 sess. 50 Cong.* pp. 91 P, 111, 114.

414. Relief of Charles W. Geddes. [§ 70.]
H. R. 9791, 1 sess. 50 Cong. "An act for the relief of Charles W. Geddes."
1888. May 2 to Sept. 28, in the House. —— Oct. 1 to Dec. 20, in the Senate.
1889. Jan. 18, vetoed.
House Journal, 1 sess. 50 Cong. pp. 1796, 2461, 2855 P. —— *Senate Journal, 1 sess. 50 Cong.* pp. 1481, 1510. —— *House Journal, 2 sess. 50 Cong.* pp. 128, 147, 174, 299, 305 O. —— *Senate Journal, 2 sess. 50 Cong.* pp. 91 P, 111, 114.

415. Pension to Bridget Carroll. [§ 74.]
H. R. 9296, 1 sess. 50 Cong. "An act granting a pension to Bridget Carroll."
1888. Apr. 4 to Sept. 28, in the House. —— Oct. 1 to Dec. 20, in the Senate.
1889. Jan. 18, vetoed.
House Journal, 1 sess. 50 Cong. pp. 1520, 2855 P. —— *Senate Journal, 1 sess. 50 Cong.* pp. 1481, 1510. —— *House Journal, 2 sess. 50 Cong.* pp. 127, 146, 174, 299, 304 O. —— *Senate Journal, 2 sess. 50 Cong.* pp. 91 P, 111, 114.

416. Pension to George Wallen. [§ 76.]
H. R. 9175, 1 sess. 50 Cong. "An act granting a pension to George Wallen."
1888. Apr. 3 to Sept. 28, in the House. —— Oct. 1 to Dec. 20, in the Senate.
1889. Jan. 18, vetoed.
House Journal, 1 sess. 50 Cong. pp. 1417, 2160, 2855 P. —— *Senate Journal, 1 sess. 50 Cong.* pp. 1481, 1510. —— *House Journal, 2 sess. 50 Cong.* pp. 127, 146, 174, 299, 305 O. —— *Senate Journal, 2 sess. 50 Cong.* pp. 91 P, 111, 114.

417. Pension to Mary Karstetter. [§ 74.]
H. R. 7877, 1 sess. 50 Cong. "An act to place Mary Karstetter on the pension roll."
1888. Feb. 28 to Sept. 28, in the House. —— Oct. 1 to Dec. 20, in the Senate.
1889. Jan. 18, vetoed.
House Journal, 1 sess. 50 Cong. pp. 957, 2079, 2855 P. —— *Senate Journal, 1 sess. 50 Cong.* pp. 1481, 1510. —— *House Journal, 2 sess. 50 Cong.* pp. 127, 146, 174, 299, 305 O. —— *Senate Journal, 2 sess. 50 Cong.* pp. 91 P, 111, 114.

418. Pension to Mrs. Ellen Hand. [§ 74.]
S. 3264, 1 sess. 50 Cong. "An act granting a pension to Mrs. Ellen Hand."
1888. July 5 to July 25, in the Senate.——July 26 to 1889, Jan. 18, in the House.
1889. Jan. 31, vetoed.
Senate Journal, 1 sess. 50 Cong. pp. 1054, 1160, 1175 P.——*House Journal, 1 sess. 50 Cong.* pp. 2472, 2481.——*Senate Journal, 2 sess. 50 Cong.* pp. 175, 187, 188, 211, 241 O, 242.——*House Journal, 2 sess. 50 Cong.* pp. 87, 300, 301 P, 331.

419. Pension to Eli Garrett. [§ 74.]
H. R. 9163, 1 sess. 50 Cong. "An act granting a pension to Eli Garrett."
1888. Apr. 3 to Dec. 14, in the House.——Dec. 17 to 1889, Jan. 25, in the Senate.
1889. Feb. 12, vetoed.
House Journal, 1 sess. 50 Cong. p. 1417.——*House Journal, 2 sess. 50 Cong.* pp. 90 P, 352, 400, 481, 484 O.——*Senate Journal, 2 sess. 50 Cong.* pp. 66, 166, 216 P, 230.

420. Relief of Julia Triggs. [§ 74.]
H. R. 5752, 1 sess. 50 Cong. "An act for the relief of Julia Triggs."
1888. Jan. 23 to Dec. 14, in the House.——Dec. 17 to 1889, Jan. 25, in the Senate.
1889. Feb. 12, vetoed.
House Journal, 1 sess. 50 Cong. pp. 493, 1156.——*House Journal, 2 sess. 50 Cong.* pp. 90, 91 P, 352, 400, 481, 484 O.——*Senate Journal, 2 sess. 50 Cong.* pp. 66, 166, 216 P, 230.

421. Pension to Clara M. Owen. [§ 74.]
H. R. 11052, 1 sess. 50 Cong. "An act granting a pension to Clara M. Owen."
1888. July 31 to 1889, Jan. 18, in the House.——1889, Jan. 19 to Jan. 25, in the Senate.
1889. Feb. 12, vetoed.
House Journal, 1 sess. 50 Cong. pp. 2508, 2631.——*House Journal, 2 sess. 50 Cong.* pp. 300, 301 P, 352, 400, 481, 485 O.——*Senate Journal, 2 sess. 50 Cong.* pp. 175, 177, 186, 216 P, 230.

422. Pension to Frank D. Worcester. [§ 74.]
S. 3451, 1 sess. 50 Cong. "An act granting a pension to Frank D. Worcester."
1888. Aug. 16 to Dec. 20, in the Senate.——Dec. 21 to 1889, Jan. 25, in the House.
1889. Feb. 13, vetoed.
Senate Journal, 1 sess. 50 Cong. p. 1297.——*Senate Journal, 2 sess. 50 Cong.* pp. 58, 92 P, 220, 238, 239, 242, 317 O, 318.——*House Journal, 2 sess. 50 Cong.* pp. 126, 138, 188, 345, 346 P, 380.

423. Pension to Michael Shong. [§ 74.]
S. 2514, 1 sess. 50 Cong. "An act granting a pension to Michael Shong."
1888. Mar. 26 to July 25, in the Senate.——July 26 to 1889, Jan. 25, in the House.
1889. Feb. 13, vetoed.
Senate Journal, 1 sess. 50 Cong. pp. 540, 1162, 1175 P.——*House Journal, 1 sess. 50 Cong.* pp. 2471, 2480.——*Senate Journal, 2 sess. 50 Cong.* pp. 220, 238, 239, 242, 318 O, 319.——*House Journal, 2 sess. 50 Cong.* pp. 345, 346 P, 380.

424. Pension to Charles J. Esty. [§ 72.]
S. 2665, 1 sess. 50 Cong. "An act granting a pension to Charles J. Esty."
1888. Apr. 11 to June 6, in the Senate.——June 7 to 1889, Feb. 2, in the House.
1889. Feb. 14, vetoed.
Senate Journal, 1 sess. 50 Cong. pp. 640, 923, 934 P.——*House Journal, 1 sess. 50 Cong.* pp. 2088, 2094.——*Senate Journal, 2 sess. 50 Cong.* pp. 248, 265, 266, 268, 324 O.——*House Journal, 2 sess. 50 Cong.* pp. 402, 403 P, 431.

425. Quieting settlers' titles on the Des Moines River. [§ 48.]

H. R. 1368, 1 sess. 50 Cong. "An act to quiet the title of settlers on the Des Moines River lands, in the State of Iowa, and for other purposes."
1888. Jan. 4 to Dec. 5, in the House. —— Dec. 6 to 1889, Feb. 8, in the Senate.
1889. Feb. 21, vetoed. —— Mar. 1, reconsidered by the House; vote, 147–104.

House Journal, 1 sess. 50 Cong. p. 193. —— *House Journal, 2 sess. 50 Cong.* pp. 49 P, 457, 466, 481, 587, 596 O, 683, 697, 702 R. —— *Senate Journal, 2 sess. 50 Cong.* pp. 41, 283 P, 290, 291.

426. Pension to John J. Lockrey. [§ 74.]

H. R. 220, 1 sess. 50 Cong. "An act granting a pension to John J. Lockrey."
1887. Dec. 21 to 1889, Feb. 1, in the House. —— 1889, Feb. 4 to Feb. 8, in the Senate.
1889. Feb. 23, vetoed.

House Journal, 1 sess. 50 Cong. pp. 79, 2184. —— *House Journal, 2 sess. 50 Cong.* pp. 402 P, 464, 476, 622, 631 O. —— *Senate Journal, 2 sess. 50 Cong.* pp. 249, 271, 285 P, 298, 299.

427. Pension to John McCool. [§ 74.]

H. R. 5807, 1 sess. 50 Cong. "An act granting a pension to John McCool."
1888. Jan. 23 to 1889, Jan. 25, in the House. —— 1889, Jan. 28 to Feb. 8, in the Senate.
1889. Feb. 23, vetoed.

House Journal, 1 sess. 50 Cong. p. 495. —— *House Journal, 2 sess. 50 Cong.* pp. 345, 346 P, 464, 476, 622, 632 O. —— *Senate Journal, 2 sess. 50 Cong.* pp. 221, 223, 235, 286 P, 298, 299.

428. Pension to William Barnes. [§ 74.]

H. R. 11999, 2 sess. 50 Cong. "An act granting a pension to William Barnes."
1889. Jan. 7 to Jan. 18, in the House. —— Jan. 19 to Feb. 8, in the Senate.
Feb. 23, vetoed.

House Journal, 2 sess. 50 Cong. pp. 164, 246, 301 P, 465, 477, 489, 633 O. —— *Senate Journal, 2 sess. 50 Cong.* pp. 175, 177, 199, 285 P, 298, 299.

429. Pension to Henry V. Bass. [§ 74.]

H. R. 11803, 2 sess. 50 Cong. "An act granting a pension to Henry V. Bass."
1888. Dec. 14 to 1889, Jan. 25, in the House. —— 1889, Jan. 28 to Feb. 8, in the Senate.
1889. Feb. 23, vetoed.

House Journal, 2 sess. 50 Cong. pp. 85, 288, 345, 346 P, 465, 477, 487, 632 O. —— *Senate Journal, 2 sess. 50 Cong.* pp. 221, 223, 235, 286 P, 298, 299.

430. Pension to Edwin W. Warner. [§ 72.]

S. 3561, 1 sess. 50 Cong. "An act granting a pension to Edwin W. Warner."
1888. Sept. 17 to Dec. 20, in the Senate. —— Dec. 21 to 1889, Feb. 8, in the House.
1889. Feb. 25, vetoed.

Senate Journal, 1 sess. 50 Cong. p. 1426. —— *Senate Journal, 2 sess. 50 Cong.* pp. 92 P, 289, 303, 304, 309, 399 O, 400. —— *House Journal, 2 sess. 50 Cong.* pp. 126, 139, 188, 459 P, 478.

431. Pension to Squire Walter. [§ 74.]

H. R. 10448, 1 sess. 50 Cong. "An act granting a pension to Squire Walter."
1888. June 9 to 1889, Jan. 18, in the House. —— 1889, Jan. 19 to Feb. 8, in the Senate.
1889. Feb. 25, vetoed.

House Journal, 1 sess. 50 Cong. pp. 2105, 2804. —— *House Journal, 2 sess. 50 Cong.* pp. 300, 301 P, 464, 477, 622, 633 O. —— *Senate Journal, 2 sess. 50 Cong.* pp. 175, 177, 209, 285 P, 298, 299.

432. Pension to George Colwell. [§ 73.]

H. R. 12047, 2 sess. 50 Cong. "An act granting an increase of pension to George Colwell."

1889. Jan. 11 to Feb. 8, in the House. —— Feb. 9 to Feb. 15, in the Senate. Feb. 26, vetoed.

House Journal, 2 sess. 50 Cong. pp. 199, 340, 460 P, 516, 529, 542, 643, 696 O. —— *Senate Journal, 2 sess. 50 Cong.* pp. 290, 300, 328 P, 334, 336.

* **433. Refunding the Direct Tax.** [§ 54.]

S. 139, 1 sess. 50 Cong. "An act to credit and pay to the several States and Territories and the District of Columbia all moneys collected under the direct tax levied by the act of Congress approved August fifth, eighteen hundred and sixty-one."

1887. Dec. 12 to 1888, Jan. 18, in the Senate. —— 1888, Jan. 19 to Dec. 12, in the House.

1889. Mar. 2, vetoed. —— Mar. 2, reconsidered by the Senate; passed over the veto, 45 to 9.

Senate Journal, 1 sess. 50 Cong. pp. 31, 58, 140, 141, 182, 183 P. —— *House Journal, 1 sess. 50 Cong.* pp. 469, 878, 953, 1138, 1407, 1445, 1533, 1552. —— *Senate Journal, 2 sess. 50 Cong.* pp. 58, 83, 84, 86, 89, 90, 288, 298, 334, 336, 340, 342, 350, 357, 380, 501 O, 509 R. —— *House Journal, 2 sess. 50 Cong.* pp. 49, 50, 54, 69, 71, 73, 76, 77 P, 120, 121, 466, 469, 531, 534, 550, 551, 558, 573, 742.

APPENDIX B.

A CHRONOLOGICAL LIST OF PRESIDENTIAL PROTESTS FROM APRIL 6, 1789, TO MARCH 4, 1889.[1]

PRESIDENT JACKSON (1829-1837).—[1 PROTEST.]

1. Censure of the Senate. [§ 20.]
A protest against the Senate resolution censuring the President for his course in the bank controversy.
1834. Apr. 15, protest signed.
Senate Miscellaneous Documents, 49 Cong. 2 sess. No. 53, p. 119 Q.

PRESIDENT TYLER (1841-1845).—[2 PROTESTS.]

2. Refusal to furnish information. [§ 26.]
A refusal on the part of the President to furnish to the House of Representatives the names of applicants for office.
1842. Mar. 23, protest signed.
Senate Miscellaneous Documents, 49 Cong. 2 sess. No. 53, p. 167 O.

3. Committee report on tariff veto. [§ 53.]
A protest against the report made by a committee of the House of Representatives upon the President's tariff veto of Aug. 9, 1842.
1842. Aug. 29, protest signed. *Congressional Globe, 27 Cong. 2 sess. p. 973* O.

PRESIDENT BUCHANAN (1857-1861).—[1 PROTEST.]

4. Covode investigation. [§ 32.]
A protest against the resolution of the House of Representatives appointing a committee to investigate the President's conduct.
1860. Mar. 28, protest signed.
Senate Miscellaneous Documents, 49 Cong. 2 sess. No. 53, p. 274 O.

PRESIDENT LINCOLN (1861-1865).—[1 PROTEST.]

5. Davis-Wade Bill.
A proclamation giving the President's reasons for not signing the Davis-Wade Bill.
1864. July 8, proclamation signed. *Appleton's Annual Cyclopædia, 1864, p. 307* O.

---

[1] This list includes those protests which have had reference to the exercise of the veto power. It is not intended to include all presidential protests.

PRESIDENT JOHNSON (1865-1869).—[1 PROTEST.]

6. Rider taking away President's war power. [§ 30.]
A protest against a rider which was tacked to an army appropriation bill, and which took from the President his direct command of the army.
1867. Mar. 2, protest signed.
Senate Miscellaneous Documents, 49 Cong. 2 sess. No. 53, p. 347 **O.**

PRESIDENT GRANT (1869-1877).—[3 PROTESTS.]

7. River and Harbor Bill. [§ 91.]
A protest against an extravagant river and harbor bill.
1876. Aug. 14, protest signed.
Senate Miscellaneous Documents, 49 Cong. 2 sess. No. 53, p. 399 **O.**

8. Diplomatic Bill. [§ 23.]
A protest against the invasion by Congress of the President's authority in foreign affairs.
1876. Aug. 14, protest signed.
Senate Miscellaneous Documents, 49 Cong. 2 sess. No. 53, p. 402 **O.**

9. Blankets for a reform school. [§ 9.]
A protest against a joint resolution of Congress which granted to a reform school army blankets which were needed by the army.
1877. Jan. 15, protest signed.
Senate Miscellaneous Documents, 49 Cong. 2 sess. No. 53, p. 404 **O.**

PRESIDENT HAYES (1877-1881).—[1 PROTEST.]

10. Fees of United States Marshals.
A protest against the failure of Congress to provide for the payment of United States Marshals.[1]
1879. June 30, protest signed.
Senate Miscellaneous Documents, 49 Cong. 2 sess. No. 53, p. 434 **O.**

---

[1] This protest occurred in the contest between President Hayes and Congress over riders. (See Ante, § 35.)

APPENDIX C.

A CHRONOLOGICAL LIST OF VETOES SENT TO THE CONGRESS OF THE CONFEDERATE STATES OF AMERICA FROM MARCH 1, 1861, TO MARCH 17, 1865.

PREPARED BY THE EDITOR FROM DATA FURNISHED BY JOHN O. SUMNER.

1. **Regulating the slave trade.** (Bill.)
1861. Mar. 1, vetoed. —— Mar. 2, reconsidered by Congress; vote, 3 states to 4 states (18 yeas to 28 nays). *Journals, Provisional Congress.*

2. **Removal of Congress to Richmond.** (Bill.)
1861. May 17(?), vetoed. —— May 17, reconsidered by Congress; vote, no states in favor. *Secret Journals, Provisional Congress.*

3. **Admiralty Court for Mississippi.** (Bill.)
1861. May 21(?), vetoed. —— May 21, reconsidered by Congress; failed to pass. *Secret Journals, Provisional Congress.*

4. **Appointment of additional assistant surgeons.** (Bill.)
1861. Aug. 22(?), vetoed. —— Aug. 22, reconsidered by Congress; vote, 1 state to 11. *Secret Journals, Provisional Congress.*

† 5. **[Subject not stated.]** (Bills.)
1861. Aug. 31, verbal statement on behalf of the President by the Attorney-General, that the President disapproved of certain bills, but was unable to prepare messages. —— Dec. 21, report setting forth the facts; tabled by Congress. *Secret Journals, Provisional Congress.*

6. **Regulation of furloughs and discharges.** (Bill.)
1861. Dec. 14, vetoed. —— 1862, Jan. 16, reconsidered by Congress; vote, 3 states to 9. *Secret Journals, Provisional Congress.*

7. **Small-arms and gunpowder.** (Bill.)
1862. Jan. 22(?), vetoed. —— Feb. 12, reconsidered by Congress; vote, 2 states to 10(?). *Journals, Provisional Congress.*

8. **Incorporation of Texan volunteers into the army.** (Bill.)
1862. Jan. 22, vetoed; Feb. 12, reconsidered by Congress; vote, 3 states to 9(?). *Journals, Provisional Congress.*

9. **Incorporation of Missouri volunteers into the army.** (Bill.)
1862. Jan. 22, vetoed. —— Feb. 14, reconsidered by Congress; vote, 7 states to 4 (1 divided). *Journals, Provisional Congress.*

10. Incorporation of Missouri volunteers into the army. (Bill.)
1862. Jan 9, passed.
Jan. 23(?), vetoed. —— Feb. 14, reconsidered by Congress; point of order that it had already been reconsidered.[1] *Journals, Provisional Congress.*

11. Furloughs. (Bill.)
1862. Feb. 1, vetoed. —— Feb. 15, reconsidered by Congress; vote, 8 states to 3 (2 divided), [not considered a constitutional two-thirds majority].
Journals, Provisional Congress.

12. Repeal of certain features of the U. S. naturalization laws. (Bill.)
1862. Feb. 5(?), vetoed. —— Feb. 5, reconsidered by Congress; vote, 3 states to 9.
Journals, Provisional Congress.

13. Creation of a commanding general. (Bill.)
1862. Mar. 15, vetoed. —— Mar. 20, reconsidered by the House; vote, 1-68.
Secret House Journal, 1 sess. 1 Cong.

14. Disposition of prize money. (Joint resolution.)
1861. Apr. 21(?), vetoed. —— Apr. 21, reconsidered by the Senate; vote unanimous against the resolution. *Secret Senate Journal, 1 sess. 1 Cong.*

15. Disposition of pay of deceased soldiers. (Joint resolution.)
1861. Apr. 21(?), vetoed. —— Apr. 21, reconsidered by the Senate; vote, 7-12.
Secret Senate Journal, 1 sess. 1 Cong.

16. Prize money. (Joint resolution.)
1862. Apr. 21, vetoed. —— Apr. 21, reconsidered by the Senate; unanimously rejected.
Senate Journal, 1 sess. 1 Cong.

† **17. [No subjects stated.]** (Bills.)
1862. Apr. 21, message to the House; no time to draw up reasons for withholding assent from three bills. *Open House Journal, 1 sess. 1 Cong.*

18. Rank of Quartermaster-General. (Bill.)
1862. Oct. 6(?), vetoed. —— Oct. 8, reconsidered by the Senate; vote, 4-10.
Open Senate Journal, 2 sess. 1 Cong.

19. Amendment of Provisional Army Act. (Bill.)
1862. Oct. 7(?), vetoed. —— Oct. 7, reconsidered by the House; vote, 1-61.
Open House Journal, 2 sess. 1 Cong.

20. Bequests to American Bible Society to go to C. S. Bible Society. (Bill.)
1862. Oct. 13, vetoed. —— Oct. 13, reconsidered by the Senate; vote, 0-16.
Open Senate Journal, 2 sess. 1 Cong.

21. Reorganization of medical department. (Bill.)
1862. Oct. 13(?), vetoed. —— Oct. 13, consideration postponed by the House. [No record of reconsideration.] *Open House Journal, 2 sess. 1 Cong.*

22. Building a vessel of war. (Bill.)
1862. Oct. 13(?), vetoed. —— Oct. 13, consideration postponed by the House. [No record of reconsideration.] *Secret House Journals, 2 sess. 1 Cong.*

---

[1] This bill had been presented to the President, who supposed that it had been superseded by the bill first vetoed; as there was no record of supersession, President Davis vetoed the bill.

*23. **Reorganization of heavy artillery.** (Bill.)
1863. Mar. 31, vetoed. —— Apr. 3, reconsidered by the Senate; passed over the veto, 18–5. —— Apr. 7, reconsidered by the House; vote, 22–59.
Open Senate Journal, 3 sess. 1 Cong.

24. **Free postage for newspapers.** (Bill.)
1863. May 1(?), vetoed. —— May 1, consideration postponed by the Senate. [No record of reconsideration.] *Open Senate Journal, 3 sess. 1 Cong.*

25. **Providing for elections in Tennessee.** (Bill.)
1863. May 1(?), vetoed. —— May 1, consideration indefinitely postponed by the House.
Open House Journal, 3 sess. 1 Cong.

26. **Appropriations for Kentucky troops.** (Bill.)
1863. Dec. 31(?), vetoed. —— 1864, Jan. 11, reconsidered by the Senate; vote, 10–8.
Open Senate Journal, 4 sess. 1 Cong.

27. **Veteran Soldiers' Home.** (Bill.)
1864. Feb. 11, vetoed. —— Feb. 13, laid on the table by the House. [No record of reconsideration.] *Open House Journal, 4 sess. 1 Cong.*

28. **Exemption of editors and employees of periodicals.** (Joint resolution.)
1864. June 7(?), vetoed. —— June 8, reconsidered by the Senate; vote, 11–10.
Open Senate Journal, 1 sess. 2 Cong.

29. **Appointment of additional officers of artillery.** (Bill.)
1864. June 7(?), vetoed. —— June 8, reconsidered by the Senate; vote, 1–22.
Open Senate Journal, 1 sess. 2 Cong.

30. **Exemption to vessels chartered by states.** (Bill.)
1864. June 10, vetoed. —— June 10, reconsidered by the House; vote, 26–43.
Open House Journal, 1 sess. 2 Cong.

31. **Claim of McDaniel and Ewing.** (Joint resolution.)
1864. June 11(?), vetoed. —— June 13, reconsidered by the Senate; vote, 9–7.
Open Senate Journal, 1 sess. 2 Cong.

32. **Funding and reducing treasury notes.** (Bill.)
1864. June 14, vetoed. —— June 14, consideration postponed. [No record of reconsideration.] *Open House Journal, 1 sess. 2 Cong.*

*33. **Increase of midshipmen.** (Bill.)
1865. Jan. 23(?), vetoed. —— Jan. 23, reconsidered by the Senate; passed over the veto, 15–3. —— Jan. 26, reconsidered by the House; vote, 40–36.
Senate and House Journals, 2 sess. 2 Cong.

34. **Newspapers to soldiers to be free of postage. (Bill.)
1865. Jan. 26, vetoed. —— Jan. 28, reconsidered by the Senate; passed over the veto, 13–4. —— Jan. 31, reconsidered by the House; passed over the veto, 63–13.
Senate and House Journals, 2 sess. 2 Cong.

*35. **Promotion of officers by general commanding in the field.** (Bill.)
1865. Mar. 9, vetoed. —— Mar. 11, reconsidered by the Senate; passed over the veto, 11–5. —— Mar. 11(?), reconsidered by the House; vote, 14–45.
Senate and House Journals, 2 sess. 2 Cong.

36. Abolition of certain offices. (Bill.)
1865. Mar. 11, vetoed. —— Nov. 14, reconsidered by the Senate; vote, 8–7.
Senate Journal, 2 sess. 2 Cong.

37. Diminishing exemptions and details. (Bill.)
1865. Mar. 13, vetoed. [No record of reconsideration.]
Senate Journal, 2 sess. 2 Cong.

* 38. Issue of $80,000,000 for payment of arrears to troops. (Bill.)
1865. Mar. 17(?), vetoed. —— Mar. 17, reconsidered by the House; passed over the veto, 39–18. —— Mar. 18, reconsidered by the Senate; vote, 11–1 (not a quorum). *House and Senate Journals, 2 sess. 2 Cong.*

APPENDIX D.

LEGISLATIVE ACTIVITY OF THE PRESIDENTS, 1789–1889.

COMPILED BY THE EDITOR.

This appendix is based upon an examination of the Statutes at Large. A note after each statute indicates whether it was signed, became law by the ten days rule, or was passed over the veto. The number of vetoes is taken from Appendix A.

	Acts and Joint Resolutions.				Bills.	
	Signed by the President.	Became law by ten days rule.	Passed over the veto.	Total.	Vetoed.	Total acts and vetoes.
1789–1793. Washington, I.	195	0	0	195	1	196
1793–1797. Washington, II.	210*	0	0	211	1	212
1797–1801. John Adams	268	0	0	268	0	268
1801–1805. Jefferson, I.	205*	0	0	206	0	206
1805–1809. Jefferson, II.	211	0	0	211	0	211
1809–1813. Madison, I.	324*	0	0	325	4	329
1813–1817. Madison, II.	569*	0	0	571	2	573
1817–1821. Monroe, I.	465	0	0	465	0	465
1821–1825. Monroe, II.	573	0	0	573	1	574
1825–1829. J. Q. Adams	501	0	0	501	0	501
1829–1833. Jackson, I.	831	0	0	831	7	838
1833–1837. Jackson, II.	848	0	0	848	5	853
1837–1841. Van Buren	679	0	0	679	0	679
1841–1845. Tyler	802	0	1	803	9	811
1845–1849. Polk	799	0	0	799	3	802
1849–1853. Taylor and Fillmore	973	0	0	973	0	973
1853–1857. Pierce	968	0	5	973	9	977
1857–1861. Buchanan	680	2	0	682	7	689
1861–1865. Lincoln	1035	1	0	1036	3	1039
1865–1869. Johnson	1446	18	15	1479	21	1485
1869–1873. Grant, I.	1756	24	1	1781	17	1797
1873–1877. Grant, II.	1319	112	3	1434	26	1457
1877–1881. Hayes	1395	0	1	1396	12	1407
1881–1885. Arthur	1716	13	1	1730	4	1733
1885–1889. Cleveland	2991	283	2	3276	301	3575
	21,759	453	29	22,246	433	22,650

* No record of the President's action on five joint resolutions.

APPENDIX E.

PROVISIONS OF STATE CONSTITUTIONS RELATIVE TO THE VETO, JULY 15, 1890.

COMPILED BY THE EDITOR.

The basis of this appendix is the analysis in Stimson's American Statute Law, §§ 305-307, 310. The tabulation in Benton's Veto Power, pp. 57, 58, has been compared. Wherever the two authorities disagree, and in the cases of the six new States, North Dakota, South Dakota, Montana, Washington, Wyoming, and Idaho, the Constitutions have been directly examined.

APPROVAL OF LEGISLATION BY THE GOVERNOR.

1. Bills submitted.
In the following States and Territories, every bill passed by the Legislature shall be presented to the governor before it becomes a law, and if he approves, he is to sign it: — *N.H., Mass., Me., Vt., Ct., N.Y., N.J., Pa., Ind., Ill., Mich., Wis., Io., Minn., Kan., Neb., N.D., S.D., Mon., Wy., Ida., Md., Va., W.Va., Ky., Tenn., Mo., Ark., Tex., Cal., Ore., Wash., Nev., Col., S.C., Ga., Ala., Miss., Fla., La.,* — 40 States. *Ariz., N.Mex., Utah,* — 3 Territories.

2. Bills not submitted.
In the following States there is no provision for submission of bills: — *R.I., Del., O., N.C.,* — 4 States.

3. Joint resolutions submitted.
In the following States and Territories, every joint or concurrent resolution, except for adjournment, is submitted in like manner: — *N.H., Mass., Me., Pa., Mich., Minn., Kan., Neb., Mon., Wy., Va., Ky., Tenn., Mo.,** *Ark., Tex., Col., S.C., Ga., Ala., Miss., La., Wash.,* — 23 States. *Ariz.,* — 1 Territory.

4. Joint resolutions not submitted.
In the following States and Territories there is no provision for submission of joint resolutions: — *Vt., R.I., Ct., N.Y., N.J., O., Ind., Ill., Wis., Io., N.D., S.D., Ida., Md., Del., W.Va., N.C., Cal., Ore., Nev., Ga.,* — 21 States. *N.Mex., Utah,* — 2 Territories.

VETO OF LEGISLATION BY THE GOVERNOR.

5. No requirement of return or statement of reasons.
The governor may withhold his signature without stating reasons in: — *Ga.,* — 1 State.

6. Return to the House in which the proposition originated.
The governor may veto a bill or resolution, when submitted, by returning it, with his objections, to the House in which it originated, in the following States and Territories: — *N.H., Mass., Me., Vt., Ct., N.Y., N.J., Pa., Ind., Ill., Mich., Wis., Io., Minn., Neb., N.D., S.D., Mon., Wy., Ida., Md., Va., W.Va., Ky., Tenn., Mo., Ark., Tex., Cal., Ore.,*

---

* Except resolutions for amending the Constitution.

Wash., Nev., Col., S.C., Ala., Miss., Fla., La., — 38 States. *Ariz., N.Mex., Utah,* — 3 Territories.

7. Return to the lower House.
In one State the bill or resolution is to be returned to the House of Representatives: *Kan.,* — 1 State.

8. Veto of items in appropriation bills.
In the following States the governor may veto certain items in an appropriation bill, and allow others to become a law: — *N.Y., N.J., Pa., Minn., Neb., N.D., S.D., Mon., Wy., Ida., W.Va., Mo., Ark., Tex., Cal., Col., Ga., Ala., Fla., La.,* — 20 States.

9. No veto of items in appropriation bills.
In the following States there is no power to veto parts of bills: — *N.H., Mass., Me., Vt., Conn., Ind., Ill., Mich., Wis., Io., Kan., Md., Va., Ky., Tenn., Ore., Wash., Nev., S.C., Miss.,* — 20 States.

10. No veto power.
In the following States there is no provision for revision of a bill by the governor: — *R.I., O., Del., N.C.,* — 4 States.

PASSING LEGISLATION OVER THE VETO.

11. Majority vote.
A vetoed bill shall become law if it receive, on reconsideration, an ordinary majority vote in: — *Ct., Vt.,* — 2 States.

12. Majority of all the members elected.
In the following States a majority of all the elected members of each House is required: — *N.J., Ind., W.Va., Ky., Tenn., Ark., Ala.,* — 7 States.

13. Three-fifths of the elected members.
In the following States a vote of three-fifths of the elected members of each House is required: — *Neb., Md.,* — 2 States.

14. Two-thirds of the members present.
In the following States and Territories a vote of two-thirds of the members present in each House is requisite: — *N.H., Mass., Me., Wis., Minn., S.D., Mon., Ida., Va., Tex., Ore., S.C., Ga., Miss., Fla.,* — 15 States. *N.Mex., Ariz., Utah,* — 3 Territories.

15. Two-thirds of the elected members.
In the following States and Territories a vote of two-thirds of the elected members of each House is requisite: — *N.Y., Pa., Ill., Mich., Io., Kan., N.D., Wy., Cal., Nev., Col., La., Wash.,* — 13 States.

16. Two-thirds of elected members in originating House, and a majority in the other House.
A vote of two-thirds of the elected members of the House in which the proposition originated, and of a majority in the other House, is required in *Mo.,* — 1 State.

17. No reconsideration.
In the following States the proposition is not submitted to the governor and hence is not subject to reconsideration: — *R.I., O., Del., N.C.,* — 4 States.

ENTRY IN THE JOURNALS.

18. Entry required.
In case of reconsideration, the votes must be entered on the Journal in the following States: — *N.H., Mass., Me., Vt., Ct., N.Y., N.J., Pa., Ill., Mich., Wis., Minn., Neb.,*

N.D., S.D., Mon., Wy., Ida., Md., Va., W.Va., Ky., Tenn., Mo., Ark., Tex., Ore., Nev., Col., S.C., Ala., Miss., Fla., La., Wash., — 35 States.

19. Entry not required.
In the following States, in which a veto may be overridden by a sufficient vote, there is no requirement that the veto be entered in the Journals: — *Ind., Io., Kan., Cal.,* — 4 States.

20. Veto not submitted.
In one State no statement of reasons is required: — *Ga.,* — 1 State.

21. No reconsideration.
In the following States there is no veto, and hence no reconsideration to be entered: — *R.I., O., Del., N.C.,* — 4 States.

LEGISLATION NOTWITHSTANDING THE WITHHOLDING OF THE GOVERNOR'S SIGNATURE.

22. Signature in no case required.
In the following States bills become law without submission to the governor: — *R.I., Del., O., N.C.,* — 4 States.

23. Kept three days without returning.
In the following States and Territories, if the proposition be kept by the governor three days without returning it, it will become a law, without his signature: — *Ct.,* Ind.,* Wis.,* Io.,* Minn.,* Kan.,* N.D.,* S.D.,* Wy.,* S.C.,* — 10 States. *Utah, N.Mex.,* — 2 Territories.

24. Kept five days without returning.
In the following States the same principle applies if it be kept five days: — *N.H., Mass., Me.,* Vt.,* N.J.,* Neb.,* Mon.,* Va.,* W.Va.,* Tenn.,* Ark.,* Ore.,* Wash.,* Nev.,* Ga.,* Ala.,* Miss.,* Fla.,* La.,* — 19 States.

25. Kept six days without returning.
In the following States the same principle applies if the proposition be kept for six days: — *Md.,** — 1 State.

26. Kept ten days without returning.
In the following States and Territories the same principle applies, if the proposition be kept for ten days: — *N.Y.,* Pa., Ill.,* Mich.,* Ida., Ky.,* Mo., Tex.,* Cal.,* Col.,* — 9 States. *Ariz.,* — 1 Territory.

EFFECT OF ADJOURNMENT ON THE TIME LIMIT.

27. Operation of the time rule prevented.
In the following States and Territories, if the legislature adjourn before the time respectively limited above, the bill does not become law: — *N.H., Mass., Vt., Ct., N.Y., Neb., Mich., Ore., Io., Minn., Kan., Md., Va., Tenn., Cal., S.C., Ga., Ala., La.,* — 19 States. *N.Mex., Ariz., Utah,* — 3 Territories.

28. Bills not to be presented within two days of adjournment.
In *Ind.,* — 1 State.

29. Bills not to be presented within three days of adjournment.
In *Vt.,* — 1 State.

30. Objections to be filed if not approved.
In *Mon.,* — 1 State.

* Sundays excepted.

31. Law unless the bill is returned with objections within five days after adjournment.
In *Ind., Neb., W.Va., Ore.*,* — 4 States.

32. Law unless returned within ten days after adjournment.
Ill., S.D., Ida., Wash., Fla., — 5 States.

33. Law unless returned within fifteen days after adjournment.
N.D., Wy.,* — 2 States.

34. Law unless returned within twenty days after adjournment.
Ark., Tex., — 2 States.

35. Law unless returned within thirty days after adjournment.
N.J.,* *Pa., Mo., Col.,* — 4 States.

36. Law unless returned within three days after the next meeting of the legislature.
Me., Ky., Miss., — 3 States.

SIGNATURE OF THE GOVERNOR AFTER ADJOURNMENT.

37. Within ten days after adjournment.
A proposition becomes law if returned and signed by the governor within ten days after the adjournment of the legislature in *Cal.*,* — 1 State.

38. Within fifteen days after adjournment.
The governor may sign a bill at any time within fifteen days after adjournment in *Mon.,* — 1 State.

39. Within thirty days after adjournment.
The governor may sign bills at any time within thirty days after the final adjournment in *N.Y., Io.,* — 2 States.

40. Within two days after the next meeting.
The governor may still sign the bill at any time up to two days after the beginning of the next meeting of the legislature in *S.C.,* — 1 State.

41. Bills passed in last five days signed within five days after adjournment.
Such bills still become law in *Mich.,* — 1 State.

42. Passed in last three days signed within three days.
Such bills become law in *Minn.,* — 1 State.

43. No provision for signature after adjournment.
In the following States there is no provision for signature by the governor after a final adjournment : — *N.H., Mass., Me., Vt., R.I., Ct., N.J., Pa., O., Ind., Ill., Wis., Kan., Neb., N.D., S.D.. Id., Wy., Md., Del., Va., W.Va., N.C., Ky., Tenn., Mo., Ark., Tex., Ore., Wash., Nev., Col., Ga., Ala., Miss., Fla., La.,* — 37 States. *Utah, N.Mex., Ariz.,* — 3 Territories.

VETO BY ANOTHER LEGISLATURE.

44. Congressional review of territorial legislation.
The laws of the following Territories are to be submitted to Congress, and, if disapproved, shall be void : — *Utah, N.Mex., Ariz.,* — 3 Territories.

* Sundays excepted.

APPENDIX F.

BIBLIOGRAPHY OF THE VETO POWER.

In this list are included the full title of all works to which reference is made in the monograph; and also some titles of books and articles relating to the veto, though containing nothing not found elsewhere. With the exception of an article by Governor Long and some brief discussions in Von Holst, Pomeroy, Cooley and other commentators on the Constitution, the author has found no secondary authorities of value. Mr. Benton's Veto Power, which is almost the only formal treatise on the subject, is an *ex parte* argument on the application of the veto to a particular case. The debates in Congress, reports of Committees, and the veto messages themselves have been the only safe guides.

Adams, Henry. History of the United States during the First Administration of Thomas Jefferson. 2 vols. New York, 1889.
American Historical Association. Papers. 3 vols. New York and London, 1886–1889.
American Whig Review. The Veto Power (x, 111).
Arnold, S. G. History of the State of Rhode Island and Providence Plantations. New York, 1859.
Bagehot, Walter. The English Constitution. London, 1867.
Bancroft, George. History of the United States of America (last revision). 6 vols. New York, 1883.
Bateman, William O. Political and Constitutional Law of the United States of America. St. Louis, 1876.
Benton, T. H. Thirty Years' View; or, A History of the Working of the American Government for Thirty Years, from 1820 to 1850. 2 vols. New York, 1854.
Benton, J. H., Jr. The Veto Power. Boston, 1889.
Blaine, James G. Twenty Years of Congress: From Lincoln to Garfield. 2 vols. Norwich, 1884.
Bolles, A. S. The Financial History of the United States, from 1774 to 1789. 3 vols. New York, 1879–1886.
Bright, J. F. History of England. 3 vols. London, 1887.
Bryce, James. The American Commonwealth. 3 vols. London, 1889.
Callender, E. B. Thaddeus Stevens, Commoner. Boston, 1882.
Conkling, Alfred. The Powers of the Executive Department of the Government of the United States and the Political Institutions and Constitutional Law of the United States. Albany, N. Y., 1882.
Conkling, F. A. Abuses of the Veto Power. *The Forum*, Jan. 1890, viii, No. 5.
Conway, M. D. Our King in a Dress Coat. *North Am. Review*, Mar. 1887.
Cooley, Thomas M. The General Principles of Constitutional Law in the United States of America. Boston, 1880.
Curtis, G. T. History of the Origin, Formation and Adoption of the Constitution of the United States. 2 vols. New York, 1860.

Curtis, G. T. Life of James Buchanan. 2 vols. New York, 1883.
Davis, Horace. American Constitutions. *Johns Hopkins University Studies*, Third Series, Nos. ix-x. Baltimore, 1885.
Democratic Review. The Veto Power (xxiv, 14; xxviii, 243, xxxvi, 35).
Desty, Robert. The Constitution of the United States, with Notes. San Francisco, 1887.
Elliot, Jonathan. The Debates in the Several State Conventions on the Adoption of the Federal Constitution. 5 vols. Washington, 1836.
Freeman, E. A. The Growth of the English Constitution. London, 1876.
Hallam, Henry. Constitutional History of England, from the Accession of Henry VII. to the Death of George II. 3 vols. New York, 1869.
Hamilton, J. C. Life of Alexander Hamilton: A History of the United States of America as traced in his Writings and in those of his Contemporaries. 7 vols. Boston, 1879.
Hart, Albert Bushnell. The Disposition of our Public Lands. *Quarterly Journal of Economics*, Jan. 1887, i, 169–183, 251–254.
Hearn, W. E. The Government of England; its Structure and Development. London, 1867.
Hildreth, Richard. The History of the United States of America from the Discovery of the Continent to the Organization of the Government under the Federal Constitution. First Series. 3 vols. New York, 1849.
Howell, T. B. A complete collection of State Trials and Proceedings for High Treason from the earliest period to the year 1783. London, 1816.
Jameson, J. A. A Treatise on Constitutional Conventions; their History, Powers, and Modes of Proceeding. Chicago, 1887.
Jefferson, Thomas. The Writings of Thomas Jefferson. Edited by H. A. Washington. 7 vols. Washington, 1853.
Johnston, Alexander. History of American Politics. New York, 1886.
Laughlin, J. Lawrence. Principles of Political Economy, by John Stuart Mill. New York, 1885.
Laughlin, J. Lawrence. Influence of the Presidents of the United States on Legislation. *Atlantic Monthly*, lv, 826.
Lawrence, W. B. Elements of International Law, by Henry Wheaton. Boston, 1863.
Long, John D. The Use and Abuse of the Veto Power. *The Forum*, Nov. 1887, iv, No. 3.
McPherson, Edward. The Political History of the United States during the period of Reconstruction. Washington, 1871.
Madison, James. Letters and Other Writings. 4 vols. Philadelphia, 1865.
Madison, James. Papers of James Madison, being his Correspondence and Reports of Debates. 3 vols. Washington, 1840.
Mason, E. C. A Defense of the Veto Power. *Forum*, July, 1890, ix, No. 5.
Massachusetts Historical Society. Proceedings for December, 1889, and January, 1890.
New York. Documents relative to the Colonial History of New York, Procured in Holland, England, and France by J. R. Brodhead, Agent. Albany, 1856.
National Quarterly. The President's Veto in 1866 (xii, 296).
Niles' National Register. The Veto Power (xxxviii, 371; xlviii, 69).
Parliamentary or Constitutional History of England. From the Earliest Times to the Restoration of King Charles II. London, 1762.
Parton, James. Life of Andrew Jackson. 3 vols. New York, 1860.

Bibliography.

Pomeroy, J. W. An Introduction to the Constitutional Law of the United States. Boston and New York, 1888.

Poore, Ben Perley. The Federal and State Constitutions, Colonial Charters, and Other Organic Laws of the United States. 2 vols. Washington, 1877.

Quincy, Josiah. History of Harvard University. 2 vols. Cambridge, 1840.

Salmon, Lucy M. History of the Appointing Power of the President. *Papers of the American Historical Association*, I, No. 5.

Sato, Shosuki. History of the Land Question in the United States. *Johns Hopkins University Studies*, Fourth Series, Nos. vii–viii–ix.

Schouler, James. History of the United States of America under the Constitution. 4 vols. Washington, 1880–1889.

Story, Joseph. Commentaries on the Constitution of the United States; with a preliminary review of the Constitutional History of the Colonies and States before the Adoption of the Constitution. 3 vols. Boston, 1833.

Story, William. Life and Letters of Joseph Story. Edited by his son William Story. 2 vols. Boston, 1851.

Stubbs, William. Select Charters and Other Illustrations of English Constitutional History. Oxford, 1876.

Sumner, W. G. Andrew Jackson as a Public Man. *American Statesman Series*. Boston, 1882.

Tacitus. De Moribus Germaniæ.

Taswell-Langmead, T. P. English Constitutional History from the Teutonic Conquest to the Present Time. London and Boston, 1881.

United States. Annals of Congress (1789–1823).

United States. Congressional Debates (1823–1837).

United States. Congressional Globe (1833–1873).

United States. Congressional Record (1873–1889).

United States. Journals of the Senate and House of Representatives (1789–1889).

United States. Revised Statutes of the United States. Washington, 1878.

United States. Veto Messages of Presidents of the United States, with the action of Congress thereon. Compiled by order of the Senate by Ben Perley Poore, clerk of Printing Records. *Senate Miscellaneous Documents*, 49 Cong. 2 sess., No. 53.

United States. Views of the Minority of the Committee on Bills S 465, 549, 739, 809, 820, 838, 1237, and the veto messages thereon. *Senate Reports*, 50 Cong. 1 sess., No. 1667.

United States. The Statutes at Large of the United States (1789–1889).

United States. Treaties and Conventions concluded between the United States of America and other Powers since July 4, 1776. Washington, 1873.

Von Holst, H. Constitutional and Political History of the United States. 6 vols. Chicago, 1877–1889.

Von Holst, H. The Constitutional Law of the United States of America. Chicago, 1887.

Von Holst, H. John C. Calhoun. *American Statesman Series*. Boston, 1882.

Webster, Daniel. Works. 6 vols. Boston, 1851.

Williams, Edwin. The Statesman's Manual. 4 vols. New York, 1854.

Wilson, Henry. History of the Rise and Fall of the Slave Power in America. 3 vols. Boston, 1877.

INDEX.

ADAMS, JOHN, legislative activity, 214.
Adams, John Quincy, legislative activity, 214; report on revenue act of 1842, 70.
Alexandria, establishment of church, 53, 142 (No. 3).
Allentown, Pa., public building at, 105, 188 (No. 294).
American colonies, veto in, 17.
Anderson, Mrs. M., pension to, 172 (No. 184).
Anderson, Sarah E., pension to, 198 (No. 368).
Anne, Queen, last English veto, 16.
Appropriations, army, 47, 162 (No. 120); civil, 47, 163 (No. 122).
Army, reduction of, 142 (No. 2); medical officers for, 108, 151 (No. 51); bounties to soldiers, 108, 155 (No. 75); appropriations, 47, 162 (No. 120).
Arner, Philip, pension to, 172 (No. 181).
Arthur, Chester Alan, Fitz-John Porter, 43, 86; Chinese, 58; ocean steamships, 94; river and harbor, 104; reasons for vetoes, 127; attempt to enlarge the veto power, 138; list of vetoes, 164, 165; legislative activity, 214.
Articles of Confederation, 19.
Ashville, N. C., public building at, 105, 179 (No. 235).
Ayers, Edward, pension to, 166 (No. 141).

BABERICK, CATHERINE, pension to, 204 (No. 413).
Baker, J. W., relief of children of, 85, 156 (No. 80).
Ball, Farnaren, pension to, 189 (No. 306).
Ballier, John F., pension to, 194 (No. 340).
Baney, Tobias, pension to, 193 (No. 338).

Bangham, Mrs. E. C., pension to, 167 (No. 149).
Bank charter vetoes, 32, 74; Second United States Bank, 74, 143 (No. 7); renewing charter, 75, 144 (No. 14); Fiscal Bank, 76, 145 (No. 22); Fiscal Corporation, 77, 145 (No. 23).
Bank notes in D. C., 79, 151 (No. 50).
Bar Harbor, Me., public building at, 105, 190 (No. 313).
Barnes, Mrs. R., pension to, 180 (No. 241).
Barnes, Rachel, pension to, 196 (No. 353).
Barnes, W., pension to, 206 (No. 428).
Bash, Major D. N., relief of, 186 (No. 282).
Bass, H. V., pension to, 206 (No. 429).
Bayard, James A., on second reconsideration of veto, 121.
Baylor, J. R., pension to, 183 (No. 260).
Beck, W. H., pension to, 170 (No. 171).
Beezeley, Mrs. L. C., pension to, 173 (No. 195).
Belding, H. K., relief of, 181 (No. 250).
Bennett, R. K., pension to, 182 (No. 254).
Benton, Jr., J. H., reasons for veto, 114.
Best, J. M., relief of, 156 (No. 84).
Bishop, William, pension to, 91, 171 (No. 177).
Blazer, Dolly, pension to, 191 (No. 319).
Bloomer, E. J., pension to, 160 (No. 104).
Bodies for dissection, 60, 165 (No. 135).
Boon, Clark, pension to, 174 (No. 200).
Boone, W., pension to, 175 (No. 209).
Botts, John Minor, influence on Tyler's veto, 77.
Bradley, Mrs. S. A., pension to, 178 (No. 229).
Bradshaw, W. S., pension to, 201 (No. 392).
Branch, D. B., pension to, 166 (No. 143).
Brimmer, W. H., pension to, 186 (No. 286).

Brock, M. W., relief of, 159 (No. 101).
Brokenshaw, W. H., pension to, 186 (No. 283).
Brown, Van Buren, relief of, 193 (No. 335).
Bryant, J. S., pension to, 199 (No. 375).
Buchanan, James, protest against Covode investigation, 45, 208 (No. 4); land grant, 62; homesteads, 63; internal improvements, 103, 106; signing constitutional amendments, 118; reasons for vetoes, 127; list of vetoes, 149, 150; legislative activity, 214.
Bundy, M. L., pension to, 175 (No. 210).
Burlingame, Anson, Chinese treaty, 58.
Burnett, John D., appointment to office, 41.
Burr, Elizabeth, pension to, 19. (No. 320).
Burritt, L., pension to, 184 (No. 270).
Burtch, A., relief of, 158 (No. 94).
Burtram, B. A., pension to, 197 (No. 365).
Bussey, Catherine, pension to, 199 (No. 381).
Butler, J., pension to, 171 (No. 175).
Butterfield, Mrs. Anna, pension to, 195 (No. 348).

CALHOUN, J. C., on adjournment of Congress, 27; on internal improvements, 95.
Campbell, Jesse, pension to, 182 (No. 258).
Campbell, Jr., William M., pension to, 193 (No. 333).
Carlin, Bernard, pension to, 196 (No. 358).
Carpenter, W. S., relief of, 198 (No. 372).
Carr, Mary A., pension to, 202 (No. 404).
Carroll, Bridget, pension to, 204 (No. 415).
Carroll, J., pension to, 177 (No. 222).
Chamberlain, C. H., relief of, 203 (No. 411).
Champlain, bridge across Lake, 109, 179 (No. 236).
Chandler, J. C., pension to, 166 (No. 142).
Charles I., vetoes, 13, 16.
Chase, C. A., pension to, 174 (No. 202).
Chase, N. D., pension to, 193 (No. 336).
China, treaties with, 58.
Chinese immigration, 58, 162 (No. 119); 164 (No. 129).
Clay, Henry, 26; on right of the speaker to vote, 95; on pocket vetoes, 113.
Clayton, 27.
Cleveland, Grover, removals from office, 41; Indians, 56, 57; bodies for dissection, 60; Des Moines River lands, 64, 66; Castle Island Park, 65; land grant to Tacoma, W. T., 65; land grant to Kansas, 66; Fort Wallace Reservation, 66; refunding the direct tax, 73; Dependent Pension Bill, 89; pension policy, 90; Springfield a port of delivery, 94; public buildings, 105; Texas Seed Bill, 107; Omaha a port of delivery, 109; bridge across Lake Champlain, 109; United States map for 1886, 110; neglect of reconsideration, 122; bills passed over the veto in one house, 125; reasons for vetoes, 128, 130; effect on parties, 131; prevention of unwise measures, 132, 133; indirect influence on legislation through veto, 133; list of vetoes, 165-207; legislative activity, 214.
Coleman, William, 142 (No. 4).
Collins, Major J. C., relief of, 163 (No. 124).
Columbia, District of, 29; vetoes affecting, 59; recording in, 29, 159 (No. 100); paving Pennsylvania Avenue, 59, 160 (No. 107); police commissioners, 60, 161 (No. 111).
Columbus, Ga., public building at, 105, 190 (No. 312).
Colwell, George, pension to, 207 (No. 432).
Confederate States of America, veto in, 119, 125, 126, 130, 136; chronological list of vetoes, 210-213.
Congress, Form, 25; regulation of session, 26, 30, 145 (No. 20).
Connecticut, 17, 18.
Connelly, Julia, pension to, 173 (No. 193).
Contractors, relief of, 155 (No. 77).
Cooper, Charles, relief of, 155 (No. 76).
Cooper, Harriet E., pension to, 193 (No. 334).
Corson, Sarah A., pension to, 195 (No. 351).
Cotton, J. D., pension to, 172 (No. 182).
Council Bluffs, Iowa, 105, 190 (No. 314).
Courts, trials in district, 27, 142 (No. 5); new trial in court of claims, 28, 157 (No. 87); special term in Mississippi, 29, 162 (No. 118).

Covode investigation, 45, 208 (No. 4).
Crawford, R. B., pension to, 156 (No. 82).
Cunningham, Maria, pension to, 177 (No. 224).
Currency and coinage, 78; inflation of currency, 80, 158 (No. 92); Bland Silver Bill, 81, 162 (No. 117).
Curtin, Mary, pension to, 197 (No. 363).
Cutler, G. W., pension to, 180 (No. 245).

DARLING, J. H., pension to, 174 (No. 201).
Dauper, John, pension to, 202 (No. 399).
Davis, Jefferson, vetoes as president of the Confederate States, 210-213.
Davis-Wade Bill, 208 (No. 5).
Dayton, O., public building at, 105, 179 (No. 234).
Dean, John, pension to, 199 (No. 378).
Debt, refunding the national, 78, 164 (No. 128).
Deck, Amanda F., pension to, 194 (No. 339).
De Krafft, Elizabeth S., pension to, 90, 170 (No. 168).
Denning, F., pension to, 177 (No. 220).
Denniston, W. H., relief of, 158 (No. 91).
Denny, Alfred, pension to, 170 (No. 170).
Dependent Pension Bill, 89, 183 (No. 261).
Dermody, W., pension to, 177 (No. 218).
Des Moines River lands, settlers' titles to, 64, 66, 165 (No. 134); 206 (No. 425).
De Witt, Hannah C., 186 (No. 284).
Dickens, W., pension to, 181 (No. 248).
Diplomatic congratulations, 39, 161 (No. 112).
Doane, R. L., pension to, 199 (No. 377).
Dougherty, Mary Ann, pension to, 192 (No. 330).
Dow, Mrs. J., pension to, 180 (No. 240).
Drake, Mary I., pension to, 204 (No. 412).
Duluth, public building at, 105, 178 (No. 227).
Dunlap, Margaret, pension to, 181 (No. 251).
Dustin, George M., removal from office, 41.

EAST TENNESSEE UNIVERSITY, relief of, 157 (No. 88).

Eaton, Lydia A., pension to, 202 (No. 398).
Edward III, 13, 14.
Edwards & Co., relief of, 150 (No. 47).
Elderkin, D. T., pension to, 172 (No. 185).
Eldridge, Mrs. R., pension to, 167 (No. 148).
Elections, testimony in contested, 28, 146 (No. 27); interference, 46, note 3, 162 (No. 121).
England, early legislative power, 12, 13; veto, 14; disappearance of the veto, 15.
Errors, correction of clerical, 109, 151 (No. 52).
Esty, C. J., pension to, 205 (No. 424).
Evans, Mrs. F. E., pension to, 178 (No. 228).
Executive departments, advertising of, 35, note 2, 161 (No. 115).

FALCONER, A., pension to, 181 (No. 252).
Farris, J. W., pension to, 169 (No. 165).
Federal Convention, 20.
Fincher, J. D., pension to, 184 (No. 267).
Fitzmorris, Mary, relief of, 193 (No. 337).
Foley, Bridget, pension to, 194 (No. 344).
Forbes, Duncan, pension to, 180 (No. 242).
Franklin, Benjamin, 18, 21.
French spoliation claims, 83, 147 (No. 32); 84, 148 (No. 36).

GARCIA, MANUEL, pension to, 195 (No. 352).
Garfield, James A., on closing consular offices, 38; reasons for failure to veto, 127.
Garrett, Eli, pension to, 205 (No. 419).
Gaven, Ester, pension to, 202 (No. 400).
Geddes, C. W., relief of, 204 (No. 414).
Georgia, State of, signing bill after adjournment of Congress, 116.
Germany, early legislative power, 11.
Gerry, Elbridge, Federal Convention, 21.
Gilmer, Thomas W., Revenue Act of 1842, 70.
Glamann, Charles, pension to, 192 (No. 326).
Glass, Eliza S., pension to, 203 (No. 405).
Godfrey, E. J., pension to, 199 (No. 376).

Goldsborough, Robert H., 27.
Grant, Ulysses S., Court of Claims, 28; recording in District of Columbia, 29; advertising of executive departments, 35, note 2; consular offices, 37; Indians, 55; paving in District of Columbia, 59; police commissioners in District of Columbia, 60; homestead entries, 64; diplomatic intercourse, 39; President's salary, 45; Inflation Bill, 80; internal improvements, 104, note 2; refusal to carry out a bill, 103; bounties to soldiers, 108; protest, blankets for reform school, 109, 209 (No. 9); post-office statutes, 109; right to recall a veto, 118; neglect of reconsideration, 122; reasons for vetoes, 128; effect on parties, 131; prevention of unwise measures, 132; River and Harbor Bill, 104, 209 (No. 7); Diplomatic Bill, 37, 209 (No. 8); list of vetoes, 155-162; legislative activity, 214.
Griggs, A. P., pension to, 182 (No. 256).
Griswold, Elisha, relief of, 190 (No. 311).
Guyse, G. W., pension to, 172 (No. 186).

HAGERMAN, MRS. M. J., pension to, 180 (No. 239).
Ham, J. D., pension to, 166 (No. 144).
Hamilton, Alexander, Federal Convention, 21; the veto in 1789, 139.
Hamilton, D. W., pension to, 167 (No. 145).
Hamilton, Mrs. Sarah, pension to, 185 (No. 247).
Hand, Mrs. Ellen, pension to, 205 (No. 418).
Hanks, Dr. John F., relief of estate of, 156 (No. 78).
Hannegan, John, relief of, 155 (No. 76).
Hannegan, William, relief of, 155 (No. 76).
Harbaugh, Mrs. S., pension to, 174 (No. 197).
Harden, S. W., pension to, 167 (No. 150).
Hardy, Lieut. J. G. W., relief of, 191 (No. 324).
Harkins, Mary F., pension to, 191 (No. 322).
Harrington, E. M., pension to, 178 (No. 231).
Harrison, W. H., reason for failure to veto, 127.

Hayes, Rutherford B., special term of court, 29; riders, 46, note 3, 47; Chinese, 58; refunding the national debt, 78; Bland Silver Bill, 81; failure to enter veto message in journal, 122; reasons for vetoes, 128; prevention of unwise measures, 132, 133; vetoes which have failed, 134; attempt to enlarge the veto power, 137; protest, fees of United States marshals, 209 (No. 10); list of vetoes, 162-164; legislative activity, 214.
Hawes, Susan, pension to, 180 (No. 246).
Hawley, G. C., pension to, 173 (No. 188).
Haworth, J. D., pension to, 167 (No. 147).
Heckler, Elizabeth, pension to, 202 (No. 403).
Heiny, Lydia A., pension to, 196 (No. 356).
Hensley, E. P., pension to, 170 (No. 166).
Herbst, Theresa, pension to, 194 (No. 343).
Hester, W. H., pension to, 188 (No. 301).
Hiar, R. J., pension to, 189 (No. 302).
Hill, A. J., pension to, 166 (No. 138).
Hill, J. A., relief of, 158 (No. 97).
Hinely, Louis, pension to, 158 (No. 95).
Hipple, Jr., H., pension to, 169 (No. 164).
Hockaday, relief of, 150 (No. 49).
Holman, William S., closing consular offices, 38.
Holsey, Robert, pension to, 171 (No. 176).
Hopkins, T. S., pension to, 168 (No. 156).
Hooper, Mary, pension to, 202 (No. 401).
Houchin, W. M., pension to, 194 (No. 342).
How, John, relief of, 184 (No. 272).
Hoxey, Mary M., pension to, 191 (No. 323).
Hunter, J., pension to, 169 (No. 159).
Hunter, Mrs. Maria, pension to, 174 (No. 196).
Hutchins, Waldo, attempt to enlarge the veto power, 138.

ILLINOIS, signing bill after adjournment of Congress, 116.
Indians, 54; Cherokee award, 55, 146 (No. 28); custody of trust funds, 55, 158 (No. 96); sale of lands, 55, 160 (No. 108); 56, 187 (No. 293); right of way for railroad, 57, 178 (No. 232); 194 (No. 345).

Indian Territory, 57.
Ingersoll, Charles J., Revenue Act of 1842, 70.
Internal improvements, general view, 105; Bonus Bill, 94, 143 (No. 8); Cumberland Road, 96, 143 (No. 9); Maysville Road, 97, 143 (No. 10); turnpike stock, 97, 143 (No. 11); light-houses and beacons, 97, 144 (No. 12); canal stock, 97, 144 (No. 13); river and harbor, 144 (No. 16); Wabash River, 97, 145 (No. 18); rivers and harbors, 99, 147 (No. 29); rivers and harbors, 100, 147 (No. 31); Territory of Wisconsin, 100, 147 (No. 33); completion of works, 101, 148 (No. 35); Mississippi River, 101, 148 (No. 38); Saint Clair Flats, 101, 149 (No. 39); Saint Mary's River, 101, 149 (No. 40); Des Moines Rapids, 101, 149 (No. 41); Patapsco River, 101, 149 (No. 42); Saint Clair Flats, 103, 150 (No. 45); Mississippi River, 103, 150 (No. 46); appropriations for salaries, 103, 159 (No. 102); rivers and harbors, 104, 164 (No. 131); 104, 209 (No. 7).
Irwin, J. T., pension to, 176 (No. 213).

JACKSON, ANDREW, session of Congress, 26, 30; bank veto, 32; treaty with the Two Sicilies, 36; proceeds of public land sales, 60; interest on state claims, 73; bank veto, 75; funds receivable for United States revenues, 79; internal improvements, 96, 106; reasons for vetoes, 127, 129; effect on parties, 131; prevention of unwise measures, 133; protest against censure by the Senate, 33, 208 (No. 1); list of vetoes, 143-145; legislative activity, 214.
Jacoby, Mrs. M. A., pension to, 176 (No. 215).
James I, 13.
Jefferson, Thomas, 26; reason for failure to veto, 126; legislative activity, 214.
Jenckes, Thomas A., tenure of office, 43.
Jennings, Nancy F., pension to, 188 (No. 297).
Johnson, Andrew, Tenure of Office Act, 42; war power, 44, 209 (No. 6); reconstruction vetoes, 46; negro, 57, 59; preempting mineral land, 64; admission of Colorado, 67, 68; admission of Nebraska, 67, 68; duty on copper, 72; bills passed over the veto, 125; effect on parties, 131; prevention of unwise measures, 132; vetoes which have failed, 134; protest against a rider, 209 (No. 6); list of vetoes, 151-155; legislative activity, 214.
Johnson, J. T., relief of, 156 (No. 79).
Jones, G. A., relief of, 155 (No. 76).
Jones, Margaret R., pension to, 184 (No. 268).
Judiciary, form of national, 27.
Jussen, Edmund, relief of, 157 (No. 86).

KABLER, J. E., pension to, 197 (No. 367).
Kansas, 55, 56; land grant, 66, 200 (No. 386); sale of Fort Wallace reservation, 66, 200 (No. 387).
Karstetter, Mary, pension to, 178 (No. 226); 204 (No. 417).
Kelley, Daniel H., relief of, 86, 161 (No. 113).
Kelly, Ellen, pension to, 202 (No. 402).
Kent, Joseph, attempts to diminish the veto power, 136, 137.
Kinney, Mrs. A., pension to, 180 (No. 243).
Kirkpatrick, J. S., pension to, 175 (No. 207).
Kyler, H. L., pension to, 176 (No. 212).

LA FAYETTE, IND., public building at, 105, 185 (No. 277).
Lane, Henry S., Revenue Act of 1842, 71.
Lang, Mary A., pension to, 193 (No. 332).
Langdon, Hannah R., pension to, 186 (No. 281).
Lanham, S. W. J., Texas Seed Bill, 108.
Latham, W. S., pension to, 202 (No. 397).
Lawrence, William, closing consular offices, 38.
Leary, John, pension to the widow of, 197 (No. 364).
Leatherbury, P. A., relief of, 195 (No. 346).
Leese, F. J;, pension to, 169 (No. 163).
Leggit, relief of, 150 (No. 49).

Leland, Edward A., relief of, 162 (No. 116).
Lewis, Edwin, 142 (No. 4).
Lewis, William J., attempts to remove the veto power, 136.
Lincoln, Abraham, bank notes in D. C., 79; medical officers for the army, 108; clerical errors, 109; signing bill after adjournment of Congress, 115; signing constitutional amendments, 117; neglect of reconsideration, 122, 125; pocket vetoes, 126; reasons for vetoes, 127; prevention of unwise measures, 132; manifesto against Davis-Wade Bill, 208 (No. 5); list of vetoes, 151; legislative activity, 214.
Liner, Peter, pension to, 201 (No. 396).
Lockrey, J. J., pension to, 206 (No. 426).
Loewinger, Johanna, pension to, 190 (No. 315).
Loomis, A. F., pension to, 176 (No. 211).
Lounsberry, C. A., relief of, 198 (No. 373).
Luce, Mrs. E., pension to, 170 (No. 167).
Luckett, E. H., relief of, 159 (No. 98).
Lutman, D. H., pension to, 198 (No. 369).
Lynch, W., pension to, 181 (No. 253).
Lynn, Mass., public building at, 105, 184 (No. 273).

McBLAIR, J. H., relief of, 165 (No. 133).
McCaleb, Sarah E., relief of, 189 (No. 305).
McCarty, Mrs. C., pension to, 178 (No. 230).
McCool, John, pension to, 206 (No. 427).
McCullah, J. A., relief of, 157 (No. 89).
McIlwain, Mrs. M., pension to, 174 (No. 199).
McKay, E., pension to, 176 (No. 217).
McKay, Nathaniel, relief of, 185 (No. 278).
McRobertson, A., pension to, 184 (No. 269).
Maddox, Laura E., relief of, 200 (No. 388).
Madison, James, Federal Convention, 20, 21, 22; appointing judges, 28; tenure of office, 43; church and state, 53, 54, 60; naturalization, 54, 59; bank veto, 74; internal improvements, 94, 105; pocket vetoes, 125; reasons for vetoes, 127, 129; effect on parties, 131; prevention of unwise measures, 132, 133; list of vetoes, 142, 143; legislative activity, 214.
Mails, subsidy for ocean, 148 (No. 37); overland, 35, note 2; 149 (No. 43); post-office statutes, 109, 160 (No. 105).
Mansfield, Betsey, pension to, 186 (No. 280).
Mantor, M. T., pension to, 186 (No. 285).
Maphet, C. T., pension to, 199 (No. 379).
Marchand, Mrs. M. D., pension to, 168 (No. 155).
Marion, John H., relief of, 191 (No. 316).
Marshals, payment of United States, 47, 163 (Nos. 123, 125, 126); 46, note 3; 164 (No. 127).
Martin, Elijah, relief of, 191 (No. 318).
Maryland, 17, 18.
Massachusetts, 16, 18.
Mead, James R., relief of, 158 (No. 93).
Melcher, Louis, pension to, 166 (No. 140).
Mertz, Anna, pension to, 190 (No. 309).
Miller, Mrs. M. A., pension to, 172 (No. 183).
Miller, S., pension to, 172 (No. 187).
Mills, Emily G., relief of, 187 (No. 292).
Mims, Samuel, 142 (No. 4).
Mississippi, land grant to a church in, 54, 142 (No. 4).
Monroe, James, internal improvements, 95, 105; reasons for veto, 127, 129; effect on parties, 131; only veto, 141; legislative activity, 214.
Monroe, J. D., pension to, 169 (No. 162).
Montana, 56; right of way for railroad, 57, 178 (No. 232).
Montgomery, M. A., pension to, 156 (No. 83).
Morehead, A., pension to, 176 (No. 216).
Morhiser, W. H., pension to, 184 (No. 271).
Morton, J. B., relief of, 192 (No. 328).
Myer, Capt. E. S., restoration of, 160 (No. 106).

NATURALIZATION, 54, 142 (No. 6).
Nebraska, 55.
Nevil, W. H., pension to, 177 (No. 219).
Newhard, Jacob, pension to, 200 (No. 384).

New York, State of, signing bill after adjournment of Congress, 116.
Norman, Mrs. M., pension to, 175 (No. 205).
Nottage, Mrs. M. J., pension to, 170 (No. 172).

OBEKIAH, B., pension to, 181 (No. 249).
Omaha a port of delivery, 109, 165 (No. 136).
O'Neal, Charlotte, pension to, 183 (No. 263).
O'Shea, James, pension to, 92, 168 (No. 153).
Owen, Mrs. A. C., pension to, 167 (No. 146).
Owen, Clara M., pension to, 205 (No. 421).

PARKER, N., pension to, 175 (No. 208).
Parker, P. E., relief of, 197 (No. 366).
Parsons, Mrs. M., pension to, 171 (No. 173).
Passengers, carriage of by sea, 94, 164 (No. 130).
Pennsylvania, 18.
Pension vetoes, 87.
Piatt, Mrs. T. M., pension to, 188 (No. 296).
Pierce, Franklin, land grant, 61; French spoliation claims, 84; internal improvements, 101, 106; what constitutes a two-thirds majority, 120; second reconsideration of veto, 121; bills passed over the veto, 125; reasons for vetoes, 127; list of vetoes, 147–149; legislative activity, 214.
Pierpont, Rachel Ann, pension to, 183 (No. 265).
Piggott, Michael, relief of, 203 (No. 407).
Pilcher, J. E., relief of, 189 (No. 307).
Pinckney, Charles, 21.
Pitner, G. W., pension to, 196 (No. 355).
Points, A., pension to, 180 (No. 244).
Polk, James K., French spoliation claims, 83; internal improvements, 100, 106; reasons for vetoes, 127; list of vetoes, 147; legislative activity, 214.

Porter, Fitz-John, relief of, 43, 86, 165 (No. 132).
Portsmouth, O., public building at, 105, 185 (No. 276).
Potts, Mrs. Jane, pension to, 200 (No. 382).
President of the United States, methods of treating a bill, 24; refusal to carry out an act, 116; right of protest, 117; signing constitutional amendments, 117; reduction of salary, 45, 159 (No. 99).
Probert, Mrs. Anna A., pension to, 174 (No. 198).
Public buildings, Zanesville, O., 105, 169 (No. 158); Duluth, Minn., 105, 178 (No. 227); Dayton, O., 105, 179 (No. 234); Asheville, N. C., 105, 179 (No. 235); Springfield, Mo., 105, 179 (No. 237); Lynn, Mass., 105, 184 (No. 273); Portsmouth, O., 105, 185 (No. 276); La Fayette, Ind., 105, 185 (No. 277); Allentown, Pa., 105, 188 (No. 294); Youngstown, O., 105, 189 (No. 308); Columbus, Ga., 105, 190 (No. 312); Bar Harbor, Me., 105, 190 (No. 313); Council Bluffs, Ia., 105, 190 (No. 314); Sioux City, Ia., 105, 168 (No. 157); 198 (No. 374).
Public lands, 60; proceeds of land sales (Clay's Bill), 60, 144 (No. 17); proceeds of land sales, 61, 146 (No. 26); grant to indigent insane, 61, 147 (No. 34); grants for agricultural colleges, 62, 149 (No. 44); Homestead Act, 63, 150 (No. 48); grant to Montana Iron Company, 64, 152 (No. 56); surveying district of Montana, 64, 152 (No. 58); homestead entries, 64, 160 (No. 110); titles to Des Moines River land, 64, 66, 165 (No. 134); 206 (No. 425); Castle Island, Boston Harbor, 65, 188 (No. 298); government purchase at Council Bluffs, 105, 190 (No. 314); grant to Tacoma, W. T., 65, 195 (No. 347); grant to Kansas, 66, 200 (No. 386); sale of Fort Wallace reservation, 66, 200 (No. 387).

QUIGGLE, CHLOE, pension to, 187 (No. 288).

RAILROADS, right of way in Montana, 57, 178 (No. 232).
Randall, Sally A., pension to, 188 (No. 300).
Randolph, Edmund, Federal Convention, 20, 21.
Reconstruction, freedman's bureau, 46, 151 (No. 53); civil rights, 46, 57, 151 (No. 54); continuation of freedman's bureau, 46, 152 (No. 57); suffrage in D. C., 46, 152 (No. 59); Tenure of Office Act, 42, 46, 152 (No. 62); Reconstruction Act, 46, 153 (No. 63); supplemental Reconstruction Act, 46, 153 (Nos. 64, 65); joint resolution on reconstruction, 46, 153 (No. 66); amending Judiciary Act, 46, 154 (No. 67); exclusion of electoral votes, 46, 154 (No. 70); discontinuance of freedman's bureau, 46, 154 (No. 71); trustees of colored schools, 46, 155 (No. 72).
Reed, Mrs. Catherine, pension to, 200 (No. 383).
Reed, John, pension to, 183 (No. 264).
Relief bills, 85.
Religious liberty, 53.
Representatives, apportionment of, 142 (No. 1).
Revenue, funds receivable for United States, 79, 145 (No. 21); cutters and steamers, 35, note 2; 147 (No. 30).
Reynolds, J. W., pension to, 198 (No. 371).
Rhode Island, 17, 18.
Richards, Mary K., pension to, 201 (No. 391).
Richardson, A. C., pension to, 181 (No. 247).
Riddle, W. P., pension to, 196 (No. 357).
Riders, army appropriations, 47, 162 (No. 120); civil appropriations, 47, 163 (No. 122); payment of marshals, 47, 163 (Nos. 123, 125, 126).
Robeson, John, pension to, 201 (No. 395).
Romahn, M., pension to, 167 (No. 151).
Romiser, J., pension to, 177 (No. 22).
Roosevelt, James I., Revenue Act of 1842, 70.
Ross, D. H., pension to, 179 (No. 233).
Rowland, Alfred, desertion of, 161 (No. 114).
Rowley, Jerome, relief of, 155 (No. 76).
Rowley, Mrs. R. V., pension to, 176 (No. 214).
Ryan, Abigail, pension to, 156 (No. 181).

SACKMAN, WILLIAM, Sr., pension to, 187 (No. 289).
Sacs and Foxes, 55.
Salt works, relief for owners of, 157 (No. 90).
Sattler, Catherine, pension to, 182 (No. 259).
Saxberry, Edson, relief of, 196 (No. 359).
Scanland, L. W., pension to, 177 (No. 223).
Schenck, Mrs. C. R., pension to, 170 (No. 169).
Schenck, Robert C., duty on copper, 72; internal improvements, 101.
Schiedel, Stephen, pension to, 191 (No. 317).
Schuler, Charles, pension to, 173 (No. 189).
Schultz, B., pension to, 173 (No. 194).
Scott, C. C., pension to, 203 (No. 409).
Seavey, S. A., pension to, 195 (No. 350).
Senate, censure of the, 33, 208 (No. 1).
Servis, D. A., pension to, 190 (No. 310).
Seward, W. H., second reconsideration of veto, 121.
Sexton, Ellen, pension to, 192 (No. 325).
Seyfforth, Caroline G., pension to, 196 (No. 360).
Shannon, Thomas, pension to, 194 (No. 341).
Shea, Ellen, pension to, 189 (No. 304).
Sherman, John, reasons for vetoes, 130.
Shong, Michael, pension to, 205 (No. 423).
Sioux City, Ia., public building at, 105, 168 (No. 157); 198 (No. 374).
Smith, Abigail, pension to, 165 (No. 137).
Smith, Eliza, pension to, 195 (No. 349).
Smith, Jacob, pension to, 183 (No. 266).
Smith, Polly H., pension to, 192 (No. 329).
Smith, Virtue, pension to, 191 (No. 321).
Snyder, John, requiring names of applicants for office, 41.
Spencer, Jacob, relief of, 158 (No. 93).
Springfield, Mass., a port of delivery, 166 (No. 139).
Springfield, Mo., public building at, 105, 179 (No. 237).

Railroads — Veto. 231

Stapleton, R. H., pension to, 177 (No. 225).
Starr, W. H., pension to, 175 (No. 204).
States, the veto in, 113, 114, 118, 136; provisions of State Constitutions, 215-218; veto in first State Constitutions, 18.
States, admission of Colorado, 67, 151 (No. 55); 68, 152 (No. 60); Nebraska, 67, 68, 152 (No. 61); Arkansas, 46, 154 (No. 68); Southern States, 46, 154 (No. 69).
State claims, interest on, 73, 144 (No. 15).
Stevens, A. F., pension to, 168 (No. 154).
Steward, J., pension to, 171 (No. 178).
Stewart, William M., second reconsideration of veto, 121.
Stillwell, J. M., pension to, 200 (No. 385).
Stone, C., pension to, 182 (No. 257).
Stricklett, Georgia A., relief of, 188 (No. 295).
Stryker, C. G., pension to, 189 (No. 303).
Stuarts, the, 14, 15.
Sullivan, Mary, pension to, 187 (No. 290).
Sweet, Franklin, pension to, 182 (No. 255).

TARIFF, 69, first Whig bill, 70, 146 (No. 24); second Whig bill, 70, 146 (No. 25); duty on copper, 72, 155 (No. 73); Tyler's protest, 70, 208 (No. 3).
Tax, refunding the direct, 73, 207 (No. 433).
Taylor, John, pension to, 169 (No. 160).
Taylor, Zachary, compromise of 1850, 57; reasons for failure to veto, 127; indirect influence on legislation, 133.
Tervin, Richard, 142 (No. 4).
Texas Seed Bill, 107, 183 (No. 262).
Tiffany, Nelson, relief of, 159 (No. 103).
Tiller, C. W., pension to, 169 (No. 161).
Tillman, H., pension to, 175 (No. 203).
Todd, Margaret B., pension to, 198 (No. 370).
Travers, Mrs. A. E., pension to, 172 (No. 180).
Treaty power, invasion of, 49.
Triggs, Julia, relief of, 205 (No. 420).
Trumbull Civil Rights Bill, 57.
Tucker, John R., closing consular offices, 38.
Tudors, the, 15.

Turly, John A., relief of widow of, 192 (No. 327).
Turner, Major J. T., relief of, 87, 160 (No. 109).
Tuttle, J., pension to, 175 (No. 206).
Two Sicilies, treaty with, 36, 145 (No. 19).
Two-thirds majority, what constitutes, 103, 119.
Tyler, G. B., relief of, 159 (No. 98).
Tyler, John, taking testimony, 28; names of applicants for office, 40; Cherokee Indians, 55; proceeds of public land sales, 61; temporary Revenue Act, 70; permanent Revenue Act, 70; bank veto, 76; fiscal corporation veto, 77; internal improvements, 99; second reconsideration of veto, 121; bills passed over the veto, 125; reasons for vetoes, 127; effect on parties, 131; prevention of unwise measures, 133; refusal to furnish information, 40, 208 (No. 2); protest against committee report on tariff veto, 70, 208 (No. 3); list of vetoes, 145-147; legislative activity, 214.

UNITED STATES, additional copies of map, 110, 197 (No. 362).

VAN BUREN, MARTIN, reason for failure to veto, 126.
Van Etten, Mrs. M. A., pension to, 171 (No. 179).
Vest, George G., reasons for vetoes, 130.
Veto, the, a legislative power, 112; pocket vetoes, 113; reasons for veto, 114; signing bill after adjournment of Congress, 115; signing constitutional amendments, 117; right to recall a veto, 118; right of the speaker to vote on reconsideration, 120; second reconsideration of veto, 120; failure to enter veto message in journal, 122; neglect of reconsideration, 122; reasons for vetoes, 126; constitutionality and expediency, 129; effect on parties, 131; prevention of unwise measures, 132; indirect influence on legislation, 134; vetoes which have failed, 134; popular objections to the veto, 135; attempts to alter the power, 136, 137; the veto in 1789 and in 1889, 138.

Virginia, 17.
Vogelsang, Mrs. Sophia, pension to, 201 (No. 394).

WALLACE, T. B., relief of, 157 (No. 85).
Wallen, George, pension to, 204 (No. 416).
Walsh, Thomas, pension to, 203 (No. 408).
Walster, Charles, pension to, 199 (No. 380).
Walter, Squire, pension to, 206 (No. 431).
Ward, Sallie T., pension to, 196 (No. 354).
Warner, E. W., pension to, 206 (No. 430).
War powers, 108; Johnson's protest against the removal of power from the President, 44, 209 (No. 6).
Washington, George, apportionment, 25, 30; reduction of the army, 108; reasons for vetoes, 127, 129, 130; prevention of unwise measures, 132; list of vetoes, 142; legislative activity, 214.
Weaver, W. H., pension to, 179 (No. 238).
Webster, D., 26; tenure of office, 43.
Welch, Mrs. H., pension to, 171 (No. 174).
Welch, Julia, pension to, 193 (No. 331).
West, C., pension to, 173 (No. 192).
Wheaton, Laban, church and state, 54.
Wheaton, W. R., relief of, 203 (No. 411).
White, J. C., pension to, 197 (No. 361).
White, Rollin, relief of, 155 (No. 74).

Wilbur, J. E., relief of, 201 (No. 390).
Williams, J. S., pension to, 168 (No. 152).
Wilson, A. J., pension to, 173 (No. 191).
Wilson, C. B., relief of, 203 (No. 406).
Wilson, H. B., relief of, 187 (No. 291).
Wilson, James, 22.
Wilson, Joseph, 142 (No. 4).
Witt, William P., pension to, 187 (No. 287).
Woodbridge, Sarah A., pension to, 200 (No. 389).
Woodson, Mrs. M. S., pension to, 173 (No. 190).
Woodworth, Mary, pension to, 201 (No. 393).
Worcester, F. D., pension to, 205 (No. 422).
Worden, L. J., relief of, 188 (No. 299).
Wright, Anna, pension to, 185 (No. 275).
Wright, Laura A., pension to, 185 (No. 279).

YAMGHEIM, E. J., pension to, 203 (No. 410).
Youngstown, O., public building at, 105, 189 (No. 308).

ZANESVILLE, O., public building at, 105, 169 (No. 158).

www.ingramcontent.com/pod-product-compliance
Lightning Source LLC
Chambersburg PA
CBHW022011220426
43663CB00007B/1041